STRATEGY & POLICY FORMATION

an integrative approach

FRANK T. PAINE
University of Maryland

WILLIAM NAUMES
Temple University

688744

W. B. SAUNDERS COMPANY • Philadelphia • London • Toronto

W. B. Saunders Company: West Washington Square
Philadelphia, PA   19105

12 Dyott Street
London, WC1A   1DB

833 Oxford Street
Toronto, Ontario M8Z 5T9, Canada

Strategy and Policy Formation   ISBN   0-7216-7047-4

Last digit is the Print Number: 9   8   7   6   5   4   3

PREFACE

The purpose of Strategy and Policy Formation: An Integrative Approach is to provide a conceptual framework for information gathering in the field of policy and for organizing and analyzing such information.

Most schools of business offer courses in business policy. A sampling of these courses indicates that many instructors consider the field of policy to be concerned with:

1. identifying relevant challenges, threats, and opportunities in the environment,
2. setting missions and broad objectives,
3. designing strategic action plans to fulfill these objectives,
4. developing and allocating the financial, human and physical resources to carry out the plans, and
5. monitoring ongoing performance to see that the desired ends are being accomplished and altering the mission, objectives and action plans as appropriate, and
6. structuring the interpersonal and intergroup relationships within the organizations to facilitate accomplishment of the desired future peformance levels.

In studying this complex field, it is easy for the student as well as the manager to be overwhelmed by the number of variables that need to be taken into account simultaneously (e.g., environmental, economic, structural, motivational, etc.). Given this complexity, many courses emphasize cases and try to identify a conceptual basis for the subject and a clearly defined normative approach to policy formation which can be used subsequently in business. While there are many fine books on policy formation at present, we feel the conceptual frameworks presented have *not* gone far enough toward (1) being based on empirical research, (2) blending into an integrated theory of management policy, (3) describing the complex processes of management, (4) integrating the behavioral and management sciences into policy. We recognize that there are some shortages of empirical evidence, but we are attempting in this book to meet the need for a practical unifying text on strategy and policy formation.

Several questions are considered: What are the problems facing managers and analysts trying to develop organizational policy? What are the questions we must ask, to orient ourselves, before seriously embarking on a program to improve organizational policy formation? Where do we look for answers? What can we learn from descriptive and normative decision theory? From management and behavioral science research and ideas? From organizational development? How may we appropriately conceptualize the policy formation process? What are the significant variables in the social and in the intellectual process of policy formation? What determinations need to be made in a framework for developing strategic plans of action? What methods are appropriate for assessing and developing the organization and its policies and strategies? The reader hopefully will be supplied with a critical appreciation of some relevant theories and methods, a knowledge of where to look for answers and some idea of what he is likely to find there.

The book is fairly short; it may be viewed as an overview about the present accomplishments in the study and development of the policy formation process in organizations, be they business or nonprofit institutions. The general management functions are emphasized. It may be foolhardy, but our hope is to turn the reader on to the potential value and excitement in the study of the crucial fields of general management and policy formation and to provide the serious student with a primer that may give impetus to further academic study. There is a great need for research and theorizing in policy formation; the book provides some ideas to the reader for carrying out rather interesting but simple studies on his own.

For whom is the book intended? The book was written primarily for use as a framework for information gathering and for organizing and analyzing such information by three main types of policy analysts:

—The top level or middle manager himself, who, on a regular basis, is involved in policy formation and implementation.

—The assessor or researcher interested in understanding and in developing the policy formation process.

—And, most importantly, for the student of policy, who, by the use of case analysis, field or library projects, computer games, and/or role plays, may be enabled to develop conceptual and administrative skills.

Thus, it is written for those who are interested not only in an intellectual appreciation of policy but also in practice in applied information processing on complex policy issues.

Though we include and discuss some practice materials (e.g., cases, role plays, case problems, discussion questions), the book, if used in a policy or management course or in a training program, may be supplemented by further case studies, a computer game, and a field and/or library project for additional information processing.

The concepts and ideas presented have been tested and modified through many different situations ranging from young students without any significant organizational experience to groups of experienced managers and staff personnel from business and public bodies. These very different sets of students, though they may vary in the emphasis they place on each aspect or variable, seem to be able to apply the concepts and ideas effectively. Some prior knowledge of core business administration subjects (i.e., organization and management, marketing and finance) is assumed.

It has been our experience that use of the book with additional practice materials would be expected to aid the reader in the following ways:

1. Conceptualizing the policy formation process as a social process in which an intellectual process is embedded.

2. Developing comprehension, skill and knowledge for diagnosing and dealing with the specific and unique policy and strategy situation.

3. Gaining understanding of the complex realities, challenging questions and conflicting responsibilities in policy making.

4. Analyzing the organization's environment and its policy-generating structure.

5. Designing and proposing approaches that will help to prevent organizational stagnation.

6. Developing administrative and communication skills in presenting and developing solutions to policy problems in the course.

7. Integrating or tying together concepts, principles and skills learned separately in other more specialized courses.

8. Being cautious in accepting the many prescriptions that exist in the literature of Policy (e.g., long range planning is good per se).

To meet these objectives of policy courses, it seems useful for the student to play the role of advisor to top management in the organization under consideration. The student steps back, asks a series of questions and analyzes all aspects of the organization and its policy making process, including the personalities and self-interests of the organization's top personnel. We ask the reader to play the role of the advisor.

It is felt that, in a rather short space, many of the more significant normative and descriptive aspects of the policy formation process have been presented to the student for scrutiny and further investigation. The emphasis is on diversity and breadth at some expense of depth of coverage. The attempt is made to interest the student: (1) in searching further into the literature, and relating what he finds to real organizational policy situations; or (2) in searching into real organizational policy situations, and relating what he finds to the literature.

In addition, and perhaps more importantly, an attempt is made to present an accurate and current picture of some of the achievements of organization development specialists in business and government, their methods of approaching and solving policy formation type problems, and some of the major unanswered questions relating to their work. In short, in this book parts of the rapidly growing field of organization development have been integrated with policy formation.

We hope the book serves the purposes for which it was intended. The demands for study and theorizing in policy formation and in organization development are great and growing, and if we can stimulate a few additional students and managers to delve seriously into such areas, we shall feel well rewarded.

It is impossible to credit all the people who have helped to create this book and shape its contents one way or another. The following are some of them: Charles Summer, Max Richards, Henry Mintzberg, Bernard Taylor, Bruce Coleman, John Sims, S. Kyle Reed, Richard Cyert, James March, Dale Zand, Raymond Bauer, William Guth, John Miner, William Newman, Bud Pederson, Robert Katz, Henry Eyring, Rocco Carzo, Jr., Robert D. Henderson, Richard M. Hodgetts, Michele Kowalchick, Billie Brick, Thomas O'Connor, and John Neifert. We will, of course, take the blame for any errors of commission or omission.

Credit should also be given to our wives, Johanne and Peggy, for all their patience and support in this project and other projects.

FRANK T. PAINE
WILLIAM NAUMES

TABLE OF CONTENTS

1

POLICY FORMATION AND THE CHOICE PROCESS 1

Questions to Ask 3
What Is Policy Formation? 4
What Are Missions, Objectives, Policies, Strategies,
    Programs and Roles? How Are They Related to
    Each Other? 5
        Basic Missions 6
        Organizational Objectives 6
        Policies 6
        Strategies 7
        Programs, Roles and Structures 8
        Need for Coherent Means-End Chain 9
The Choice Process — Some Ideas on What *Should*
    Happen 10
        Normative Framework for Policy Formation 13
The Choice Process — Some Ideas on What *Actually*
    Happens 15
Theories Relevant to the Choice Process 18
Overview of Decision Theories — Normative and
    Descriptive 18
        Group Theory and Elite Theory 20
A Case Study 20
Some Ideas on the Univis Case 21
Summary 22
Discussion Questions 23
Appendix. Univis, Inc. 24

2

**CONCEPTUALIZING THE POLICY FORMATION
PROCESS** 44

Policy Formation and Decision Making 44
A Descriptive Model of the Policy-Formation Process 47
    Inputs — Environmental Forces 49
    Structure — Roles and Programs 50
        Self-interests 51
        Political Resources 53
    Interaction of Structure and Environmental
        Pressures 54
    Circular Effects of Policy Formation 57

Applying the Model to Business and Public
Bodies.. 58
Illustration of Model — A Role Play 59
Social Responsibility and the Model — A Debate........ 61
Summary.. 63
Intergroup Policy Exercise................................... 64
Discussion Questions.. 65

3

LEARNING ABOUT POLICY 67

Case Study 69
The Case System in Business Education................. 70
Case Analysis.. 72
Using the Case Method 72
The Diagnostic Process...................................... 75
Diagnosis — Case Study 76
The Live Case 79
Field Projects.. 80
Field Research 83
Dynamic Computer Models................................. 88
Role Playing 90
Timing a Case in the Future with Science Fiction 93
Summary.. 94
Discussion Questions.. 95

4

ASSESSMENT GUIDES 97

Objectives of Assessment of Policy Formation.................. 98
Use of Guides 98
Framework for Assessing Policy Formation 99
Part A. The Current Situation.............................. 101
Current Organizational Mission and Current
Basis of Support 101
Organizational Objectives and Outcomes........ 106
Policy-generating Structure.......................... 111
Part B. The Changing Situation............................ 119
Environmental Forces — Problems,
Opportunities, Demands........................... 119
Economic Considerations.................... 119
Technological Advances...................... 121
Social Influences.............................. 122
Political Inputs................................. 123
Competitive Factors........................... 124
Social Responsibility.......................... 125
Summary.. 129
Discussion Questions.. 129
Appendix 1. A Program for Analyzing Some Aspects of
the Present Financial Conditions of the Organization...... 131
Appendix 2. A Program for Determining Top
Management Effectiveness Dimensions........................ 140

5

REFORMULATING CORPORATE STRATEGY: OBJECTIVES FOR CHANGE AND THE ACTION PLAN

REFORMULATING CORPORATE STRATEGY: OBJECTIVES FOR CHANGE AND THE ACTION PLAN 143

Outline of Corporate Strategy 144
Formulating Objectives for Change 145
Priority of Objectives 149
Making Trade-offs on Objectives 149
Problems to Overcome 150
The Action Plan: Setting Strategic Alternatives 152
Developing and Profiling Alternatives 153
Major Opportunities 153
Obvious Limitations 155
Narrowing the Choice 155
Synergistic Possibilities 156
Strategic Changes and Corporate Policies 157
Detailing Provisions for Procuring and
Allocating Resources: Linking Overall Strategy
with Operations 161
A Computer Program for Reformulating Corporate
Strategy 166
Summary 168
Discussion Questions 169

6

ASSESSMENT AND DEVELOPMENT METHODS— AN ACTION-RESEARCH PROGRAM

ASSESSMENT AND DEVELOPMENT METHODS— AN ACTION-RESEARCH PROGRAM 172

Why Assessment and Development? 173
Evaluation Approaches 174
What Is an Organization Development Approach to
Policy Formation? 177
Action-Research Program 179
Use and Limitations of Methods 179
Information Gathering and Processing 181
Forecasts 183
Publications and Reports 184
Informal Information Networks 185
Observation 188
Interviews 189
Interview Item Content 191
Sample of Structured Interview 193
Questionnaire 197
Questionnaire Item Content 198
Content Related to Organizational Effectiveness 199
Policy-Formation Practice Questionnaire 200
Breakout of Returns and Use of Results 203
Market Segmentation Breakouts 204
Summary 206
Discussion Questions 208

7

MANAGEMENT SCIENCE AND COMPUTER PROGRAMS ... 210

Use of Management Science Approaches in Strategy Formation ... 211
    Quantitative Problems in Policy ... 212
    Discounting and Present Value ... 212
    Personal Probability ... 213
    Case Problem I ... 214
    Establishing Priorities and Rates of Return ... 215
    Cost of Delay ... 215
    Tracing Decisions into the Future ... 216
    Case Problem II ... 217
    "What If" Questions ... 218
    Forecasting Models and Methods ... 220
    Simulations ... 222
    Combining Expert Opinion ... 224
Reasons for Success and Failure of Management Science Programs ... 225
Computer-Aided Decision Making ... 228
    Applications of Computers ... 229
    Creativity and the Computer ... 229
    Complex Systems ... 230
    Human Reaction to Complex Systems ... 230
Summary ... 231
Discussion Questions ... 233
Appendix 1. Solution to Problem 1 ... 235
Appendix 2. Solution to Problem 2 ... 236

8

THE ACTION THRUST IN STRATEGY FORMATION: DEVELOPING INDIVIDUAL AND GROUP INVOLVEMENT ... 237

Patterns for Effective Change and Implementation ... 238
Individual and Group Problem Solving ... 241
Overall Structuring of the Activity ... 243
Timing of the Activity ... 245
Selecting Problem-Solving Situations ... 246
Types of Structured Activities—Individual and Group ... 248
    Strategy Formation Process ... 249
    Assessment of Leverage Points ... 249
    Manager Functioning ... 250
    Stating and Analyzing Objectives ... 251
    Priority Setting and Action Planning ... 251
    Progress Review ... 251
Effective Group Sessions ... 253
Feed-in of Action Research and Management Science Data ... 254
Questions and Answers Regarding the Action Components ... 258
Summary ... 263
Discussion Questions ... 263
Appendix 1. Questionnaire on Managerial Functioning ... 266
Appendix 2. Organizational Effectiveness Form ... 270

9

STRATEGY AND STRUCTURE 272

Trends in Strategy and Structure 272
Designing the Organization 274
Environmental Demands 275
Related Influences on Design 276
Differentiating by Organizational Level.................... 278
Keeping the Corporate Strategy in Mind 280
Overall Summary 281
Practical Problems for You to Solve 281
Questions to Answer... 282
Policy Makers 283
Discussion Questions.. 284
Appendix. Some Action Steps.. 285

Author Index... 289

Subject Index.. 293

1

QUESTIONS TO ASK

WHAT IS POLICY FORMATION?

WHAT ARE MISSIONS, OBJECTIVES, POLICIES, STRATEGIES, PROGRAMS AND ROLES?

HOW ARE THEY RELATED TO EACH OTHER?
    Basic Missions
    Organizational Objectives
    Policies
    Strategies
    Programs, Roles and Structure
    Need for a Coherent Means-End Chain

THE CHOICE PROCESS – SOME IDEAS ON WHAT SHOULD HAPPEN

Normative Framework for Policy Formation

THE CHOICE PROCESS – SOME IDEAS ON WHAT ACTUALLY HAPPENS

THEORIES RELEVANT TO THE CHOICE PROCESS

OVERVIEW OF DECISION THEORIES – NORMATIVE AND DESCRIPTIVE
    Group Theory and Elite Theory

A CASE STUDY

SOME IDEAS ON THE UNIVIS CASE

SUMMARY

DISCUSSION QUESTIONS

APPENDIX 1. UNIVIS INC.

POLICY FORMATION AND THE CHOICE PROCESS

Two seemingly disparate events jolted a large diversified company last week. On Monday, in a surprise move, directors of the giant named a new man as president. On Wednesday the company sold its computer equipment business for $10.6 million to a smaller concern.

The new president was vaulted into the top spot largely because of his intimate identification with "strategic business planning," a technique that treats an organization's array of ventures with systematic analysis, sorting out the winners and the losers.

This true story, which actually occurred a few years ago, illustrates an important aspect of the field of policy, a subject that has received much attention recently. The field involves an in-depth analysis of such elements as growth prospects, competition, special organizational capabilities and requirements, and resource allocations. Many companies feel that such analysis will help to foster corporate growth. The systematic analysis, with some modification of course, would seem to be especially useful to nonprofit organizations in sifting through their own various activities and resource allocations.

A new manager of an organization, whether business or nonprofit, may be given the challenge of applying concepts from the field of policy on a continuing basis. Applying them, moreover, is one of the most important and complex challenges and opportunities with which a manager may be faced. For example, there may be forecasts to be made on changes in economic conditions, consumer behavior, social values, technology, politics and even pollution standards. In fact, there are a large number of environmental factors that may be of importance to the organization. Their significance for the organization must be determined, and time and effort must be spent in studying their impact on the organization's activities now and in the future. In addition to the difficult job of proper identification of the challenges and opportunities, the organization is faced with (1) setting missions and broad objectives; (2) designing action plans to fulfill these objectives; (3) developing and allocating the financial, human and physical resources to carry out the plans; (4) monitoring the results of the plans made and the organization to see that the desired ends are being accomplished and, when necessary, altering the plans or organization to more nearly accomplish the objectives; and (5) structuring the interpersonal and intergroup relationships within the organization to facilitate accomplishment of the desired future performance levels. These several elements constitute the field of policy.

As you can see, managers at the policy level are dealing with weighty and complex matters. The manager will have some of these matters within his grasp, but some are part of the broad framework of society and include various interest groups and various uncertainties.

This book is concerned with what the policy analyst or manager can do in a business or nonprofit institution to study and to improve the process of dealing with these complex policy issues. Recognition is given to the similarities in top management functions and responsibilities in all types of performance-oriented organizations. The book deals with ideas useful to organizations of various sizes and organizations with various technologies. Its focus is on managers with significant policy-making responsibility. It has application, as well, to managers and staff with broad responsibilities in a significant segment of an organization (e.g., a profit center or an operations bureau). It covers the more general policy-making issues and problems that affect the long-term development of the performance-oriented organization. The emphasis tends to be on private business firms, and the book deals to only a limited extent with important but specialized topics such as labor relations policy, executive staffing and mergers.

The manager, even at the top level, is influenced by policies and activities other than his own. Sometimes, if he is at or near the top, he has opportunities to influence his organization's major policies and to take part in activities that contribute to the vitality of the total organization. His actions, however, must be responsive to requirements and changes outside his control. Nevertheless, he shapes his own policy formation process to meet internal requirements and to respond to specific situations. He must help individual policy analysts and policy formation groups to achieve a proper understanding of their role in the total organization (perhaps vis-à-vis other individuals or groups) and to improve their effectiveness in identifying and making choices.

QUESTIONS TO ASK

Assume you are being hired to help to design and to implement an approach for improving the policy formation process in a private or public organization. You should be sufficiently informed and self-critical to be aware of the flimsy base on which prescriptions for strategic management have been posed.* Some advances are now being made in behavioral and management science concepts and in assessment and development techniques to replace relatively unsystematic observations and anecdotal evidence. Still, a cautious, "I don't know for sure" approach seems to be appropriate. This book will use such a cautious approach, but hopefully will provide some guidance in establishing a model and a frame of reference for your thinking and your search.

There will be many questions to ask in your search for an approach to improving policy formation. One set of questions that you might be asking has to do with the nature of the choice process and policy formation.

1. What is "policy formation"?
2. What are missions, objectives, policies, strategies, programs, roles?
3. How are they related to one another?
4. By what methods and processes *should* significant decisions or choices be made?
5. How are choices *actually* made in policy formation?
6. Of what relevance is normative and descriptive decision theory?

Study of this chapter should provide the reader with some answers to these questions.

Another set of questions has to do with conceptualizing the policy formation process and is taken up in the second chapter. The second chapter questions are aimed at uncovering and describing what the policy formation process actually involves:

1. How does policy formation relate to typical decision-making models?
2. What are environmental demands and environmental support?
3. What are some significant aspects of the policy generating structure?
4. What is the role of the manager in coordinating conflicting sets of interests?
5. How do the structure and the environment interact to form organizational objectives, organizational strategies, and so forth?

You would surely want to deal with a set of questions on the ways of assessing and improving the policy product or, from a different perspective, with questions dealing with approaches to study

---

*P. H. Grinyer: Some dangerous axioms of corporate planning. *Journal of Business Policy*, 3 (No. 1) 3–9, 1973.

of the process of policy formation. In other words, the questions aim at guides and methods for studying and developing the policy process and policy product.

1. How does one learn about policy? (Chapter 3)

2. What are some guides for assessing the current situation of the organization and its environment? (Chapter 4)

3. What are some guides for reformulating organizational objectives and action plans? (Chapter 5)

4. What are some methods for assessment and development of the organization, its strategies and its policy formation process? (Chapter 6)

5. What is the role of management science and the computer at the policy level? (Chapter 7)

6. By what processes is there an "action thrust" in strategy making that involves others in planning actions, coordinating actions, executing actions and evaluating actions? (Chapter 8)

7. What are some of the factors related to the structural form of the organization? What are some stages in the development of the organization? How may one take a planned approach to action? (Chapter 9)

This chapter will introduce you to the choice process and policy formation. It provides background material helpful to understanding the nature of this important but complex subject. The material following this chapter suggests answers to some of the additional questions you may have about conceptualizing, assessing and developing the policy formation process.

WHAT IS POLICY FORMATION?

Definition

Important broad definition.

Policy formation involves the decision making and the activities in an organization which tend to (1) have wide ramifications, (2) have a long-time perspective, and (3) use critical resources toward perceived opportunities in a changing environment. Policy formation is a dynamic social process within which an intellectual process is embedded.

It involves wide ramifications. Policy formation activities are related to the total system (or a large segment of it), such as a change in organization goals, or managerial strategies that have implications throughout the organization (e.g., a major change in the direction or scope of the business or activity the organization is in).

It involves a long-time perspective. The directional decisions in policy formation can be expected to have effects on the organization for an extended period of time.

It uses critical resources toward perceived opportunities in a changing environment. The most important human, financial and other resources are brought to bear in certain situations seen as providing the organization with an opportunity to manage the elusive environment. To understand how effective the policy formation process has been, it is necessary to have some criteria for what an effective policy formation process would look like. This question will be dealt with in a later chapter.

It is an intellectual process. In policy formation, key individuals perceive, analyze and choose between alternatives, interrelating such policy elements as basic missions, broad organizational goals, policies and strategies.

It is a continuing dynamic social process. Policy formation is not just a chore to be undertaken a few times each year when top management meets to decide critical issues. Policy formation is a continuing dynamic social process of implementing and revising policies in the human organization as changes occur in resources and in the environment.

All these characteristics of policy formation will be examined with the view toward understanding and improving the choice process, which significantly affects the welfare of the organization and the individual. Before looking at what *should* happen in the choice process, however, it is important to make a few comments on how the various components of the policy formation process may be described or defined.

WHAT ARE MISSIONS, OBJECTIVES, POLICIES, STRATEGIES, PROGRAMS AND ROLES? HOW ARE THEY RELATED TO EACH OTHER?

In the conduct of business or agency operations a hierarchy of rules for conduct may exist either explicitly or implicitly. The hierarchy in descending order is referred to here as missions or scope, objectives, policies, strategies, programs and roles. In the following discussion we shall present a few highlights of the nature of these elements so that the policy analyst can differentiate between them. Later these topics will be discussed in more detail. You will notice that the phrases "policy formation" and "strategy formation" are being used interchangeably to refer to a number of kinds of significant activities and elements in an organization. There is no classification of elements or of activities that has a common acceptance. However, many writers and practitioners will agree that, while it is not essential for all to distinguish between elements in the same way, it is essential that one see the means-end relationships among such components as missions, objectives and policies. One of the ways of distinguishing between the elements and examining the means-end relationship is what follows next. Alternative ways will be discussed throughout the book.

What is the hierarchy of rules of conduct?

Terms used interchangeably!

Basic Missions

Scope of operation—product and market or service and client.

As mentioned, policy formation includes the making and interrelating of decisions on the use of limited resources with potential opportunities, risks and threats in a changing, uncertain environment. On the basis of information about such environmental factors and taking into consideration personal values or self-interests of top managers and/or "influentials" in the organization or associated with it in some way, decisions are made on the basic mission or direction of the organization. The mission may be described as the scope of operations in terms of product and market or of service and client. An organization may define its mission as the railroad business. However, it will be one thing if its mission is commuter or passenger business near a large metropolitan area and quite another if it is freight hauling in the midwest. Deciding upon the basic mission is a *fundamental* component in policy formation. For example, the Southern Pacific Railroad Company decided it was in the transportation business (not just the railroad business) and expanded its activities into trucking and pipelines. Too broad a mission may be dangerous, since problems tend to increase in relation to opportunities.

Organizational Objectives

Hoped for results, goals or targets.

Organizational objectives may be described as "hoped for results, goals or targets." They can be quite general (e.g., quality service) or very specific (e.g., reduction in force—(RIF), 5 per cent by June 30th). The more specific the goal, the easier it is to appraise how well it has been fulfilled.

Objectives or goals can be derived from different considerations. They may be based on extensive analysis of the external environment, or they may be dictated, without any research analysis, by the top manager or other influential people associated with the organization. They may also have been derived from complex power plays within the organization. However, if the basic mission is, in fact, desired, the objectives need to be based on fulfilling such a mission. We shall return to this point in a minute.

Policies

Broad guides.

Policies may be described as broad guides for managers, supervisors and other employees for the achievement of objectives. It is important to recognize that the policies stem from fulfilling objectives. For example, an objective of quality service may have a policy of extensive monitoring of service activities. Obviously, each objective may require more than one policy in the attempt to reach the objective; thus, another policy stemming from the objective of quality service may be the decision to recruit only the very top-rated management personnel. It may be a decision to allow divisions to acquire only other quality oriented companies, after approval of the central office.

Now one may see the hierarchy or means-end chain in basic missions, objectives and policies. In the above example the extensive monitoring was a *policy* designed to fulfill a basic objective of quality service. If we use our previous example of a basic mission being the transportation of goods and passengers, the hierarchy looks as follows:

Transportation of Goods and Passengers
Quality Service
Extensive Monitoring

The means-end chain is a reflection of the fact that every step in the hierarchy is a means to an end. The chain occurs because all the missions, objectives, policies (and strategies) are linked to one another.

Strategies

While policies are seen as broad guides to action, strategies may be viewed as specific *major* actions or patterns of action for attainment of objectives. They may be planned ahead of time or emerge over time based on ad hoc decisions.* A strategic decision for a company might be to deploy resources into new operations in Germany; another might be to compete head to head with another company for the instant photography business, such as Eastman Kodak's decision to develop a technically superior in-camera development process. Such strategic decisions may result in the need for strategies for marketing, technology, finance, geographic area definition, and so forth; in other words, a cluster of strategies may be required.

Specific major actions or pattern of actions.

A cluster of strategic decisions over time might involve, for example, (1) picking a particular product-market segment or niche that is propitious in view of the needs of society and the organization's capabilities, (2) selection of the underlying technologies and ways for attracting financial and other inputs, (3) deployment of resources into a particular geographic or major research area, and (4) disposing of a particular line of products which do not fit acceptable levels on significant criteria (e.g., our initial example of the computer equip-

What is a cluster of strategies?

Corporate strategy may be viewed as an integrative concept.

*As we shall see later in this chapter, an overall strategy (or corporate strategy) may be defined as a plan which encompasses not only the mission, policies, objectives and more specific goals of the organization, but also a plan of action for achieving those objectives and goals. Subsequent decisions are based on the plan. On the other hand, corporate strategies may be described as a stream of significant decisions which emerge over a period of time into a pattern. In this case the decisions, made on an ad hoc basis while trying to adapt to various uncertainties, determine the strategy.

ment business). An overall strategy, then, is the sum total or pattern of these past and present actions or decisions.

An example of a strategic decision stemming from our previous means-end chain would be the decision for greater integration of the organization by adding assessment and development activities formerly purchased from other organizations. The activities might be seen as a systematic attempt toward planned change in the organization to fulfill the policy of extensive monitoring. The actions might include market research and auditing of the rapidly changing external environment, as well as additional auditing of the internal environment of the organization.

Programs, Roles and Structures

Programs—generalized procedures in response to particular actions.

Programs can be described as generalized procedures that are used in response to a particular type of stimulus.* You have heard of programs being "built" into the computer, which takes inputs, executes a set of steps and produces outputs. Humans, as well as machines, learn and use programs as an economical (they are not new each time but reflect the learning of past actions) way of responding. For example, the financial analyst in response to a request carries out a capital budgeting program, or a manager in response to a difficulty carries out a problem-solving program.

As with strategies, there are sets of programs linked to each other. One set might describe the various assessment and development activities used to measure progress in terms of time, resources, quality and quantity. Another related set might describe such methods as periodic status reports, data analysis, interviews, questionnaires and problem-solving conferences. Thus, to the above means-end chain could be added:

Assessment and Development Activities
Problem-solving Conferences, and so forth

The means-end chain could be extended to the level of the individual manager, supervisor or employee in the organization. If it were extended, the individual's role prescription as well as his actual role performance would be added. The role prescription includes the pattern of behavior expected and the functions, duties, authorities and responsibilities assigned to the holder of the position. For example, part of the role prescription for a manager might be as follows:

Determine whether significant factors have been included in goal or target setting of subordinates.

---

*We elaborate on the concept of program in Chapter 4.

The role performance is a description of the actual pattern of behavior that is followed by the individual and the actual functions and duties he performs. It may be quite specific. For example:

> In carrying out his leadership role, he frequently chats informally with his subordinates. Through this contact he keeps current on important milestones and he uses his recognized competence to influence the pattern of activities among his subordinates.

Roles—behavior patterns of the individual.

The structure of an organization deals with the coupling of the roles (and programs) of various members of the organization and the resulting flow of information and authority. It is important to note that in carrying out roles, managers and other influentials use programs to make determinations on the other aspects of the hierarchy, such as missions, objectives, policies, and strategies. We shall return later to the policy making structure of the organization and discuss roles and programs more fully.

The means-end chain that has been constructed to this point, appears as follows:

Transportation of Goods and Passengers
Quality Service
Extensive Monitoring
Assessment and Development Activities
Problem-solving Conferences
Determinations on Whether Significant Factors
Are Included in Target Setting
Frequent Informal Chats with Subordinates

The means-end chain, of course, is a simplification in that even in the smallest agency, department or business concern there are a number of interrelated objectives, policies and programs. It seems important to recognize the fact that, contrary to an assumption sometimes made in economics, there is no such thing as a single objective for a company or organization. Each organization has a network of goals and a network of means to attain those prescribed goals.

While evaluating an organization and its "policy formation process," the classification of basic missions, objectives, policies, strategies, programs, role prescriptions and role performance is difficult and inexact. Evaluation, however, cannot proceed effectively without knowledge of these elements and how they are interrelated.

Classification difficult and inexact but must have knowledge of elements.

Need for Coherent Means-End Chain

We have indicated that for each organizational situation the means-end chain needs to be examined for interrelationships and for mutual supportiveness. That is, do the review procedures generate useful data for strategy formation? Are the clusters of strategies designed in such a way as to facilitate policy fulfillment? Is, say, centralized decision making congruent with expected participative lead-

TABLE 1-1 SOME ORGANIZATIONAL FEATURES THAT ARE
LIKELY TO VARY WITH A CHANGE IN STRATEGY

Centralization versus decentralization of authority

Degree of division of labor

Size of self-sufficient operating units

Mechanism for coordination

Nature and location of staff

Management information system

Characteristics of key personnel

ership practices? Are pay and promotion procedures supporting desired role performance?

The determination of mutual consistency is, needless to say, a difficult task. Strategies, for example, are subject to continuing formation, implementation, interpretation, change and obsolescence over time. With each shift in strategy the appropriateness of the means-end chain needs to be examined anew. One of the comparisons for the business policy analyst is: Do we have the right organizational structure for our new strategies? To complicate the matter there are several structural features (among other types) that are likely to vary with a change in strategy, as William Newman has discussed.* At this point we shall just show you a sample of features (Table 1-1).

This discussion of the means-end chain has given you a preliminary indication of the information processing that the policy analyst must do in dealing with complex policy issues. The nature and importance of these issues necessitate attention on a continuing basis to the choices that are being made.

The choice process is the next subject to be examined. After a brief introduction to the choice process, some ideas on what *should* happen will be discussed, following which some ideas on what actually happens will be indicated.

THE CHOICE PROCESS—SOME IDEAS ON WHAT *SHOULD* HAPPEN

Assume that you have agreed to accept the challenge of trying to develop an approach for improving policies and the policy formation process. Assume further that you are asking some of the questions that were outlined previously in this chapter in order to get a

---

*William H. Newman: Strategy and Management Structure. Presented at the Annual Meeting of the Academy of Management, Atlanta, Georgia, 1971. See also A. D. Chandler: *Strategy and Structure,* Cambridge, MIT Press, 1962.

general orientation as to the nature of the present policy situation. The development of an approach for improvement in policy formation demands some early analysis of the choice procedure; that is, given the fact that resources and capabilities are limited, choices must be made between competing alternative strategies or policies. We ask then by what methods and processes should significant decisions or choices be made?

What methods and processes should be used?

Some ideas on what should happen can be derived by examining organizations such as Digital Equipment Corporation (D.E.C.), American Motors, and HMH Publishing Co. (Playboy). They have aimed their products at *particular niches in a larger market.* D.E.C., for example, decided against attempting to compete directly with I.B.M. Instead, it built expertise in a much smaller market, that of mini-computers. While I.B.M. was building larger machines, D.E.C. took the opposite approach and built smaller, more compact machines for lower prices. It felt that the mini-computer market would expand once the computer had become fully accepted. The mini-computer was felt to be the answer for those large and small corporations that have problems that could best be solved by use of computers — problems, however, that could not be programmed economically on the large full scale machines.

Find a niche.

The success of D.E.C. over the last several years points to the effectiveness of its corporate strategy. This strategy, as we can see, was designed to take advantage of competitive factors in the environment. D.E.C. hoped it could *match its own internal strengths* in computer design, as well as company size, *with a perceived need in the environment.* In this manner D.E.C. tried to turn a potential weakness, its size and the competitive situation, into an opportunity *by formulating a set of objectives and an action plan that skirted its weaknesses and these threats* and *capitalized on its strong points in the total environment.*

Match internal strengths and perceived need in environment.

Skirt weaknesses and threats.

The above example shows the desirability of a *well defined corporate strategy or strategic posture* from which the organization can work. Effective use and communication of such a strategic posture allowed D.E.C. to channel its resources into a particular area. This use and communication enabled subordinates in all areas of the organization to gain a knowledge of the direction that the organization was to take and to make tactical (or implementing), as well as strategic, policy decisions in a consistent manner.

Work from well defined corporate strategy.

Additional examples of directing product appeal to particular market segments as mentioned are American Motors Corporation and Playboy Enterprises. A.M.C. found, in the late 1960's, that it did not have the resources to compete head-on with the Big Three in the auto industry. It saw its sales and market share decline as it spread its efforts and image over a broad range of models. It made a decision to return to its formerly successful strategy of producing small quality cars. A.M.C. felt that this niche strategy, combined with the knowledge that imported subcompacts were selling well, would help it to regain its lost share of market and profits. This strategy has proved relatively successful for the company.

What is A.M.C.'s current corporate strategy?

Playboy Enterprises, on the other hand, has attempted to tie its diversification efforts into a consistent image of the company. Its products and services are all tied in to its philosophy of the kind of life style the successful urban male should follow. The various enterprises of the firm are designed to enhance that life style.

These examples, however, only give us some insight into parts of what we should consider as a total strategy for an organization. They do not really give us a picture of the framework that the analyst should use during the strategy formation process.

The approaches taken by most policy texts are really concerned with what should be done during the policy formation process.* Although their definitions differ, they are meant to provide a framework to be followed by the policy analyst to provide an effective corporate strategy.

What are the common threads?

There are common threads that can be traced through many of the various statements on the strategy or policy formation process. The process is felt to be both continuous and creative. It involves the individual or group in a constant process of creatively applying information to the future of the organization. The corporate strategy adopted by an organization should encompass not only the objectives and more specific goals of the organization, but also a plan of action for achieving those objectives and goals. This plan of action should contain the degree of detail appropriate to the time span relevant to the particular strategy, as well as the function of the analyst involved in the process.

The example from D.E.C.'s planning demonstrates that the corporate strategy should also consider both the external and internal factors in the environment affecting the future course of the firm. Too often an organization fails to consider the external environment fully when discussing its future direction. Even when internal and external areas are explored during the policy formation process, the question of integrating the total analysis is often not considered. The analyst frequently neglects to consider internal factors as they relate to external opportunities and threats. This, then, detracts strongly from the feasibility of the total plan. It also tends to create inconsistencies within the corporate strategy ultimately adopted.

---

*See, for example, H. I. Ansoff: *Corporate Strategy*, New York, McGraw-Hill Book Co., 1965; W. H. Newman and J. P. Logan: *Strategy Policy and Central Management*, Cincinnati, Southwestern Publishing Co., 1971; F. Gilmore: *Formulation and Advocacy of Business Policy*, Ithaca, Cornell University Press, 1970; R. Katz: *Management of the Total Enterprise*, Englewood Cliffs, N. J., Prentice-Hall, Inc., 1970; C. E. Sumner, Jr., and J. O'Connell: *The Managerial Mind*, Homewood, Ill., Richard D. Irwin, Inc., 1969; J. T. Cannon: *Business Strategy and Policy*, New York, Harcourt, Brace & World, Inc., 1968; R. H. Buskirk: *Business and Administrative Policy*, New York, John Wiley & Sons, Inc., 1970; W. Glueck: *Business Policy: Strategy Formation and Management Action*, New York, McGraw-Hill Book Co., 1972; F. J. Bridges, K. W. Olm and J. A. Barnhill: *Management Decisions and Organizational Policy*, Boston, Allyn & Bacon, Inc., 1971; H. N. Broom: *Business Policy and Strategic Action*, Englewood Cliffs, N.J., Prentice-Hall, Inc., 1970; E. P. Learned, C. R. Christensen, K. R. Andrews and W. D. Guth: *Business Policy, Text and Cases*, Homewood, Ill., Richard D. Irwin, Inc., 1969; T. J. McNichols: *Policy Making and Executive Action*, New York, McGraw-Hill Book Co., 1972.

The question of an effective framework, therefore, often can be difficult to resolve. The framework should include a general structuring of the policy or strategy formation process. It should also include a method of presenting this framework to the user of the process. The examples and literature included in this book present the arguments for different types of frameworks and the need for a total framework.

Integrate the analysis of external and internal factors.

Normative Framework for Policy Formation

Figure 1–1 presents a framework demonstrating the interrelationships between some of the various factors mentioned above that are involved in strategy making.

STRATEGY FORMATION

Figure 1–1 *In particular, this figure demonstrates the need for a thorough analysis of the total environment when carrying on the strategy formation process. The environment affects all phases of the process, objectives, actions, and results and, in turn, is affected by them.*

The objectives are determined by a composite of the values of the principles involved as well as the capabilities of the organization and the analysis of the external environment. These objectives, in turn, determine the more specific goals or results for which the firm may be aiming.

In addition, both the environment and the objectives provide constraints on the alternative actions available to the organization. The commitment of resources at this stage represents the beginning of a total action plan designed to achieve results consistent with the objectives originally proposed.

All this, in turn, affects the environment, both internal and external. These environmental changes could alter the basic values of the individuals involved in the strategy. This could then lead to a revised strategy. The entire process, therefore, develops into a continuous, iterative procedure causing changes by the very nature of the process itself.

A continuous iterative process.

The key to this framework is the manager or policy analyst himself. He stands in the middle of the environment, exploring the situation around him in order to plan — hopefully — for an "optimal" fit between resources and objectives.

The next point that should be considered is the consistency of fit of the objectives with the environment, both internal and external. After finding a competitive niche in the automobile market, A.M.C. decided to take on the Big Three across the board. It felt that to be an effective competitor, it should also produce a full line of cars. What the firm failed to consider was the total environment facing it. It failed to consider its own weakness with respect to its competition. The other firms were better able to compete, financially and in other ways, in the general auto market. A.M.C. had allowed itself to take its previous success in one particular submarket as a sign of strength in the total market.

We now see that one phase of strategy formation involves a more general determination of objectives. Another phase looks for specific areas of strength and weakness in the total environment. A third phase involves formulation of an action plan consistent with the previous analysis. Included in the total process must be a method of evaluating the total strategy to ensure the success of that strategy.

The development of this planning framework is only one part of the total framework, however. The action plan resulting from this framework can be arrived at only if the analyst is able to comprehend the entire planning process. An effective method of utilizing this framework must, therefore, be determined. This should include the ordering of the framework and the mechanical means of presenting the ordered framework to the analyst. There are, naturally, differences of opinion as to the approach that is most effective in ordering and presenting the framework.

What is a "wholistic" approach?

One school of thought is to approach strategy formation from the top down. This opportunity-oriented or "wholistic" approach has been suggested by several authors and studies. The analytical process in this approach begins with a general, overall view of the organization and its strategic position in its environment. It then works toward creating, through an iterative process, a feasible strategy for the organization by matching strengths with opportunities, and suppressing or overcoming weaknesses and threats.

What is an "incremental" approach?

A somewhat different approach is also possible, however. The "incremental" or "tactical" approach is more useful in some instances. This approach attempts to explore the environment from the bottom up. The detailed and specific resources of the organization are first studied; then this analysis is used to develop possible courses of action for the organization to follow.

The problem with the former method is that the analyst could possibly become too engrossed with the overall picture and fail to produce a detailed corporate strategy. A lack of specifics could then lead to the strategy's becoming infeasible through a lack of fit with the particular environment in which it must exist. Also, if the strategy lacks specific details concerning crucial or key issues, the potential for change of the strategic posture of the organization from below is increased. Lower levels of management, after all, are supposed to be utilizing the corporate strategy for guidance. If there is ambiguity or lack of specificity in the plan or objectives, they will substitute their own strategy for that of the organization. This could lead to suboptimal use of the organization's resources.

The incremental method also has problems, however. These are very close to the reverse of the problems associated with the top-down approach. In taking an incremental approach, the analyst often fails to get a global view of the environment. To use an old cliché, he often fails to see the forest for the trees. There is also a tendency for inconsistency in the final strategy. This can come about from a lack of fit between the individual areas studied. There is also a potential for suboptimization if the analyst fails to tie the individual analyses together.

When we realize the potential problems emanating from both methods, we see the opportunity for combining the two methods and, hopefully, eliminating the problems. McKinney, for example, found that use of the wholistic approach followed by the incremental approach provided superior results when student analysts had several problems to solve.*

The approach that is taken by this book is a modified form of this integrative method. The framework of the approach to be used includes essentially a wholistic method of presentation, with incremental-type questions added to attempt to overcome the problems previously noted.

An integrative approach is taken.

THE CHOICE PROCESS—SOME IDEAS ON WHAT *ACTUALLY* HAPPENS

We have briefly introduced a normative, theoretical framework for policy or strategy formation. If we were living and managing in a theoretical world, this framework would produce ideal strategies for organizations.

As we well know, however, we operate in a world with a wide variety of uncertainties and difficulties. These factors can lead to considerable variance from the process as we have outlined it. This should not lead us to scrap the entire process, however. It should lead us to try to understand why the variances occur and how we can adapt the basic process to account for these variances. A brief anecdote concerning policy formation in practice might help to highlight some of these problems and solutions.

Recently a large electronics firm decided to diversify into related areas. A financial planner was included in a new ventures division. His primary responsibility was to cooperate with the engineering department for planning for large scale, capital improvements.

He and an engineer proceeded to gather information concerning the future direction and objectives of the total organization forecasts regarding sales and expense constraints, although, with some degree of difficulty. The difficulty appeared to be primarily politically motivated within the organization. They were, however, finally able to obtain all the technical data they felt was necessary from a planning standpoint.

Based on this data, which they were able to get all relevant managers within the organization to agree on, they proceeded to formulate a consistent and feasible plan of action. After several weeks of consultations and revisions, they presented their plan to the plant and division managers.

The plan took into consideration the various constraints the firm had to face. The final figures of the plan were presented in terms of total square feet

*George W. McKinney, III: *An Experimental Study of Strategy Formulation Systems* (Stanford, California, Graduate School of Business, Stanford University, 1969), p. xi. (Unpublished doctoral dissertation.)

of building area and equipment required to achieve division objectives from a capital improvements point of view. This information was designed to fit into an overall strategy for diversification and expansion.

To the surprise of the analysts, the upper level managers were unimpressed with the presentation. The analysts left the presentation session determined to find out why this "well formulated" plan had not been accepted. Further discussions with other top managers in the corporation led the analysts to what they felt was a solution. They discovered that the symbols of status and success within the organization revolved around the numbers and growth of the personnel beneath a given manager on the organization chart. They felt that this could well have influenced the managers' reactions to the formulated plan.

With this knowledge, the analysts reconstructed their presentation to point up the numbers of people involved in the proposal. Fortunately this was relatively simple to chart since this information was a necessary basic consideration in arriving at the original plan. Effectively, all they did was to make the same presentation but to use different terms in defining their purposes. The result was that the superiors accepted the presentation and included it in the total strategy.

What this demonstrates is that all decisions are not made in a vacuum. Eventually human managers must make a commitment of resources for a particular strategy. These commitments are not always based on a rational analysis of a completely known environment.

In this factual example the decision of the managers was influenced by status factors that would not necessarily affect the overall success or failure of the strategy. Moreover, the analysts did not have this information available to them at crucial stages of the policy formation process.

In this instance, this part of the strategy could be reformulated with relatively little waste of time and energy. Many times, however, much time and energy seem to be wasted because of lack of proper understanding of all the factors affecting how significant decisions are actually made in an organization.

Prescriptions are meaningful only when grounded on valid description.

Theories and concepts may provide a solid foundation for understanding the basic strategy formation process. They are very practical or useful if they give us an appropriate framework for thinking and for making policy choices. However, prescribing what we should do is meaningful only when it is grounded in valid description.

Behavioral theory of the firm.

Thus, as we have asked: What actually happens in the choice process? Descriptive decision theory and, in particular, the behavioral theory of the firm* provide us with some additional clues.

Organization is a coalition.

One point of departure is to view the organization as a coalition. It includes a variety of individuals and subcoalitions, e.g., bureau chiefs, product managers, engineering managers, members of the

---

*R. M. Cyert and J. G. March: *A Behavioral Theory of the Firm,* Englewood Cliffs, N.J., Prentice-Hall, Inc., 1963. For empirical support see E. E. Carter: The behavioral theory of the firm and top-level corporate decisions, *Administrative Science Quarterly, 16* (No. 4):413–428, Dec., 1971. See also T. Petit: A behavioral theory of management, *Academy of Management Journal,* Dec., 1967, pp. 341–350.

Board of Commissioners, heads of research, union officials, vice presidents, stock holders, and others. They are all participating in the organization because they share some goals; there is presumed to be some net benefit for their participation. However, there may be conflict over unshared goals and over the distribution of benefits. Different organizational units (say two service bureaus) have different functions or activities but are rivals. This conflict can become a motivation for constructive thought and analysis based on in-depth research and detailed information (experiments have shown interpersonal conflict to be associated with this rivalry).

Conflict over unshared goals.

However, the managers or executives involved, caught up in the organizational rivalry, learn to maintain their viability in organizational life. First, they learn that it is better not to have a proposal turned down. "No's" may get to be a habit; the "no's" may damage their image, their effectiveness and their future. Second, they learn that for many issues or proposals the uncertainty is so great that a slight change in the calculations or emphasis may mean that the organizational standards or cut-off points may be met or missed. For example, breakeven analysis is frequently used in financial planning. A slight change in the predicted expenses and capital outlays might produce a breakeven point at a level below the predicted volume of sales. Third, the executive may learn that in his organization analytical time is a scarce commodity. That, together with a common—as opposed to rational—thinking about sunk cost may mean that once a study is authorized, written up and reviewed, it becomes, as time goes on, increasingly difficult to reject. Thus, the initial authorization to make such studies is a key leverage element. Finally, and most generally, the executive heading up an organizational unit is viewed as changing his aspirations, postponing goals, making trade offs, developing allies and attempting to change the aspirations of others. He is responding to the costs and benefits in the social context.

Learning to maintain viability.

Thus, if our description is accurate we have a situation in which the sum of the proposed projects is not necessarily combined into a set which is meaningfully consistent with the organization's mission or objectives. To the contrary, given that subgoals exist and are important, the executives are bargaining and negotiating, trying to maintain a winning coalition. A coalition is sought that provides support for the proposal and for the right of the executive to go ahead and proceed with the proposal. Much time may be spent writing up the proposal so that it meets the agency or corporate standards, but this may be a time-consuming and relatively unimportant part of the game.

Bargaining and negotiating to maintain a winning coalition.

The manager or policy analyst needs to understand the process. The informal descriptive postulates presented are exceedingly limited. More normative as well as descriptive content is needed for prescriptions. The calculations are (and should be) made in comparing strategy proposals, but it may be far more useful to compare and

Need to understand more about the choice process.

check proposals against the profile of the basic mission and the objectives of that mission. Later we shall again refer to this comparison. We shall take it up in more detail in the section in which we indicate ways of assessing policy formation.

THEORIES RELEVANT TO THE CHOICE PROCESS

In summary to this point in our analysis of the choice process, we see policy initiators making an analysis and choice but doing so within a dynamic social process. Policy makers (or initiators) are seen as allocating and mediating among conflicting sets of interests. They form judgments specific to the situation, balancing each issue off against a wide range of other issues, present and future. And in doing so, they attempt to maintain a coalition of support.

You may want to investigate the theories further.

Furthermore, in our discussions to this point we have developed some considerations from theories relevant to the choice process. These approaches have been reviewed elsewhere (for an excellent review see Bauer and Gergen),* so we shall not review them extensively here. Moreover, later in this book use will be made of some of the more important variables (e.g., programs, roles, self-interests) from previous studies, with explanations provided where appropriate.

The next section will provide a brief summary of the type of theories relevant to the choice process. It may be appropriate for the student of policy formation to conduct further investigation of many of these theories. This overview is included to indicate the range of possibilities.

OVERVIEW OF DECISION THEORIES—NORMATIVE AND DESCRIPTIVE

The way they "ought to" versus the way they actually do.

Decision theory may be separated into two categories, normative and descriptive. Normative theory is concerned with the particular decisions an organization ought to make, and descriptive theory is concerned with the way organizations actually go about making decisions. Further, normative theory has as its purpose the provision of rules that will hopefully improve choices and consequences, while descriptive theory sets out to describe the patterns of behavior that characterize action.

Normative theory is, in essence, the theory of rational choice in complex situations. The mathematical or statistical method is frequently used to analyze relationships among valued con-

---

*R. A. Bauer and K. J. Gergen (eds.): *The Study of Policy Formation.* New York, The Free Press, 1968. See also F. Kast and J. Rosenzweig (eds.): *Contingency Views of Organization and Management.* Palo Alto, Science Research Associates Inc., 1973.

sequences. Normative theory characteristically involves an individual decision maker and decision values expressed in dollars. Using normative theory, management scientists propose ways of guiding the decision maker in business or public bodies in what he ought to do; that is, given an explicit statement of the decision maker's preference, exposition of the alternative actions open to him, and an indication of how the alternatives are related to the preferences, management scientists develop programs or generalized procedures which will indicate an optimal choice. As a practitioner or student of management and policy formation you probably are familiar with some of these programs or generalized procedures, such as statistical decision making, simulation and mathematical modeling.*

It is disturbing that these programs as publicized in some quarters might appear to give clear solutions to major policy problems. Such is not the case; exact solutions actually are not provided and should not be expected. The major weakness in providing a policy formation model is that normative theory may rely too heavily upon the concept of a single best solution. Management science programs can be helpful—as a point of departure. The strengths as well as the inadequacies of some of the procedures will be discussed in the next and subsequent chapters.

Major weakness of normative approach is that exact solutions are not provided.

Descriptive theory is more behavior oriented and may have a more pragmatic value to policy initiators in that it attempts to improve understanding of what actually is occurring. Furthermore, it tends to describe the complexities of a set of interrelated problems requiring solutions or in need of decisions. Thus, it has a better quality to fit to the complex policy formation situation.

Descriptive theory has better quality of fit.

Descriptive theory itself is further broken down into two categories that are particularly adaptive to the business and government world, theories of individual choice and theories of collective choice. Theories of individual choice obviously involve single decision makers and are exemplified by the classic theory of economic man, the theory of consumer demand and the classic theory of the firm.

Theories of collective choice often refer to decisions made by a coalition of several decision makers, and rivalry and conflict between decision-making units. Such approaches are typified by the Harvard Business School and the Stanford Business School case studies, the institutionalists (e.g., Selznick†), the experimental economists (e.g., Fouraker‡), the Carnegie group (the behavior theory of the firm already mentioned) and the McGill group.§

Individual choice and collective choice.

However, though these descriptive approaches show promise, they may be criticized as either not testable or not yet adequately tested.

---

*These procedures and others will be amplified as we proceed.
†Phillip Selznick: *Leadership and Administration.* New York, Harper & Row, 1957.
‡L. E. Fouraker: Level of aspiration and group decision making, in Messick and Brayfield, (eds.): *Decision and Choice: Contributions of Sidney Siegel.* New York, McGraw-Hill Book Co., 1958.
§H. Mintzberg: The Nature of Managerial Work. New York, Harper & Row, 1973.

Group Theory and Elite Theory

In addition, descriptive decision theory is frequently viewed as including two particular categories, group theory and elite theory. Group theory places heavy emphasis on interaction within a group and sees the group as the primary source of influence over the attitudes and behaviors of individual policy makers. A major criticism of group theory is that it tends to subordinate the individual.

In contrast, elite theory places considerable emphasis on the individual. Elite theory often includes concern for the recruitment of elites, their socioeconomic characteristics, their perception and communication patterns and their circulation habits and, most importantly, their patterns of decision making. The theory hopes to explain expectations of elites and, therefore, the values they can be expected to pursue.* Elite theory, while isolating important analytical variables such as perceptions and decision-making patterns is criticized for not being tied to dynamic process variables. Policy making, so the argument would go, needs to be seen as a process of turning inputs into outputs.

Policy making needs to be seen as a process of turning inputs into outputs.

Our brief review of decision theory is designed only to provide a sample of the approaches that might be useful to the study of policy making and a sample of the criticisms that seem to reduce the appropriateness of these approaches for our purposes. That is, though the approaches have considerable merit, they do not provide rigorous support for prescriptions in policy making. Either the approach was based on nonoperational assumptions (e.g., a single decision maker) or it was devoid of acceptable normative content and could not be used alone to support prescription.

In short, any theory relevant to choosing policies and strategies is in its infancy. It would seem that, as already alluded to, advances in descriptive theory would be a major help in the development of a sound base for normative theory. It would seem also that we need field research allowing the comparison of policy formation in many types of organizations. Advances in field research would probably be aided and abetted by advances in normative theory. Better normative and descriptive content is needed for policy prescriptions.

What is needed for policy prescriptions?

A CASE STUDY

One way of adding to our descriptive content and learning about policy is through the use of case materials. A case study of an actual organization is given in the Appendix to this chapter to illustrate some of the elements in the policy formation process. Reading of the case on the Univis organization will aid in the understanding

---

*See, for example, W. D. Guth and R. Tagiuri: Personal values and corporate strategies, *Harvard Business Review*, September-October, 1965, pp. 123–132, and G. W. England: *Personal Value Systems of Managers—So What?*, Minneapolis, Industrial Relations Center, University of Minnesota, January, 1973.

of the need for consistency between such policy elements as follows: (1) mission (e.g., "Univis, Inc. is engaged in providing products and services used in the protection and improvement of human vision"), (2) fundamental objectives (e.g., "maximize owners' common share price and pursuit of growth"), (3) policies (e.g., "superior performance through excellence in generalized *professional management*"), (4) strategies ("pursue growth primarily through *compatible* exploitation of ongoing environmental change although opportunities otherwise commensurate with our standards will be considered"), and (5) programs (e.g., "the paramount phase in the planning program is in the reduction of preferences, insofar as useful, into a clear, precise and formal goal statement, with due regard to priority order and consistency in the arrangement of multiple facets"). There are several other phases in the Univis planning program such as determining the "gap" that existed between the company's objectives and the expected performance over the period of the planning cycle.

The Univis case does illustrate some of the practical problems that can be expected during the policy formation process. As we proceed in subsequent chapters we shall refer not only to this case, but provide anecdotes based on actual policy formation experiences in other organizations. The objective is to demonstrate real life problems and potential solutions.

SOME IDEAS ON THE UNIVIS CASE

Study and discussion of the Univis case, in particular, will demonstrate some of the problems inherent in implementing a theoretical approach to planning. The company had carried on no formalized planning prior to the employment of the new analyst. Changes in some areas and lack of changes in others can be viewed readily by discussing aspects of the case.

Particular emphasis in the discussion should be placed on the attitudes of the various executives toward planning as it has been implemented. Some see it as a threat to their autonomy and power. Others feel it will be totally ineffective and, therefore, ignore it. Others still are willing to go along with anything the "boss" says.

These kinds of responses by executives may be expected toward any planning process. The key may be to look for symptoms of these responses and to try to counter them before they become hardened into obdurate attitudes.

To be sure, however, the method of implementing a process of this type in the organization was not optimal. Attention may also be given to the time, effort and monetary cost put into the format. This may be compared with the benefits that are being seen after an appropriate period of time (e.g., three years) with the new process.

The style and method of using risk and opportunity tables could also be analyzed. More mention will be made of these factors in later chapters (particularly Chapter 7). A study might be made concerning the realism and feasibility of the criteria for deciding new directions for the organization.

Finally, the overall consistency of the strategy of the organization should be explored. Questions involving the fit between the stated objectives of the firm and the methods or action plan designed to achieve those objectives should be explored fully. Justification for the direction this firm is taking have been stated by management. The feasibility and consistency of these moves should be critically analyzed, not only from the perspective of the internal resources of the firm, but also from the viewpoint of the external environment.

SUMMARY

"Policy formation" is a general term referring to a dynamic social process of which an intellectual process is an integral part. Policy formation deals with such crucial questions as, "What can this organization do better than anyone else?" A hierarchy of rules of conduct exists explicitly or implicitly, including basic missions, objectives, policies, strategies, programs and roles. The key directional decisions in this hierarchy (1) have wide ramifications, (2) involve a long-time perspective, (3) affect the use of critical resources toward perceived opportunities and threats in a changing external and internal environment and (4) need to be checked for consistency. These characteristics necessitate continuous attention and emphasis on policy making by top management.

This book is concerned not simply with intellectual appreciation of these complex issues but with developing conceptual and administrative skill in dealing with them. The book deals with ideas useful to organizations of various sizes and various technologies. Its focus is on managers with significant policy-making responsibility. It has application, moreover, to managers and staff with strategy and policy responsibilities in significant segments of an organization. For students, the book is designed to provide some guidance for (1) case analysis, (2) field and library projects and (3) role playing. In the third chapter we shall discuss these and other important ways of learning about policy.

A person searching for an approach to improve policy formation would ask a number of questions including those on relevant theory and method, on the significant variables and relationships in the social process and the intellectual process of policy formation, and on alternative ways of assessing and developing policies and organizational processes. A mere beginning is made in this chapter at answering some of these questions.

The choice process is analyzed on a preliminary basis, first in terms of normative ideas and approaches and then in terms of describing what actually seems to happen. Management science programs, for example, have provided some useful ways of dealing with uncertainty. The normative approaches at the present time, however, do not give exact solutions to major policy issues. A check into what actually happens in some policy choices in real organizations provides useful insight.

We see policy makers analyzing choices but also allocating and mediating among conflicting sets of interests. Not only are they dealing with conflicting sets of interests, but they must balance each issue against a wide range of other issues, present and future.

Finally, this chapter gives an overview of some of the types of theories relevant to choice activities, points the way for further background study and provides a case study and some ideas for discussion. Next we shall compare policy formation with a typical cognitive model of decision making and then extend our conceptualization of the policy formation process. The conceptualization will help you to identify some of the significant variables that affect the complex problem solving involved in formulating policy.

DISCUSSION QUESTIONS

1. Discuss the importance of strategy and policy formation. What factors should be analyzed before attempting strategy formation?

2. What are the key elements that define decisions as having strategic importance?

3. Discuss the difference between strategies, policies, objectives, missions, programs and roles. How do they relate to one another?

4. How should organizations relate strategies to their environment? What relationships should be considered when defining an effective strategy formation process?

5. Discuss the relative merits of "wholistic" and "incremental" methods of analysis.

6. What are some practical problems that can inhibit effective strategy formation? How can they be overcome?

7. Discuss the applicability of decision theory to the strategy formation process. What are the major problems in utilizing these theories?

8. Discuss the strategy formation process as exemplified by the Univis, Inc., case. What are the strengths and weaknesses exemplified here? What recommendations would you suggest to improve the process?

APPENDIX TO CHAPTER 1

UNIVIS, INC.*

During 1966, Univis, Inc., a Fort Lauderdale, Florida firm primarily engaged in the ophthalmic lens and frame business, published a booklet for the financial community that included the following statement about the company's business philosophy:

A formalized philosophy underlies our planning and operations at all levels, indicative excerpts from which are presented below for your further Univis orientation.

Objective

Acknowledging the limitations thereto, it is our contention that over a reasonable period, the single most comprehensive indicator of a public company's performance, though not the only one, is the price-earnings ratio of its common stock share. Thus as a reflection of intended long-run excellence, our fundamental objective is

Maximize Owners' Common Share Price

PURSUIT OF GROWTH

Within the context of our circumstances, we feel it appropriate that:

We identify ourselves, through adherence to requisite prudent performance standards, as a *growth company,* and contend that this will cause our common share, through continuity in earnings increases, to be viewed as a *growth stock.*

We intend to maintain such superior

performance first through excellence in generalized *professional management,* whereby specialized endeavor is subordinated and utilized as deemed desirable to achieve fundamental corporatewide goals. Furthermore, in view of our resource, risk, and yield propensities, we will pursue growth primarily through compatible exploitation of ongoing *environmental change,* although opportunities otherwise commensurate with our standards will be considered.

FLEXIBILITY

To further clarify our managerial stance, two additional precepts are embraced.

We view our organization resources as a *homogeneous* pool, untied to specific endeavors except by limitation in skills and commitments, neither of which we underestimate.

Thus, while we acknowledge ophthalmics as our core industry, we feel that our organization resources are applicable to *any business opportunity* which meets

---

*Case material of the Harvard Graduate School of Business Administration is prepared as a basis for class discussion. Cases are not designed to present illustrations of either effective or ineffective handling of administrative problems.

our standards of desirability, and these include preference for activities characterized by common interests.

DIVIDEND POLICY

Recognizing the inverse relationship between self-generated funds to finance expansion, and cash dividend payout to provide current income to shareholders, and given the ultimate precedence of our fundamental objective and its supporting commitment to growth, we consider it desirable to

> Maintain cash dividend payout at the dollar quantity already established, increasing this when permitted by ability to sustain such increments.[1]

This explicit statement of business philosophy was one of the more recent steps taken by Univis to improve corporate performance through the use of "business planning." Although the company had talked in terms of business planning ever since its new management took over in late 1955, it was with the decision to set up a department of formal corporate planning in September, 1963, that steps were made toward formalizing the objectives and philosophy in "the way they should have been."[2]

Of the company's commitment to formal planning, Mr. R. O. Barber, Univis' president, said in 1965,

> In 1955 we had no one devoting full attention to formal planning.

Today our corporate planning department is composed of three professional planners and three service personnel and is headed by a company officer.

Is there a secret to growth? We don't think so. But there is a best way to grow. We call it corporate planning.[1]

The Company

BACKGROUND

Univis, Inc., began in 1911 as the Stanley Optical Company of Dayton, Ohio. This company, which was privately owned, subsequently changed its name to the Univis Lens Company. In 1955 working control was purchased from the founding family by four of the company's staff. Sales at the time were slightly over $4 million and in the first year of the new management the company suffered an operating loss of $290,000. See the table at the bottom of the page for the company's sales and profit from 1950–1955.

In 1960 the company changed its name to Univis, Inc., and moved its headquarters from Dayton, Ohio to Ft. Lauderdale, Florida. In 1966 three of the original four purchasers—Robert O. Barber (President), Arthur J. Sowers (Vice President and Treasurer), and Stanley A. Emerson (First Vice President)—were still with the company. Together they formed Univis' executive committee. In 1966 35 per cent

---

[1]*Facts about Univis*, 1966.
[2]Barber, Robert O.: Plan those Profits. *The Presidents Forum*, fall/winter 1965, p. 29.

[1]*Ibid.*, p. 32.

TABLE 1   SALES AND NET PROFIT UNIVIS LENS CO.—1950-1955

	1955	1954	1953	1952	1951	1950
Sales ($000's)	4,220	4,360	5,163	4,909	4,749	4,497
Net profit ($000's)	(292)	(89)	257	131	257	293

Source: Moody's *Industrials*

of the company's common stock was held by the directors and officers. The rest, traded over the counter, was widely distributed among approximately 2000 shareholders.

From the small beginning in 1955, sales had climbed to $16.3 million in 1966; net earnings had risen to $1,005,118. These figures represented the latest in a series showing continuous growth in both sales and earnings since the new management had acquired control. Only in 1960, when the company moved its corporate headquarters from Dayton to Fort Lauderdale, and again in 1963 did the earnings show a temporary decline. Since 1960 net earnings had grown at an average yearly compounded rate of 33.5 per cent on an average yearly compounded sales growth of 16.6 per cent. Exhibit 1 shows comparative income statement items for the years 1956–1966. Exhibit 2 is a similar comparison for balance sheet items, while Exhibit 3 shows market data on stock as well as the growth comparison of selected parameters.

PRODUCT LINE

The company produced both glass and plastic lenses. It offered a complete range of glass lenses from single vision through bifocal to cataract[1] and had introduced the industry's first straight-top bifocal *plastic* lens in 1963. Expansion into the frame business took place in 1961 with the acquisition of the Bishop Company. This commitment was further increased with the inclusion of the Zylite Corporation into the Univis group in 1962. Univis was then able to offer a complete line of men's, women's and children's frames, comprising in all about 2000 different items.

PRODUCTION FACILITIES

The company had four production facilities. The Fort Lauderdale plant made

[1]Single vision lenses have only one power of magnification. Cataract lenses are designed for patients who suffer from aphakia, a condition resulting from the absence of the eye's crystalline lens. Bifocal lenses combine two powers of magnification in a single lens. Straight-top bifocals have the break in magnification running in a straight line horizontally across the lens face.

special-purpose and single-vision glass lenses. A factory in Guayama, Puerto Rico, specialized in producing the standard range of bifocal glass lenses. A facility in West Babylon, New York, made plastic lenses and another in North Attleboro, Massachusetts, manufactured Univis spectacle frames. The combined output of these factories, comprising nearly 10,000 different items, was warehoused and shipped from the Fort Lauderdale headquarters. The total number of employees in 1965 had risen to 1398.

MANAGEMENT

Exhibit 4 gives some information on the background and experience of the company's corporate officers, while Exhibit 5 shows the company's organization chart. Although there was no formal management development program, the company encouraged interested personnel to attend management seminars and to develop their experience and training as each one saw fit.

Ophthalmic Industry and Market

The U.S. retail market for ophthalmic goods and related services was estimated, by the Better Vision Institute, at over one billion dollars per year. Factory sales of conventional eyeglass products plus imports amounted to over $150 million annually. At the consumer level this was equivalent to $1,050 million annually.

The potential of the industry was outlined by the Better Vision Institute which estimated that, although nearly 54 per cent of the American population over the age of six utilized some form of corrective lenses, about 40 million eyeglass wearers had not had their eyes examined in the last four years, and that of those, 28 million needed new prescriptions. Univis' corporate planning department estimated that the 1970 Optical Manufacturers Association ophthalmic lens sales would probably be 40.8 million pairs, or 39 per cent above 1965's figures. This represented an average annual compounded growth rate of 6.8 per cent.

The ophthalmic industry was dominated by four firms, American Optical, who

(Text continued on page 31.)

Exhibit 1

UNIVIS, INC.

Comparative Income Statements 1956–1966
($000's)

	1966	1965	1964	1963	1962	1961	1960	1959	1958	1957	1956
Sales and other income											
Net sales	16,293	15,456	13,944	12,258	10,378	8,844	7,141	6,449	5,675	5,665	5,030
Discounts earned, etc. (net)	95	58	66	73	64	34	42	30	26	33	14
Total	16,388	15,514	14,010	12,331	10,442	8,878	7,183	6,479	5,701	5,698	5,044
Costs and expenses											
Cost of sales	9,856	8,896	8,360	7,251	5,846	4,849	3,682	3,259	3,222	3,415	3,116
Selling, general & admin.	4,500	4,659	4,231	3,918	3,318	3,317	2,950	2,338	1,994	1,871	1,707
Depreciation	167	158	165	190	143	138	133	116	111	174	167
Interest and debt	–	–	10	22	8	8	13	20	38	39	48
Total	14,523	13,713	12,766	11,381	9,315	8,312	6,778	5,733	5,365	5,499	5,038
Earnings before taxes on income	1,865	1,801	1,244	950	1,127	565**	405	746	336	199	6
TAXES ON INCOME	860	842	622	468**	552**	127†	49†	285†	145†	65	(31)
Net earnings	1,005	959	622	482	575	439	356	461	191	134	37
Shares outstanding*	712,272	702,425	674,300	667,252	661,484	646,447	646,447	646,447	635,250	635,250	635,250
Earnings per Share ($)	1.42	1.38	0.93	0.72	0.88	0.68	0.55	0.72	0.30	0.21	0.06
Dividends per Share ($)	.625	0.54	0.38	0.26	0.26	0.24	0.21	0.30	0.11	0.04	0.02

Notes: 1. *Adjusted for 1-for-2 stock distributions (same adjustment as for 3-for-2 split) July 31, 1964, and July 31, 1965, and 2 per cent stock dividends December 31, 1962, and December 31, 1963.
2. **Restated to reflect adjusted Federal income tax provisions needed in earnings reinvested in the business in 1965.
3. †Restated 1958 through 1961 for elimination of deferred taxes on undistributed earnings of Puerto Rican subsidiary.
4. Earnings per share adjusted 1959 through 1964 for issuance of 11,197 shares in 1965 for the minority interest in a subsidiary.

Source: Company records.

Exhibit 2

UNIVIS, INC.

Comparative Balance Sheet Items 1956–1966
($000's)

	1966	1965	1964	1963	1962	1961	1960	1959	1958	1957	1956
Cash and marketable securities	1,456	1,467	885	542	531	657	314	1,111	432	339	211
Receivables	1,681	1,697	1,365	1,383	976	910	901	768	892	759	681
Inventories	3,159	2,915	2,803	2,556	2,138	1,773	1,861	1,429	1,272	1,562	1,463
Current assets	6,296	6,079	5,053	4,481	3,645	3,340	3,076	3,308	2,596	2,660	2,355
Current liabilities	1,760	1,726	1,589	1,233	653	600	647	405	131	304	258
Total assets	8,033	7,412	6,309	5,694	4,797	4,066	3,929	3,913	3,328	3,592	3,571
Gross plant	3,084	2,500	2,371	2,198	1,886	1,549	1,442	1,203	1,120	1,187	1,176
Net plant	1,510	1,069	1,007	950	789	606	631	469	488	592	674
Long-term liabilities*	154	188	643	770	673	491	433	715	566	752	860
Common equity**	6,119	5,498	4,076	3,691	3,471	2,976	2,849	2,793	2,631	2,536	2,453
Book value per share ($)	8.59	7.12	6.27	5.72	5.25	4.60	4.40	4.32	4.14	3.99	3.86
Common equity return (%)	16.5	17.4	15.3	13.1	16.5	9.3	7.2	12.3	6.1	5.2	1.5
Total net assets return (%)	12.5	12.9	9.9	8.5	12.0	6.8	5.2	8.8	4.8	3.7	1.0

Notes: *Prior to 1965 includes deferred Puerto Rican taxes, deferred executive compensation, and long-term notes payable.
**1965 and 1966, following a ruling by the U.S. Internal Revenue Service, includes $500,000 of previously deferred Puerto Rican taxes.

Source: Company records.

Exhibit 3

UNIVIS, INC.

Information on Common Share Market Valuation

Year	Stock price—Adjusted			Thousand Shares Transferred	Price/Earnings		Price/cash Flow		Yield	
	High	*Low*	*Close*		*High*	*Low*	*High*	*Low*	*High*	*Low*
1966	31 1/2	13 3/4	N.A.	N.A.	26	12	22	10	3.3%	1.5%
1965	35 1/4	16 1/2	27	286,680	18	8	14	6	5.1	2.3
1964	16 1/2	7 1/2	16 1/4	327,985	13	10	9	7	3.6	2.7
1963	9 1/2	7 1/4	7 1/2	237,785	10	7	8	6	4.2	2.9
1962	8 7/8	6 1/8	8 7/8	263,166	17	11	11	7	5.1	3.3
1961	7 1/4	4 3/4	7 1/8	338,295	23	12	14	8	5.2	2.8
1960	7 1/2	4	5 1/8	440,817	14	5	10	4	10.9	4.1
1959	7 1/4	2 3/4	7 1/4	—	14	6	8	3	8.0	3.1
1958	3 1/2	1 3/8	3 1/4	—	10	7	4	3	2.8	2.0
1957	2	1 3/8	1 3/8	—	35	19	7	4	1.8	0.9
1956	2 1/8	1 1/8	1 3/8	—						

Source: Company records.

Selected Growth Comparisons

	% Average Yearly Compound 1960 QII–1965 QIII
U.S. Gross National Product	6.1
U.S. Personal Consumption Expenditures	5.3
U.S. Ophthalmic Market Revenue	7.8
Univis Revenue	16.6
U.S. Manufacturing Corporations Profit, post-tax	14.3
Univis Profit, post-tax	33.5
Standard and Poor's Composite Earnings per Share	10.7
Univis Earnings per Share	29.9

Source: Company records.

Exhibit 4

UNIVIS, INC.

Management Profile

Person	Age	Education	Length of Service	Experience
A	60	College	15	Marketing
B	62	Graduate degree	30	Optical and Scientific
C	55	College	15	Diversified Finance
D	45	College	15	Marketing
E	45	College	10	Manufacturing
F	55	College	15	Scientific
G	45	College	15	Market Research
H	45	High School	27	Production
I	54	College	28	Sales and Personnel
J	47	College	6	Scientific
K	43	College	6	Scientific
L	50	College	5	Finance and Accounting
M	36	Graduate degree	3	Business

Average Age: 49.3 yrs.

Average length of service: 14.6 yrs.

Source: Company records.

because of their size effectively set the prices, Bausch & Lomb, the Shuron-Continental Division of Textron, and Univis. Each company produced and sold ophthalmic lenses, spectacle frames, and associated products, although Univis' major competitors were more highly diversified in terms of technology, industry and product. Because of the consolidation of divisional figures in annual reports, Univis was the only company for which sales data were available. Univis' sales were made through wholesalers or, occasionally, directly to the U.S. or a state government.

Planning at Univis

Prior to the introduction of a formal corporate planning department, the company had always emphasized planning as a key aspect of effective management. The first decision to institute a series of formal controls was made when the new management took over working control of the company in 1955. The President, Mr. Barber, explained the decision as follows:

> ...Our immediate concern was to put Univis in the black. As a start, we established a cost-cutting program that eliminated most of the fat while sparing most of the muscle. We wrote job descriptions for all jobs and set up performance standards for key people. (For the past several years these standards have been the basis for payment of incentive bonuses.)

> We spelled out our company creed [see Exhibit 6], the first in our history, and defined our business:

> "Univis, Inc. is engaged in providing products and services used in the protection and improvement of human vision."

Exhibit 5

UNIVIS, INC.

Partial Organization Chart

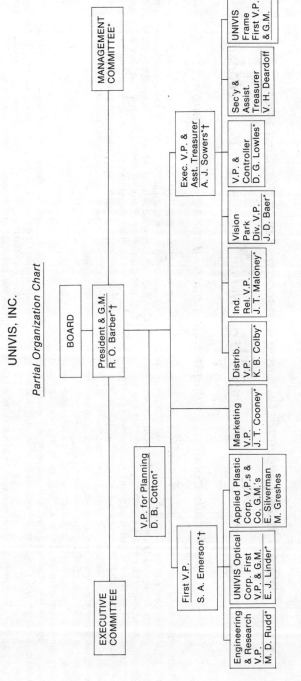

*Member Management Committee (11)
†Member Executive Committee (3)

Source: Company records.

Exhibit 6

UNIVIS, INC.

Univis Creed

We at Univis believe that we owe a responsibility to our Customers,

Personnel, Shareholders, Community and our Nation. In accepting this responsibility

we specifically detail our obligations in each of these areas as follows:

I To bring to our Customers, products and services of such merit and so competitively priced that the Customer will find his Univis Distributorship to be valuable both from a profit as well as a prestige standpoint; to remain constantly aware that the sale of our goods and services to our Customers is not enought but that we must make available to them the kind of programs and assistance which will assure the adequate movement of these goods and services from our Customers to their Customers; to create and support constructive marketing policies which will strengthen our Customers' position in the industry and justify their continuing confidence in Univis as a supplier; to constantly upgrade the quality of our Distribution to the end that the climate in which our Customers function is of the highest order.

II To pay our Personnel as high a wage as their skills merit in the labor market in which they offer their services; to maintain a benefit program consistent with our industry and our area; to support programs inside and outside the Company organization which will help develop the inherent capabilities of our Personnel; and to so select, train, supervise, control and motivate our Personnel that the job will be performed with maximum efficiency with a full measure of satisfaction going to those who perform it.

III To recognize that our Shareholders are individuals or institutions who have shown confidence in the management of this Company and its products, and that it is our responsibility to conduct our Corporate affairs in such a manner that they will receive a fair return on their investment; to keep our Shareholders properly informed through Annual and interim reports and such other communications as are necessary regarding Company progress and condition.

IV To make a sensible allotment of our time and abilities to the service of our Community to the end that our Community receives support for those activities which contribute to its material progress, spiritual growth and cultural environment.

V To take advantage of opportunities to actively interest ourselves as individuals, or as a Company, in State and National issues so that our contribution may also be made in the continuing struggle for survival of our freedom and our way of life.

This statement changed management's concepts and broadened the horizon for future planning and growth.

Because we believe that decisions are never any better than the information on which they are based, we set up controls to give managers at all levels timely and adequate, but not excessive, information about the jobs for which they were responsible.[4]

In line with this early emphasis on formal control, the company had written job descriptions for all the major functions in the company. These descriptions, 124 in all, were kept in a three-inch thick organization manual that was broken down into eight company divisions. Each of the divisions, such as top management, marketing, engineering and research, had an organization chart showing the positioning of all the people in that division and a series of job descriptions for the relevant tasks. Exhibit 7 illustrates a typical job description format for the Assistant Vice President for corporate planning. Most of these descriptions were written by the personnel department and involved talking to both the person involved and his "boss" in order to produce an accurate prescription of the task to be performed.

In addition to the detailed organization manual, the company also set "standards of performance" for managerial and administrative functions and determined a "job rating" for all the factory tasks.

The "standards of performance" were negotiated between the superior and subordinate and were aimed at ensuring that the particular person under review played his role in achieving the division objectives set for the year. Consequently, each person was set a "performance standard" for the ensuing year. The actual performance of the individual versus this standard was evaluated four times a year, and if the subordinate was not measuring up to requirements he would be asked to write his superior a memo describing how he planned to do a better job. As an incentive to meet the standard, a dollar bonus was calculated by comparing *actual* managerial performance with the standard. To calculate the size of the bonus the person under review was rated by his superior along several dimensions, and a point number was obtained somewhere in the range between 0–15, with 9 being the average. The bonus was then obtained by using the score obtained as a percentage of the base pay (i.e., if the score was 9 then the bonus for the period would be +9 per cent of the salary).

Because the nature of some tasks made them harder to evaluate effectively or because they carried more responsibility, there were two special incentive "clubs" in operation. The first, the "Key Club," was for staff people, and members of it were evaluated more informally owing to the difficulty of setting meaningful performance standards. The maximum bonus here was one month's pay, or a maximum of an $8\frac{1}{3}$ per cent increase on the base pay. The second, the "Fulcrum Club," was set up for individuals like the advertising or data processing manager, who could more directly affect the company's profitability. In addition to their evaluation against a performance standard, which held out the possibility of achieving a maximum bonus of 15 per cent, they also participated in a scheme based on return on investment. If the return on investment goal for the year had been set at 10 per cent and the actual achieved was 26 per cent, then members of the "Fulcrum Club" would receive an additional 16 per cent bonus.

Factory positions, on the other hand, were all "job rated." This was done along such dimensions as education required, experience required, complexity of the task, supervision received, and the possibility of errors. People were then hired to suit particular jobs or classes of jobs. In this way the personnel department attempted to match people to the formalized system of job requirements. Factory personnel did not receive a bonus. They were, however, presented with a Christmas turkey every year.

Under the old planning system that was in effect until 1963, the executive committee[5] formulated the objectives once each year for the coming year. These were based upon budget forecasts from the division and upon top management's under-

---

[4]Barber, R. O.: *op. cit.,* p. 29.

[5]See Exhibit 5 for membership.

standing of business conditions and market opportunity in the period ahead. This over-all plan was passed down to the division heads in the form of division objectives. These objectives were then translated into the "standards of performance," just described, for each and every managerial position. Thus the growth and progress of the company and the bonuses paid were directly related to the original objective and goal setting determined by the executive committee. As the company grew, Mr. Barber came to believe that it was becoming important to improve upon the methods of goal setting.

> Clearly [he wrote], the company's progress since 1955 was primarily the result of planning. However, much of our planning was intuitive.

> Forecasts were not sufficiently sophisticated and our objectives were not formalized the way they should have been. We realized that the employment of capital in the years ahead would assume a new and greater significance and we needed constraints which would help guide future decisions.[6]

The decision was made in September, 1963, to institute a corporate planning department.

Corporate Planning

The corporate planning department was located in the organization structure so that it reported directly to the president (see Exhibits 5 and 7). All the material, in the form of reports and requests, that was produced by the planning department was either specifically addressed to or approved by the president. The company felt that this support by the president was key to the successful functioning of the department. Mr. Barber appointed Donald B. Cotton to the position of director of corporate planning in 1963.

Gradually [he said], Cotton's professional skills and top management backing (he reported directly to me) won him the confidence of our top management team and the cooperation of divisions.[7]

The Purpose of Planning:[8]

The primary purpose of corporatewide planning is to increase the probability that corporatewide objectives will be attained. Toward this end, plans for future deployment of Corporate resources are appraised to assure their compatibility with the basic Corporate objectives.[9]

This view of corporatewide planning was restated in the more fundamental terminology of the organization as follows:

> We view *planning* as a prescriptive process, intended to guide decision making in the deployment of organization resources, through continuing surveillance and adjustment of goal attainment behavior.

> In their full capacity, these endeavors are characterized by a total systems concept resting in identification, description, and manipulation of substantive behavioral, technological, and pecuniary parameters.

> In our opinion, the paramount phase in the planning process is in the reduction of preferences, insofar as useful, into a clear, precise, and formal goal statement, with due regard to priority order and consistency in the arrangement of its multiple facets.[10]

---

[6]Barber, R. O.: *op. cit.*, p. 29.

[7]Barber, R. O.: *op. cit.*, p. 30.

[8]The remainder of this section on "Corporate Planning" is drawn from material generated by Mr. Cotton as he set up Univis' planning function. Only specific quotations from this material will be fully referenced.

[9]*Corporatewide Planning Guide,* November 1, 1965, Section 1, p. 1.

[10]Cotton, D. B.: *Our Management Philosophy, Report 1,* August 20, 1964, p. 1.

Exhibit 7

UNIVIS, INC.

ICH 13G132
AM–P
250

POLICY, ORGANIZATION AND PROCEDURE BULLETIN	NUMBER: 0-1025
	DATE EFFECTIVE 7/12/65
Title: Assistant Vice President for Corporate Planning	PAGE 1 of 2

Reporting

The Assistant Vice President for Corporate Planning reports directly to the President, to assist in development and control of corporate goals, policies, and plans.

General Responsibility

The Assistant Vice President for Corporate Planning furnishes expertise, coordination, and integration for design of corporate goal attainment activity. He applies management science, executes management research, and performs management consulting relevant to corporate planning. These endeavors will be characterized by a total systems concept resting in identification, description, and manipulation of substantive social, technological, and pecuniary parameters.

Duties

In carrying out his general responsibilities, the Assistant Vice President for Corporate Planning performs the following duties:

1. Develops objectives, policies, and programs for approval of the President.

2. Confers in relevant situations in all functions, echelons, and locales encompassed by the Corporation.

3. Executes assignments from the President regarding:

   a. Formulation of corporate goals, policies, and plans.

   b. Impact simulation of major corporate alternatives.

   c. Macro and micro-economic analyses.

   d. Macro-organization structure and process.

4. Offers, in a consistent and timely manner:

   a. Surveillance of general macro-economic environment.

   b. Interindustry comparisons.

   c. Commentary on capital markets.

5. Administers corporatewide long-range planning activities.

ICH 13G132
AM–P
250

Exhibit 7 *(Continued)*

UNIVIS, INC. POLICY, ORGANIZATION AND PROCEDURE BULLETIN	NUMBER: 0-1025
Title: Assistant Vice President for Corporate Planning	DATE EFFECTIVE: 7/12/65
	PAGE 2 of 2

6. Participates in relations with the Financial Community, in general, and specifically is responsible for:

   a. Development, interpretation, and communication of underlying technical analyses.

   b. Liaison with relevant personnel internal to and external to the Corporation, in which comprehensive knowledge of the aforementioned is desirable.

7. For the above purposes, serves in the collateral capacities of:

   a. Member, Corporatewide Planning Committee

   b. Member, Management Committee

Scope and Limits of Authority

The Assistant Vice President for Corporate Planning has authority derived from the President. He plans, organizes, directs, and controls the activities of his office. He is limited in the exercise of this authority in the following ways:

1. Current established company objectives, policies, and procedures.

2. Changes in objectives, policies, or procedures must be approved by the President.

3. All expenditures are limited by approved budgets. Expenditures for any amount in excess of $150.00 must be approved by the President.

4. Employment, promotion, transfer, and release of department personnel are limited by approved organization plans.

5. Compensation of personnel is limited by pay policy with any exception therefrom to be approved by the Executive Committee.

Supervisory Relationship

The Assistant Vice President for Corporate Planning directly supervises the activities of the following positions:

1. Corporate Planning Analyst (General)

2. Corporate Planning Analyst (Marketing)

3. Research Assistant

As can be seen from the diagram (Figure 1), planning was aimed at determining the "gap" that existed between the company's objectives and the expected performance over the period of the planning cycle. The expected performance could come from two sources: (1) the existing business in which the firm was engaged after making due allowance for "normal" growth (the passive projection)[11] or from planned expansion in this business, or (2) from planned diversification into other industries. If the plan showed that a gap existed between the objectives and the expected performance, the theory was that management could then either change the objectives or improve the performance so as to close the gap.

Conceptual Background of the Plan:

A particular organization is delineated from the general social system by its participants' (1) interrelations and (2) *goal orientation.*

The integration of human behavior can be viewed as a process which occurs in three decisional depths: (1) *substantive* planning prescribes the values and boundaries for subsidiary decisions; (2) *procedural* planning establishes mechanisms which channel subordinate activities into conformance, (3) *routine* endeavors are executed within the framework structured by the procedural plan.

In consonance, the goal structure of the organization can be visualized as a pyramid wherein three horizontal hierarchical layers, from the top down, are (1) *substantive goals,* (2) *procedural goals,* and (3) *routine goals.*

Substantive goals are *fundamental,* procedural goals are *strategic,* and routine goals are *tactical.* In that order value content diminishes and fact content, especially

as regards immediate environment and resources, increases.[12]

In *Organization Study Report 3,* it was amplified that the behavior of large U.S. corporations suggests derivation from the institutional assumptions of private enterprise ideology, capitalistic economics, and bureaucratic administration, and that these have their common focus in *rational economic productivity of capital.* On this basis, it was submitted that, therefore, substantive goal parameters would be amount, risk, time and yield of capital employed. Further, acceptable bounds would be specified through circumscription of activity scope and depth.[13]

In addition to this report regarding basic substantive goal parameters, other reports defined the company's concept of risk, time, capital employed and yields. Of these four, perhaps the risk concept most requires further clarification here.

To obtain some measure of useful risk categories, Mr. Cotton performed a series of experiments with the executive committee in order to gain an idea of what they meant by risk. He used several gaming and chance analogies with which to classify their concept of risk into three categories: conservative, normal, and speculative. See Exhibit 8 for the results of these experiments. This table was used by the executive committee to help appraise the risk inherent in new ventures.

Given the risk category of a new project the committee then assigned a "yield on assets employed" figure that the venture had to meet. (See Corporatewide Goals, below, for yield requirements.) Knowing the yield that was required, the committee had to evaluate whether the project would in fact provide this yield on the assets employed.

Using the substantive goal parameters outlined above, this basic requirement was more formally stated in the company's organization study as: given the assets employed (active and/or passive), achieve the yield on the assets employed over the time

---

[11]A passive projection is an estimate of future business generated from the normal growth of existing product lines. It does *not* include the possibility of expanding into other product categories or markets.

[12]Cotton, D. B.: *Organization Study Report 3,* p. 1.

[13]Cotton, D. B.: *Our Capital Markets Viewpoint,* August 20, 1964, p. 2.

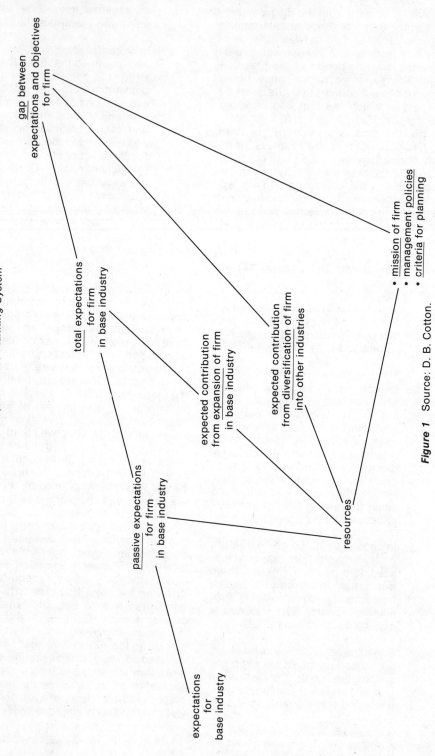

UNIVIS, INC.

Comprehensive Planning System

gap between expectations and objectives for firm

- mission of firm
- management policies
- criteria for planning

total expectations for firm in base industry

expected contribution from expansion of firm in base industry

expected contribution from diversification of firm into other industries

resources

passive expectations for firm in base industry

expectations for base industry

Figure 1 Source: D. B. Cotton.

Exhibit 8

UNIVIS, INC.

Our Standards for Risk Classification

The purpose of this typology is to prescribe broad magnitude categories wherein risk judgments on projects throughout the organization would be cast into more consistent and precise channels so as to facilitate the systemwide comparison of alternatives in the deployment of organization resources. If risk is considered, as herein, through the parallel aspects of *probability of success* and *confidence in data*, then one of these may cause rejection of a decision alternative when its characteristics in these respects are deemed beyond the tolerances implied by preset value preferences for risk.

CLASS	CONSERVATIVE	NORMAL	SPECULATIVE
probability requisites	More than 85 but less than 100 chances of success in 100.	More than 70 but less than 85 chances of success in 100.	More than 50 but less than 70 chances of success in 100.
confidence requisites — information	Quite confident of all estimates, due to comprehensive experience in same circumstances.	Fairly confident of most estimates, based upon reasonably complete knowledge.	Little confidence in estimates, because of fragmentary knowledge.
information	Satisfactorily reliable and complete. Routinely available and processed in standard manner.	With some reservations, adequately reliable and complete. Requires some nonroutine selectivity, integration, and synthesis.	Questionably reliable and incomplete. Data preponderantly unavailable and/or unprocessed.
techniques	Existing techniques satisfactory.	Some nonroutine analysis and/or modification of existing techniques.	Present techniques untried in new circumstances and/or new techniques.
constraints	Acceptance of nondiscretionary constraints, with no contest.	Questioning recognition of nondiscretionary constraints, with some peripheral maneuvering.	Recognition of nondiscretionary constraints, with active confrontation.

The rationale underlying differentiation of confidence requisites is that confidence decreases as innovation relative to in-company routine increases. While it is recognized that this is not necessarily so, the probability is deemed sufficient to warrant this hypothesis in most cases.

Source: D. B. Cotton, Our Concept of Risk, July 21, 1964

span for assets employment and at the appropriate risk category all within the scope and depth of prescribed behavior. It was proposed that "properly aligned supporting statements should [then] be assigned component organization units"[14] in order to achieve over-all corporatewide goals.

Corporatewide Goals

From the fundamental corporatewide objective of maximizing owners' common share price through the medium of growth company behavior, management had derived a set of quantitative goals. These goals were expressed in terms of four variables related to the assets employed: (1) amount, (2) risk, (3) yield, and (4) time span. Specifically these corporatewide goals had been tentatively formulated as follows:

1. Expected yield on assets employed will be at least 20 per cent at the standard risk mix, wherein
   a. Expected yield on conservatively employed assets will be at least 17 per cent,
   b. Expected yield on normally employed assets will be at least 21 per cent,
   c. Expected yield on speculatively employed assets will be at least 25 per cent,
2. Earning per share will increase at an average annual compounded rate of at least 7 per cent.[15]

By late 1966 these quantitative goals had undergone minor clarification to include the word *pretax* after each of the yield percentages, and to change the wording of part 2 to read:

3. Earnings per share will increase at a rate, on the average over a significant period of time, substantially greater than that characterizing the broad stock market averages.[16]

PROGRESS TO DATE:

The first step toward relating the planning concepts and objectives with actual performance projections was accomplished on March 18, 1966, with the completion of the "Univis Passive Projections, 1966–1970." The "passive projections" were simply estimates of business activity resulting from an extension of the existing operations through the ensuing five-year period.

The projections were based on the assumptions of normal market growth without diversification into other lines and industries. These passive projections were in the process of being replaced by the first five-year plan covering the period 1967–1971.

> The purpose of the Univis Five-Year Plan, 1967–1971, is to present estimates of the *most probable* expected Univis performance during the period, with respect to Univis management objectives and parameters, subject to the assumptions and constraints specified subsequently in this text.
>
> Acknowledging the compromises induced in this corporatewide planning effort by resource limitations, personnel availabilities, and schedule deadlines, it is intended that
>
> The Univis Five-Year Plan, 1967–1971, is a *working document* for operations during that period.[17]

This "first" plan was different from the passive projections in that it allowed the division managers to exploit the opportunities in the environment as they saw fit, subject, of course, to certain specified constraints and later management approval. The corporate planning department supplied information regarding economic trends and the basic guidelines upon which the plan was to be built.

Each division was required to produce an *operations* plan for its own activities during the period, while marketing and distribution, in particular, were to produce *function* plans (prior to the development of operation plans) as a guide in the con-

---

[14]Cotton, D. B.: *Organization Study, Report 3*, p. 3.

[15]*Univis Five-Year Plan*, second estimation, October 1, 1965, p. 6.

[16]Cotton, D. B.: *Standards for Expected Performance Illustration*, September 1, 1966.

[17]*Univis Five-Year Plan, 1967–1971, Context, Requirements and Schedule*, Corporate Planning Department, August 18, 1966, p. 3.

Exhibit 9

UNIVIS, INC.

Corporatewide Planning Cycle Plan

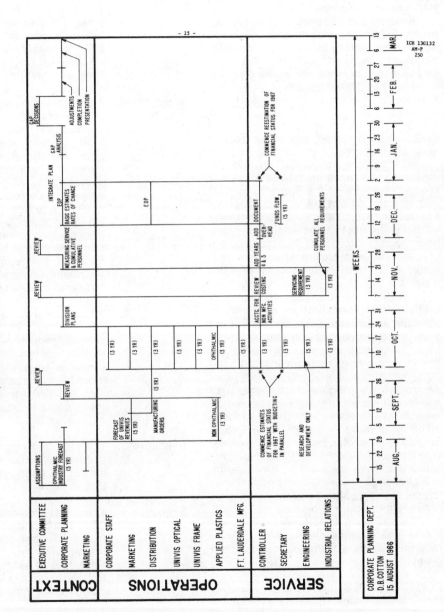

struction of these operations plans. Exhibit 9 shows the planning cycle in more detail. It will be seen there how the industry assumptions preceded the Marketing and Distribution Division's function plans which, in turn, preceded the division's operation plans.

Analysis and discussion of the gap between expected performance and corporate objectives by the executive committee was scheduled for early February, while the final presentation of the plan was to be held on March 13, 1967.

EXECUTIVE COMMENT AND REACTION:

Although the actual cost involved in instituting the planning function was not known, estimates of the figure suggested that it was somewhere in the range of $75,000 to $100,000 a year. This range included the cost of the additional man-hours required in each division to generate the planning information which was estimated at 300 to 600 man-hours a year per division.

Reaction among the management group to the formalization of company planning was mixed. Some people felt the planning department's requirements had been introduced too quickly. Some felt that as yet no worthwhile results had been obtained. Almost everybody agreed, however, that the setting up of a five-year plan had forced people to think and to question aspects of the status quo that had been taken for granted. Although the final form of the five-year plan had not yet been set (see Exhibit 9 for schedule), the managers seemed to take pleasure in the freedom and challenge provided by the opportunity to plan five years ahead and thus to take an active role in determining their *own* future.

The following quotations are all comments regarding the planning function by different members of the top management group.

Executive 1: The plan forced people to think, to estimate things for themselves and to participate for themselves. It gives a goal and a sense of accomplishment. In fact it's funny how it makes the men in my department think more about life, what it's all about and where they're going from here. I guess they'd never thought of those things before. In a roundabout way you could say that it gives a fellow a sense of confidence in the company, also he tends to be an expert in his own field. Strangely enough they all fought it originally, now they love planning.

Executive 2: Formal planning puts you in a frame of thinking that unconsciously makes you think further ahead and puts you in position to question things. We've been operating for 46 years and we did O.K. However, this really increased thought. On your question of the plan causing some rigidity; this is always a problem but its effect will depend upon top management's administration of the plan.

It could've been sold a little more carefully in the initial stages, probably through better communication. I would've tried to avoid a directive type approach myself, but I'm not sure that this would've been any more effective.

Executive 3: The plan lacks personality. It doesn't portray the feelings of the people and what they achieve.

Executive 4: The first reaction was "We're bringing the brains trust in." No one discounted the activity. I'm not sure what they're doing but if Bob Barber thinks it's worth doing then it must be worth doing.

Executive 5: It helped personnel expand horizons. It made us list our assumptions and constraints. Forced us to realize areas of responsibility. Really sharpened up on forecasting. Excellent management training.

Executive 6: It hasn't provided us yet with too much more than we were getting previously with the 12 months' forecast, even though it now projects out into the future. There is a lack of sophistication down the line and because of the difficult terminology they can't understand what's going on. In any event I'm not yet convinced that the form of corporate planning we have is necessarily the best. I'm not negative on planning, but some people feel that less sophistication would have achieved the same results.

Executive 7: There are several benefits that the introduction of planning has brought us. It has helped educate division management by broadening their horizons and clarifying what is happening. It has pointed out areas that need improvement to maintain our past growth and it has emphasized the need to think logically. On the other hand, however, it is very time consuming, although not all the time is extra. I feel it has really just formalized what we were doing before, but I definitely hope that the plan will initiate new policies.

The President, Mr. Barber, summed up his feelings when he said:

I think the introduction of corporate planning is a very good investment. However, we have always planned to one degree or another. I guess I just really believe in it.

Suggested References for Further Research

Emery, J. C.: *Organizational Planning and Control Systems — Theory and Technology.* New York, The Macmillan Company, 1969.

England, G. W.: Personal value systems of American managers. *Academy of Management Journal,* March, 1967.

Glueck, W. F.: Business Policy: *Strategy Formation and Management Action.* New York, McGraw-Hill Book Company, 1972.

Holden, P., Pederson, C., and Germane, G.: *Top Management.* New York, McGraw-Hill Book Co., 1968.

Jerome, W. T.: *Executive Control — The Catalyst.* New York, John Wiley & Sons, 1961.

Leavitt, H. J., Dill, W. R., and Eyring, H. B.: *The Organizational World.* New York, Harcourt, Brace, Jovanovich, Inc., 1973.

McNichols, T. J.: *Policy Making and Executive Action.* 3rd ed. New York, McGraw-Hill Book Co., 1972.

Mintzberg, H.: A new look at the chief executive's job. Organizational Dynamics *1* (No. 3):21–30, 1973.

Newman, W. H., and Logan, J. P.: *Strategy, Policy, and Central Management.* Cincinnati, Southwestern Publishing Co., 1971.

Steiner, G. A.: *Top Management Planning.* New York, The Macmillan Company, 1969.

POLICY FORMATION AND DECISION
MAKING

A DESCRIPTIVE MODEL OF THE POL-
ICY-FORMATION PROCESS
    Inputs — Environmental Forces
    Structure — Roles and Programs
        Self-interests
        Political Resources
    Interaction of Structure and
      Environmental Forces
    Circular Effects of Policy
      Formation

Applying the Model to Business
    and Public Bodies
Illustration of Model — A Role
    Play
Social Responsibility and the
    Model — A Debate
SUMMARY
INTERGROUP POLICY EXERCISE
DISCUSSION QUESTIONS

2

CONCEPTUALIZING THE POLICY-FORMATION PROCESS

POLICY FORMATION AND DECISION MAKING

We have considered to this point some basic aspects of policy formation and the choice process. We have given some examples of what *should* be done and what *is* done in policy formation. We have provided a case, Univis, Inc., for preliminary study and analysis.

Assumptions of decision-making model.

Let us now elaborate a bit to develop further a conceptualization of the policy process. We shall start by comparing some basic assumptions of a typical decision-making model with those of a policy-formation model. The term "decision making" as frequently used by management scholars and psychologists implies a specific model of cognitive activity. This cognitive model may assume (1) a problem statement, (2) a single decision-making unit, (3) a single set of utility preferences, (4) a knowledge of a full range of alternatives and consequences, (5) the intention to select alternatives toward maximizing utility, and (6) the opportunity, disposition and capacity to make appropriate calculations.*

Assumptions violated.

A practical consequence that would follow from conceptualizing policy formation in the same way as decision making would be a hampering of understanding. This impediment to understanding occurs because, as a matter of fact, each of the assumptions of the decision-making model may be violated in policy formation. Thus, the student of policy formation as previously discussed from a different point of view would not have a description of what is actually occurring. Furthermore, another consequence is that the cognitive decision-making model may confuse the policy maker on how he ought to proceed with the process.

---

*See M. Patchen: Decision theory in the study of rational action: Problems and a proposal, *Journal of Conflict Resolution*, June, 1965.

TABLE 2-1   POLICY FORMATION AND A TYPICAL DECISION MODEL

Element	Decision Model	Policy Formation
Problem or issue	Problem statement	Lack of unity in problem statement; two or more interrelated issues
Organization	Single decision-making unit	A coalition of two or more units
Objectives	1. Single set of utility preferences	1. Two or more sets of interests and values (not translatable into a common set)
	2. Intention to select alternatives that will maximize utility on issue	2. May trade off for benefits on other issues
Alternatives and consequences	Knowledge of full range	Uncertainty, risk, relationships with other issues unclear
Calculation	Opportunity, disposition and capacity to make appropriate calculations	Uncertainty and the diversity of interests and values may preclude calculations of determinate solutions

In Table 2-1 we indicate some ways in which the assumptions of the decision-making model may be violated. The policy formation process is seen as occurring in an organization. An organization is viewed as a coalition of subcoalitions and individuals, including, as mentioned, officials representing different functions or projects along with a board of commissioners or directors, union officials, workers, and clients or customers. Drawing a definitive and permanent boundary is impossible when circumstances change frequently. The various interest groups participate, as we have indicated, because the sharing of goals allows some benefits. To illustrate this conflict from a different perspective, consider the current controversy over the extent and type of social responsibility expected of American corporations.*

If a corporation allocates more resources to fulfill its social responsibilities, should wage earners and shareholders receive less or should customers pay more? The top manager in publicly held cor-

*See for example W. J. Baumol, R. Likert, C. Wallich, and J. McGowan: *A New Rationale for Corporate Social Policy,* Committee For Economic Development, Supplementary Paper No. 31, 1970; M. J. Green et al.: *The Closed Enterprise System,* Nader Study Group, June, 1971; The American corporation under fire, *Newsweek,* May 21, 1971, pp. 74–85; G. Lodge: Top priority: Renovating our ideology, *Harvard Business Review,* Sept.–Oct., 1970, pp. 43–55; B. J. Kolasa: *Responsibility in Business,* Englewood Cliffs, N.J., Prentice-Hall, Inc., 1972; S. Prakash: *Up Against The Corporate Wall: Modern Corporations and Social Issues of the Seventies,* Englewood Cliffs, N.J., Prentice-Hall, Inc., 1971.

porations is responsible to the owners, customers, employees, competitors, local, state and national governments, and so forth. If policies are devised that pursue the interests of any one group exclusively, the interests of others may suffer, at least in the short run, and sometimes over a prolonged period.

Modification in decision-making model.

Of course, the decision-making model can be modified and it has been. For example, as indicated in the Univis case, adjustments can be made to deal formally with uncertainty and "risk" by using rather sophisticated modern approaches from management science. Nevertheless, even these adjustments tell an individual decision-making unit only what *ought* to be done; it does not describe fully what actually *is* done so that we may understand the process better.

The basic difficulty.

Another modification in approach might be to have the coalition (e.g., top management executives at Univis) work toward more agreement on the problem or issue statement. Through definition and redefinition it might be possible to develop a consensus on an operational definition. However, the perceptions of problems change over time. The basic difficulty is conceiving what would constitute the single set of interests and values against which to judge solutions. Members of a group will not have identical values (e.g., the executives at Univis reacted in various ways to formal planning). Furthermore, individuals with substantially the same values may be located at different points in the organization and receive different benefits. Often benefits are widely distributed and costs are highly concentrated. Consider a proposed reorganization of agencies in the Federal government. Benefits may be widely spread to many citizens across the country, but costs may be highly concentrated among relatively few bureaucrats; a few Congressmen might even lose some political muscle if Congressional Committee responsibilities are altered to match the new agencies.

Is there an optimal policy?

In policy formation, then, involving allocating and mediating among conflicting sets of values and interest, judgments are formed specific to the situation, balancing each issue off against a wide range of other issues, including present issues and those that might exist in the future. Is there an optimal policy? No! Different perceptions of the critical problems and the diversity of interests and values preclude the determination of a single "best" policy. For example, the high cash dividend policy at Univis may be "best" for some stockholders but not "best" for those more concerned with plowing back earnings for growth.

Of course, improvements can be made toward more effective and consistent policies. What would the reader, hired to improve the policy-formation results and the policy-formation process, need besides the conceptualization of the policy formation developed to this point, to develop an effective improvement program? The remainder of the book is designed to present the reader with some information to help him to focus on significant variables and relationships as well as to answer critical questions.

The approach that is suggested is to see the policy issues as involving a complex social process and then to converge on the cognitive aspects rather than hope that the issues can be understood in terms of solely intellectual components. This approach has been proposed by Bauer.* He suggests two reasons for not working outward to the social context:

What is the approach suggested?

1. Much of the record and people's verbalization of what has happened and is happening is highly rationalized (e.g., the President of Univis says "I think the introduction of corporate planning is a very good investment.").

Why?

2. Much of what occurs will not make sense in the more limited context (e.g., what is meant in the Univis case by, "The plan lacks personality. It doesn't portray the feelings of the people or what they achieve"?).

In the first instance the analyst may be deceived about the policy process. In the second, he may label the behavior of the businessman or government official as "irrational" when, in fact, the individual involved is concerned with more issues than the analyst has taken into account.

A DESCRIPTIVE MODEL OF THE POLICY-FORMATION PROCESS

In an attempt to clarify and to describe some of the more significant variables in the policy-formation process, an input-output model is presented in Table 2–2. This model of policy formation is designed primarily from the standpoint of the policy maker(s). The policy makers are seen in the role of planning and coordinating to find solutions to policy issues which will (1) capitalize on opportunities and gain or utilize external and internal support, (2) satisfy environmental demands or requirements, and (3) partially satisfy the policy makers' own interests and desires.

Summary of descriptive model.

The model assumes that the key inputs affecting policy makers are environmental forces and that these forces interact with a given policy generating structure to *produce outputs (organizational objectives and actions)* which are designed to adjust to and adapt to these pressures on the structure. The outputs became part of the environment, and the cycle continues. The structure is a political one in which an authoritative allocation of benefits takes place; that is to say, those in authority allocate benefits to relevant parties in exchange for this support. Four concepts related to structure with which the model deals are roles, programs, self-interests and political resources.

The model further assumes an open and dynamic situation

---

*R. A. Bauer: Social psychology and the study of policy formation, *American Psychologist, 21* (No. 10):933–942, 1966.

TABLE 2-2   A DESCRIPTIVE MODEL OF POLICY FORMATION

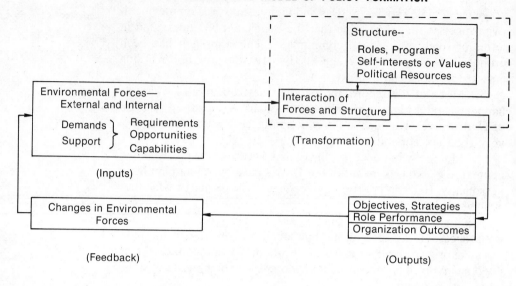

whereby the environment and the structure continually interact. The interaction is such that certain environmental forces such as technology or uncertainty may be associated with particular types of organizational forms, administrative practices, organizational objectives or strategies. This contingency approach has been suggested by several studies.* For example, Lawrence and Lorsch† argue that organizations facing a stable environment may find a centralized "bureaucratic" organization structure adequate for achieving proper coordination and specialization of activities, while a more uncertain environment would preclude effective use of the same form.

Contingency approach.

Other researchers have focused on different dimensions. Hage and Aiken‡ considered the interrelationships between technology and structure and conclude that organizations with routine work are more likely to have greater formalization (i.e., the extent rules are used in the organization) of organization roles. At the present time, however, we do *not* completely understand all the various rela-

---

*See J. Woodward: *Industrial Organization: Theory and Practice.* London, Oxford University Press, 1965; T. Burns and G. M. Stalker: *The Management of Innovations.* London, Tavistock Publications, Ltd., 1961; J. D. Thompson: *Organizations in Action,* New York, McGraw-Hill Book Co., 1967; R. Hall: *Organizations: Structure and Process,* Englewood Cliffs, N.J., Prentice-Hall, 1972; F. E. Kast and J. E. Rosenzweig (eds.): *Contingency Views of Organizations and Management,* Palo Alto, California, Science Research Associates, 1973.

†P. R. Lawrence and J. W. Lorsch, *Organization and Environment,* Homewood, Ill., R. D. Irwin, Inc., 1969. See also H. Tosi, R. Aldag and R. Storey: On the measurement of the environment: An assessment of the Lawrence and Lorsch Environmental Uncertainty Subscale, *Administrative Science Quarterly, 18* (No. 1):27–36, March, 1973.

‡J. Hage and M. Aiken: Routine technology, social structure and organization tools, *Administrative Science Quarterly, 14* (No. 3), September, 1969.

tionships and contingencies. Thus, the model is presented in a general and simplified form. As we proceed through the book, we shall refer to and elaborate upon some of the concepts depicted by the model, and we shall discuss some of the possible contingencies and relationships.

Simple model—elaborations throughout the book.

The cognitive process of intellectual analysis of internal capabilities and alternative strategies is not denied by the model. It is, however, not emphasized at this point. Later, of course, it will be more fully explored.

Inputs—Environmental Forces

The concept of interchange or data input to the structure has been taken from Easton* with some modification. Easton assumes two inputs to a political structure:
1. Demands for scarce resources.
2. Support, i.e., support of the right to decide and support for specific decisions.

This model treats demands both as *external* environmental pressures, opportunities or threats (e.g., public policy, public opinion, unions) and *internal* environmental pressures (e.g., subordinates, peers). Support for the decisions and actions may come from customers buying products or services as well as from subordinates or peer groups with appropriate competence and motivation. Support for the right to decide may come from stockholders, for example. Changes in such environmental components as the economy, the culture, technology, customers, competitors, subordinates, and unions are the input data to the structure. Monitoring and predicting the environmental changes are important for policy formation.

What are external and internal forces? factors

Two additional concepts are depicted by the model. First, the outcomes, goals and objectives of the organization are filtered by the environment and must be acceptable to it. Otherwise, the environment will not allow the organization to continue. For example, pollution standards are now being raised and are being enforced to a greater extent. Some plants have had to shut down for failure to comply. Second, the elements that make up the organization's environment are not isolated from and independent of one another. Rather, the opposite is true: they are interdependent, so that a change in one factor flows to each of the other factors until all are altered in some respect. For example, a governmentally induced legislative change in the area of racial relations in this country has led to changes in the mores of our society and has caused other changes in some aspects of our attitudes toward racial questions. At

Environment filters outcomes.

Environmental forces interdependent.

*D. Easton: An approach to the analysis of political systems, in S. S. Ulmer (ed.): *Introductory Readings in Political Behavior,* Chicago, Rand-McNally, Inc., 1961, pp. 136–147.

the same time, aspects of our cultural environment have influenced the government to enact legislation. Also affected by this legislation are the personnel policies and practices that are part of the output which has been forced to alter itself to meet the new legal requirements.

Structure—Roles and Programs

The entrepreneur, the planner and the adaptor.

Some managers dominate the organization, seek bold opportunities and quickly decide to enlarge their empire (the entrepreneur). Others (e.g., the President of Univis, Inc.) more concerned with the planning process, follow a highly analytical one-step-at-a-time method of making policy (the planner). Still others react when opportunities and threats come "over the transom" (the adaptor). They adapt to the environment and treat policy formation as an incremental process (i.e., adding on to what presently exists).

What is a primary concern of the model?

These behavioral patterns are examples of role behavior for managers. There are, of course, nonmanagerial roles. They will be discussed later. A primary concern of this model is to explain the behavior of individuals (managerial and nonmanagerial) and, to a lesser extent, coalitions of individuals confronted with policy formation.* It should be noted, however, that for some organizations the structure may include just one dominant individual who makes the choices. Even the single policy maker must deal with the environmental forces such as influential individuals outside the organization.

Policy formation, as explained, involves choices among conflicting sets of values. A vehicle for managing this conflict in an organization is the structure. Parsons and Shils point out that the most significant unit of social structure is the role. "The role is that organized sector of an actor's orientation which constitutes and defines his participation in an interaction process. It involves a set of complementary expectations concerning his own actions and those with whom he interacts."† Thus, we can look at the structure as a set of interacting roles. In addition, as mentioned in the first chapter, generalized procedures or *programs* are devised to provide a course of action in response to some stimulus or pressure. Thus, for example, a manager carrying out his role when he hears of a difficulty may use a problem-solving program that includes scanning the environment for information on relevant factors. Self-interests, political resources and tactics, however, affect how the roles and programs are carried out. The discussion of "what actually happens" in the

---

*For additional insight into the behavior of coalitions of individuals, see J. D. Thompson: *Organizations in Action,* New York, McGraw-Hill Book Co., 1967.
†T. Parsons, and E. A. Shils: *Toward a General Theory of Action.* Cambridge, Harvard University Press, 1962, p. 23.

previous chapter illustrated this interplay. The activities were adjusted to account for self-interests and political resources.

Many formulations of the role concept assume that role consensus exists on the expectations applied to incumbents of particular positions; that is to say, there is a high degree of agreement among others on the patterns of behavior that are expected of the incumbent. However, role consensus need not be present and frequently is not. Members of a coalition or a policy-generating structure may have divergent expectations of the role of any one individual. For example, some expect the President to be very conservative; others expect a more liberal orientation. In addition, roles for the individual may vary across policy issues and vary with the political subsystem. For example, some issues are utterly crucial for their advocates, and they adjust their role performance accordingly. Their role performance is adjusted for issues of low salience. Thus, role conflict may come about because an individual simultaneously occupies two or more role positions (interrole conflict), or because of contradictory role expectations for the individual as incumbent of a single role position (intrarole conflicts).

Role consensus.

Role conflict.

To an extent these role conflicts are resolved in the process of policy formation.*

The major factors that come into play in the resolution of role conflict are legitimacy and sanctions. The first refers to the individual's feelings about the legitimacy or illegitimacy of each of the incompatible expectations that he perceives is held for him in the situation. The second refers to his perception of the sanctions to which he will be exposed for nonconformity to each of the incompatible expectations. For example, he may be told to be innovative and to take risks. At the same time, however, he may note that those who have taken visible actions that fail, find their own future careers in jeopardy. It seems to be a common story in government bureaucracy, for example, that you make that "one visible mistake" and "your career is dead." If a manager feels that he is judged (legitimately) on the "no mistake image" he creates, there is plenty of reason to believe that this has a profound effect on his behavior and on the policies he supports or adopts.

Resolution of role conflict.

Self-interests

Our model shows that self-interests or values of top managers are basic and fundamental premises which have affected the policy process. For example, the influential manager may have said, "I want this agency to be best known for its innovations," or he may have said, "I want this company to be much bigger in five years." Or he may have written on a subject such as the socioeconomic purpose

---

*For discussion see N. C. Gross, W. S. Mason and A. W. McEachern: *Explorations in Role Analysis*. New York, John Wiley & Sons, Inc., 1958.

of the organization. Edward Cole, as President of General Motors wrote: "The big challenge to American business—as I see it—is to carefully evaluate the constantly changing expressions of public and national goals. Then we must modify our own objectives and programs to meet—as far as possible within the realm of economic and technological feasibility—the new demands of the society we serve."* Sometimes these kinds of statements are not articulated, but nevertheless "come through" to the organization by the actions of the top executive(s). For instance, it may be known that the top executive wishes to not "rock the boat" or take any serious risk. Each of these interests rooted in top management has provided a frame of reference for others who occupy positions of less importance.

In considering the individual as a policy maker and the choices he will make, March and Simon feel that man behaves rationally only with respect to his own abstractions of the real world dependent on personal values and his own unique modes of perceiving. Therefore, choice is always exercised with respect to a limited, approximate simplified "model" of the real situation.†

Three aspects of a model of self-interest are:

1. Who is the self under consideration?
2. What value is being pursued?
3. Over what time period?‡

Many individuals do not have the information to be clearly aware of their self-interest and to clearly answer these questions. Their "interests" are multiple and complex. In the absence of complete information about these dimensions of self-interests, the policy maker is forced to adopt "tactics" that can be altered by new information. New information may change what the policy maker perceives to be his own best self-interest.

As we have indicated, we cannot assume a single and unchanging goal and rational decision making. Individuals have preferences that impose themselves in the policy-making process. Imbalances result in rejecting, clarifying, redefining or changing both individual aspirations and *organizational objectives*. This behavior can be seen as an ongoing series of testing and feedback processes by which the individual both guides his interests and determines his effectiveness. The information sources and perceived self-interests (along with roles and programs) are thus determinants of the behavior of policy makers in the model.

Determinants of behavior of policy makers.

---

*Edward N. Cole: Management priorities for the 1970's, *Michigan Business Review* 22:1, July, 1970.

†J. G. March and H. A. Simon: *Organizations.* New York, John Wiley & Sons, Inc., 1958, Chapter 6.

‡R. Bauer, I. Pool and L. Dexter: *American Business and Public Policy.* New York, Atherton Press, 1963, Chapter 9.

Political Resources

A political resource is a means by which one member of a policy-generating structure can influence the behavior of others. Political resources may be derived directly from his official position in the structure (e.g., legitimate authority) or from other sources (e.g., competence or charisma); other political resources include control of information, social standing, friendship and money.

What are political resources?

Political resources may be used at varying rates by an individual according to differences in rewards anticipated for resource use, the degree of optimism associated with the probability of achieving a desired objective, and the opportunity costs associated with the resource use.*

The higher the value of the anticipated reward and the more optimistic the outlook for objective achievement, the more readily resources are employed. The opportunity cost associated with the use of a resource is the sacrifice required of alternative uses.† Furthermore, the opportunity costs associated with political resources can be changed by environmental pressures. For example, the opportunity cost of the goodwill used to support a new product promotion strategy is the cost associated with not having the same goodwill for use in supporting enlargement of the budget for a new market research approach. Environmental pressures may make the new market research strategy more important, and the *opportunity cost* of not supporting it increases. Since the reservoir of goodwill is not unlimited, it must be used judiciously, considering the present and future salience of each issue.

How are they used?

Various political tactics may be used in the policy-formation process. For example, a partial list of "advice" on political tactics might include:

1. Always act like a boss, maintain some social distance; otherwise, you may lose power.
2. Be confident; appear to know what you are doing.
3. Stay flexible; have maneuvering room; keep your options open.
4. Channel, withhold and time information carefully. The policy initiator with pertinent, current, reliable information has power.
5. Form alliances for protection, communication and publicity above, diagonally, and below in the organization. For those above, find out which issues are salient and what you can do for them. At other levels, build the status of your allies with privileges, title, pay, and public endorsement, to name a few.
6. Take counsel only when you desire, from whom you desire; don't say that you "will hear advice from anybody" or you may have pressure and you may have conflicting alignments in your own ranks.
7. When faced with an unfavorable policy proposal:
   a. Don't give in; you will lose power.
   b. Use negative timing, delay.

Political tactics.

---

*R. A. Dahl: *Who Governs?* New Haven, Yale University Press, 1961, p. 274.
†J. C. Harsangi: "Measurement of social power opportunity costs and the theory of two person bargaining games, *Behavioral Science,* 7 (No. 1):71, January, 1962.

    c. Don't refuse; you may have a crisis.
    d. Compromise on minor matters.
    e. Move off on tangents.
    f. If it looks like you are going to suffer a reverse, give in. You use
       political resources built up from giving in as a trade-off later.

These political tactics are, of course, commonly used by some organization members for their own private gain as well as for maintaining a winning coalition. Some of the tactics are in contrast to the proposals of some behavioral scientists and practitioners for open communication, participation and a democratic atmosphere. A rationale needs to be developed for the nonhypocritical use of power or political tactics. However, the tactics are presented here merely to provide a more complete description of the realities in policy making.

Interaction of Structure and Environmental Pressures

Personal decision.

The interaction of structure and environmental pressures has two parts: The first involves the individual policy makers and their personal decisions regarding resolution of role conflicts, furtherance of self-interest and conservation of political resources. It has been assumed that consciously or unconsciously each decision is the result of an effort on the part of the policy maker to satisfy his conflicting personal demands. A trade-off of political resources in light of perceived self-interests and the degree of role conflict may be made.

Coordinating with others.

The second part of the interaction of structure and the environment is the carrying out of the coordination function in obtaining a solution on priority allocation issues while maintaining a winning coalition. Policy makers are seen as coordinating to find solutions that will win external support (e.g., customers), internal support (e.g., peers) and partially satisfy self-interest. The coordination and planning is like "muddling through"* when considered as a social process, and it is impossible to determine in advance exactly what the solutions should be. Thus, there must be sensitivity to *feedback* and a disposition to change tactics. For example, feedback affecting the budget might involve a strike, government wage-price controls, a competitor's technological advance or a crisis of any kind. Adjustments in resource allocation are made, using the "muddling through" process of coordination and planning.

Various methods are used by policy makers in attempting to deal with or to coordinate conflict situations of resource allocation. A challenge is to prevent the conflict from becoming dysfunctional while at the same time retaining the stimulation and challenge of

---

*C. E. Lindblom: The science of muddling through, *Public Administration Review,* 19:79–88, Spring, 1959.

competition and conflict. Out of conflict may emerge distinctive and constructive differences in values, objectives and methods. Unmanaged conflict, however, may get out of hand. Methods for coordination include the following:

Clarity and acceptance of roles. Clear and definite expected patterns of behavior can serve to help policy makers to become more autonomous and to reduce jurisdictional disputes. There is a risk of loss of flexibility and, of course, conflict situations may still develop. If the role assignments have been accepted as legitimate, however, they are likely to serve as one basis for resolution of differences.

How is conflict managed?

Some evidence exists showing that role conflict and ambiguity have detrimental effects on organization members and organization success.*

Hierarchical coordination. A frequently used method in coordination is to rely on legitimate authority or the formal right to command. There is, in many instances, the major advantage of decisive and quicker action. Again, however, there is a risk of lack of flexibility and also a risk of lack of acceptance of the decision. Political resources, such as expertise and charisma, may exist in locations other than where the formal authority rests. In this situation, the one with formal authority may accommodate or negotiate.

Pros and cons of reliance on legitimate authority.

Structural integration. There are a variety of structural arrangements that are used to mediate potential conflicts over values, objectives and allocations. Integrators or link pins may serve as contacts and communicators between organizational units or between organizations. Examples include project managers, sales-production expeditors, political lobbyists, interdepartmental committees and joint labor-management teams. One difficulty of link pins may be a tendency for each to represent his own self-interest and thus fail to collaborate in any meaningful sense. Of course, if the reward structure is adjusted so that successful accomplishment of coordination provides a real payoff, this difficulty may be overcome.

Use of "linking pins."

Some evidence on the relationship between structural integration and organization success is provided in a study of six firms in the plastics industry.† An index of integration was closely associated with measures of profit change, sales volume and the number of new products developed over a five-year period.

Superordinate goals and shared values. Superordinate goals are compelling goals which cannot be obtained by the resources and energies of the parties separately. For example, departments work-

---

*For a review of such studies, see J. Rizzo, R. House and S. Lirtzman: Role conflict and ambiguity in complex organization, *Administrative Science Quarterly*, 15:150–163, 1970; and A. Filley and R. House: *Management Process and Organizational Behavior*, Glenview, Illinois, Scott, Foresman, and Company, 1969.

†P. R. Lawrence and J. W. Lorsch: *Organization and Environment: Managing Differentiation and Integration*. Boston, Graduate School of Business, Harvard University, 1967.

ing jointly on a project involving a new service or product may force a dilemma on such issues as flexibility versus stability of operations, short run versus long run considerations, and objective measurements (e.g., costs) versus subjective measurements (e.g., employee attitudes). The policy initiators may take stands on issues according to their subgoals, and this fact in relation to their "strategic" position (political resources) is one of the determinants in initiating action. When a superordinate goal (e.g., share of market, continuation of the organization, identifying reasons for perceptual distortion, developing a cheap and highly desirable product) can be introduced or mobilized in a given situation, it may serve as a coordination device.* On the other hand, if goals and values are shared and cohesiveness fostered merely within the group, the result may have negative implications for coordination.

Coordinating actions through development of shared values.

Bargaining. Bargaining and negotiating a solution are identified with threats, trading off, falsification of position and, in general, gamesmanship. It requires persistence and strength in the struggle between two parties or two coalitions. The negotiator has a problem: If he takes bold action, he is liable to violate the norms of his group and lose status, so his group loyalty may overwhelm organizational logic. On the other hand, if the negotiations stall, he is liable to lose his acceptability to the other group.

A major shortcoming of bargaining, then, is the tendency to move to a distributive relationship in which there are fixed goals for each side. What is one party's gain is the other party's loss. When the bargaining turns out to be of such poor quality, it often results in a "limited war" in which interparty tension is not resolved.† Additional machinery is needed for conflict adjudication, e.g., hierarchical coordination. The emphasis is then on control.

Bargaining: creating as well as resolving tensions.

Under certain conditions bargaining is an effective coordination method. It can be effective where there are common or complementary interests. Then integrative potential for joint problem solving exists, permitting solutions benefiting both parties, or at least where one party's gain does not represent an equivalent loss for the other party.

Research evidence supports the effectiveness of bargaining, specifically where two individual policy initiators bargain to work out their differences and where group interaction is limited to studying issues rather than planning strategies.‡ The conference approach discussed next, however, suggests somewhat broader applicability.

Conference or joint problem-solving approaches. A joint prob-

---

*Muzafer Sherif: *In Common Predicament*. Boston, Houghton-Mifflin Company, 1966.

†For a discussion see E. Schein: *Organizational Psychology*. Englewood Cliffs, N.J., Prentice-Hall, Inc., 1972.

‡B. M. Bass: Effects on the subsequent performance of negotiators of studying issues or planning strategies alone or in groups. *Psychological Monographs, 80* (No. 6): 1–3, 1966.

lem-solving approach to coordination which has achieved considerable impact in recent years involves meetings of potentially or actually conflicting parties attempting to gain an open and frank discussion of issues and policies. The conferences are designed (frequently by neutral third parties) to open lines of communication and to establish personal and group commitment to improving organizational functioning and organizational policies. This approach has at least part of its origin in organization development.*

Groups as effective policy formation agents.

A key requirement in the confrontation between parties is to build an atmosphere of trust and to develop a form of leveling in discussion of perceived organizational problems. A low key approach is often used to bring differing objectives, values and perceptions out into the open where they can be dealt with constructively. Also, a basic tactic in problem solving is to find the goals upon which the parties can agree and thereby establish effective interaction. Frequently the group provided with data input is asked to identify priority issues, barriers to actions, plans of actions for themselves and recommendations on plans for others. Evidence exists of the success of this approach in improving coordination and policy formation in both industry and government settings.†

Circular Effects of Policy Formation

The outputs from the interaction of the structure and the environmental forces include objectives, strategies, role performance and organizational outcomes.

The strategies, as mentioned, are specific major actions or patterns of action (sometimes ad hoc, sometimes planned) to attain objectives. Objectives are targets or hoped for results. Role performance means the actual patterns of behavior of participants relevant to the organization. Role performance would include the interpretation, implementation and acceptance of strategies, and organizational outcomes would include such performance measures as growth, stability, flexibility, return on investment and social responsibility.

Furthermore, the model assumes that once a strategy is formulated it becomes part of the environment. The implementation of the strategy and the reaction to it by the organization member and by individuals and groups outside the organization will comprise new environmental pressures which may necessitate modification of existing strategy and, perhaps, the creation of new strategy. The

Feedback in a dynamic process.

---

*G. Dalton, P. Lawrence, and L. Greiner (eds.): *Organization Change and Development.* Homewood, Ill., Richard D. Irwin, 1970.

†R. T. Golembiewski and A. Blumberg: The laboratory approach to organization change, *Academy of Management Journal,* Vol. II, 1968; F. T. Paine: A conference approach to assessing public management, *Personnel Administration,* June, 1972, pp. 47–52.

Policy process is incremental.

feedback of output effects and organizational outcomes is necessary since strategy formation is a dynamic process. What was decided yesterday will already exist in a new light today.

The feedback is used in such a way as to make the policy process interrelated, cumulative and consistent — in short, incremental.* Existing levels of support for various activities are more or less taken for granted and incremental changes considered. This situation is associated with the widely shared value of mitigation of conflict (or "don't rock the boat"). Such a view of the policy process seems to fail to account for new policy departures. Such events could be treated as random disturbances. A dominant manager may come along and seek bold opportunities. A planning manager may carefully reformulate a corporate strategy. However, old patterns of the interaction process may reassert themselves.

Core issue — need to prevent stagnation.

The organization might not be able to adjust to opportunities and challenges in a rapidly changing environment. A built-in provision for self-criticism, for challenging present policies and practices, for auditing the environment, and for revising and reformulating strategies is needed. This is a core issue; the organization needs to seek a deliberate way of preventing dry rot or stagnation.

Applying the Model to Business and Public Bodies

The model is seen as applicable to business as well as non-business organizations. Both types of organizations have structures which (1) scan the changing environment for opportunities, threats and risks, and (2) based on premises about the environment and considering self-interests, develop basic missions, objectives and strategies.

The policy analyst should keep in mind, however, that significant differences do exist which affect the nature of his assessment. Bernard Taylor, a well known policy analyst from Great Britain, notes some significant differences between business and public bodies as follows:†

	Business	*Public Bodies*
Main objective	Profit	Public service
Economic objectives	Profit required; bankruptcy possible	No profit required; bankruptcy not possible
Structure	Frequently decentralized into profit centers	Usually a centralized bureaucracy
Accountable to	Shareholders	Congress/Parliament
Control of strategy	Management	Government

---

*For discussion see A. Wildavsky: *The Politics of the Budgetary Process,* Boston, Little, Brown and Co., 1964.

†Bernard Taylor: Personal communication, July 17, 1972.

Scope of activity	Unlimited; no monopoly	Limited; state monopoly
Major source of funds	Shareholders/banks	Government

These differences, significant as they are, do not preclude treatment of these business and public bodies with the same model. Adjustments can and should be made, adapting the critical analytical variables to the specific organization.

Illustration of Model—A Role Play

In order to "bring to life" the model of policy formation you may want to devise and implement a role play or exercise involving one or more groups to illustrate roles, self-interests, conflicts, political resources, trade-offs, coalitions and environmental pressures. Such an exercise might contain the following:

1. A basic description of the organizational policy situation.
2. An analysis of alternative policy opportunities.
3. A description of the policy makers, their self-interests, political resources and environmental pressures.
4. Private information known only to a limited number (one or more) policy makers.

The description of the Slimey Oil Co. situation which follows illustrates such a role play or exercise. The secret information is not included.

SLIMEY OIL COMPANY (SOCO)

1. SOCO is a large, independent oil refinery located in Baltimore, Maryland. 1969 sales, $100M; profit, $2M.
2. A controlling interest in SOCO was recently acquired by a large conglomerate, Amalgamated Industries. Amalgamated is interested in SOCO because of its asset base ($300M) and has put one of its young executives on SOCO's board to watch over its interests.
3. SOCO is reasonably profitable and internally sound, both financially and managerially.
4. SOCO's key competition comes from the Philadelphia Refining Company (PRC) of Philadelphia, Penna.
5. Because of the switch in 1971 by all the major auto makers to engines that will use unleaded gas, SOCO must rebuild portions of its facilities or lose its customers. This changeover is tying up all of SOCO's cash reserves ($5M) and some of its credit ($3M). The refinery will not have to shut down for this conversion. PRC already makes unleaded gas and is unaffected by the switch.
6. SOCO has learned through its lobbyist that the state of Maryland will pass a law in the next general assembly which will require all companies to cease pollution. This law will take effect in 1974 and would require SOCO to expend a great deal of money on antipollution equipment. This money would have to be borrowed and interest rates are at record highs. Further, a six months' shutdown in production would be required to complete the necessary modifications. Much of the rebuilding necessary to make unleaded gas would also have to be redone. Finally, PRC is under no pressure from Pennsylvania to stop polluting.

After much debate and under pressure from Baltimore area conservation groups and from its stockholders, the Board of Directors decided to meet in executive session and adopt a strategic plan of action.

There are only three alternatives open:

A. Support the law fully and comply. This requires borrowing $20M at 9 per cent and six months' shutdown.

Effects   1. High interest costs ($1.8M/yr.).
             2. Put in bad competitive position vs. PRC.
             3. Socially acceptable choice.
             4. Don't pay for unleaded change twice.

B. Take law to court and fight for delay. Legal costs would be high, but much, much less than interest costs. The future of interest rate is uncertain and it is unknown if pending Federal antipollution laws will cause the same problems for PRC.

Effects   1. Maintain competitive position vs. PRC.
             2. Bad public relations; a socially unacceptable choice.
             3. Potential serious financial and legal consequences if court battle is lost; particularly bad if lost early.
             4. Pay for unleaded change twice.

C. Compromise. Fight for delay but also spend some for antipollution. Requires spending $5M but very little shutdown—four weeks. Would still have to pay twice for unleaded change.

Effects   1. Although costs are greater than choice B, still less than choice A.
             2. Better competitively than A.
             3. Still reasonably bad public relations.
             4. Largely avoids legal problems.

MEMBERS OF THE BOARD OF DIRECTORS (7 MEMBERS)

CHAIRMAN _____ Is founder of the company, independently wealthy, *very* civic minded. Has been chairman for 30 years. Strongly supports plan A.

PRESIDENT _____ Has been president for 20 years, during which time the company has enjoyed unprecedented growth and earnings. Supports plan B all the way and has taken public position that if it is not adopted he will retire on the spot.

EXECUTIVE VICE PRESIDENT _____ Son-in-law of president but also MIT honors graduate with M.S. Chem. E. and MBA. Highly competent and well thought of. It is suspected there is strong pressure on him from his wife to support the president. He supports plan B.

CONGLOMERATE REPRESENTATIVE _____ It is known that he supports plan C; Amalgamated doesn't want to rock the boat. He will vote against A or B unless new arguments are presented that give him a better option. Amalgamated will not overthrow the Board.

MRS. _____ A large independent stockholder. Adamantly supports plan A both emotionally and intellectually (believes in conservation). Willing to compromise only as a last resort. She is a civic-minded widow with children in college.

COMPTROLLER _____ Also a stockholder; has been with company since founding. Because of bad financial position that would, in his opinion, result from either plan A or C he strongly supports plan B.

MR. _____ A prominent Baltimore businessman with an independent income. A member of the Sierra Club and a staunch conservationist. Supports plan A all the way. He is a personal friend of the Chairman, the comptroller and Mrs. _____.

Instructions

Your instructor may assign you to play one of the roles as indicated in the exercise. He might also assign some members of the class to be observers of the policy-formation process. Such observers would note their perceptions of the activities in the complex problem-solving situation and report to the class.

In addition, your instructor may wish to provide private information to be known to only a limited number of the policy makers during the meeting. For example, the executive vice president might be given the following information:

If the President wins the vote and you vote against him, he will fire you. He holds a $30,000 note payable on demand on some of your real estate. If he loses and you voted against him, he will call the note.

You are secretly a member of the Sierra Club and strongly support conservation and therefore Plan A, but you must publicly support B initially.

This kind of information would be divulged to all participants only after the observers make their reports. The class discussions will include the question of how the factors (e.g., roles, self-interests, conflicts, differing perceptions of the problem, political resources, trade-offs, coalitions, capabilities and environmental pressures) have affected the complex problem-solving process.

Social Responsibility and the Model — A Debate

There are various points of view on corporate or organizational social responsibility. This section of the chapter assembles some of the more important statements about the role of the corporation in society in order to facilitate comparison and discussion.

In the final analysis, the policy maker is left with questions of judgment, influenced by his role perception and self-interests, and constrained by various environmental forces, all of which he must take in consideration in adapting the organization to social responsibilities.

His judgment may have been affected by one or more of the points of view which we will bring out. You may wish to study and to discuss them. In a classroom situation a debate might be staged with students gathering additional information and examples.* One individual or group might start the argument as follows:

Various points of view.

1. The businessman has no way of determining what his social responsibility should be, how much he should spend on it or how he should evaluate the results. If he spends funds in a way other than the way those to whom he is responsible (the shareholders) would

Businessman should seek profit for stockholders benefit?

---

*There is a lack of systematic research on impact of public responsibility on formulation of corporate strategy. Read Robert W. Ackerman: Public responsibility and the businessman, *Harvard Business School*, 4 - 371–520, BP 1033, 1971.

have spent it, he is in effect imposing a tax and deciding on the use of proceeds.

2. Public functions should not be exercised by the managers of private enterprises, lest, if democracy is to be preserved, they become civil servants to be duly elected by the people or appointed by the state.*

Another individual or group might take a different view of corporate responsibility as follows:

1. Yes, there are economic constraints and the possibility of sacrifices in short-term profitability. However, social responsibility should be included as a factor influencing the formulation of policy and strategy. This explicit inclusion of social responsibility is an expression of corporate conscience.

Express corporate conscience?

2. In the long run, those firms that will earn the right profits for their stockholders are discharging their responsibilities to society.†

A third position might be as follows: Business is better qualified than government to find solutions to many urban and other problems provided (1) it is adequately controlled and (2) given economic incentives to do so. Once government has decided on the goals, social problems can be converted into economic opportunities which business can deal with effectively.

Convert social problems into economic opportunities?

Still another position that might be brought up is one relating to how social responsibility can be rendered manageable in the complex organization. Joseph Bower argues as follows: "The central source of motivation, the career system, is so designed that virtually all measures are short run and internally focused. Men are rewarded for performance, but performance is almost always defined as short run economic or technical results. The more objective the system, the more an attempt is made to quantify the results, the harder it is to broaden the rules of the game to take into account the social role of the executive."‡

Reward social role of executive?

Finally, the recommendations of the National Affiliation of Concerned Business Students might be used as a starting point for discussion. The ten "essential first steps" to integrate planning for social action into regular corporate functions are:

(1) *Corporate philosophy*—formulate a philosophy in order to define the role of the corporation in meeting economic and social objectives; (2) *social objectives*—formulate social objectives as part of the yearly and long-range economic growth goals, taking these down to the operating units so every manager knows "where he comes in"; (3) *social accountability*—develop a

---

*Milton Friedman: The social responsibility of business is to increase its profits; *The New York Times Magazine,* September 13, 1970.

†K. Andrews: The company and its social responsibilities: Relating corporate strategy to the needs of society, in *The Concept of Corporate Strategy,* Homewood, Ill., Richard D. Irwin, 1971, pp. 118–177; and Henry Ford, II: *The Human Environment and Business,* New York, Weybright and Talley, 1970, p. 63.

‡J. L. Bower: The amoral organization, mimeographed paper, August, 1970. See also Jules Cohn: Is business meeting the challenge of urban affairs, *Harvard Business Review,* July-August, 1965.

system to evaluate employees and managers on their progress toward social objectives; (4) *social audits* — develop a system of social auditing to allow a corporation to determine what social needs are most critical, and where the corporation can best use its own resources, and evaluate its progress toward the social objectives it has set up; (5) *social reports* — publish a social progress report as part of the corporate annual report, on the basis that social performance is part of the overall corporate performance; (6) *top executive advocate* — name a high level advocate or watchdog for social considerations within the corporation; (7) *social staff* — set up noneconomic senior executive for social concern to do research and planning to determine social needs and corporate programs; (8) *broaden board of directors* — include groups not now generally represented in order to get needed additional perspectives; (9) *lobbying* — use existing political power to lobby for needed social legislation; (10) *executive brainstorming committee* — appoint a top-level group of executives to study the corporation's role in society, allowing the group time away from daily operations to deal with social considerations in depth.*

Integrate planning for social action into corporate functions.

The discussion of these points of view may center on organizational objectives, including the balancing of economic and noneconomic considerations, personal values or interests and social responsibilities, and the environmental and structural forces affecting the implementation of social responsibility in the complex organization.

SUMMARY

We have elaborated a bit on conceptualizing the policy formation process in organizations. Specifically, we indicate that a typical cognitive model of decision making may hamper understanding and may confuse students of the policy-formation process. In contrast to this decision-making model, a policy-formation model to be descriptive must include, at least, the lack of unity on problem statements, two or more issues, two or more sets of interests and no single best solution.

The general approach to be followed in this book is to see the policy issues as involving a complex social process and then to converge on the cognitive aspects. To begin, an input-output model is presented emphasizing the dynamic social process. The model assumes that key inputs affecting policy are environmental forces (support and demands) and that these forces interact with a given policy-generating structure. Policy makers, though they make an intellectual analysis of alternative policies, are affected by their role perceptions, their perceived self-interests, and the use of political resources. They monitor and predict changes in the internal and external environment.

The interaction of structure and environment pressures has two parts: The first involves the policy makers' decisions regarding reso-

*Stanford University Graduate School of Business, *Alumni Bulletin*, Summer, 1972, p. 13.

lution of role conflicts, furtherance of self-interests and conservations of political resources. The second part involves the coordination function in obtaining solutions to priority allocation issues while maintaining a winning coalition of support. Various methods for dealing with coordination are discussed, such as role clarity and acceptance, structural integration, superordinate goals and joint problem solving.

The feedback of output effects and organizational outcomes is used in such a way as to make the policy process incremental. This may result from a widely shared value of mitigation of conflict. If such be the case, the organization needs some provision to rejuvenate itself and to prevent stagnation. Appropriate review and evaluation of the policy-formation process would determine the need for revisions in the adaptions to the environment. Subsequent chapters will deal with some guides to such reviews and evaluations. They will help you to answer some of your questions on learning about policy in general and on using a framework and methods appropriate to a specific situation.

The next chapter discusses learning about policy. We feel it very important to understand the variety of ways one may develop knowledge, information-processing skill and other skills useful in the complex problem-solving process of policy formation.

To add realism and practicality, this chapter has provided (1) an illustration of the model of the policy-formation process, and (2) a potential class assignment that includes various points of view on social responsibility.

INTERGROUP POLICY EXERCISE

Policy formation is seen by some as a bargaining process. Certain people interact in the establishment and implementation of policies. There is a need (1) to negotiate, (2) to gain acceptance, and (3) to have leadership skill in spelling out to potential members of a coalition how the policy will serve their interests.

The instructor will set up three or four groups with four or five students in each. He will assign the groups an important policy choice, e.g., selection of one from three or more types of term projects or a determination of the sequence in presenting individual or group reports. It is necessary that the policy choice have a high potential for provoking both interest and disagreements. Each small group will proceed as follows:

1. Make a decision in favor of one of the alternatives.
2. Choose a reporter who will present his group's preference and views to the whole group.
3. Choose a delegate who will meet with other delegates to make a final decision for the whole group. The final decision is binding.

4. Be prepared to discuss the decision-making process within the small group and within the meeting of delegates.

Time limits will be set for each of the activities, based on the complexity of the policy issue and on the class requirements. Discussion of the exercise may include such aspects as the effects of conflicts on the intergroup decision-making process.

DISCUSSION QUESTIONS

1. Compare and contrast strategy formulation with the typical decision-making model discussed in the text.

2. Why does it seem appropriate to view strategy issues as involving a complex social process and then to converge on the cognitive aspects rather than to hope that strategy issues can be understood in terms of solely intellectual components?

3. What are some of the ways the assumptions of the decision-making model may be violated?

4. How do self-interests and political resources affect strategy making?

5. Discuss the methods of coordination used in resource allocation conflict situations.

6. What is meant by the circular effects of strategy formation?

7. Discuss political tactics that may be used in the strategy-formation process. Do you agree with the appropriateness of their use? Why?

8. Discuss differences in the application of the strategy-formation model to business organizations and to public bodies.

9. Devise a descriptive theory that explains the behavior of the participant in the policy-formation process.

Suggested Additional References for Further Research

Anshen, M.: Price tags for business policies, *Harvard Business Review, 38*(No. 1): 71–78, 1960.

Barber, R. J.: *The American Corporation; Its Power, Its Money, Its Politics.* New York, E. P. Dutton and Company, 1970.

Bauer, R. A., and Gergen, K. J.: *The Study of Policy Formation.* New York, Free Press, 1968.

Brooks, J. G.: *1846–1938, The Conflict Between Private Monopoly and Good Citizenship.* Boston, Houghton Mifflin Company, 1939.

Cannon, J. T.: *Business Strategy and Policy.* New York, Harcourt, Brace & World, 1968.

Elbing, A. O., and Elbing, Carol J.: *The Value Issue of Business.* New York, McGraw Hill Book Co., 1967.

Farmer, R., and Hogue, W. D.: *Corporate Social Responsibility.* Palo Alto, Cal., Science Research Associates, Inc., 1973.

Galbraith, J. K.: *The New Industrial State.* Boston, Houghton Mifflin Company, 1967.

Kapp, K. W.: *The Social Costs of Private Enterprise.* Cambridge, Harvard University Press, 1950.

Kaufmann, C. B.: *Man Incorporate: The Individual and His Work in an Organized Society.* New York, Doubleday and Company, 1967.

Kristol, I.: Professor Galbraith's New Industrial State, *Fortune,* July, 1967, pp. 90–91, 194–195.

Lawrence, P. R., and Lorsch, J. W.: *Organization and Environment.* Cambridge, Harvard University Press, 1967.

Lindblom, C. E.: *The Intelligence of Democracy.* New York, Free Press, 1965.

Lindblom, C. E.: *The Policy Making Process.* Englewood Cliffs, N.J., Prentice Hall, Inc., 1968.

Luthans, F., and Hodgetts, R. M.: *Social Issues in Business.* New York, The Macmillan Company, 1972.

March, J. G., and Simon, H. A.: *Organizations.* New York, John Wiley & Sons, Inc., 1958.

Nader, R.: *The Consumer and Corporate Responsibility.* New York, Harcourt, Brace Jovanovich, Inc., 1973.

Parsons, T.: Power, party, and system. *In* Ulmer, S. S. (ed.): *Introductory Readings in Political Behavior.* Chicago, Rand McNally & Company, 1961, pp. 127–136.

Parsons, T., and Shils, E. A.: *Toward a General Theory of Action.* Cambridge, Harvard University Press, 1962, p. 23.

Riker, W. H.: *The Theory of Political Coalitions.* New Haven, Yale University Press, 1962.

Riley, J. W., Jr., and Levy, M. F. (eds.): *The Corporation and Its Publics: Essays on the Corporate Image.* New York, John Wiley & Sons, Inc., 1963.

Simon, H. A.: On the concept of organizational goal, *Administrative Science Quarterly* 9:1–22, 1964.

Simon, H. A.: The new science of management decision, in *The Shape of Automation.* New York, Harper & Row, 1965.

Thompson, J. D., and Bates, F.: Technology, organization and administration, *Administrative Science Quarterly* 2(No. 3): 1958.

Trebing, H. M.: *The Corporation in the American Economy.* Chicago, Quadrangle Books, 1970.

Weissman, J. I. (ed.): *The Social Responsibilities of Corporate Management.* Hempstead, New York, Hofstra University Press, 1966.

Vaill, P. B.: Industrial and socio-technical systems, *Journal of Industrial Engineering,* Volume 18, September, 1967.

3

CASE STUDY
    The Case System in Business
      Education
    Case Analysis
    Using the Case Method

THE DIAGNOSTIC PROCESS
    Diagnosis — Case Study

THE LIVE CASE

FIELD PROJECTS

FIELD RESEARCH

DYNAMIC COMPUTER MODELS

ROLE PLAYING

TIMING A CASE IN THE FUTURE
WITH SCIENCE FICTION

SUMMARY

DISCUSSION QUESTIONS

LEARNING ABOUT POLICY

As previously discussed, there is much to learn about policy formation and the environmental forces affecting an organization. This is a complex subject about which there are volumes of information on practice, and about which there is some theory and research which is relevant. We have expressed the caution, however, that the theory is in an infant stage and that the limited research available does not provide rigorous support for current prescriptions in policy making. Thus, it should be recognized that you will be developing tentative answers to your questions on policy. Research and theory building going on right now will eventually add to our fund of knowledge.*

There are a variety of specific approaches to research and theory building in the field of policy now being used that promise useful results in the next decade or so. Some emphasize a description of what is going on, or, in other words, try to gain some understanding of why policy makers do what they do. Other approaches emphasize adding more depth to an existing normative framework. In both the descriptive and the normative approaches there should be more empirical research. The policy process should be observed and studied in a systematic way. (Note that we are being normative here.)

Some of the major research strategies as summarized by William Guth are:†

1. "Illumination of the interaction between knowledge — science and art — judgment in coping with problems of policy formulation

---

*See, for example, P. H. Grinyer: Some dangerous axioms of corporate planning, *Journal of Business Policy 3* (No. 1):3–9, 1973.

†William D. Guth: U.S. perspectives on the teaching of business policy, in *Some Selected Working Papers from the International Seminar for Teachers of Business at the Irish Management Institute,* Norman, Oklahoma, Academy of Management, Division of Business Policy and Planning, 1971, p. 90.

*Major research
strategies.*

and implementation." (Direct empirical investigation of top-management behavior in relation to specific policy formation and implementation problems would be the principal methodology commitment here.)

2. "Development and empirical testing of normative models of decision making in relation to policy formulation and implementation problems." (Guth points out that empirical testing of normative models for decision making on such problems is at least difficult, if not impossible, in anything other than experimental settings. In spite of the limitations of experimental research designs, however, it is accepted that they can provide at least some modest corroboration or refutation of the effectiveness of normative methodologies.)

3. "Historical-empirical testing of hypotheses about the relationships between major variables under managerial control and the growth and profitability of the firm." (As an example, the stages of corporate development.)

4. "Exploratory study of the interface between the private and public institutions, and problems of social justice and the general quality of life leading to a greater understanding of present and potential relationships."

*Need for
updating your
knowledge.*

At some point these approaches will no doubt provide significant additions to existing information and theory on policy. Thus, what you learn about policy making now will need updating from time to time, i.e., assuming you have a continuing intellectual or practical interest in this important subject.

Thus far we have been focusing attention on information and theory about complex problem solving, that is, problems that affect the long-term development of the organization. These problems are complex because of the factors pointed out in Chapters 1 and 2. In order to develop skill in handling these problems, it is important that the reader actually process complex problems; that is, more information-processing activity seems to lead to greater skills in the policy-formation process.

*Link theory with
practice and
develop skill with
information-
processing
activity.*

The manager and the staff analyst or technocrat have opportunities for on-the-job experience in such information-processing activities. He or she may assess the relevance of theory in practice or, in other words, link the theory with practice. In universities and in development programs, the students may link theory with practice and develop skill in information-processing activities in a variety of ways. They may play a business game, pretend to start a company, observe and analyze reality firsthand via a field study, have a role play discussion of social issues facing managers, read practical and applied type readings,* or use some form of case study method. However, three methods appear to predominate in linking theory

---

*For example see A. D. Chandler: *Strategy and Structure,* Cambridge, Mass., MIT Press, 1962; J. W. Bonge and B. P. Coleman (eds.): *Concepts for Corporate Strategy,* New York, The Macmillan Co., 1972; J. G. Hutchinson: *Readings in Management and Strategy and Tactics,* New York, Holt, Rinehart & Winston, 1971.

and practice and in developing skill in processing information — dynamic computer models, field projects and the case study method. Of these, clearly the case study method is most often used at present for policy courses in universities and colleges and in development programs.

CASE STUDY

In the case study method learning takes place as the students try to discover, define and answer critical questions, using real life situations described on paper. The end goal of case analysis is suggested management actions based upon the analysis.

How effective is this method? In the expert opinion of training directors* in a recent study, the case study method was rated highly effective for the training objective of improving problem-solving skill. Unfortunately the research on effectiveness of case study as a training approach is very limited. Only a few studies have been found that involved more than an attempt to obtain testimonials from course participants.

How effective for various objectives?

Solem† found that the case study method was effective for learning how to derive solutions to complex problems. Fox‡ found that about two thirds of the students exposed to case study analysis improved moderately or significantly in their ability to handle cases; the other one third made no improvement.

Another training objective of case study analysis is knowledge acquisition. The training experts mentioned previously rated the case study method quite high for attaining this objective. Again, the scientific research in this area is limited. However, in a well controlled study§ in which a class taught by the case method was compared to a class taught by the lecture and discussion approach, the case study section scored significantly higher on achievement tests.

In the pure case study method, theories are ignored and specific knowledge acquisitions are not expected. However, the case method may include a rigorous conceptual structure (or theory) as a basis.** Thus, the conceptualization may be linked to the described practice.

In the past, cases sometimes have not had adequate coverage of

---

*Stephen J. Carroll, Frank T. Paine and John J. Ivancevich: The relative effectiveness of training methods — expert opinion and research, *Personal Psychology*, Fall, 1972.

†A. R. Solem: Human relations: Comparisons of case study and role playing, *Personnel Administration* 23(s):29–37, 1960.

‡W. M. Fox: A measure of the effectiveness of the case method in teaching human relations, *Personnel Administration* 26:53–57, 1963.

§E. D. Butler: An experimental study of the case method in teaching the social foundations of education, *Dissertation Abstracts* 26:3712, 1966.

**The Harvard Business School, which has a central commitment to cases, is developing an increased conceptual-analytical rigor in its approach.

certain concepts such as the policy-generating structure, budget allocations and organizational outcomes. Thus, the policy analyst using these cases is somewhat limited. He must do the best he can with what he has and add to his information where possible. Sometimes current information from the library, newspapers, business magazines or the organization itself is available and proves helpful.

Cases developed in the last few years are giving greater attention to the role, stakes and pressures of managers at different organization levels, including especially the middle manager affected by strategy implementation. In addition, more attention has been shown recently to the stages of organization development and to relating those stages to product-market scope, to resource allocation processes and to various aspects of organization structure.

The variety of purposes and techniques which may be associated with the case method are discussed in the following material developed at Stanford University in 1958. It is still quite useful today.

THE CASE SYSTEM IN BUSINESS EDUCATION*

Cases used to find problems as well as solutions.

The use of the case system in academic programs of training for business is not primarily to help students accumulate a store of knowledge, nor to acquaint them with current business practices. It does that. But the first purpose is to help the students to develop skills in discovering and defining the vital questions which ought to be answered, then to learn how to go about answering such questions. In the ordinary course of business they will find themselves compelled to take action before they can get all the facts which they would like to have in deciding what is the right action.

The case system does not aim to give the student ready-made answers to the problems which it is assumed his business life will present to him. Such an enterprise would be futile for the questions which he will have to answer have not yet been asked. It's vitally important to develop the ability to ask the key questions. The question that has not been asked is not answered, and frequently represents the vital problem which was not solved with resultant loss of profit. Most advances in science have been made by challenging the obvious. So in business the ability to ask the problem-solving question frequently requires a greater flash of insight than that needed for finding the answer.

Learn by doing.

1. The case system is essentially teaching by the project method. The mere act of listening to wise statements and sound advice is not enough. The student learns by doing, by working in dynamic cooperation with others to solve real problems in the form in which they actually arise. Such is, however, not automatic. It has to be stimulated and given space and time in the course. Therefore, students are not given general theories or hypotheses to criticize. Rather, they are given the specific facts, the raw materials, on the basis of which decisions are reached. Fundamental here is, of course, student initiative and participation through free channels of communication constantly kept open between students and students, and between students and teachers.

---

*Copyright, 1958, by the Board of Trustees of Leland Stanford Junior University.

2. The case system is a system of learning. The student is given real problems for *his* analysis and discussion; for *his* solution and decision. Like a minor business executive, he must find answers and explain them orally or write reports on questions such as the following: What, if anything, should be done? Why? How would you get it done? What facts would you like before you decide what to do? Will it be worth your while to get them? Can you afford to wait? If you decide now, what are your calculated risks? What is your "out" in the event you are wrong or conditions change?

3. The case system, while it cannot create or enhance intelligence, does give exercise to it. The business executive fails or succeeds, not so much by what he knows, as by what he does. In business, knowledge divorced from action is sterile. Ability and willingness to take action soon enough is frequently more important than being 100 per cent right when it is too late. Inaction frequently constitutes action of the wrong kind. For example, to hold savings in cash because one is uncertain in what to invest may in a period of inflation involve considerable loss.

Case analysis gives exercise to intelligence.

4. The case system does not limit instructional techniques. It can include lecturing where necessary, report writing, collateral reading, laboratories, field trips and field work, assignment and intensive study of text material, individual and group conferences, and visual aids. It is usually more expensive than the conventional lecture system. Grading is difficult and time-consuming. Objective tests are difficult to develop. There are frequently several good answers, all partly valid and none completely and demonstrably accurate. Reports must be evaluated on the basis of the logical processes, whereby questions are raised and answers are presented, particularly the balance, judgment, and awareness shown of the intricacies of the problem.

5. Not all students are capable of handling cases. Those do best who have adult background knowledge of business operations. Foreign students, undergraduates, and those without work experience often feel at sixes and sevens. The lack of authoritative answers and the agony of being compelled to make decisions which neither the student nor anyone else can incontrovertibly demonstrate as wrong, leave them up in the air. Sometimes they feel no sense of solid accomplishment, at least at first. With no benchmarks, it is difficult to detect forward motion. Additions to one's power to act are not as noticeable as additions to one's store of facts. It is harder to be aware of an increase in the faculty of intelligent improvisation than to show a sheaf of lecture notes.

Outside knowledge is valuable.

Moreover, everyone hates to undertake the intolerable toil of thought. *Mais l'appetit vient en mangeant.* After a time the student acquires more confidence in his own ability to face the unknown. Indeed, there may be times when he falls a victim to brazen, sophomoric overconfidence. But he is learning his job as a business man, that of evaluating risks and bearing uncertainty. In the process of hunting around for solutions he finds that a considerable accumulation of factual knowledge rubs off on him. He learns to appreciate the unpredictabilities of business and economic problems. He learns the value of constant experimentation, constant reappraisal of results, goals, and methods, constant dissatisfaction with results, and constant striving for improvement.

6. Good cases are hard to get. The intangibles, the fragmentary apprehensions which are all that is available when one must exercise foresight are difficult to put into the case, collected from and by men enjoying the omniscience of hindsight. Merely selecting what now are known to be "relevant" facts eliminates many considered major at the time but now patently of minor importance. Facts *a priori* rarely carry neat labels or identification certificates of actual weight.

Cases are as varied as the uncertainties and problems facing business. Only in rare instances are business cases identical with law cases. It is the latter that gave rise at Harvard to the use of the case system in the strict sense. To be sure there are such — particularly in the relationships of business to government. They vary with the legal system, even of individual States. Legal cases have the enormous value inherent in the judicial rule of *stare decisus*. The lawyer's great advantage is that he can cite such decisions as authority, and often win for his client. But business men can rarely thus compel solutions to their problems. Everything changes so rapidly that old ways of handling uncertainties may provide useful analogies but rarely definitive answers.

Usually business cases represent descriptions of particular situations that a particular firm had to meet in the past. The materials are obtained from their files. An expert interviewer strives to induce the business executives involved to remember what happened, and in particular what they thought was happening. Major issues are clarified. The actual adjustment made may be included, particularly if, as is the usual instance, it was both satisfactory and unsatisfactory. Most business cases are of that type and are available though not equally useful, for each of the functional fields in business: accounting, finance, pricing, distribution, production, statistics, industrial relations, public relations, and adjustment to the changing rules of governments, local, state and federal.

Finally, there are cases that consist for the most part of presentations of data on problems. In increasing measure the business executive faces uncertainties that are external, rather than internal. In order to appraise the business situation, whether general or for his type of enterprise, he often has to pick the crucial facts out of business periodicals, statistical services, surveys of current business, congressional hearings, new legislation, administrative rulings, legal decisions, commission reports and government publications in general.

Case Analysis

In case courses students are frequently expected to participate in class discussion and to make oral and written reports on cases. To provide some guidance, handouts describing the problem identification and problem solution process are frequently used. Many of these handouts include material similar to that which is used at the University of Maryland. We shall give a sample of what is used at Maryland to help students to get started; then we shall proceed to discuss the important *diagnostic process* that the student or analyst is expected to go through.

Using the Case Method

I. INTRODUCTION

1. This method of learning calls for the maximum individual participation in class discussion. One cannot learn as an observer, he must be a participant.

Critical participation required.

2. In class discussion, one must accept a critical atmosphere and be willing to submit his conclusions to rebuttal.
3. While learning under the case method is a group process to which one must adjust, this does not imply conformity to group opinion.

4. One must be willing to accept the risks of stating one's conclusions and overcome the fear of making and admitting a mistake.
5. Intelligent analysis calls for the recognition and identification of assumptions.
6. Effective classroom case discussion and analysis can be realized only if each participant has the "facts" of the case in his analysis well in hand. One does not seek to uncover facts or use his analysis during the discussion, although modifications of the facts and analysis will evolve through the insights provided by the group's efforts.
7. The teacher is a discussion leader, not a lecturer or major contributor of facts and analysis.

Requirements for successful case discussion.

8. Decisions have to be made without all the data one would desire, and this is an asset, not a liability, in case analysis—for it reflects the condition management often faces.
9. There may be several acceptable solutions to a problem in a case. Definitive answers are rarely, if ever, available. The solution is not as significant as the basis from which it is derived.
10. Learning by the case method, or any other educational approach, is in the final analysis an individual proposition calling for a maximum of personal effort and responsibility.

No single approach to case problem solution is ideal; however, the student may use the following procedure in handling the cases assigned in this course:

II. SITUATIONAL ANALYSIS

The first step consists of recognizing the existence of a problem(s) and determining the significant issues with which management must deal. Please remember that the firm's strategies and policies are derived from its basic purposes and objectives which in turn are influenced by the various constraints of the company's internal and external environments.

Diagnose the situation.

An analytical study of the case facts is required to determine why and when the problem arose, who is concerned, and how critical the situation is. In addition, the adequacy of company resources and the probable impact on organizational performance capability must be properly evaluated.

III. USE AND ANALYSIS OF EVIDENCE

A. Support from Evidence Other than Quantitative
1. Adequacy. A persuasive analysis usually provides an accumulation of evidence to support its position. A particularly dangerous weakness in this area is the excessive reliance on generalizations and principles rather than cases.
2. Balance. An analysis which consistently recognizes only evidence favorable to its own conclusions leaves the critic or evaluator with a feeling that the analyst did not see the other side and so cannot have properly considered its merits.

Evaluate available qualitative evidence.

3. Validity. Some of the evidence in a case is established fact. Other evidence is in the form of statements, opinions, estimates, feelings and the like. The validity of such evidence must be examined to determine its value.
4. Reasonableness of Interpretations. The analyst takes the facts before him and through a series of interpretations arrives at a judg-

ment as to their effect on the issues. At each step he applies his own judgments supported by case evidence and/or general knowledge.

5. Objectivity. First, there are the analyses which omit arguments other than those favoring their position. Second, there are those in which interpretations appear to be based on prejudices or preconceptions of the analyst which blind him to other interpretations. These analyses frequently rely on strong generalizations rather than sufficient consideration of case evidence.

6. Thoroughness of Reasoning. The degree of thoroughness required for each point is determined by such questions as "How important is this point?"; "How controversial is it?"; and "How deep must I go to be convincing?"

B. *Support from Quantitative Evidence*

1. Adequacy. Though figures such as cost data and market statistics should be as conclusive and precise as possible, rough estimates and approximations should not be omitted if they are the only figures available and might give valuable evidence.

Analyze relevant quantitative data.

2. Accurate Usage. In a particular case several methods of calculation will usually be possible to make a given set of figures useful. You should especially beware of applying textbook techniques mechanically without establishing their value in the immediate problem.

IV. IDENTIFICATION AND EVALUATION OF ACTION ALTERNATIVES

What can be done to solve these problems? (Or expressed in another way, what are the alternatives of action?) Some alternatives are clearly infeasible; these can be discarded at once.

All others must be formally evaluated. This requires a determination of yardsticks by which their feasibility, utility, and risk may be evaluated. It is not enough that a given action would reduce costs; there may be other offsetting disadvantages. Human factors are always significant, and a lack of capital might prohibit certain courses of action.

V. CONCLUSIONS AND/OR RECOMMENDATIONS

Alternatives lead to actions.

A. Relation to Analysis. The decisions should follow directly from the analysis. If they come as a surprise, either because they are inconsistent with, or not related to, the analysis, the effect of the discussion is weakened.

B. Detail of Development. In this respect you should be careful in the use of generalities or panaceas like "the manager should get better staff help or environmental audits should be made more effective." Indicate the specific means for carrying out your recommendations. For example, "Have the manager take the following steps:

1._____   2._____
3._____   4._____ "

C. The Action Decision. Logical reasoning and evaluations will eventually narrow the several feasible alternatives to the one with the least risk and/or the greatest potential reward. This should be adopted. It must solve the problem faced, tend to optimize profits and costs, and be feasible in terms of people satisfaction, existing functional relationships, and resources available.

D. Implementation of the Action Decision. The decision is not complete until operational plans for its implementation have been drawn up. An effective date for initiation of action must be stipulated. Market factors and the business cycle must be favorable. Resources must be assembled. Finally, all persons involved in the action program must be sold on its timeliness and validity.

THE DIAGNOSTIC PROCESS

We have said that the policy maker is sensitive to feedback from the environment. He runs a great risk of not finding the right problem or opportunity. The risk here is probably greater than the one involved in determining how to solve the problem or exploit the opportunity once it is recognized.* The diagnostic (or intelligence) process must be given careful consideration.

The diagnostic process is defined as the art or act of recognizing the problem, opportunity or threat from symptoms, signs, intuitive insights and/or analytical findings. This is the task facing the policy analyst or student. The task requires keeping all the diverse aspects of the situation in mind while searching for the problem, opportunity or threat or reviewing a situation that has presented itself. *Definition.*

One method of diagnosis is to: (1) accumulate the significant facts and opinions, (2) review or evaluate them, and (3) generate a diagnosis which pinpoints the problem, opportunities or threats.† *Method of diagnosis.*

Facts and opinions are accumulated by scanning the environment, and perhaps by some in-depth analysis of the data developed. The integration of this information which has been fed in, using various techniques and sources, is critical. If various aspects of the situation are described, it is usually possible to find out how the aspects are interrelated and why they exist. For example, in pinpointing a problem (opportunities and threats may be handled in the same way) it is desirable to list all the suspected problems and review the evidence for reliability and adequacy to support their existence as problems. The problems will be seen to exist in a hierarchy; i.e., "lower level" problems are interrelated and can be stated as a "higher level" single problem. With precise statements of these *Pinpointing a problem.* larger problems it is possible to diagnose the causes of some or all of them. For example, the interrelated "lower level" problems of excessive inventory, rising sales costs and declining cash flow may be combined into a product obsolescence problem. The cause may be an inferior product. Or, on the other hand, the same lower level problems may be combined into a marketing effectiveness problem. The cause in this instance may be some of the characteristics of the marketing program. From a variety of possible causes, the most

---

*See G. Steiner: *Comprehensive Managerial Planning,* Oxford, Ohio, Planning Executives Institute, 1972, p. 13.

†See John W. Bonge: Problem recognition and diagnosis: Basic inputs to business policy, *Journal of Business Policy 2* (No. 3):45–53, Spring, 1972.

Which "cause" explains the symptoms or signs?

likely cause or causes must be identified by testing tentative causes and by searching for statements that explain the existence of symptoms and signs.

Before we illustrate the diagnostic process in more detail we shall indicate some cautions for the policy analyst to observe in the process as follows:

1. There may be incomplete data on the problem, opportunity or threat. It may be possible (perhaps costly, though) to gather the appropriate data or, on the other hand, to make certain assumptions and proceed. As indicated before, however, managers have to make choices with respect to a limited simplified "model" of the real situation.

Cautions to observe.

2. There may be a failure to thoroughly evaluate the symptoms and signs. Premature judgment, acceptance of the opinions of a few as general facts, failure to test tentative causes, and failure to search for exceptions which can be found for the explanations of the problem are elements of this error.

3. There may be a tendency to express the diagnosis in terms consistent with self-interests, such as market researchers indicating a need for more market research or trainers diagnosing the situation as requiring more training. Attempts should be made to have an open-minded and a systematic approach.

4. The knowledge and skill for diagnosis of a complex situation may be missing. The resultant diagnosis may include false "causes," and much time and effort may be wasted in trying to correct them. Advice and assistance from expert or experienced sources may be needed. The case analyst may ask his colleague or his instructor. The manager may call in a staff specialist or a consultant.

Diagnosis—Case Study*

This case study illustrates the process of diagnosis. The case study follows the development of a core problem or issue which emerged in a review of policy formation at a small government agency.

The Issue

As a result of a policy review a number of significant issues had been identified for consideration by the top manager in developing a plan for improved management. A key issue involved the roles of (1) the three Assistant Executive Directors, and (2) an Executive Group made up of several Bureau Chiefs and other selected top managers. The Assistant Executive Directors and the Executive Group assisted the Executive Director in giving policy direction to 30 "programs" and activities included in carrying out the agency's basic missions. Lack of a clear definition of the executive group's role and delegation of authority to the Assistant Execu-

---

*This case is based on a real organization situation, but the organization's identity has been disguised.

tive Director had resulted in slow decision making, "end runs" which destroyed planning efforts, and lack of communication up the line from "program" managers.

Development of the Issue — The Roles of the Assistant Executive Directors and the Executive Group

1. During the briefing by the review staff of the Executive Group, considerable curiosity was expressed about the scope of the review. A question was raised as to whether the review would include such matters as the relationships between Assistant Executive Directors and the Executive Director. At the time, this question was regarded by the review staff as purely exploratory rather than suggestive of a problem area.

2. In the first of several meetings of the review staff with a group of managers, statements of major issues which represented barriers to effective management were developed. In sum, the statements were rather general in nature, pointing to "loose" management, poor planning, inadequate communication, and so forth. However, some comments were aimed directly at the executive group and Assistant Executive Directors. Such comments included the following: "Managers of major programs are not represented at policy-making levels." "Better staff work is needed at the top," and "There is a lack of confidence in the Executive Group among Engineers."

3. Discussion of the issue statements by members of the review group and managers was primarily concerned with basic management issues. Judgment was needed to keep these discussions in perspective and to avoid assigning all the "blame" to people not participating in the meetings. The discussion did not narrow down the role of the Executive Group at this point. However, specific criticism was directed at one program manager who was aggressive, had the ear of the Assistant Executive Directors, and had managed to involve himself in nearly every program area. Although not completely evident at the time, this "end-running" was symptomatic of ill defined roles at the top management level.

4. The review team began to collate information from the meetings with that collected through interviews and through reviews of records and reports. Much of this information supported that brought out in the meetings. The information was organized into rough categories:

    a. Planning and priorities
    b. External environment
    c. Work organization
    d. Procedures
    e. Budgeting

These categories were essentially a grouping of symptoms. These symptoms were not yet tied to any particular centers of responsibility. Many of the problems later identified as arising from lack of role definition and delegation of authority at the top levels of management were associated at this time with planning, work organization, and procedures.

5. The consolidated list was checked for accuracy and relevance by the managers. The managers, in some cases, provided more specificity and supporting examples. The review team was satisfied that the major symptoms had been clearly identified, but the *roots* of these problems had to be found. Each problem was reviewed to isolate causes, e.g., if program managers felt they were not represented at policy levels, why was this so?

It was concluded that the key program managers had no well defined line of authority between them and the Executive Director—it was not clear whether the Executive Group or the Assistant Executive Directors were functioning as an executive body or were more nearly staff advisors.

A detailed review of delegations of authority and position descriptions supported this conclusion. Written delegations did not exist or were obsolete and position descriptions were contradictory on this point.

Issue Statement and Implications

This statement lays out the issue discussed in the case study in detail and shows some of its significant implications:

Absence of Enough Information and Authority at Operational Levels to Set Plans into Action

Part A

Lack of Clear Delineation of Responsibility and Delegation of Authority

Results

— Decisions slow in coming or not made through normal channels.
  o Role of the Executive Group?
  — — Role misunderstood, unclear. Is not functioning as a *decision-making board of directors*. What is it supposed to be?
  — — *Makeup* of Executive Group needs review. Should have broad perspective (e.g., made up of representatives of all segments of the agency) in order to set policy and priorities, to evaluate new ideas.
  — — Advocates of specialized programs: Are they appropriate members of the Executive Group?
  o Role of Assistant Executive Directors
  — — Confusion widespread re: whether Assistant Executive Directors are line or staff.
  — — Need to delineate authority of Assistant Executive Directors to:
    · decide policy
    · aid Bureau Chiefs
    · arbitrate and decide between programs.
  — — Need to ensure that Assistant Executive Directors aid communications between Executive Director and Bureau Chiefs.
— "End-runs" destroy planning efforts. Decisions are often made on individual projects but then not coordinated throughout the agency.
— Program Managers are sometimes bypassed in funding decisions and in the acceptance and assignment of projects.

Part B

Lack of Communication up (Especially from Bureau Chiefs and Program Managers)

Results

— Program Managers feel they are not represented at decision-making levels.
— Engineers feel they do not have steady communications up the line.
— Agency staff expertise not always utilized.

Possible solutions

— Re-examine and redefine role of Executive Group and Assistant Executive Directors. Are they line or staff? If they are staff, designate the line access to the Executive Director. Make this clear to all levels of the agency.

— Clarify lines of authority.
— Further delegation of authority.
— Require point of coordination to stop "end-runs":
  o Empower executive level individual to see that plans are set into action and that feed-back is received.
  o Need to clearly establish relationship of this position to Executive Director and Assistant Executive Directors.
— Better staff work before programs are presented to Executive Group for decision.

The Issue Statement resulting from the diagnostic process as shown becomes important input to the complex problem-solving process in policy formation. The statement, if properly developed, can clarify and focus attention on significant variables. To reiterate, there is a great risk in not finding the right problem, threat or opportunity. Considerable attention needs to be given to the diagnostic process. This is true, of course, not only in case analysis but in doing field projects, a subject to which we shall turn later.

Issue Statement becomes important input to problem solving.

THE LIVE CASE

A specific example of a case study that can be utilized in the business policy type of course is the live case. In this situation, as practiced at several schools, a case-type situation is developed utilizing a real organization and its managers. The organization allows itself to be studied by students at the time of the use of the case in the classroom. Typically, a case would be developed around the organization, basing the data on the up-to-date information and problems of that organization. The organization agrees to send its executives to the school for a period of time to act as consultants to the students in the policy course. The assignment to the students, which would take two or three weeks of the course, would be to present a corporate strategy for the organization for the next four to five years. The students would be assigned the task of researching the company both from the material presented in the written analysis of the case and from data available from published sources. Based on this research and analysis they are then asked to develop a preliminary strategy for the company. This preliminary strategy would be used as a basis for a final strategy that would be presented before top executives of the corporation or organization. To further define this preliminary strategy the students would have the potential of interviewing and discussing the strategy with middle and upper management levels within the company. Typically, this process would take about three or four days. After they have defined the strategy they then present their ideas to the faculty in charge of the course, who choose the best strategies for presentation before the top management of the organization. The top management would include the top executive and his immediate subordinates.

Gains for
students and
executives.

The gain on the part of the student in this type of situation includes active consultation and interaction with top management executives, as well as a more realistic approach to developing strategies in real life situations. The usual problem or complaint of students has been that the case situations are dated and don't provide a real life setting; the live case overcomes some of these problems. The advantages for the organization itself are that it has a better opportunity to talk with and interact with students, as well as a fresh outlook on its problems. There are also goodwill advantages for the organization in participating in this type of situation. As an example, we would cite the case in which a major railroad participated in a live case discussion at a well known graduate business school recently. One of the suggestions of a student group was that the railroad should actively participate in real estate development because of its large real estate holdings. At the time of the presentation several managers in that company felt that that was not the goal or objective of the company. It was interesting to note, however, that less than a year later that very same company had set up a real estate subsidiary to develop some of their land which was lying idle.

FIELD PROJECTS

Many students respond quite favorably to the challenge and to the opportunity to engage in a field project. Learning about policy in the field is one step from learning on the job. Field projects can focus on different aspects of learning. The student can test out specific theories, ideas and techniques that he has learned in the policy course and elsewhere. The student may also focus on the opportunity to find out what an organization actually needs to do to improve its policy-making situation. Moreover, the student may be asked to describe the organization in terms of the theory and thereby to refute, support or ideally extend the theory.* The student may also gain proficiency in the use of a particular management science program (e.g., modeling).

What are two
favorable forces?

If these specific purposes are attained, then knowledge is acquired and problem-solving skills are developed. However, to our knowledge there has been no specific scientific research on the effectiveness of this learning approach. The field project approach to learning was not included in the previously mentioned study by Carroll, Paine and Ivancevich in which expert opinion and research was reviewed. However, Lynton and Pareek† have studied the approach in industry and community development programs in the U.S.A. and

---

*See H. Mintzberg: Field project outline, in *Teaching and Research in Business Policy,* Working Group Report, Bradford, England, European Association of Management Training Centers, Appendix B4, 1971.

†R. P. Lynton and U. Pareek: *Training for Development,* Homewood, Ill., Richard D. Irwin, Inc., 1967, p. 120.

in India. They conclude that, "two favorable forces emerge as the training in the field gets under way. Most participants feel intensely stimulated by it and respond to the opportunity with unexpected initiative and devotion. If anything, they exaggerate their part in what happens. For its part the organization usually responds warmly to the participants' earnestness and good sense, and values their thoughtful questions and comments, this even before recommendations get focused and embodied in a formal report."

Student response, as well as the response of many members of the organization under study, is reported as enthusiastic at McGill University in Canada. Henry Mintzberg* uses the field project approach there specifically in the policy course.

The experience with the field project approach in the policy course at the University of Maryland appears to have met with success. Over 100 organizations in the Baltimore–Washington, D.C., area have participated. It is our observation that more and more instructors of policy (and other courses) are starting to use the project method. Many that we have talked to comment favorably about their experience. If one can believe these sketchy self-reports, the field project is a key integrating and learning device which provides a systematic way to focus on the process of top management and gives an opportunity to assess the relevance of the policy theory which is being developed.

Key integrating and learning device?

It should be pointed out, of course, in terms of the feasibility of usage, that there are many sections of the country where there is a limited number of organizations to investigate. Thus, other methods would need to be relied on.

Feasibility?

If feasible for use, extensive and detailed preparation is necessary. Four areas for thought and action need special attention in the field project method according to Lynton and Pareek:†

1. Clarification of roles of the students.
2. Clarification of the instructor's role.
3. Choosing the organization for the field project.
4. Preparing the students.

Extensive and detailed preparation.

For a policy course we see the student's role in field projects as basically that of an interested outsider or helper. It should be made clear that in exchange for the opportunity to carry out an investigation, the student is expected to offer something that he feels is of value to the organization. The student, of course, has no legitimate authority for declaring recommendations to be valuable. The organization itself decides on whether to accept, modify or reject the ideas.

The instructor plays the role of resource person or consultant to the individual student or to the team of students doing the diagnostic

---

*H. Mintzberg: Policy as a Field of Management Theory, Working Paper, McGill University, June, 1971, p. 36. See also C. E. Gregory: *The Management of Intelligence,* New York, McGraw-Hill Book Co., 1967.
†R. P. Lynton and U. Pareek: Training for Development, *op. cit.,* pp. 116–122.

project. The instructor must make a judgment on how much leeway to allow the students.

The students can learn from making up their own minds. On the other hand, the instructor needs to be accessible for consultation to make sure at least minimal standards of quality are being met.

The choice of organization is largely a function of the chosen roles. We feel that, in part, policy is the study of entrepreneurship. That is why we join other instructors who give the students the opportunity of finding an organization or industry, making arrangements with it, and executing those arrangements. The success they achieve is determined by their own initiative and effort.

It must be remembered that for some the use of major field projects is a rather new approach to classroom instruction and learning in policy. Careful preliminary briefing and orientation is necessary to improve the quality of effort for many students. It is especially important, then, to thoroughly explain the objectives, class organization, methods of instruction and grading of criteria and methods. In addition, time is needed in class: (1) to focus on policy theory—the conceptual understanding of the topic and its application to existing organizations, and (2) to assist in preparation for the team project.

The field project approach may be used effectively by groups or individuals. The choice is up to the instructor. However, in classes of 40 or more it seems advisable to help the students to organize themselves into groups of four to six. In classes with smaller enrollments, such as graduate seminars, it may be appropriate to have students do individual projects. It has been our experience, however, that interaction within a team working on a project usually seems to stimulate the learning process. It also, of course, reduces the number of organizations which are contacted in any one semester.

Scientific inquiry and instruction.

What constitutes an acceptable field project? The answer to this question will vary with the instructor of the policy course. We feel, however, that the student should be engaged in scientific problem solving. The approach is simultaneously a method of *scientific inquiry* and *instruction*. We feel the project should be intellectually challenging, should deal with a question of policy, should be based on theory, and should involve an intensive study of the literature. With these constraints, we feel "anything goes," and creativity is encouraged. Projects might involve one or more organizations or an industry and focus on such topics as:

1. Strategy formation and implementation.
2. Goal formation.
3. Coalition formation.
4. Reorganization.
5. Management science programs applied to top management.
6. The role of top management.
7. Decision making in policy.
8. Organization development applied to the field of policy.
9. The overall management and organization design.

10. An industry forecast.
11. Social responsibility.
12. Planning, programming and budgeting.
13. The use of computer models in policy making.

Field projects, then, may constitute one of the central elements in a policy course. The course may focus on our conceptual understanding of important aspects of policy (such as strategy making, complex problem solving, goal formation, the role of top managers) and their application to existing organizations and industries. Along with the field projects there may be readings, cases, and class and team discussions. The field project, as indicated, may provide an integrating device for learning about policy. In the field, the student uses his knowledge and skill to carry out an analysis, and in the class and team meetings he shares and compares his findings with those of other students.

FIELD RESEARCH

We have mentioned that the field project, in addition to being a method of instruction, is a method of scientific inquiry. For advanced undergraduates, graduate students and academic or corporate researchers, the field project may be a rather sophisticated and perhaps long-term study, and add substantially to our learning about strategy. The learning may have implications for the individual organization but also may be generalizable to other situations.

One example of such field project research is provided by Professor Henry Mintzberg. He proposes *analyzing streams of significant decisions* in organizations over long periods of time in an inductive fashion. Specifically, the research proceeds in three steps: (1) a chronology of decisions and events, (2) inference of strategies, and (3) analysis of strategy making.

Analyzing streams of significant decisions.

A chronology of decisions and events is produced by tracing every significant action taken by the organization and every important event and trend during the period of study (e.g., government action, competitive activity, economic upturn). The chronology of decisions, or decision streams, is then analyzed for patterns or strategies that have emerged over time. For example, Mintzberg* recommends demarcating periods of strategy development as a *groping* period, when the organization appears to be searching for a strategy; a period of *continuity* of strategy, during which decision streams are relatively unchanged; a period of *global* change in decision streams, during which strategies in all or many areas (e.g., product, production, pricing) appear to be changing; and *piecemeal* change, during which only one or a few areas are changing. The source of informa-

Periods of strategy development.

Groping.

Continuity.
Global change.

Piecemeal.

---

*H. Mintzberg: Research on strategy-making, *Professional Papers, 1972 National Meeting,* Minneapolis, Minnesota, Academy of Management pp. 2–6.

tion for this study is varied and may include analytical background material such as annual reports, articles, books, internal reports, personal interviews, and so on. The various pieces of information on the strategies and on the environmental events is brought together to help to explain the development of strategy.

For the analysis of strategy making, a whole group of questions may be asked which serve to focus on conceptual issues under study. Among the questions which might be included are the following:

What is the role of external forces — demands and supports in the development of strategies?

What is the role of the strategy-generating structure?

Is there validity to the strategy formation/strategy implementation dichotomy? So-called implementation — making a series of resource commitments — may simply be a set of decision streams which leads to reformulation of strategies

Under what conditions does the strategy-generating structure react and when does it seek out opportunities in the fashion of an entrepreneur?

To what extent, if any, are formal analysis and planning actually used and actually effective?

What are the characteristics of the various periods of strategy development (e.g., groping, piecemeal, global, continuity)? In what sequence do these periods occur?

What seem to be the most effective strategic responses to various challenges in the environment?

How does the organization avoid stagnation and enhance creativity and innovation?

Aim is to describe strategy-making.

A number of other questions may be devised from portions of this book and from other sources. This field project research for the advanced undergraduate, the graduate student and for the academic or corporate researcher is quite exploratory and open-ended. It is aimed at description of strategy making in such a way that we shall come to understand the complex process of strategy or policy formation. As we have argued before, we must avoid the temptation of arming ourselves with simplistic *prescriptions* (e.g., long-range planning is good per se). The field project research, though, may help us to bring some structure to an area about which we know very little and may provide grounding for the development of hypotheses and prescriptions.

Mintzberg and his associates have completed a number of studies using the aforementioned approach to field project research (e.g., Canadian Military Strategy, 1945–1970; McGill University Strategy, 1821–1972; Canadian Government Foreign Policy, 1961–1965; U.S. Vietnam Strategy, 1950–1968). To illustrate the results of his work he summarizes the strategy development of *Volkswagenwerk,* 1934–1969 as follows:

1934–1947 — a period of flux; the basic product designed by Porsche; plant built by Nazi regime; went into wartime production, and was destroyed during war; British opened the operation after war; in 1947, had a product and a market strategy but no organization.

1948 — a period of development; Nordhoff placed in charge of operations; service and distribution components integrated with basic product-market strategy; organization structure established.

1949–1958 — a period of continuity; aggressive pursuance of explicit strategy; massive growth of dealerships, exports, etc.

1959 — a period of adjustment, small signs of change in strategy; forced to become public company; a wholly new model developed; advertising campaign launched in U.S.; increase in plant investment.

1960–1964 — a period of continuity; more advertising, more demand; no change in basic strategy but pressures to change increasing (competition, etc.).

1965–1969 — a period of flux, of groping for new strategy; two new firms acquired; many new models introduced, most incompatable with beetle design; new lines of business started; no clear strategy emerges.

Subsequent to the Mintzberg study, the firm seemed to be developing a new integrated strategy by consolidating some of the disjointed elements. The student may wish to investigate the current strategy situation at Volkswagenwerk as part of his learning activity. The current strategy and current environment may be compared with previous strategy patterns and environmental conditions. The study of *current events,* of course, seems to be an interesting and informative way of learning about policy.

Integrated strategy.

Current events.

Through this kind of chronological study of several organizations Mintzberg has been able to come up with some tentative conclusions describing the strategy process. For example, he has observed frequently a push-pull model of strategy development. In general terms, the top strategy maker(s) state(s) an explicit strategy à priori (perhaps a diversification strategy) and is then pulled into a significant commitment by the rest of the strategy-generating structure. Meanwhile, the demands and/or support in the environment begin to change and forces build up for a change in strategy. At first the structure appears to ignore the signals (as was the case with Volkswagenwerk), perhaps because of a certain organizational momentum or perhaps because of a psychological commitment to the strategy on the part of top strategy makers. Later, the environmental threats become clearer, and the organization begins to grope for a new strategy. The seeds of a new strategy appear to develop as the organization reacts with a series of apparently disjointed decisions testing out alternatives (see Volkswagenwerk, 1965–1969). These alternatives gradually suggest new strategies, and eventually one strategy is made explicit. Thus the organization is given a push and the push-pull phenomenon continues.

Push-pull model of strategy development.

One may wonder whether or not this is a valid model of strategy development. By tracing the patterns of strategy change as Mintzberg has done we may be able to answer this question, and perhaps many more questions, about strategy.

Another approach to field project-research, however, is exemplified by an *opinion survey* of top executives by Professor George Steiner. Over 250 executives holding responsible positions in 202

Opinion survey.

organizations were given a list of 71 factors which could be grouped into the categories of general managerial, financial, marketing, engineering and production products, personnel and materials. They were asked to rate each factor on a scale for how strategic (or important) it was likely to be to the success of their company over the next five years. In addition, the executives were asked to rate in similar fashion their degree of satisfaction with the current performance of their company on each factor.

Most important strategic factors are in general management category.

Figure 3–1 lists the importance and satisfaction data for the 10 factors that received the highest importance ratings for the total group survey. Based on this evidence the most strategic factors or factors of greatest future importance are, first, several in the general managerial category (getting and training top managers, managerial drive for profits, managerial judgment, perception of new product opportunities, long-range planning). Second in importance are marketing factors (service to customers, knowledge about markets, and

Strategic Factors

Get high quality top management
(General managerial)
Importance
Satisfaction

Train future domestic managers
(General managerial)
Importance
Satisfaction

Managerial drive for profits
(General managerial)
Importance
Satisfaction

Better judgment — top management
(General managerial)
Importance
Satisfaction

Perceive new product opportunities
(General managerial)
Importance
Satisfaction

Service to customers
(Marketing)
Importance
Satisfaction

Better long-range planning
(General managerial)
Importance
Satisfaction

Knowledge about markets
(Marketing)
Importance
Satisfaction

Vigor in sales organization
(Marketing)
Importance
Satisfaction

Competitive stockholder return
(Financial)
Importance
Satisfaction

1.0 1.2 1.4 1.6 1.8 2.0 2.2 2.4 2.6 2.8 3.0 3.2 3.4 3.6 3.8 4.0 4.2 4.4 4.6 4.8 5.0

Mean Rating

Figure 3–1 *Mean importance for 10 strategic factors rated as of greatest future importance compared with mean satisfaction ratings for same factors. (Adapted from G. A. Steiner:* Strategic Factors in Business Success. *New York, Financial Executives Research Foundation, 1969, pp. 58–59.)*

vigor in sales organization). On these factors considered to be most important, the respondents do not view their organization as currently doing a highly effective job. Naturally, being somewhat dissatisfied with performance on a specific factor may give it higher importance.

Of all the 71 factors, those that received the highest satisfaction rating included: financial (raise short-term capital, raise debt at low cost), material (continuity of material supply) and personnel (good relations with the union). Performance was also viewed as fairly good in the engineering and production areas.

These results and those shown in Figure 3–1 are mean ratings by managers from many industries and from many functional areas. A given manager in a particular organization may be at variance with the results. The most pronounced differences in the Steiner data emerged between industries. For example, "better long-range planning" was viewed as quite strategic in chemicals, electronics and utilities; less so in financial institutions and pharmaceuticals.

Difference in importance between industries.

Still another approach to a field project research would *relate formal strategy planning practices to organizational success.* This approach was used by Professor Ross Stagner as part of a questionnaire study on corporate decision making involving 217 vice-presidents from 109 of the largest American corporations.

Relating practices to organizational success.

The questionnaire included four questions directly related to strategic planning. The answers to these questions were compared for respondents in the more successful firms and in the less successful. Measures of success included profit as a per cent of sales, profit as a per cent of invested capital, and organizational size as a measure of growth. The comparisons, as indicated in Table 3–1, give support to the view that *formal, shared* strategic planning by top management does contribute to corporation success.

Formal shared planning seems to help sometimes.

A second study* using the same approach, which compared the success of 36 companies with and without formal long-range planning within six industries — steel, oil, food, metal-working, pharmaceutical and chemicals — was completed by a graduate student. Questionnaires were used to determine formal planning activity. Measures of success included earnings per share of common stock, increases in stock prices and other profit and growth measures.

In the oil and steel companies there was no relationship between formal planning and performance. However, in the food companies there was some relationship on certain measures. For the metal working, pharmaceutical and chemical companies, which were doing more formal planning, there was consistently more organizational success. Thus, at least for several of the companies

---

*Thune, S.: *An Investigation into the Effect of Long-range Planning in Selected Industries.* MBA Thesis, New York, Bernard M. Baruch School of Business, City University of New York, 1967. Also see D. H. Herold: Long-range planning and organizational performance: A cross validation study? *Academy of Management Journal 15* (No. 1): 91–102, March, 1972.

TABLE 3-1 STATISTICALLY SIGNIFICANT RELATIONSHIPS
BETWEEN QUESTIONS RELATED TO FORMAL PLANNING AND
INDEXES OF CORPORATE SUCCESS*

	Success Index		
	---	---	---
Question	Profit as Per Cent of Sales	Profit as Per Cent of Capital	Size
Concern over formal steps in decision making at top level (regular meetings, written records, etc.) [Much attention to formal routines]	X		
Estimates of cost and anticipated profit to result from a decision [Always carefully computed]	X		X
Discussion among all top executives [Yes]	X		
Use of top-level strategy committee [Yes, active]		X	X

*Adapted from R. Stagner: Corporate decision making: An empirical study, *Journal of Applied Psychology*, 53:10–11, 1969.

studied, the strategic factor of formal long-range planning seemed to be of considerable value.

These studies then, in addition to adding substantially to our learning about strategy with methods of scientific inquiry, represent the field project with potential of being a rather sophisticated method of instruction. Learning how to learn would seem to have durable educational value. The caution should be raised again, however, that considerable expertise (and time) is needed to successfully design, implement and conclude field projects of the kind illustrated.

Caution.

DYNAMIC COMPUTER MODELS

Still another element in a policy course may be the use of dynamic computer models. There is considerable interest in the United States and Europe in learning about policy through the use of dynamic computer models. Many schools use this approach as part of the policy course. Few schools, however, have made major commitments in this direction. A dynamic computer program simulates the environmental realities for an organization or industry. Competing groups of students make decisions on such matters as financial requirements, strategies, prices and inventory. The results and their competitive situations are fed back periodically. Thus, the students may test their concepts in a simulated practice situation. The principal arguments favoring this use are stated by William Guth* as follows:

1. They can provide students with a dynamic experience in decision-making, simulating more closely the reality of decision-making processes than is possible with cases.

Arguments for effectiveness.

2. Student progress in the development of heuristics for problem-solving can be more easily controlled in relation to the computer model than in relation to reality since the instructor knows what is in the model. Also, those advocating this approach insist that since current reality will change, there is little point in teaching students about it. Teaching them about how to go systematically about finding out what current reality is and about making decisions under varying degrees of uncertainty over time, they argue, does have lasting value.

Training directors in the Carroll, Paine, Ivancevich study ranked the computer models, or business games as they are sometimes called, as being an effective method for developing problem-solving skills. However, there is little research support for this point of view. A student self-report study† indicated that the students did not seem to learn much about specific problem-solving solutions or strategies that could be used in other situations.

Little research evidence.

Raia found that experience with a business game did not improve the ability to handle cases.‡ In this study, however, the comparison groups used case material. A study of students in class sections that used games plus lectures indicated that those students understood the interrelationship between organizational factors better than students in sections using cases plus lectures.§

It is obvious that we need more study of dynamic computer models (and other methods) before we can be completely sure of their effectiveness. It would seem logical, however, that students would be assisted somewhat in developing their skills as policy analysts through the use of dynamic computer models.

An example of this type of model is the STRATANAL program currently being utilized at Temple University and other schools of business.** The STRATANAL computer program is designed as a question and answer program that assists the students in developing and evaluating corporate strategies. The program, through an interactive computer system, asks the usual questions designed to ensure that significant areas of the strategy formation

Use of computer based models to develop strategies.

---

*William Guth: U.S. perspectives on the teaching of business policy, op. cit., p. 91.

†W. R. Dill and M. Doppelt: The acquisition of experience in a complex management game, *Management Science, 10*:30–46, 1963.

‡A. P. Raia: A study of the educational value of management games, *The Journal of Business, 39*:339–352, 1966.

§J. L. McKenney: An evaluation of a business game in an MBA curriculum, *The Journal of Business, 35*:278–286, 1962.

**W. Naumes: *Effects of Responsive Computer Interaction in the Strategic Planning Process.* Dissertation, Stanford University, California, 1971.

process are covered by the student. The questions are general enough in nature that they can be used with any strategic planning problem, case-oriented or otherwise. Based on the replies given by the user, the program will determine which questions should be asked next. In some instances the program develops questions on its own, using replies given by the student.

The timing of the various questions is designed to lead the user through the strategy formation process from analysis of the environment faced by the organization to be studied through to a final corporate strategy, including measures designed to promote creativity by the student over the short and long range. Experience seems to indicate that this type of computer programming can materially assist the student in learning the strategy formation process. It seems to help to promote within the student an understanding and appreciation for the use of computer models and programs in the decision-making process. It is felt that the development of such heuristic computer programs would be of material assistance, not only in the teaching, but also in the planning process as it is applied in ongoing organizations.

ROLE PLAYING

A simulation method of learning about certain aspects of policy is role playing. Role playing is a controlled experience in which the participants actually talk *with* people rather than *about* people and actually start some actions rather than talking or writing *about* doing something. The main requirement is that of assuming roles and actually playing them out.

Role playing is a very flexible method that allows learning opportunities with various degrees of preplanning. The action may be carefully prepared, with specific roles assigned to be played over a given time, e.g., a structured debate with a plan and counterplan and with advocates for each serving for one hour. Or the instructor can encourage spontaneous role playing during some session; e.g., he may assign a "devil's advocate" on a board of directors responding to a student team report.

How effective is role playing? Role playing is rated fairly high in effectiveness for the training objectives of changing attitudes and developing problem-solving and interpersonal skills.* The research is somewhat limited in this area, but what there is gives support to the expert opinion in the Carroll et al. report. Several studies do show that role playing can be effective in changing attitudes of students.†

---

*S. J. Carroll, F. T. Paine, and J. J. Ivancevich, The relative effectiveness of training methods, *op.cit.*

†For example, see O. Harvey and G. Beverly: Some personality correlates of concept change through role playing, *Journal of Abnormal and Social Psychology* 63:125–130, 1961.

Furthermore, if participants in the role playing situation are asked to take a point of view opposite to their own and to verbalize this opposing point of view, the results seem to be especially effective.* Furthermore, role playing has been shown to be effective for learning how to derive solutions to problems and also to be *more* effective than case studies in teaching participants about how to gain acceptance of solutions.† Several studies indicate that problem-solving skills of both students and managers can be improved with the use of role playing.‡

How effective is role playing?

Another training objective of role playing is the development of interpersonal skills. Studies have shown that role playing can be effective in (1) increasing sensitivity to motivations,§ (2) improving interview skills,** and (3) improving group leadership skills.++ Thus, since policy courses include the objectives of changing attitudes, developing problem-solving skills, developing the ability to gain acceptance of solutions, and sometimes even developing interpersonal skills, role playing may be considered as one of the several effective methods.

With this method, as with others, careful preparation is necessary. Areas for thought and action that need special attention would include:

Careful preparation.

1. Selection of the situation for the role play.
2. Clarification of the role of the students.
3. Clarification of the instructor's role.
4. Final analysis.

For the policy course we see the need for a situation of complex and challenging nature which is of concern to those participating in the role playing. Quite frequently a conflict situation may prove effective, one in which different points of view or perspective may be clearly delineated. In any event, a situation should be chosen that will get the role players involved. Their involvement will depend, in part, on an adequate briefing so that they understand the types of persons they are expected to be. Written briefing sheets may be prepared and supplemented with an oral briefing regarding the general situation and the group atmosphere.

The instructor has a difficult assignment in being the role play

---

*For example, see F. Culbertson: Modification of an emotionally held attitude through role playing, *Journal of Abnormal and Social Psychology* 54:230–233, 1957.

†Solem, A. R.: Human relations training comparisons of case study and role playing, *Personnel Administration* 23 (5):29–37, 1960.

‡For example, see N. R. F. Maier and C. R. Hoffman: Quality of first and second solutions in group problem solving, *Journal of Applied Psychology* 44:278–283, 1960.

§R. A. Balda and C. H. Lawake: Evaluation of role playing, *Personnel Administration* 2 S (2):40–42, 1962.

**H. Van Schacck, Jr.: Naturalistic role playing: A method of interview training for student personnel administrators, *Dissertation Abstracts* 17:801, 1957.

++For example, see N. R. F. Maier and C. R. Hoffman: Using trained developmental discussion leaders to further improve the quality of group decisions, *Journal of Applied Psychology* 44:247–251, 1960.

director. He should check to see if the action is illustrating what was expected. He may cut in from time to time to interview role players to show the observers, for example, what assumptions are being made or some inconsistencies in how various role players are expressing their feelings. The instructor should try to guide the session so that certain principles or practices are demonstrated. When the instructor ends the role play he will lead a discussion, allowing interaction between and among the role players and the observers. Finally, the instructor will comment on his own analysis and evaluation of the situation just presented.

What are some examples of role playing in policy formation? Probably the most common role for the student is that of a planning expert or top level manager who presents a critique of a case analysis or a field project. For example, a presentation that argues for a particular corporate strategy is made to those playing the roles of members of the planning committee or some other top level group. The role players seek to make their opposition to the prepared approach logical. The assumption is that both sides will gain a better understanding of the complexities involved, the problem-solving process, and the underlying assumptions made in the presentation.

Most common role.

Some instructors may prefer a more structured debate which attempts to aid the process of generating new assumptions once old ones are exposed as being inadequate or are demolished. This dialectical approach, proposed by R. O. Mason,* is a legitimate strategy formation procedure as well as a vehicle for role play. What actually happens in the role play is this: A plan and a counterplan are developed and presented, with role play advocates for each.

Dialectical approach.

As the presentations proceed, the underlying assumptions as they relate to environmental demands and support and the strategy-generating structure are explored. Opposing role players interpret relevant information as supporting their views. In most cases, what seems to develop is either clear support for one alternative or a new composite approach that is superior to either of the original plans. In any event, the assumptions underlying a given corporate strategy are given a detailed study and new assumptions are generated.

Another approach to role playing is one in which group situations are set up to illustrate various complexities faced by top managers and the processes they may go through to resolve these difficulties. The emphasis in this approach is more an illustration of a process than problem solving.

The previously described model of policy formation has been "brought to life" or illustrated with a role play or an exercise such as can be found in Chapter 2.

---

*R. O. Mason: A dialectical approach to strategic planning, *Management Science* 15:403–414, 1969.

TIMING A CASE IN THE FUTURE WITH SCIENCE FICTION

Most case discussion techniques, as has been shown, involve analysis of past events in the history of an organization. This can often lead to inhibition of creativity on the part of students. This is usually because of a knowledge of the developments that have taken place since the time of the case. This has a tendency to constrain the student to standard solutions of case problems. Also, it is difficult for students to divorce themselves of the knowledge of events that transpire in the economy and general environment.

Constraints on students.

One method of attempting to overcome this problem is to set the timing of the case in the future. This forces the student to place himself in an alien environment and to reconstruct events that must have occurred to reach this point in time. This situation, if treated properly by the discussion leader, can lead to significant increases in the creativity of solutions presented by the students.

A source of potential future-oriented cases comes from the talented ranks of science fiction writers. There are many short stories with business orientations. These stories can be so enhanced as to provide a working environment for case discussions. The spirit of the science fiction case must be entered into by all involved, however.

An example of science fiction would be the use made of a short story written by Paul Anderson. His story, "A Sun Invisible," has been employed as the background for a case designed to foster discussion of several different strategic problems.

The short story involves the attempts of an entrepreneurial robber baron of the 26th century and one of his assistants to subdue an allied group of races found on the outskirts of known space. These allies have been preying on the outposts of the entrepreneur and his business colleagues.

The entrepreneur finally succeeds in defeating the allies and implementing a tenuous peace. The short case, O.R.A.C.L.E., expands on some of the problems hinted at in the story, and is designed to bring out a discussion of the problems of controlling a rapidly expanding, formerly entrepreneurial, organization.

The company has outgrown the efforts of the entrepreneur to control all its various enterprises. He is being forced to delegate authority to subordinates. The organization has to be changed if his objective of expansion is to be met. Methods of implementing this change are brought out in ensuing discussions. These discussions seem to be relatively unhindered by constraints that normally occur when discussing a traditional type of case.

Timing in future may reduce constraints.

The O.R.A.C.L.E. case discussions lead to many potentially interesting organizational strategies. One involves a two-tier structure with a group of loosely knit, semi-independent divisions run by entrepreneurial assistants. This exploratory group uses the resources of a more traditional organization to further their geographic and product designs.

Methods of staffing these organizations also prove quite interesting. Some students have suggested combing the ranks of cashiered officers from the space fleet for material for the entrepreneurial assistants required for the upper tier of the organization. Recruiting, training and controlling this new organizational structure can lead to a discussion of methods of teaching business courses in the future. The dichotomy between present methods of teaching students to be managers as opposed to entrepreneurs can also be a particularly revealing area for discussion.

SUMMARY

We have attempted to describe various methods of learning about the policy-formation process. The traditional approach of the case method requires active participation on the part of both student and teacher in all phases of the learning process.

The case method, as described, involves the class in active discussions concerning the present position and problem of the organization being discussed. These discussions are not relegated to simply retelling the case, however. Analysis of material gathered from sources other than the written case provide a great deal of the learning effect from the case method.

The purpose of the case method is to allow the student to be able to integrate problem analysis, solution, evaluation and presentation into a consistent process. It is designed to give the student practice in all these crucial areas of the policy-formation process.

The traditional case method has been modified by several innovations in style and format. All are designed to add realism to the learning process. The live case brings executives into the class to demonstrate the problems of selling ideas and also brings the case up to date from an information standpoint.

Field projects, however, rely more on the student's leaving the discussion to gather information from organizations with problems to solve. The projects are designed, once more, to add to the realism of the policy-formation process. The students are often actively involved not only in defining the problem, but also in designing and implementing solutions to those problems with the individuals actually involved with the problems.

The problem with the more realistic and interactive forms of the case method involve the time and expense of the learning process. Large amounts of resources are required of both the faculty and student to provide a worthwhile situation.

Methods of presentation complementary to the case method

include various behavioral and decision-making techniques Dynamic computer programs such as STRATANAL are designed to provide a guide to students while developing solutions to case problems.

Role playing is designed to demonstrate behavioral problems in the policy-formation process. Difficulties encountered in working with groups and individuals while trying to formulate solutions to complex problems are discovered through active participation in problem-solving scenarios by students.

Finally, other methods have also been integrated into the standard case method format. Science fiction, as a new method that may overcome the time problems of the case method, is only one of these techniques. It is presented as an example of what can be done to stimulate the search for creative problem solving on the part of students.

This chapter has looked into some general methods of learning about strategy and policy. The remaining chapters will discuss guides and methods used in the formation and evaluation of strategies and policies.

DISCUSSION QUESTIONS

1. Discuss various objectives of courses and training programs about business policy and strategy formation. Discuss the effectiveness of various methods (e.g., cases, computer games, field projects) in attaining these objectives. Which methods do you prefer and why?

2. Why do some students have difficulty in handling cases? What should be done about it?

3. Discuss the diagnostic process as it applies to cases and to field projects. Why is the diagnostic process so important for managers, for influentials and for analysts in an organization?

4. Discuss some of the cautions which the analyst or manager should observe in the diagnostic process.

5. Discuss the field project as a method of instruction *and* as a method of scientific inquiry.

6. What seem to be some of the significant advantages and limitations of learning about policy through the use of dynamic computer models?

7. Why should role playing be considered? Why should the use of "science fiction" be considered in learning about policy?

8. In your judgment, what are the most significant aspects of strategy making that need attention from students and researchers interested in the subject of strategy? What research strategies would you propose?

Suggested Additional References for Further Research

Ansoff, H. I.: A quasi-analytic approach to the business strategy problems, *Management Technology 4* (No. 1):67–77, 1964.

Bauer, R. A., and Gergen, K. J. (eds.): *The Study of Policy Formation.* New York, The Free Press, 1968.

Cyert, R., Simon, H., and Trow, D.: Observation of a business decision, *Journal of Business 29*: 1956.

Friedman, J.: A conceptual model for the analysis of planning behavior, *Administrative Science Quarterly, 12*:225–252, 1967.

Gross, N. C., Mason, W. S., and McEachern, A. W.: *Explorations in Role Analysis.* New York, John Wiley & Sons, Inc., 1958.

Lorsh, J. W., and Lawrence, P. R.: *Managing Group and Intergroup Relations.* Homewood, Ill., Richard D. Irwin, Inc., 1972.

Moffei, D. J., and Levin, R. I.: Experimental evaluation of a computerized management game. *Atlanta Economic Review 18:*7–11, 1968.

Murdick, R. G., Eckhouse, R. H., Moor, R. C., and Zimmerer, T. W.: *Business Policy; A Framework for Analysis.* Columbus, Ohio, Grid, Inc., 1972.

Myers, C. A. (ed.): *The Impact of Computers on Management.* Cambridge, The MIT Press, 1967.

Taylor, D. W.: Decision making and problem solving, in March, J. G. (ed.): *Handbook of Organizations.* Chicago, Rand McNally and Company, 1965.

Towl, A. R.: *To Study Administration by Cases.* Cambridge, Harvard Business School, 1969.

Uyterhoeven, H. E. R., Ackerman, R. W., and Rosenblum, J. W.: *Strategy and Organization: Text and Cases in General Management.* Homewood, Ill., Richard D. Irwin, Inc., 1973.

4

OBJECTIVES OF ASSESSMENTS OF
POLICY FORMATION

USE OF THE GUIDES

FRAMEWORK FOR ASSESSING
POLICY FORMATION
    Part A. The Current Situation
      Current Organizational
      Mission and Current
      Basis of Support
      Organizational Objectives
      and Outcomes
      Policy-generating Structure
    Part B. The Changing Situation
      Environmental Forces —
      Problems, Opportunities,
      Demands

Economic Considerations
Technological Advances
Social Influences
Political Inputs
Competitive Factors
Social Responsibility

SUMMARY

DISCUSSION QUESTIONS

APPENDIX 1. A PROGRAM FOR
ANALYZING SOME ASPECTS OF THE
PRESENT FINANCIAL CONDITIONS OF
THE ORGANIZATION

APPENDIX 2. A PROGRAM FOR
DETERMINING TOP MANAGEMENT
EFFECTIVENESS DIMENSIONS

ASSESSMENT GUIDES

Policy makers have been seen as planning and coordinating to find solutions to policy issues that will (1) satisfy environmental demands or requirements, (2) win external support (e.g., customers) and internal support (e.g., peers), and (3) partially satisfy self-interests. Coordination and planning has been described as sometimes like "muddling through," with the impossibility of determining in advance what the solution should be. Thus, policy makers are sensitive to feedback from the environment. They analyze their present situation and forecast what environmental demands and support will be; then, with their self-interests as basic premises, they make choices that may emerge into patterns of decisions or strategies.

This chapter contains general guides for assessment of this policy- (or strategy-) formation process and policy-formation product. Again we are using the phrase "policy formation" as a broad one, including in it decision making and activities related to the long-term development of the organization. Our descriptive model of policy formation allows us to see a complex social process and then converges on the cognitive aspects rather than hoping that policy issues can be understood solely in terms of intellectual components. Our reasons for this approach were elaborated in Chapter 2. Moreover, we have recognized the importance of the cognitive activities of analysis and choice. Our guides to analysis, here, will be seen as putting together the intellectual activities and the social process activities and will be associated with various phases of the model.

General guides.

*Putting together
intellectual and
social activities.*

97

They are organized into three parts as follows:

Part A   The Current Situation
          Current Organizational Mission and Basis of Support
          Organizational Objectives and Outcomes
          Policy-generating Structure

Part B   The Changing Situation
          Environmental Forces — Problems, Opportunities,
                                    Demands

Part C   Reformulating the Corporate Strategy
          Objectives for Change
          The Action Plan: Setting Strategic Alternatives

Parts A and B are covered in this chapter; Part C is covered in the next.

Since these guides are intended for general use in both business and nonprofit bodies, certain features of the policy formation process for more basic strategic questions are referred to in this book. More detailed agenda for review of special policy areas (e.g., labor relations policy) are discussed in other books, and should be consulted when warranted in specific analyses.

OBJECTIVES OF ASSESSMENT OF POLICY FORMATION

What are the objectives of the assessment?

The primary objective in conducting overall assessments of policy formation is to identify problems, threats and opportunities in the organization's environment and structure and to devise plans that include practical responses to the environmental and structural situation. The second important objective of the overall assessment process is to evaluate the operation of specific strategies and specific managers for corrective action by the organization where necessary. An appraisal of policy goes hand-in-hand with an appraisal of management. Management appraisal may use standards of excellence revealed by the success of policy.

USE OF THE GUIDES

Use by three main types of analysts.

The assessment guides are intended for use as a framework for asking questions and for organizing data by three main types of policy analysts:

Top level and middle level managers who on a regular basis are involved in policy formation and implementation; it is recognized, of course, that they may desire and may need staff assistance in information gathering and analysis.

Assessors or researchers interested in understanding and in developing the policy-formation process.

Students doing case analysis, field projects or role plays to develop conceptual and administrative skills in the policy-formation process; it is recognized that students may find some of the information required to do a complete assessment unavailable from the subject organization or inadequately covered in the case; nevertheless, a partial assessment may be made and will probably be useful.

The guides are broadly problem-oriented in that they are aimed at analysis of policy problems, their implications and root causes. The guides are also opportunity-oriented in that they are aimed at analysis of opportunities, their requirements for success and plans for dealing with them. It should be said that the guides are not all-inclusive but are intended to suggest a number of possible elements that may be considered in the assessment process. The reader should keep in mind the limitations of these guides in the process of isolating critical problems, threats and opportunities. The guides are intended to be supplemented liberally by expertise and judgment as well as to be tailored closely to the unique circumstances in a particular organization. Cost precludes monitoring every variable and using every method. Some elements may be judged *more important* than others for particular analyses. Also some methods or variables may be *eliminated* or de-emphasized for specific assessments. For example, analysis of sales data would be eliminated for most government organizations; analysis of consumer income may be relatively unimportant to an aerospace company. Consideration of the important elements developed in the review and analysis of the relationships between the present position, the achievements, problems, opportunities, capabilities and requirements for success should permit an overall assessment of policies and the policy-formation process and the development of action plans.

General guides are problem- and opportunity-oriented.

Some elements are more important; some may be eliminated.

Considerable judgment will be required to arrive at the proper balance and perspective of present position and desired position (where the organization would like to be) in making the overall assessment. Organization and reporting of the corporate strategy will require distillation of the findings resulting from the evaluation into major issues and opportunities and translating recommendations into specific actions on the part of relevant organization participants.

Considerable judgment needed.

FRAMEWORK FOR ASSESSING POLICY FORMATION

Part of an approach for systematic improvement in policy formation demands an examination of the present "state of things" and a forecast of the future "state of things." The examination and the forecasts are not a one-shot effort but need to be more of a continual monitoring of the organization mission, objectives and plans as well as subsystems, processes and results. The subsystems may include functional groups, top managers, members of the board of directors, middle managers, and members of the work force, or they may be "outsiders" such as union officials, government officials, product or

Examine present "state of things."

service trend-setters and community leaders.* The processes include decision-making activities, policy-planning methods, relationships with interfacing groups and communication patterns. The results include such things as competitive position, effective service, share of market, image, budget success, inventory position and patents.

Forecast future "state of things."

In addition to examining the present conditions and forecasting "futures," an approach to improvement would include a more or less continuous indication and modification of the desired position and desired organizational effectiveness. In other words, the approach would include a statement of (1) where the organization would like to be (short-term and long-term objectives and goals), and (2) the differential or gap existing between the present position and the desired position. These statements would provide food for thought on where to concentrate efforts.

Identify gap between desired position and present position.

A framework serves as a general guide for those concerned with policy improvement in asking questions and organizing data. Such a guide is provided in this chapter and the next. While a few illustrative devices or instruments are discussed here, subsequent chapters will cover specific methods for assessment and development. As indicated in Chapter 1, many frameworks or agendas have been proposed for assessing policy. Compared to other frameworks the following framework has more emphasis on role and program variables which are useful in understanding and developing the process of policy formation.† In addition, objectives-outcomes, financial-accounting, competition, product-market and other important variables are included.

The following presentation of elements in the assessment process does not indicate a hard and fast sequence of steps to be followed by a policy analyst. For example, some analysts may wish to start with an examination and description of the current policy-generating structure and the social processes involved therein. They may feel that these processes and their effectiveness would affect what markets and service-product the organization intends to develop. Similarly they may feel that examination of the structure prior to an examination of the goals and action plans is appropriate. On the other hand, if General Motors were to decide to go into a new business by acquisition, then it would appear that a new structure would be appropriate to deal with achieving that goal, not that given

---

*Some analysts classify the internal subsystems as follows: (1) production, concerned with the work that gets done; (2) supportive, for procurement and disposal and for institutional relations; (3) maintenance, for tying people into their functional roles; (4) adaptive, concerned with organizational change; and (5) managerial, for the direction, adjudication and control of the many subsystems and activities. See D. Katz and R. Kahn: *The Social Psychology of Organizations,* New York, John Wiley & Sons, Inc., 1966, p. 39.

†C. Saunders: *What Should We Know About Strategy Formulation?* Professional Papers, Division of Business Policy and Planning, Academy of Management National Meeting, August, 1973.

a structure, goals should be established. Our feeling, therefore, is that in this dynamic continuous process of strategy formation the analyst has some choice in where to begin. Elements of the present situation may be studied concurrently or one at a time. The fact is that a structure already exists in the organization and is generating strategic decisions. Describing the structure will help in understanding the basis of the existing organization goals and action plans and suggest possible changes in them. It is fully recognized, on the other hand, that a given structure may need alteration after strategies are generated by that structure. Thus, the policy analyst is required to keep all the diverse elements of the present situation in mind, and it is a matter of judgment where to begin. Any recommendations that the policy analysts make, moreover, are meaningful only when grounded on valid descriptions of the current situation.

Matter of judgment where to begin.

Keep all diverse elements in mind.

Part A. The Current Situation

Current Organizational Mission and Current Basis of Support

A variety of information is involved in an analysis of the current position of the organization. First of all, as our model has assumed, once a strategy (e.g., on resource deployment) is formulated and implemented, it becomes part of the environment. In addition, this deployment has received a certain amount of environmental support or the organization would cease to exist. Two questions to help us to consider the present environment of the organization are:

Present deployment of resources.

1. What is the present deployment of resources?
2. Where in the environment does the support come from?

These questions may be answered with an analysis of budgetary, sales and other data. At least part of these data are available (1) in some case write-ups for case analysts, or (2) from some existing organizations for field project investigators. Consider the usefulness of the following breakouts of data:

Location of support.

   a. Budget and/or sales by service or product category.
   b. Division of budget among major units and among major activities.
   c. Percentage of time spent on major functions, e.g., providing technical services.
   d. Sales by customer category and/or budget by client category.
   e. Sales and/or budget by channel of distribution of service or product.
   f. Cash flows, return on investment, and/or perceived benefits produced by each major unit of activity.
   g. Major sources of financial and budgetary support, e.g., banks, stockholders, congressmen, government officials.
   h. Support from employee groups and unions.

The breakouts and the specific categories to use will depend on (1) judgment of what is relevant and important in the situation and, of course, (2) the availability of data. It is recognized that some data will not be available in case write-ups or in empirical investigations. The importance of the information is not diminished by this lack.

What analysis identifies mission?

The result from the analysis of whatever data are available will be at least a partial indication of the actual position of the organization in receiving support and in deploying resources. This actual position is important for knowing the way the organization and the environment have defined the organizational *mission* at the present time.

In addition, some cases and some organizations will allow a comparison of present records with records from the past several years. Thus, for example, one may investigate the rate of growth or decline or the change in product/service mix. Trend information is more helpful in spotting potential difficulties and in judging why results occurred than is one-point-in-time data. For instance, one may notice that the sales trend for Product A is leveling off and the share of market for Product A is declining. These circumstances may be symptoms of a problem, and the causes of the problem need identification so that resources may be applied to finding and implementing solutions.

Both trend information on missions and the present definition of missions have implications in developing future corporate strategies. The missions may need to be changed. For example, National Distillers at one time deployed its resources into and received most of its support from manufacturing alcoholic beverages. Shortly after World War II it defined its mission in terms of technological knowledge. This knowledge was said to be fermentation chemistry. The firm deployed its resources in a different manner, received support and became a major chemical and pharmaceutical company. In this instance, a narrower definition of mission might have reduced growth potential.

Western Union recently did a thorough analysis of its future environment, resources deployment and environment support. The decision was reached that support for its present mission would be declining and that it would change from a "telegram" firm to a communications firm. Resources were deployed into such technology as communications satellites.

The Office of the Budget was analyzed by federal administrators for possible ways to strengthen its program toward improving effectiveness and efficiency in government. The decision was made to broaden the mission into nonbudgetary factors in management that are closely related to the budgetary factors and can be overseen concurrently. The Office of the Budget became the Office of Management and Budget, with more authority over agency policies and practices. As mentioned in the first chapter, broadening of the mission may be dangerous, and the threats or risks tend to increase as the organization gets farther away from its present services and/or products and clientele and/or markets. A solid position in a narrower field where the organization has strength may be more appropriate.

Basis of support. The current position of the organization includes, in addition to resource deployment and location of support, the basis of support or reasons for support. The question is: What are the organization's primary distinctive competences, competitive advantages or special organization knowledges? Later we shall ask: To what extent will these factors continue to provide environmental support in the future? The former question may be answered by a comparison of information on current missions with information on environmental factors.

Basis of support.

What information should be gathered and how interpreted? We are looking for factors that stand out as providing a basis for support to the organization. We can save fact-finding time if we restrict ourselves to the key ingredients or requirements for success in the situation.

Restrict information gathering to key requirements for success.

A key requirement for a toy manufacturer might be capability to innovate. It might be, on the other hand, responsiveness to the clients' needs for education, or assistance for a government agency. Control of sources of supply might be the key for a natural gas company; financial flexibility for the conglomerate; location of bases for the military unit. There are a variety of possibilities that may merit consideration. Some of the breakouts of information that may be relevant and important are as follows:

1. Market and product/service situation (e.g., share of market, location, patents, advertising, new products and/or services, scope of line of products and/or services).
2. Market definition in terms of user benefits (e.g., what are the main reasons clients utilize the services of the organization?).
3. Production and supply situation (e.g., technological position, inventory control, sources of supply, labor relations).
4. Financial situation (e.g., holding and use of assets, working capital, budgeting, solvency and use of financial leverage).*
5. Research and development situation (e.g., payoffs from previous research and development, new possibilities).
6. Legal basis for activities and degree of concurrence with public policy (e.g., accountable to shareholders or Congress/Parliament, EEO position, antipollution activities).
7. Structural situation† (e.g., use of management science programs in carrying out managerial roles).

A pattern of results that may be helpful in determining the organization's strengths or competitive advantage may emerge from the analysis. Such a pattern in simplified form for a business organization might be like that shown in Table 4–1.

---

*Appendix 1, A Program for Analysing Some Aspects of the Present Financial Condition of the Organization, is useful for this section of the assessment.

†We shall give special attention to roles and programs later.

TABLE 4-1   INVENTORY OF ORGANIZATION CAPABILITIES*

Financial strength	Money available or obtainable for financing research and development, plant construction, inventory, receivables, working capital and operating losses in the early stages of commercial operation.
Raw material reserves	Ownership of, or preferential access to, natural resources such as minerals and ores, brine deposits, natural gas, forests.
Physical plant	Manufacturing plant, research and testing facilities, warehouses, branch offices, trucks, tankers, etc.
Location	Situation of plant or other physical facility with relation to markets, raw materials or utilities.
Patents	Ownership or control of a technical monopoly through patents.
Public acceptance	Brand preference, market contracts, and other public support built up by successful performance in the past.
Specialized experience	Unique or uncommon knowledge of manufacturing, distribution, scientific fields or managerial techniques.
Personnel	Payroll or skilled labor, salesmen, engineers, or other workers with definite specialized abilities.
Management	Professional skill, experience, ambition and will for growth of the company's leadership.

*From C. H. Kline: The strategy of product policy, *Harvard Business Review,* July-August, 33 (No. 4): 91–100, 1955.

Sears Roebuck did an analysis of its basis of support and built its business on a "money-back-and-no-questions-asked" guarantee to its farm customers. To the ingredients of a successful mail-order business, a simple statement of confidence in the customer provided a unique or distinctive touch. This statement of trust helped to build a favorable competitive image, adding support for their products and services.

How does the user benefit?

IBM has an organization that thoroughly analyzes its basis for support and defines the market in terms of user benefits. It is quite effective and efficient in design of product and in production. However, it is not the leader of the office equipment industry because of its physical product. IBM's analysis indicates that it is the leader because it excels in the management of data and information for business and government needs. What it gets paid for is a service rather than a product. It earns its livelihood with its knowledge of business processes.

Another way to come to grips with defining organizational competence or knowledge is to analyze those things that the organization has done well and those it has done poorly. An internal comparative analysis is illustrated by the following example:

A medium size company working on high-speed planes and missile components had an uneven performance record. There were great successes in electronics but also great failures. Again guidance controls witnessed the same results. A new, technologically ignorant president was brought in. An analysis of manpower and responsibility accounting proved of little insight. Only when each project was investigated did the answer appear. Whenever the company had a tight deadline, the company did well. Its specific ability was to work under pressure. Without this inducement no one, it seemed, cared about the project or contract. Ironically, to achieve a leisurely, non-pressure attitude management worked hard to get government contracts. Apparently its strategy succeeded only too well.*

Some case materials provide the opportunity to analyze two or more comparable organizations in the same business, industry or government area which have had opposite results with similar undertakings. Peter Drucker, for example, contrasts what two quite successful organizations, General Electric and General Motors, can do well and can do poorly.

Analyze comparable organizations.

He cites these two companies as excelling in the field of development of new businesses. GE, for example, during World War II when diamond imports were declining, decided to start from scratch and make their own. In the short time span of five years, they were making synthetic diamonds commercially. In 10 years, GE became one of the largest suppliers of industrial diamonds in the world.

General Motors, on the other hand, does an excellent job of making existing businesses it has acquired more successful than they were. It has the talent to improve companies that have already achieved a fair size and leadership position in an industry. (For this activity they have been accused of antitrust violations.)

However, the talent of GE and GM has not worked both ways. GE has not excelled at successfully building a business acquired. GM has not been a starter of businesses.† Thus, we have two firms successfully developing new business but using different competitive strategies, that is (1) starting from scratch, and (2) acquiring new organizations. Careful examination of aspects of "policy formation" other than competitive strategy, such as existing financial and personnel policies, the way objectives are set or the way they are organized may unearth reasons for differences in success when using comparable competitive strategies, and for comparable successes when using different competitive strategies.

These examples demonstrate the importance and the complexity of identifying the *present* basis of support in relationship to the other elements we have just discussed — resource deployment and location of support. Before we turn to the question of environmental changes that may affect the organization's mission and the basis of support for that mission, we shall extend our guidelines to examine

---

*P. F. Drucker: *The Effective Executive*, New York, Harper & Row, 1967, p. 116.
†P. F. Drucker: *op. cit.*, p. 115.

current objectives and outcomes and the existing policy-generating structure.

Organizational Objectives and Outcomes

Objectives are hoped-for results or goals to be achieved, usually within a specific time period. The attainment of these standards or the lack of attainment are important aspects of the present position of the organization. In assessing the present situation one must not set up some arbitrary external criteria or standards that may not be applicable; critical judgment of the appropriateness of such criteria and standards is necessary.

Our model has recognized that goals or objectives arise from complicated power plays involving various coalitions in the organization and in the environment; that is, we have said that bargaining to achieve goals takes place among top managers, between top managers and other influentials, between managers and regulating agencies, and so forth. We are assuming here, however, that top management has the largest say in which objectives are emphasized. Furthermore, if a coalition forming goals has a dominant member, the organization objectives will be close to his personal goals.* One question with a high degree of relevance then is: What are management's objectives and targets?

What are management's objectives and targets?

Of major importance is what management wants to achieve. Many cases give indications of managements' intentions. To the degree these general management objectives are or can be translated into operational targets and articulated to the organization, they provide fundamental standards against which actual performance can be measured. There is, as mentioned, a need to judge the extent to which the objectives are consistent with the current milieu. To make this judgment requires information from other elements in the policy process such as audits of the external environment and determinations on requirements for success. The policy analyst then needs to check back and forth on different elements. Long-term objectives (e.g., five years) need to be considered, but also existing deployments and environmental support for shorter term objectives (e.g., six months) need to be considered and reconsidered.

Are these fundamental standards consistent with environment?

Setting objectives and targets is something that is done all the time. Many managers do it informally when they resolve to do something about the budget picture, go after new areas to explore, try to increase the rate of growth in sales and in share of the market, improve the service to the public, be more socially responsible, push flexibility in relation to the uncertainties of political, social and technological change, improve stability in resisting declines in the busi-

---

*See W. Hill: The goal formation process in complex organizations, *Journal of Management Studies, 6* (No. 2):198–209, 1969.

ness cycle, and so forth. Pressures from various groups may have affected their decisions. Objectives and targets are interrelated and multifaceted; they may be congruent or in conflict with one another; they may be crystal clear or not definitively delineated.

An evaluation of objectives is intended as a means for assuring that intentions are on an appropriate basis—to improve the predictability that the objectives will eventually be met. Since the clarity, challenge and acceptance of the organization's objectives (as well as perceptions of the reward system) help to determine its direction of effort and its effectiveness,* it is appropriate for the policy analyst (to the extent information is available) to:

Need for clarity, challenge and acceptance.

1. List the main current objectives being concentrated on during the next suitable time period. Include major areas that contribute to the success or failure of the organization. (It is necessary to include inputs on the future environment and requirements for success.) For example:

Growth—What new areas are being explored?

Profitability—A 10 per cent return on investment.

Technical and Market Leadership—A certain number of new research projects and new products this year.

Service—Our clients and supporters (e.g., government officials) remain satisfied.

Management—What specific patterns of behavior (roles) are appropriate to expect in the future? What patterns of behavior are associated with effective management in this situation?

2. Analyze each objective in terms of being clear, measurable, and realistic but challenging. For example:

Clear—What will be the end product? Who is going to take action? When?

Measurable—What is acceptable evidence that there has been accomplishment?

Realistic but Challenging—Is it possible to complete the stated goals? Do they strain each area a bit beyond what key parties believe to be the limits of their capabilities and resources at the moment?

To detect whether an objective is challenging may require technical expertise in the area and may be a task that depends on technology which is stable and predictable. There are many instances, moreover, in research and development, marketing, engineering and other areas where even the most astute analyst will not be able to determine whether the objectives are challenging. The implementation of this guide is then somewhat restricted, however worthwhile theoretically.

Can you tell if objective is challenging?

3. Analyze each objective in terms of its relevance to the broader objectives of the organization. Does it directly support and contribute sufficiently to the overall mission of the organization? Is it socially

---

*See, for example, C. Perrow: *Organization Analysis,* (Belmont, Calif.; Wadsworth Publishing Co., 1970; and E. Locke et al.: Studies of the Relationship between satisfaction, goal setting, and performance, *Organizational Behavior and Human Performance,* 5:135–138, 1970.

responsible? Consider the priorities and whether it will be more effective if emphasis is placed on a limited number (say two or three) within a given time frame. For example:

Benefits — What will be received if objective is accomplished?
Costs — How does the cost compare with benefits expected?
Trade-offs — Is it appropriate to add emphasis on one objective at the expense of less emphasis on another?

Determine if the objectives agreed upon are consistent with the action plan designed to achieve those objectives. For example, applying this guide would have been informative to the management in the Univis case. One of their objectives was to promote the image of a growth-oriented company. Part of their action plan, however, involved the payment of a relatively large dividend on their common stock. This is inconsistent with the view of a growth-oriented company as taken by investment analysts. The management of the firm either did not realize the inconsistency of this position or chose to ignore it. This position endangered the future capability of the firm to raise money through a stock offering.

It is also possible that two or more objectives might be inconsistent. The same could be true for two or more parts of the action plan. It is possible that these apparent inconsistencies are actually meant as counterbalancing forces within the strategy. An example of this might be the inclusion of profit "maximization" and imposition of costly quality measures over and above what would be necessary to uphold sales of a product. There could be specific reasons for the inclusion of these two inconsistent objectives. If they are to be counterbalancing, they should be rated; one should be given primary importance over the other. If not, the inconsistency should be resolved and one or the other of the inconsistent factors should be dropped.

4. Review whether the objectives and methods are appropriate for today. Is what is being done now appropriate to the end results that the organization is trying to achieve? Where does the organization go from here? Determine whether significant factors have been included in the objectives setting, e.g., who was involved, what power plays were appropriate, what alternatives were considered, what assumptions have been made.

Caution — goal displacement.

Caution should be observed, for example, in checking objectives that have been made as specific as possible by quantifying them. While such quantification is often possible and desirable, studies have shown that goal displacement and inefficiency may sometimes result.* Managers may tend to overconcentrate their efforts in areas for which objectives have been quantified. Areas in which it is seldom possible to write quantifiable objectives, such as innovation and interpersonal relations, may be de-emphasized, especially if the reward system supports the attainment of the quantified objectives.

---

*See, for example, A. P. Raia: A second look at management goals and controls, *California Management Review,* 1966, pp. 49–58.

An example of excessive emphasis on quantifiable objectives is given by Steve Kerr as follows: "Attempting to measure and reward accuracy in paying surgical claims, one insurance firm requires that managers set objectives about the number of returned checks and letters received from policyholders. However, underpayments are most likely to provoke cries of outrage from the insured, while over-payments are often accepted in courteous silence. Since it is often impossible to tell from the physician's statement which of the two surgical procedures, with different allowable benefits, was performed, and since writing for clarification will interfere with other objectives concerning 'percentage of claims paid within two days of receipt,' the new hire in more than one claims section is soon acquainted with the informal norm: 'When in doubt, pay it out!' The managers of these sections regularly meet or exceed their objectives in the areas of both quality (accuracy) and quantity."*

One approach to evaluating the present situation and to helping the organization to become more effective is to involve participants in the organization (or an important segment of it) in deliberately and systematically analyzing the objectives, activities and results. This may be a group effort, or it may be a collection of individual analyses of the situation. The group effort provides the opportunity for an interchange of ideas, recognizes the complexity and the interrelatedness of objectives and provides opportunity for recognizing some relevant areas of agreement and disagreement. The top manager may, of course, reserve the right to decide. He may be subject to pressure and need to trade-off on certain issues. In any case if there is involvement of top managers and staff in the examination of present objectives and the development of new ones, it is a far cry from methods in which *the* top manager sets objectives arbitrarily and then concentrates his efforts on getting people to follow through. In contrast, evidence supports the involvement-of-others approach, which recognizes that people are more likely to commit themselves and to contribute more effectively when they have helped to shape the organization's purpose and direction and have set standards for measuring the results.†

Involve others in analysis?

Whether an individual is doing the analysis or there is a group interchange of ideas, there are many additional aspects to organizational objectives and outcomes that may require attention. Consider the relevance of the following questions to the current organizational situation.

Other aspects may require attention.

1. What was the actual performance compared to previously established standards? Also, if the objectives have been analyzed

---

*S. Kerr: Management by objectives and other children's stories, *Presented at the Academy of Management Meeting,* Minneapolis, Minn., 1972.

†See, for example, H. Tosi and S. Carroll: Management reaction to management by objectives, *Academy of Management Journal, 11*:415–426, 1968. They discuss some of the difficulties of using an objectives approach as well (e.g., the interdependence of goals).

and clarified, was it possible to use these new standards (after a reasonable time period) for comparison with actual accomplishment? Were the objectives accomplished? If not, what led to being off target? What can be learned from an analysis of practices and structural arrangements in the past period?

2. What are the trends in performance indicators? Comparison of present records with records over a period of the last several years may indicate changes in external demands, product mix, financial records, physical facilities, types of grievances, union activity, and so forth. As indicated, trend information is more helpful in spotting potential difficulties and in judging why results occurred than is one-point-in-time data.

3. What are the records and practices of comparable organizations or comparable units in the organization? Frequently the relative success or failure of an organization is rooted in broad factors that pervade an industry or a geographic territory. Within the industry or territory there may be sizable differences in individual organizations' performances. Careful examination of comparable organizations' practices and policies may unearth reasons for such differences.

Compare with other organizations in same market.

If possible, the analyst might rank two or more comparable organizations or organizational units in terms of effectiveness measures. Are there any policies or practices in these units that help to differentiate between them? Are there apparent differences in the way they set objectives and determine policies?

Are there performance differentials? Are there industry performances and organization performances that differ in products, services, application, geography, or distribution channels? Are there differences in types of customers?

Are there differences in competitive strategies? Are there distinct types of market policies, product policies, financial policies or research policies?

As an illustration of the overall assessment of the objectives and organizational outcomes we shall cite Peter Drucker's discussion of three chemical companies.* The three successful companies have many qualities in common and appear very much alike to the outsider. They are all in the same line of chemistry, have big research centers, plants and sales organizations, are about equal in capital investment, sales and return on investment. Yet each has special and peculiar abilities. One company does well at bringing a product to consumer markets. Another develops many new industrial chemical specialties but fails to "make it" in consumer markets. A third does well in neither market but derives great income from licensing developments from its research to other chemical firms.

These companies have experimented with their basis of sup-

*P. F. Drucker, *The Effective Executive*. New York: Harper & Row, 1967, pp. 115–116.

port. But they have come to understand what they do best and what their limitations are. They set their objectives and measure their organizational outcomes accordingly in terms of their special ability: the first firm in the consumer market, the second in terms of the industrial chemicals it develops, and the third in terms of fees received from its research and development.

Policy-generating Structure

As shown in our model, a description of the policy-generating structure would include (1) the roles and commitments of relevant organizational participants, and (2) programs or generalized procedures that are used in the organization. A description of this structure, if extensive, involves making several determinations. These determinations or questions indicate part of the knowledge and skill needed by those who engage in bargaining and negotiation over time in strategy formation *and* implementation. The answers provide a description of how the choices are made in the current situation.

Questions indicate knowledge and skill needed for bargaining and negotiating.

There are limits, of course, on what the policy analyst can and should describe. He should consider the questions for (1) the extent of their relevance in the situation being examined, and (2) the extent to which valid descriptive content exists or can readily be obtained.*

Several areas that could be explored in examining the current policy-generating structure are as follows:

1. Determine the pattern of distribution of perceptions of problems or issues and changes in these patterns. The organization is an open system subject to a number of competitive, economic, government and other forces that help to shape its character. Participants in the organization will tend to define and redefine the problems and issues from time to time. In addition, they may disagree, as the Univis executives did, on what the issues are and what their relative importance is, and what the barriers are to their solution.

Perception of issues.

2. Determine whether the choices are made by one person or by a process of bargaining. Determine who are the most relevant participants, or those in positions of leverage. The individual in the organization has gone through a socialization process or, in other words, has been affected by the organizational culture, the management philosophy and the organization's social philosophy. He has been socialized into a political orientation or way of thinking and feeling about the allocation of power. There may exist a series of power centers, both formal and informal, in the organization. It is important to know not only where they are located but also the nature of their political resources.

How are choices made? Who has leverage?

3. What amount and kind of political resources are located at the various points or positions of leverage? The level of effective-

Political resources.

---

*The fact that some teaching materials (e.g., cases) do not give detailed information of the kind needed does not lessen the importance of this information.

ness will vary and the base upon which the leverage exists may include competence, information and charisma as well as official position.

4. What are the sets of "interests" at various locations? How have these "interests" affected the organizational goals? The "interests" are multiple and complex, so much so that individuals at certain locations may end up on any side of an issue. The fact that prediction is difficult means that a continual monitoring is appropriate if a participant or policy analyst is to have pertinent, current, reliable information. In addition, of course, there may be conflicting sets of interests. A simple example would be a firm in which the sales group was interested in greater variety in the product line (to improve sales) and the production group was interested in less variety (to reduce costs).

Interests.

Questions directed at individual as well as group interests may be used. The organizational participants' behavior is influenced by the way they see their own self interest. A more extended example may help here. Consider the following list of statements* relating to reward criteria. Determine which ones best describe the extent to which the organization uses such criteria as a basis for rewards.

What are existing reward orientations?

*These statements have been adapted from J. Thomas Cannon: *Policy and Strategic Action.* New York, Harcourt, Brace Jovanovich, 1968. They are used here merely for illustrative purposes.

PARTICIPANTS ARE REWARDED FOR	OPINION				
1. Complying closely with policy	YES	yes	?	no	NO
2. Maintaining tranquility	YES	yes	?	no	NO
3. Allocating efforts and resources to long-term development activities	YES	yes	?	no	NO
4. Responsible management, e.g., staying within budget	YES	yes	?	no	NO
5. Being responsive to top management	YES	yes	?	no	NO
6. Making desired innovations	YES	yes	?	no	NO
7. Relating functional excellence to the marketplace	YES	yes	?	no	NO
8. Developing awareness and capability of subordinates for strategic work	YES	yes	?	no	NO
9. Maintaining high work standards	YES	yes	?	no	NO
10. Isolating strategic work for objective analysis and profiling of strategies	YES	yes	?	no	NO
11. Making progress toward goals and objectives	YES	yes	?	no	NO
12. Maintaining flexibility in strategic plans	YES	yes	?	no	NO
13. Knowing the right people	YES	yes	?	no	NO
14. Keeping subordinates informed on current objectives	YES	yes	?	no	NO
15. Relating functional excellence to the operating goals	YES	yes	?	no	NO

If the participants feel their rewards are based on not rocking the boat or getting to know the right people, they may feel justified in spending much of their energy in that direction. If the participants feel that they need to achieve impressive short-run results, their efforts in this direction may be at the expense of a willingness to allocate time to long-term projects. Opportunities may be missed. For example, there may be delayed but substantial returns for allocating resources to regional service effort and program refinements, but at the expense of current service.

Thus, the policy analyst may want to know what the reward orientations or sets of interests are at various locations and to check on their appropriateness related to organization goals and action plans.

5. Determine the approaches used in handling conflicting sets of interests. Various ways of handling conflict such as using hierarchical coordination, structural devices, superordinate goals and joint problem solving were indicated in the discussion of the model of policy formation. An understanding of the approaches used in managing conflicting sets of interests in making strategic choices provides an important base for analysis and development of improvements in the policy-formation process.

Is conflict handled constructively?

The following simply stated guidelines* are suggestions for evaluating and understanding the conflict resolution process:

a. Within and between groups (e.g., divisions, departments, unions, stockholders) is some conflict considered inevitable and subject to resolution or even as a source of creative thought and action (or is it considered bad and consequently suppressed)?

b. Do the intragroup and intergroup relationships focus extensively on conflict or are they also aimed at bilateral problem solving and generation of new mission opportunities?

c. Are there regularized arrangements for continuous surfacing of conflicts, problems and new opportunities? Do these arrangements include concerted auditing of the external and internal environment?

d. Are there regularized arrangements for continuous resolution of conflicts, for problem solving and for generating and seizing new opportunities?

e. Are information and administrative systems open, visible and understandable to both unions and management?

As well as the specific patterns of behavior in dealing with conflict, description of the role performance of key participants may be made.

6. Determine how participants in the strategy-formation process are playing their roles and how these roles are linked to each other.

An organization may be described in terms of four basic partici-

---

*Some of these guides could be applied to evaluating labor relations policy. See C. A. Newland: Collective Bargaining and Public Administration: System for Changing and the Search for Reasonableness, presented at the National Conference of the American Society for Public Administration, April, 1971.

Four basic participants.

pants: operators, technocrats, managers and influencers.* They are all playing roles in the organization. Operators carry out the basic, routine work (e.g., clerks, janitors, truck drivers). Technocrats perform technical work toward maintaining and adapting the organization (e.g., management analysts, organization development specialists, budget analysts, long-range planners). Influencers are those in formal or informal positions of leverage (stockholders, public interest groups, regulatory agencies, union officials, managers themselves). Managers are those with formal authority or the right to direct the organization toward effectiveness and efficiency (e.g., Board of Directors, executive director, president, vice-president, division head).

Later we shall concern ourselves with the coupling of the roles (and programs) of operators, technocrats and managers in the organization structure. You are probably familiar with some forms of coupling such as the traditional—functional, product, and geographic— forms and the newer, results-oriented and matrix forms. These will be discussed later when we deal with the question of carrying out the corporate strategies generated. Our main concern at this point is with the pattern of behavior of the managers, especially general managers.

Strategic, coordinative and operating levels of activity.

One way to understand the managerial role is to examine the organization at various levels of activity such as strategic, coordinative and operating.† In a smaller enterprise it is more probable that various aspects of the managerial role will be carried out by one individual. That individual would be involved in determining basic missions, organizational objectives and performance specifications, in planning his activities over the short and long run, and then in executing them to achieve the objectives. In other words, his managerial activity would range from strategic to operating.

In larger, more complex organizations the activities may be assigned to managers at different levels. At the strategic level the managerial role includes relating the organization to its environment and designing comprehensive action plans. At the operating level the managerial focus is on effective and efficient implementation of plans to achieve stated objectives. At the coordinative level the role behavior ranges from strategic to operating in trying to integrate the internal activities that have been differentiated by function and/or level.

Basic general management activities.

Every manager, regardless of level, within the discretionary limits of his position, is involved to some degree in the three basic general management activities mentioned before:

1. Defining the scope of his unit's activity (what it will emphasize).

---

*For an excellent discussion see H. Mintzberg: *Policy as a Field of Management Theory.* Working Paper, McGill University, June, 1971.

†See T. Petit: A behavioral theory of management, *Academy of Management Journal,* December, 1967, pp. 341–350.

2. Specifying performance criteria for his unit (what standards, limits, policies and procedures will be enforced and reinforced within his unit; what performances will be rewarded or punished and how).
3. Procuring, conserving and then deploying resources among competing demands within his unit.*

The purpose of the policy analyst here is to describe in more specific terms the characteristics of general management work (e.g., what activities, how much time in each, with whom do they spend their time) and to analyze variations in managerial jobs and in effectiveness.

The complexity of the managerial role has been captured by Leonard Sayles in his book, Managerial Behavior.† Many other studies of the management role have been done. However, after a review of such studies describing the managerial role, Campbell and his associates conclude that we do not have but do need a "set of fundamental dimensions to describe or measure the job behaviors desired at a particular time and for a given situation.‡

The policy analyst may proceed in a number of ways. He may attempt to find out how general managers view their own role and how they view the roles played by other parties. To illustrate, what is their concept of the principal role or roles for themselves and for others? Is it:

Need specific characteristics of general management role.

To drive for better service?
To drive for profits?
To set objectives and targets for a strategy group?
To design the structure and assign the work?
To do objective analysis and profiling of policies?
To formulate and reformulate long-range plans?
To train and develop future managers?
To obtain high quality top management?
To perceive new product opportunities?
To raise short-term capital?
To maintain good relations with unions?
To raise equity at low cost?

As discussed in Chapter 3, the factors indicated by these questions are those rated by top executives in a recent survey as some of the most important strategic factors in business success.§ The factors may be used (with some modification for nonprofit organizations) in

---

*R. L. Katz: *Cases and Concepts in Corporate Strategy,* Englewood Cliffs, N.J., Prentice-Hall, Inc., 1970, p. 98.
†L. Sayles: *Managerial Behavior,* New York, McGraw-Hill Book Co., Inc., 1964.
‡J. P. Campbell, M. D. Dunnette, E. E. Lawler, Jr., and K. E. Weick: *Managerial Behavior, Performance and Effectiveness,* New York, McGraw-Hill Book Co., Inc., 1970, p. 99. For a more recent study, see H. Mintzberg: *The Nature of Managerial Work,* New York, Harper & Row, 1973.
§These are adapted from G. A. Steiner: *Strategic Factors in Business Success,* New York, Financial Executives Research Foundation, 1969, pp. 58–59.

examining various role perceptions illustrated in various case materials.

In field investigations, key participants could be asked what roles they expect to play themselves and what roles they expect others to play. They could be asked to rank or rate the roles as to importance and as to how well they are being carried out in the organization. Comparison may be made on the relative importance of the factors, on the relative satisfaction with success in carrying out the roles, and on the differences between self-established roles and those patterns of behavior expected by others. Perhaps there will be role conflict. Perhaps there will be evidence that the assumptions made regarding certain roles need to be altered. The format suggested is admittedly an oversimplification, but it may provide insights into operating methods and agreements and disagreements among key parties.

The broad strategic factors or dimensions suggested by Steiner could be transformed into more specific managerial behavior dimensions for various types of settings. The broad dimensions are only a first approximation of the roles played by managers; the actual tasks appropriate for the managers in a particular setting could be more clearly defined and made highly specific by using phrases suitable for individuals in the situation.

Other questions and other procedures may also be developed and used to provide more depth to the analysis. We shall discuss such questions and procedures as part of a program for determining top management effectiveness dimensions in Appendix 2 of this chapter.

7. Determine the significant programs that are used in the organization and how they are linked together.

We have discussed programs as generalized procedures that are used in response to a stimulus.* The manager, for example, carries out a decision-making program in response to information which indicates that he should analyze the environment. (See example in Figure 4–1, An information-processing program.) The technocrat carries out a sales forecast program in response to a request from management. The computer carries out a program in response to directions from a policy analyst.

A program response to stimuli is economical in that it includes execution steps and outputs, both of the kinds which have proved useful in past experience. There are general programs and more specific programs. The steps in case analysis previously discussed illustrate a general program. In fact, the whole set of guides and methods for review and evaluation of strategy formation included in this

General programs and more specific programs.

---

*For discussion see R. M. Cyert and J. G. March: *A Behavioral Theory of the Firm,* Englewood Cliffs, New Jersey, Prentice-Hall, Inc., 1963. Also see H. Mintzberg, D. Raisinghani and A. Theoret: *The Structure of "Unstructured" Decision Processes.* Professional Papers, Division of Business Policy and Planning, Academy of Management National Meeting, August, 1973.

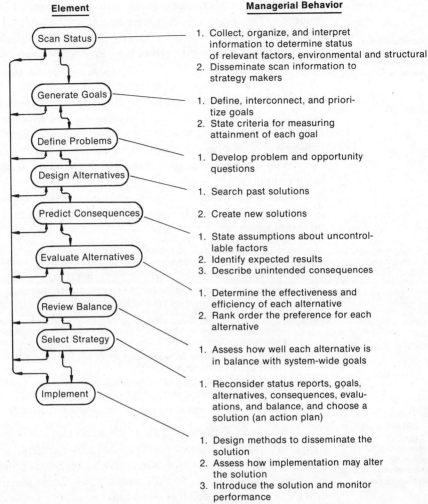

Figure 4-1 *An information-processing program. (Adapted from D. E. Zand: Policy formulation and managerial behavior: An information processing model, NYU Working Paper, No. 72-22, p. 8.)*

book represent a general program (or a group of programs). Some other programs that the organization may use are more specific (i.e., more programmed). We have previously mentioned rather specific programs in capital budgeting, simulations, market research, forecasting and mathematical modeling. We could add specific procedures in planning and coordination, using pro forma profit and loss statements, pro forma balance sheets, breakeven charts, cash flow summaries and current operating budgets. Thus, any generalized procedure that is used by the organization in response to a stimulus is a program.

A good illustration of a decision-making program is one that

An information processing program that is iterative.

emphasizes the information-processing orientation of strategy formulators. This program has nine elements or behavioral aspects, as indicated in Figure 4–1. The orderly procedure would be to follow the sequence suggested. However, in complex problem solving there may be flashes of insight that occur at any one of the stages in the process. Thus, the program shows that management strategy behavior may iterate through loops and subloops until it generates a satisfactory strategic decision. Furthermore, the program illustrates management strategy behavior with a wide scope of problem-solving responses. The program recognizes that for strategy formulation there is a need for thorough managerial questioning of expectations, assumptions, goals, values, alternatives and criteria of evaluation.

Several questions may be raised about this program and other programs in describing the strategy-generating structure. Consider, for example:

1. How are they actually used?
2. How important or relevant are they to the organization?
3. How are they linked together horizontally and vertically? For example, the informational output from one program may be the input to another; or more general programs may include two or more rather specific programs.
4. How effective are they in aiding the strategy-formation process? How costly are they?
5. Is the organization not availing itself of significant programs which could prove effective and efficient?
6. What triggers managers to respond with strategy behavior?
7. What is the present system for scanning status?
8. How are goals and action plans reviewed for balance?

CAUTION: *sometimes formal planning procedures are dysfunctional.*

Findings in a study of a large research and development company, for example, suggest that freedom to depart from formal planning procedures improves management's ability to contribute strategy recommendations.* In this company, apparently being "bogged down" in formal procedures of annual budget projections, quarterly revisions with detailed explanations of the revisions, and monthly reviews of technical progress, reduced the time for scanning the environment and developing creative strategy recommendations.

We have already indicated the need to study the role of general managers and the programs they use to carry out their roles. The top management role is not fully understood at this time. Management programs, as well, are generally complex in nature and ill defined at the present time. Work needs to be done toward understanding the dimensions of effectiveness for top managers.

The analyst studies the policy-generating structure with its variety of roles and programs and, in general, analyzes the current mission, the basis of environmental support and the organizational objectives and outcomes and gains an indication of the current "state

---

*As reported in D. Zand: *Policy Formulation and Managerial Behavior,* N.Y.U. Working Paper No. 72–22, 1972, p. 9.

of things." The policy analyst, of course, goes beyond this and forecasts what the environmental demands and support will be.

Part B. The Changing Situation

Environmental Forces — Problems, Opportunities, Demands

Changes in technology, legislation or social demands may affect entire industries and result in dramatic changes. In-camera development of pictures has significantly affected the photography industry. Recent Equal Employment Opportunity legislation has affected federal government agencies. Pressure from some citizen groups concerned with safety and pollution problems represents a potent factor in corporate and governmental planning. A lack of perceptive managers who can recognize such environmental changes may be disastrous. For example, the Baldwin Locomotive Works stuck with the making of steam locomotives until it lost environmental support and went out of business.

Predicting or recognizing change is difficult, of course, and requires constant vigilance. One problem is that the number of environmental factors (e.g., the domestic and international economy, competition, technological developments, government, legal and political changes and social issues) is so great that it is necessary to determine which are the most significant and to spend time and effort in analyzing them. (A large part of the work of corporate planning staffs is performed in these areas.) The opportunities, threats and requirements for National Beer are far different than those for Pittsburgh Plate Glass. The forecast of legislation may be very important to a government agency. The forecast of disposable personal income may be very important to an automobile company. The forecast of change in preferences of hair length and hair style is of extreme importance to those owning barber shops. (Short hair seems to be coming back in some locations.) Monitoring activities must focus on those environmental areas or variables that are deemed critical to the particular organization. In other words, those areas that will have a significant impact on the survival of the organization need consideration. The range of possibilities is broad, as the following discussions indicate.

Select and monitor critical environmental factors.

Economic considerations. A significant factor in any compilation of environmental forces must include economic considerations. All too often we hear of the new enterprise or diversification move taken by an organization only to have it fail because of changes in the economy. Many small electronics firms were founded in the late 1960's with high hopes for participating in the growing aerospace and computer industries. Much to their dismay, these new firms soon found that they had made their move just as the economy tumbled into a recession, taking with it these two relatively volatile industries.

Many of the managers in these new firms assumed that the economy would expand forever. They did not really examine what the effect of a declining economy might be upon their operations. In the case of the small electronics firms, the recession was a prime factor in many of the cuts in capital spending made by their large customers. Aerospace firms found both private and public sector contracts difficult to procure. Large companies everywhere were cutting back on orders for new computers in order to trim their overhead costs. These factors led to a declining market for the struggling young firms, many of which were undercapitalized to start with.

There may have been bright spots in the misfortunes of the recession, however. There were many companies supplying goods for so-called countercyclical industries. These are product industries which do especially well when the economy is down. Examples would include used cars, low priced food and auto parts. However, many of the firms supplying these products were caught short when the recession hit.

Effect of economic conditions.

Other similar examples could also be listed, including the inability of producers to fully supply the housing industry during its recent, dramatic turnaround. The point to be made is that the manager or analyst who is responsible for formulating strategy within the organization must have a thorough understanding of the effects of the economy on the industry and on his particular firm. The manager who does understand these interactions will have a distinct advantage over his competitors.

The analyst must also be able to distinguish between long- and short-term economic factors. In the previous examples of the small electronics firms, we should see that some of the problems confronting the organizations were short term in nature. The economy was not going to stay down forever. If the analysts had had the foresight to take into account a recession of relatively short duration, many of the firms might still have survived. If the factors had been longer lasting or even relatively permanent, such as a total change in the structure of the economy, it is conceivable that nothing might have been able to save the firms. Such shifts would include changes in savings and spending patterns brought about by psychological, technological and other factors. An example of these latter factors would be the "depression psychosis" that leads to increased personal savings. This, in turn, leads to a decrease in spending by consumers. If the products of the firm are sensitive to this type of change, its environment could be permanently altered.

Long or short term?

Perceived effects.

The analyst should consider the following points when analyzing economic effects on the firm:

1. How does the course of the economy affect sales of the product of the firm? Are short-term or long-term economic effects more important?
2. Are economic effects direct or indirect? What is the timing of these effects? Do they lead, coincide with or lag behind economic trends?

3. Are these economic effects real or perceived? Can perceptions be altered before economic effects take hold?

Technological advances. Economic inputs are not all that is required for a thorough environmental analysis. Among other key factors to be analyzed one would have to include technological advances. We are living in an age of rapidly advancing technology. How those advances might affect the opportunities available to the individual or the organization is a key input in the policy-formation process.

The story is sometimes told of the Boston patriarch who labored many years to build up a worthwhile estate to pass on to his children. When it came time for him to draw up his will, he chose to set up a rather complex, but unbreakable, trust for the benefit of his family. He left firm instructions as to how his estate should be used to provide for his heirs; he made what he felt was a thorough analysis of then current (turn of the century) conditions and stipulated that his assets should be invested in electric street railway companies. As might be guessed, it was not too long after his death that his required investments started going awry.*

The upshot of the story is that the plans for financial security laid by the head of the family were destroyed because of his lack of understanding of the nature of technological advance in a given area. The strategy adopted by the Bostonian proved inflexible when confronted with new ideas and innovations in the transportation field.

Flexible strategy?

The analyst must have a clear understanding, not only of the present state of technology affecting his products, but also of potential future advances. The analyst must also be able to consider the effect that seemingly irrelevant technological changes may have on his organization.

Many organizations have found, to their dismay, that technological events in seemingly unrelated areas have shattered supposedly carefully planned strategies. The previously mentioned example of the steam locomotive firm demonstrates this to some extent. Other examples would include many textile firms which were forced out of business because they could not see the effects that various, newly developed petroleum and chemical-based derivatives would have on their products. Synthetic fibers gained a foothold in clothing and related markets, and many organizations that had not previously been a factor in the market became significant competitors or supply agents. In these roles, they were able to determine the future direction of the industry, even to the point of having significant inputs in styling owing to constraints or the lack of constraints on the new materials. Early permanent press garments, for example, could not be repressed or altered but had to be worn as manufactured.

Seemingly unrelated technology.

---

*C. Amory: *Proper Bostonians*. New York, E. P. Dutton & Co., Inc., 1947.

Some questions that should be asked can be grouped in two categories:

1. How are new products methods, new materials, new equipment, new products and/or services likely to affect the organization (e.g., automatic data processing equipment, plastics, electric automobiles, transistors, and information retrieval systems)?

2. What use should be made of technological forecasts? The methodology for this type of forecast, which will be discussed later, ranges from mathematical formulas to informed judgment. It may be necessary to use in-depth analysis to develop useful information.

Finding answers to these types of questions will enable the analyst to grasp the potential direction of technological change in the environment. As we may see by analyzing these questions, however, answers may require information on other areas and topics. One of these areas would involve the various social factors in the environment that are shaping the direction of future change.

Social influences. The composition and thinking of society as a whole plays a significant part in the policy-formation process. The values or demands of society are used as inputs in the objective-setting phase of reformulating corporate strategy. The resources or support available in a changing society can seriously affect the action plan of an organization when the plans are designed to achieve only previously acceptable objectives.

We have seen many organizations forced to alter their corporate strategies, or cease operations altogether, because of changing social factors. The changing size and geographic location of the population has led to a wrenching change in agriculture in this country during this century. Large corporate farms have taken over the role of primary producer formerly held by small family units. This has, in turn, led to an entirely new industry often called "agribusiness."

Changes in education level and access to information have also led to differing effects on many organizations and industries. No longer can the analyst assume that the consumer has to rely on point-of-purchase information. Markets have expanded rapidly, so that analysts now must consider not only local social influences, but also those of a regional, national or even international origin.

Obviously many of the changes we are discussing here are related to change in other areas. It is quite difficult, however, to distinguish which changes were caused by what factors; the relationship and direction of effects between economic, social, technological and other factors is often quite hazy. This should not make the analyst feel that knowledge of social influence is too difficult to obtain; it should spur him on to seeking better answers to questions affecting his organization originating from social changes.

Examples of the kinds of questions and areas of interest to the analyst would include:

1. How are the size, location and age make-up of the population changing?
2. How is the educational level changing?
3. How are the values and norms of the population changing (e.g., attitudes toward the desirability for goods and services and the attitudes toward work)?
4. To what extent are such changes and other social changes likely to have an impact in the products and/or services of the organization (e.g., demand for mass transit facilities, social welfare services, investment advisory services, second homes, public insurance protection, and marijuana cigarettes)?
5. To what extent and how should survey research forecasting be formulated and used?

Political inputs. Social influences usually affect the organization in several different ways; besides some of the methods already discussed, social changes eventually show up as political influences on all levels of government.

An analyst working in the aerospace industry might have used a great deal of insight in formulating strategies by noticing social trends taking place in the mid-1960's. A growing antiwar mood in the United States could have been a forecast of decreasing defense spending. This change in the views of society eventually led to a slowdown in United States involvement in the Vietnam conflict as a result of political pressures. This slowdown had adverse effects on both aerospace and defense industries.

Political factors are not relegated to appropriations by various legislative units. Large blocs of the economy are regulated to varying degrees by governmental agencies. Present regulations must be analyzed thoroughly to determine legal constraints on the planning process. Future trends in regulations must also be anticipated. The analyst is, after all, interested in future directions and actions of the organization. For this reason, trends in outside political influences should be forecast as much as possible.

There are very few governmental actions that come as complete surprises to the economy.* Foreknowledge of these actions can often give the analyst the added competitive advantage he needs to create and implement a successful corporate strategy. Questions to be answered to help in forecasting and understanding such actions include:

Forecast government actions.

1. What agencies now hold some type of regulatory power in

---

*The obvious exception would be President Nixon's announcement of the imposition of economic controls in August, 1971. There are other less known examples, such as the delayed announcement of policy changes by the Federal Reserve Board's Open Market Committee, which affected interest rates and the money supply.

the area into which we are heading? Is there leeway in the interpretation of these regulations? Are the agencies receptive to innovation in the industry?

2. Who are the individuals involved in setting regulations or legislation in our future areas of competition? What might be their personal and professional views on our projected moves? Are these individuals likely to be replaced through electoral or other means? What other pressures or groups must they face?

3. Are there indications of wholesale changes in the governmental process (i.e., change of party in power, shift in power from Congress to the President, etc.)? What are the possible predictors of change? Can these predictors be spotted well in advance of changes? How can they be measured?

Competitive factors. The various environmental inputs discussed to this point cannot be considered as if they are affecting only the organization you are considering; all these inputs are felt to one degree or another by any organization in competition with your organization. Their reactions to these inputs must be considered if a corporate strategy is to be feasible and well rounded. Included in any analysis of competitive factors must be a knowledge of the reactions to the strategic moves planned by the organization. Once again the policy formation process is, of necessity, an interactive procedure.

Reactions to our strategic moves.

Competitive reactions play an integral part in determining the constraints on strategy formation. American Motors must consider what its giant competitors might do if it decided to attack a new segment of the auto market. Its most profitable years have occurred when it was not competing head on with the full line of products carried by the Big Three. Similar examples can be seen in other industries dominated by a small number of relatively large firms.

For these reasons, an analysis of the strengths and weaknesses of competitors is extremely useful. In the case of American Motors, it would be helpful to realize that its competitors might view its continued existence as a potential defense against antitrust action against the industry. The industry somehow looks more competitive with relatively small firms still operating. This potential weakness of competitors could be turned into a strength on the part of American Motors to fortify their strategic moves in the future.

Polaroid Corporation found itself in a position where it had to weigh heavily the reaction of its huge competitor in the home picture business, Kodak, when it made decisions relating to future camera and film developments. It decided to begin producing its own film, knowing that the loss of the market to Kodak could well force Kodak to try to develop its own instant cameras.

As these examples demonstrate, a thorough knowledge of the policies and strategies of competitors is necessary during the policy-formation process. Questions that should be asked include:

1. What is the competitive environment of the industry? Is competition concentrated among a few firms or is it spread over many firms? How are the competitors geographically dispersed?
2. What policies and strategies are followed by individual firms in the industry? Do they lead the industry in developing new production methods and pricing? What are their strengths in research and development, marketing, promotion, etc.? What are their production strengths?
3. What is the financial condition of the various competitors? Will they be vulnerable to strategic moves because of lack of financial resources?*

The basic idea is to determine what peculiar strengths or weaknesses competitors might have that would affect any potential actions by an organization. The human, material and financial resources available to the competition must be analyzed to be able to provide contingency plans in the corporate strategy against any moves initiated by that competition.

The combination of these external environmental inputs is designed to give the manager an understanding of the constraints facing an organization. The strategy-formation process is dependent upon an integration of the analyses of the various internal and external factors in the current and changing situation. Bringing together an understanding of these factors provides the basis for redeveloping objectives for the organization. It also enables the analyst to reformulate alternate plans for achieving those objectives.

Social responsibility. The combination of the external environmental trends and internal behavioral influences can lead to decisions that often do not directly affect the productive capability of the organization. The concept of social responsibility within the firm involves one of these areas. Nevertheless, this issue must be faced in a society where increasing emphasis is placed on the responsibility of the organization towards its environment.

Problems may arise, however, in attempting to implement these policies regarding the social responsibility of the corporation. The corporation, although legally a separate entity, is nevertheless comprised of many individuals. The question arises as to the feelings of these individuals regarding their combined social responsibility. Just as agreeing on an overall strategy for the firm is difficult to arrive at, so is determining the social goals of the organization. First, the question arises as to whether the firm even has as an objective the betterment of the society within which the firm operates.

The claim is made that corporations are limited to performing operations as described in the corporate charter. The philosophical argument put forth is that the corporation is restricted to these areas alone. The rejoinder to these arguments follows the lines of the com-

---

*It was speculated that the fierce price competition started by A & P in consumer food marketing would cease only when the company had exhausted its large and carefully gathered financial reserves.

ments made previously in Chapter 2: The corporation operates within its environment; if that environment prospers, then the firm will probably prosper along with that environment.

Whose evaluation to use?

However, the question still arises as to whose evaluation of social responsibility the firm should follow. A strictly rational discussion would lead the firm to choose corporate strategies that would lead to its own economic advancement. Examples of this point of view would include the advantages to the lumber industry of reforestation. This industry requires a continuous supply of raw materials for its long-run viability. It would, therefore, be economically sound for it to develop resources for further reforestation projects. The lumber industry assumes that there will be a long-run need for its products. However, it also draws much of its raw material from federal lands. The stipulations attached to these timber sales require reforestation. Also, the government holds title to the land, decreasing the capital investment of the lumber industry. All firms within the industry are faced with similar constraints. This is not true for all industries, however.

There are several factors that the individual firm must consider when faced with socially oriented investments, particularly those designed to improve the physical environment. One involves the actions of competing firms, both at home and abroad.

Some policies rationalized on profitability or on legal grounds.

If the environmental actions are not required by law, the question arises as to the competitive position a firm might find itself in if it were the only firm taking environmental action. The policy analyst must question whether the various image, personnel and product gains, if any, will overcome potential cost disadvantages relative to competition. At this stage, the individual firm must truly test its commitment to environmental betterment.

On a larger scale, the country itself must test its commitment when it requires environmental protection through regulations and legislation. If these actions place an entire domestic industry at a disadvantage relative to foreign competition, the country must consider who will be asked to pay for that disadvantageous position.

The analyst working in any of these situations must eventually evaluate the effectiveness and feasibility of his corporate strategy. To do this, he must have some idea of the long-term demand for his product; often, however, social and environmental considerations inhibit his ability to forecast the long-term demand. The petroleum industry, as an example, finds that it needs more refining capacity domestically to meet a growing demand for its various products. It feels constrained in investing in increased capacity, however, because it does not know what types of regulations the federal government may place on its various products, such as gasoline. This problem becomes particularly acute since the cost of an efficient

Social issues add to uncertainty.

refinery is in excess of $100 million and requires three years to build. This kind of uncertainty present in the environment makes strategic decisions extremely difficult, if not impossible, to make.

The utility industry finds itself in a similar position. The main differences are that the time involved is longer and the costs are greater. These factors heightened the investment problems and led to a virtual halt in planning for new nuclear power plants in 1971.

The policies just related have all involved commitments directly related to the product itself, or government regulations involving the product or the production process. As such, these environmental and social policies can be rationalized on profitability or legal grounds.

Less easily rationalized policies involve decisions to support local, regional and national causes not directly related to the product or service supplied by the firm. The question arises not only as to what extent the firm should support various charitable, educational and social causes, but whether they should be supported at all. *Support which causes?*

During past centuries support of these causes was often the sole responsibility of the private sector. During this century, however, the government has assumed support in many of these areas. This has led many firms to withhold resources from what are considered nonessential actions. Basically, the decision eventually facing the firm breaks down into three different questions.

1. Who within the organization is to decide what is the position of the firm on social responsibility?
2. To which social causes should the firm commit its resources?
3. What percentage of its resources should be allocated to fulfilling the social responsibilities of the firm?

These questions have to be considered by the policy analyst if he is to be successful. Likewise, the student of policy formation has to consider these questions if he is to present a total analysis of the environment surrounding *any particular situation.*

The problem arising with the strategic importance of social responsibility issues is that investments in this area are usually long term in nature. Also, the returns from these investments rarely show up on any financial statements except as expenses. The question arises as to how to take advantage of these investments in the eyes of the investing public. *Usually long-term investment.*

One solution arrived at by some authors, consultants and businessmen is to perform a social audit for the firm.* The purpose of the social audit is to measure "the impact of its [the firm's] social programs in terms of costs, benefits, performance, or even profits."† Although no specific ground rules or regulations have been developed for the social audit, examples have been developed. One such example is reproduced here (Fig. 4–2). It was developed by Abt Associates, Inc., to measure their own resources available for social issues. *Measure and demonstrate social contribution.*

This type of policy aid could prove to be quite valuable to top

*For a more extensive discussion, see, R. A. Bauer and D. H. Fenn, Jr.: *The Corporate Social Audit,* New York, Russell Sage Foundation, 1972.
†The first attempts at a corporate "social audit, *Business Week,* September 23, 1972, p. 89.

Abt Associates Inc. Social Balance Sheet

Year ended December 31, 1971 with comparative figures for 1970

Social Assets Available	1971	1970
Staff		
Available within one year (Note I).....................	$ 2,594,390	$ 2,312,000
Available after one year (Note J)......................	6,368,511	5,821,608
Training Investment (Note K)..........................	507,405	305,889
	9,470,306	8,439,497
Less Accumulated Training Obsolescence (Note K)	136,995	60,523
Total Staff Assets	9,333,311	8,378,974
Organization		
Social Capital Investment (Note L)..................	1,398,230	1,272,201
Retained Earnings.......................................	219,136	–
Land...	285,376	293,358
Buildings at cost	334,321	350,188
Equipment at cost	43,018	17,102
Total Organization Assets	2,280,081	1,932,849
Research		
Proposals (Note M)......................................	26,878	15,090
Child Care Research.....................................	6,629	–
Social Audit...	12,979	–
Total Research	46,486	15,090
Public Services Consumed Net of Tax Payments (Note E)...	152,847	243,399
Total Social Assets Available............................	$11,812,725	$10,570,312
Social Commitments, Obligations, and Equity		
Staff		
Committed to Contracts within one year (Note N)	$ 43,263	$ 81,296
Committed to Contracts after one year (Note O)	114,660	215,459
Committed to Administration within one year (Note N)	62,598	56,915
Committed to Administration after one year (Note O)	165,903	150,842
Total Staff Commitments......................	386,424	504,512
Organization		
Working Capital Requirements (Note P)	60,000	58,500
Financial Deficit...	–	26,814
Facilities and Equipment Committed to Contracts and Administration (Note N).........	37,734	36,729
Total Organization Commitments...........	97,734	122,043
Environmental		
Government Outlays for Public Services Consumed, Net of Tax Payment (Note E)........	152,847	243,399
Pollution from Paper Production (Note Q)........	1,770	770
Pollution from Electric Power Production (Note R)...	2,200	1,080
Pollution from Automobile Commuting (Note S)	10,493	4,333
Total Environmental Obligations	167,310	249,582
Total Commitments and Obligations	651,468	876,137
Society's Equity		
Contributed by Staff (Note T)	8,946,887	7,874,462
Contributed by Stockholders (Note U).............	2,182,347	1,810,806
Generated by Operations (Note V)	32,023	8,907
Total Equity.......................................	11,161,257	9,694,175
Total Commitments, Obligations and Equity	$11,812,725	$10,570,312

Figure 4–2 How one company measures its social contributions. (From Business Week, *September 23, 1972.)*

managers in plotting strategic decisions. Much study must be done before a realistic social audit can be accepted and implemented for all firms. The lack of an effective measurement device should not deter firms from engaging in socially responsible efforts, however.

The key factor is not to feel unnecessary psychological constraints. The students should include a realistic analysis of the social trends of the environment, as previously indicated, as an input into the strategy-formation process. The fact that this topic is included in the Business Policy course should not be considered as simply a gesture toward salving the social conscience of the instructor, the students or the business community as a whole. Social responsibility should be designed to provide an important constraint, or opportunity, for the strategy-formation process.

Constraint or opportunity.

SUMMARY

The general assessment guides introduced in this chapter are intended to help the reader to begin the process of understanding and analyzing an organization's present situation and to forecast what the environmental demands and support might be. The guides, intended for general use in both business and public bodies, include many of the more basic strategic variables or questions that may be pursued in an assessment.

Considerable judgment is required, however, in tailoring the assessment to the unique circumstances of the organization. Some methods or variables may be eliminated for specific assessments; some may be added; some may be judged as more important than others. Consideration of the selected elements in the review and analysis of the relationships between the current position, desired position, achievements, problems, opportunities, threats, capabilities and requirements for success should permit an overall assessment of corporate strategies (organizational objectives and action plans) and the strategy formation process and aid in the reformulation of those strategies. We now turn to that reformulation process, which is Part C of our assessment guides, Reformulating the Corporate Strategy.

DISCUSSION QUESTIONS

1. Discuss the need for assessment guides. Who uses them? In what manner are they used by different groups?

2. In what manner does assessment tie in with the strategy-formation model presented in Chapter 1, and with the descriptive model of policy formation presented in Chapter 2?

3. What effect does the current position of the organization have on the overall assessment? Where does the statement of missions occur in the assessment?

4. Discuss the purpose of objectives in the assessment of cor-

porate strategies. What factors should be considered when determining the effectiveness of stated objectives?

5. How are conflicts resolved in the objective-setting process?

6. Discuss the relevance of external factors in the strategy-formation process. What key questions should be considered when relating corporate strategy with these external factors?

7. Take a stand on the questions of the type and degree of social responsibility for business corporations. Defend your position. What pressures might you be under as a manager in an attempt to effectively implement your ideas?

Suggested Additional References for Further Study

Ackerman, R. W.: *Social Responsiveness in the Large Corporation.* Professional Papers of the Academy of Management, Division of Business Policy and Planning, Boston, 1973.

Adams, E. S.: Public role of private enterprise, *Michigan Business Review,* May, 1969.

Almond, G. A.: Comparative political systems, *Journal of Politics, 18:*391–409, 1956.

Argyris, C.: *Interpersonal Competence and Organizational Effectiveness.* Homewood, Ill., Richard D. Irwin, 1962.

Barnard, C. I.: *The Functions of the Executive,* Cambridge, Harvard University Press, 1938.

Brown, C. C.: *The Ethics of Business:* Corp Beh in the Mark Place, New York, Columbia University Press, 1963.

Business fights the social ills — in a recession, *Business Week,* March 6, 1971.

Collins, J. W.: *Formulating Corporate Social Policy: Consideration of the Effect of Social Attitudes.* Paper presented at Academy of Management, Division of Business Policy and Planning, Boston, 1973.

Dearborn, D. C., and Simon, H.: Selective perception: A note on the departmental identification of executives, *Sociometry,* June, 1958.

Freedman, R.: The challenge of business ethics, *Atlanta Economic Review,* May, 1962.

Friedman, M.: The social responsibility of business is to increase its profits, *New York Times Magazine,* September 13, 1970.

Fry Consultants, Inc.: *Social Responsibilities,* 1970. (Pamphlet; study of 78 companies.)

Guffin, C. E.: The locus of social responsibility in the large corporation, *Michigan Business Review,* March, 1971.

Jerome, W. T.: *Executive Control — The Catalyst.* New York, John Wiley & Sons, Inc., 1961.

Kluckhohn, C., et al.: Values and value-orientation in the theory of action, in Parsons, T. and Shils, E. (eds.): *Toward a General Theory of Action,* Cambridge, Harvard University Press, 1951.

Landaw, P.: Do institutional investors have a social responsibility? *Institutional Investor,* July, 1970.

Levison, H.: Management by whose objectives? *Harvard Business Review, 48:*4, 1970.

Levitt, T.: The dangers of social responsibility, *Harvard Business Review,* September–October, 1958.

Manne, H. G.: The myth of corporate responsibility, *Public Relations Journal,* December, 1970, p. 6.

Nadler, P. S.: Public deposits and social goals, *Banking,* December, 1970.

Odell, H. R.: *What Does Social Responsibility Mean?* Paper presented at Academy of Management Meeting, Division of Business Policy and Planning, Boston, 1973.

Scheinfeld, A.: Social investment; A new concept of corporate philanthropy, *Management Review,* July, 1968.

Stover, C. F.: Corporation and public good, *Conference Board Record,* December, 1970.

APPENDIX 1 TO CHAPTER 4

A PROGRAM FOR ANALYZING SOME ASPECTS OF THE PRESENT FINANCIAL CONDITION OF THE ORGANIZATION

We have previously discussed financial strength as one aspect of the requirements for success in pursuing alternative opportunities in the environment. For example, the analyst may need to determine the extent to which money is available or obtainable for financing research and development, plant construction, inventory receivables, working capital and operating losses in the early stages of a new venture. Analyzing the present financial state of the organization will provide a sound basis for making such a determination.

The following generalized procedures and examples provide a useful guide to the analyst or manager. The procedures are not exhaustive but do provide the kinds of information most commonly used during strategy formation. Potential outside sources of funds such as banks would re-

quire a thorough and professional analysis, including the kind of information generated with the financial analysis program, before deciding to provide financial support to the organization.

The authors acknowledge the cooperation of Merrill Lynch, Pierce, Fenner and Smith, Inc., in supplying these examples. A more detailed analysis can be found in their pamphlet, *How to Read a Financial Report.*

To illustrate the program we shall provide a balance sheet and profit and loss statements for the Typical Manufacturing Company, Inc. Then we shall discuss concepts and procedures such as those involving net working capital, current ratio, inventory turnover, capitalization ratios, leverage, net profit ratio and cash flow.

Exhibit 1

TYPICAL MANUFACTURING COMPANY, INC., AND
CONSOLIDATED SUBSIDIARIES

Balance Sheet—December 31, 1969

ASSETS		
Investment in Unconsolidated Subsidiaries		$300,000
Property, Plant, and Equipment		
Land	$ 150,000	
Buildings	3,800,000	
Machinery	950,000	
Office Equipment	100,000	
	$5,000,000	
Less: Accumulated Depreciation	1,800,000	

Net Property, Plant, and Equipment	$3,200,000
Prepayments and Deferred Charges	100,000
Goodwill, Patents, Trademarks	100,000
Total Assets	$9,700,000

LIABILITIES AND STOCKHOLDERS' EQUITY
Current Liabilities

Accounts Payable	$1,000,000	
Notes Payable	850,000	
Accrued Expenses Payable	330,000	
Federal Income Tax Payable	320,000	
Total Current Liabilities		$2,500,000
Long-term Liabilities		
First Mortgage Bonds, 5% Interest, due 1975		2,700,000
Total Liabilities		$5,200,000

Net Working Capital

There is one very important thing that we can find from the balance sheet (Exhibit 1); that is net working capital, sometimes simply called working capital.

Net Working Capital or Net Current Assets is the difference between the total current asset and the total current liabilities. You will recall that current liabilities are the debts due within one year from the date of the balance sheet. The source from which to pay those debts is the current assets. Therefore the working capital or net current assets represents the amount that would be left free and clear if all current debts were paid off. In Typical Manufacturing, the figures are:

WORKING CAPITAL

Current Assets	$6,000,000
Minus Current Liabilities	2,500,000
Working Capital or Net Current Assets	$3,500,000

Current Ratio

Probably the question in your mind is: "Just what is a comfortable amount of working capital?" Well, there are several methods used by analysts to judge whether a particular company has a sound working capital position. To help you to interpret the current position of a company in which you are considering investing, the current ratio is more helpful than the dollar total of working capital. The first rough test for an industrial company is to compare the working capital figure with the total current liabilities. Most analysts say that minimum safety requires that current assets should be at least twice as large as current liabilities. This means that for each $1 of current liabilities, there should be $2 in current assets.

The Current Ratio is current assets divided by current liabilities. In the Typical Manufacturing balance sheet, the figures are:

CURRENT RATIO

$$\frac{\text{Current Assets}}{\text{Current Liabilities}} \quad \frac{\$6,000,000}{\$2,500,000} = \frac{2.4}{1} \text{ or 2.4 to 1.}$$

Therefore, for each $1 of current liabilities, there is $2.40 in current assets to back it up.

There are so many different kinds of companies, however, that this test requires a great deal of modification if it is to be really helpful in analyzing companies in different industries. Generally, companies that have a small inventory and easily collectible accounts receivable can operate safely with a lower current ratio than those companies having a greater proportion of their current assets in inventory and selling their products on credit.

Quick Assets

Current Assets	$6,000,000
Minus Inventories	1,500,000
Quick Assets	$4,500,000

Net Quick Assets

Quick Assets	$4,500,000
Minus Current Liabilities	2,500,000
Net Quick Assets	$2,000,000

Quick Assets Ratio

$$\frac{\text{Quick Assets}}{\text{Current Liabilities}} \quad \frac{\$4,500,000}{\$2,500,000} = \frac{1.8}{1} \quad 1.8 \text{ to } 1$$

Thus, for each $1 of current liabilities, there is $1.80 in quick assets available.

Inventory Turnover

How big an inventory should a company have? That depends on a combination of many factors. An inventory is large or small, depending upon the type of business and the time of the year. An automobile dealer, for example, with a large stock of autos at the height of the season is in a strong inventory position; yet that same inventory at the end of the season is a weakness in his financial condition.

There are dangers in a large inventory position. In the first place, a sharp drop in price may cause serious losses. And second, it may indicate that the company has accumulated a big supply of unsalable goods.

How can we measure adequacy and balance of inventory? One way is to compare it with sales for the year to arrive at Inventory Turnover. Typical Manufacturing's sales for the year are $6,500,000, and the inventory at the balance sheet date is $1,500,000. Thus the turnover is $4\frac{1}{3}$ times, meaning that the goods are bought and sold out more than four times per year on the average. (Strict accounting requires computation of Inventory Turnover by comparing annual Cost of Goods Sold with Average Inventory. Such information is not readily available in the published statements; hence, an approved substitute is Sales Related to Inventory.)

Inventory as a Percentage of Current Assets. Another comparison may be between inventory and total current assets. In Typical Manufacturing the inventory of $1,500,000 represents 25 per cent of the total current assets, which amount to $6,000,000. But there is considerable variation between different types of companies, and thus the relationship is significant only when such comparison is made among companies in a similar industry.

Proportion of Bonds, Preferred and Common Stock

Capitalization Ratios. Before investing, you will want to know the proportion of each kind of security issued by the company you are considering. These proportions are sometimes referred to as Capitalization Ratios. A high proportion of bonds sometimes reduces the attractiveness of both the preferred and common stock, while too large an amount of preferred can detract from the value of the common. The principal reason is that bond interest must be paid before preferred stock dividends, and the preferred stock dividends before common stock dividends.

The Bond Ratio is found by dividing the face value of the bonds, $2,700,000 for Typical Manufacturing, by the total value of the bonds, preferred stock, common stock, capital surplus, and accumulated retained earnings, amounting to $7,200,000. This shows that bonds amount to $37\frac{1}{2}$ per cent of the total capitalization. Capitalization means the face value of bonds and par value of stocks (both preferred and common) that a company has outstanding. But we must include also the amount of capital surplus and the accumulated retained earnings which have been plowed back into the corporation. The capitalization of Typical Manufacturing therefore consists of:

CAPITALIZATION

Bonds	$2,700,000
Preferred Stock	600,000
Common Stock	1,500,000
and	
Capital Surplus	700,000
Accumulated Retained Earnings	1,700,000
Total Capitalization	$7,200,000

The Preferred Stock Ratio is found in the same way: Divide the preferred stock of $600,000 by the entire capitalization of $7,200,000. The result is $8\frac{1}{3}$ per cent.

Naturally, the Common Stock Ratio will be the difference between 100 per cent and the total of the bond and preferred stock ratios—$54\frac{1}{6}$ per cent in our example. The same result is reached by combining the common stock, capital surplus, and accumulated earnings and dividing by the total capitalization. Both capital surplus and accumulated earnings represent additional backing for the common stock. The capital surplus usually indicates the amount paid by stockholders in excess of the par value of the common stock; the accumulated retained earnings are undistributed profits plowed back to help the corporate growth. For Typical Manufacturing we add to the common stock of $1,500,000 the capital surplus of $700,000 and the accumulated retained earnings of $1,700,000 for a total of $3,900,000. This figure divided by $7,200,000 total capitalization gives $54\frac{1}{6}$ per cent as the common stock ratio.

To summarize, the proportion of bonds, preferred, and common stock for Typical Manufacturing is:

CAPITALIZATION RATIOS

	Amount	Ratio (%)
Bonds	$2,700,000	$37\frac{1}{2}$
Preferred Stock	600,000	$8\frac{1}{3}$
Common Stock	3,900,000	$54\frac{1}{6}$
(Including capital surplus and retained earnings)		
Total	$7,200,000	100

Generally speaking, it is considered desirable for an industrial company to have no more than 25 per cent bond ratio, and for the common stock ratio to be at least as much as the total of the bond and preferred stock ratios. If these proportions are not maintained, a company may find it difficult to raise new capital. Banks are reluctant to lend money to companies with relatively large debts, and investors are reluctant to buy their common stock because of all the bond interest or preferred dividends that must be paid before the common stockholder receives any return.

Railroads and public utility companies are exceptions to most of the rules of thumb that we use in discussing Typical Manufacturing Company. Their situation is different because of the tremendous amounts of money they have invested in their fixed assets, their small inventories, and the ease with which they can collect their receivables. Senior securities of railroads and utility companies frequently amount to more than half their capitalization.

Leverage

A stock is said to have high leverage if the company that issued it has a large proportion of bonds and preferred stock outstanding in relation to the amount of common stock. Speculators are often interested in companies that have a high proportion of debt or preferred stock because of the Leverage Factor. A simple illustration will show why. Let us take, for example, a company with $10,000,000 of 4 per cent bonds outstanding. If the company is earning $440,000 before bond interest, there will be only $40,000 left for the common stock after payment of $400,000 bond interest ($10,000,000 at 4 per cent equals $400,000). However, an increase of only 10 per cent in earnings (to $484,000) will leave $84,000 for common stock dividends, or an increase of more than 100 per cent. If there is only a small common stock issue, the increase in earnings per share will appear very impressive.

You have probably realized that a decline of 10 per cent in earnings would not only wipe out everything available for the common stock, but result in the company's being unable to cover its full interest on its bonds without dipping into accumulated earnings. This is the great danger of so-called high-leverage stocks and also illustrates the fundamental weakness of companies that have a disproportionate amount of debt or preferred stock. Investors will do well to steer clear of them. Speculators, however, will continue to be fascinated by the market opportunities they offer.

The Income Statement

Some companies refer to this statement as The Earnings Report or The Statement of Profit and Loss. We have called it Income Statement. It appears as Exhibit 2, p. 139.

While the balance sheet shows the fundamental soundness of a company, reflecting its financial position at a given date, the Income Statement may be of greater interest to investors because it shows the record of its operating activities for the whole year. It serves as a valuable guide in anticipating how the company may do in the future.

The income statement matches the amount received from selling the goods and other items of income, on the one hand, against all the costs and outlays incurred in order to operate the company, on the other hand. The result is a Net Profit for the year or a Net Loss for the year.

For example:

Sales for the Year and Other Income	$6,610,000
Costs Incurred	6,255,000
Net Profit	$ 355,000

The costs incurred usually consist of cost of the goods sold; overhead expenses such as wages and salaries, rent, supplies, depreciation; interest on money borrowed; and taxes.

The most important source of revenue always makes up the first item on the income statement. In Typical Manufacturing, it is Net Sales. If it were a railroad or a utility instead of a manufacturer, this item would be called Operating Revenues. In any case, it represents the primary source of money received by the company from its customers for goods sold or services rendered. Net sales is the amount received after taking into consideration returned goods and allowances for reduction of prices.

A secondary source of revenue referred to as Other Income or Miscellaneous Income comes from dividends and interest received by the company from its investments in stocks and bonds, which are carried as assets in the balance sheet.

Cost of Sales and Operating Expenses

In a manufacturing establishment, Cost of Sales represents all the costs incurred in the factory (including depreciation, which we have stated separately for Typical Manufacturing) in order to convert raw material into a finished product. These costs include raw materials, direct labor, and such factor overhead items as supervision, rent, electricity, supplies, maintenance, and repairs.

Depreciation is the decline in useful value of an asset due to wear and tear. Each year's decline in value of a machine used in the manufacturing process is a cost or a loss to be borne as an expense chargeable against the production as an additional outlay.

Net Income

After we have taken into consideration all income (plus factors) and deducted all costs and expenses (minus factors), we arrive at Net Income for the year. In condensed fashion, the income statement looks like this:

CONDENSED INCOME STATEMENT

Plus Factors		
Net Sales	$6,500,000	
Other Income	110,000	
Total		$6,610,000
Minus Factors		
Cost of Sales and Operating Expenses	$5,800,000	
Interest on Bonds	135,000	
Provision for Federal Income Tax	320,000	$6,255,000
Net Income		$ 355,000

Net Income is the amount available to pay dividends on the preferred and common stock and to use in the business. To the extent that dividends declared by the board of directors are less than the net income, the excess is plowed back into the corporation and is reflected in the accumulated retained earnings. From the balance sheet, we have learned a good deal about the company's stability and soundness of structure; from net profit from operations, we judge whether the company is earning money on its investment.

The figure given for a single year is not nearly the whole story, however. The historical record for a series of years is more important than the figure for any single year. This is just as true of net income as any other item.

Even though a company shows no profit in a particular year or winds up with a loss for the year, the board of directors may deem it prudent to continue to pay a dividend to the stockholders. Such distribution comes from the accumulation of earnings of former years.

Analyzing the Income Statement

The income statement, like the balance sheet, will tell us a lot more if we make a few detailed comparisons. The size of the totals on an income statement doesn't mean much by itself. A company can have hundreds of millions of dollars in net sales and be a very bad investment. On the other hand, even a very modest profit may make a security attractive if there is only a small number of shares outstanding.

Before you select a company for investment, you will want to know something of its Operating Margin of Profit and how this figure has changed over the years. Typical Manufacturing had sales for the year of $6,500,000 and showed $700,000 as the operating profit.

Net Profit Ratio is still another guide to indicate how satisfactory the year's activities have been. In Typical Manufacturing, the net profit was $355,000. The net sales for the year amounted to $6,500,000. Therefore, Typical Manufacturing's profit was $355,000 on $6,500,000 of sales or

NET PROFIT RATIO

$$\frac{\text{Net Profit}}{\text{Sales}} \quad \frac{\$\ 355,000}{\$6,500,000} = 5.5\%$$

This means that for every $1 of goods sold, 5½¢ in profit ultimately went to the company. By comparing the net profit ratio from year to year for the same company and with other companies in the same industry, we can best judge profit progress. For example:

The American Iron and Steel Institute and United States Steel Corporation give the following figures of Profits per Dollar of Sales (that is, net profit ratio):

Year	Steel Industry Percentage	U.S. Steel Percentage
1965	6.0	6.2
1966	5.9	5.6
1967	4.9	4.2
1968	5.3	5.5
1969	4.5 (est.)	4.5

The margin of profit ratio, the operating cost ratio, and the net profit ratio, like all those we examined in connection with the balance sheet, give us general information about the company and help us to judge its prospects for the future. All these comparisons have significance for the long term, since they tell us about the fundamental economic condition of the company.

Interest Coverage

The bonds of Typical Manufacturing represent a very substantial debt, but they are due many years hence. The yearly interest, however, is a fixed charge, and one of the first things we would like to know is how readily the company can pay the interest. More specifically, we would like to know whether the borrowed funds have been put to good use so that the earnings are ample and therefore available to meet the interest cost.

The available income representing the source for payment of the bond interest is $810,000 (total income before interest on bonds and provision for income tax). The annual bond interest amounts to $135,000. Therefore:

TIMES FIXED CHARGES EARNED

$$\frac{\text{Total Income}}{\text{Interest on Bonds}} \quad \frac{\$810,000}{\$135,000} = 6$$

meaning the annual interest expense is covered six times.

Before an industrial bond can be considered a safe investment, most analysts say that the company should earn its bond interest requirement three to four times over. By these standards, Typical Manufacturing has a fair margin of safety.

Preferred Dividend Coverage

To calculate the Preferred Dividend Coverage (the number of times preferred dividends were earned), we must use net income as our base, since federal income taxes and all interest charges must be paid before anything is available for stockholders. Since we have 6,000 shares of $100 par value of preferred stock that pays a dividend of 5 per cent, the total dividend requirement for the preferred stock is $30,000. Dividing the net income of $355,000 by this figure, we arrive at approximately 11.8, which means that the dividend requirement of the preferred stock has been earned more than eleven times over, a very safe ratio.

EARNINGS PER SHARE OF COMMON

Net Income for the Year	$355,000
Less Dividend Requirements on Preferred Stock	30,000
Earnings Available for the Common Stock	$325,000
Number of Shares of Common Outstanding	300,000 shares

$$\frac{\text{Earnings Available } \$325,000}{\text{Number of Shares } 300,000} = \$1.08^{1/3} \text{ Earnings per Share of Common}$$

Earnings Available for Common Stock	$325,000
Dividends Paid Out on Common	120,000
Current Year's Undistributed Earnings Allowed to Accumulate in the Corporation	$205,000

Cash Flow

You will observe from the net profit shown on the income statement that Typical Manufacturing was $355,000 better off by reason of the year's operating results. One of the elements of cost that was taken into consideration was depreciation in the amount of $900,000. Now, this amount does not represent an actual outlay of cash; it represents rather the annual write-off of an investment in fixed assets, showing the decline in value due to use during the year. Therefore, we can regard the current year as having generated $1,255,000 in cash, thus:

Net Profit for the Year	$ 355,000
Restore Depreciation Write-off, Which Is Not an Outlay of Funds	900,000
Profit for the Year on this Basis – Cash Flows	$1,255,000

Source of Funds and Their Application. A more significant presentation of cash flow for a corporation should show how the funds were used during the year. For example:

Source of Funds		
Net Profit for the Year		$355,000
Add Back Depreciation		900,000
Total Source of Funds		$1,255,000

Application as follows:

To purchase new plant equipment	$675,000	
To redeem long-term debt	150,000	
To pay dividends	$150,000	975,000
Balance remaining added to working capital		$ 280,000

Exhibit 2

TYPICAL MANUFACTURING COMPANY, INC., AND CONSOLIDATED SUBSIDIARIES
Income Statement—1969

Net Sales			$6,500,000
Cost of Sales and Operating Expenses			
Cost of Goods Sold		$4,400,000	
Depreciation		900,000	
Selling and Administrative Expenses		500,000	5,800,000
Operating Profit			$ 700,000
Other Income			
Dividends and Interest			110,000
Total Income			$ 810,000
Less: Interest on Bonds			135,000
Profit before Provision for Federal Income Tax			$ 675,000
Provision for Federal Income Tax			320,000
Net Profit for the Year			$ 355,000

ACCUMULATED RETAINED EARNINGS STATEMENT
(EARNED SURPLUS)—1969

Balance January 1, 1969		$1,495,000
Add: Net Profit for the Year		355,000
Total		$1,850,000
Less: Dividends Paid		
On Preferred Stock	$ 30,000	
On Common Stock	$ 120,000	150,000
Balance December 31, 1969		$1,700,000

APPENDIX 2 TO CHAPTER 4

A PROGRAM FOR DETERMINING TOP MANAGEMENT EFFECTIVENESS DIMENSIONS

At this point we should like to suggest a program (or a set of programs) for determining more precisely the work done by effective managers as "policy makers" in the strategy-generating structure. The program is possible for skilled technocrats with access to existing functioning organizations. The detailed information needed is not available in cases. Teams of students using computer games to study policy could, with their instructor's assistance, go through the program (or part of it). They could obtain a better understanding of behavioral patterns in simulated management teams. It is important, nevertheless, as students of policy to understand the concepts involved in management effectiveness even though it may not be possible to process the information on the subject.

The search for managerial effectiveness dimensions has lead to all sorts of descriptive variables and to all sorts of managerial style and role perception questionnaires developed by behavioral scientists.* The appropriate language, however,

may not be forthcoming from behavioral scientists. It may come from individuals in the situation (though not necessarily by reporting their own behavior). One approach to improving the descriptions is to use a modification of Smith and Kendall's retranslation method* in developing job behavior observation scales for use in describing the job effectiveness of policy makers. Summarizing the actual steps taken in developing the scales will illustrate the method:

1. In conferences or workshops attempt to identify and to gain consensus on the problems and issues in the present organizational situation.
2. Then major dimensions involved in strategy making would be defined and related to the problems and issues.
3. After the dimensions are identified, critical incidents are discussed with a view toward isolating and scaling rather specific effective and ineffective strategy maker's behavior.
4. The dimensions and their definitions and scales are reviewed and revised independently by a second conference group.
5. Where there is substantial agreement between groups on definitions and scales, they are retained. The other definitions and scales are eliminated.

The resulting task definitions would be job centered and behaviorally based statements which would seem to be useful in evaluating role performance. Moreover, the requirements for judging top manag-

---

*L. Sayles: *Managerial Behavior*, New York, McGraw-Hill Book Co., 1964; R. Stewart: *Managers and Their Jobs*, London, The MacMillan Co., Ltd., 1967; S. Carlson: *Executive Behavior*, Stockholm, Strombert, 1951; J. P. Campbell, M. D. Dunnette, E. E. Lawler and K. E. Weick: *Managerial Behavior Performance and Effectiveness*, New York, McGraw-Hill Book Co., 1970; J. K. Hemphill: Job descriptions for executives, *Harvard Business Review*, 37:55–67, 1959; T. A. Mahoney, T. H. Jerdee and S. J. Carroll: The jobs of management, *Industrial Relations*, 4 (No. 2):97–110, 1965; R. H. House and J. R. Rizzo: Toward the measurement of organizational practices: A scale development and validation, *Experimental Publications System*, June, 1971, 12, Ms. No. 481–1.

*P. D. Smith and L. M. Kendall: Retranslation of expectations: An approach to the construction of unambiguous anchors for rating scales, *Journal of Applied Psychology*, 47:149–155, 1963; M. D. Dunnette, J. P. Campbell and L. W. Heleriik: *Job Behavior Scales for Penney Co. Department Managers*. Minneapolis, Personnel Decisions, 1968.

ers or policy makers, if they are to be helpful for developmental purposes, need to meet several criteria:

1. Tasks must be directly relevant to what managers do themselves in terms of effective allocation of resources.
2. Must not be deficient in that major behavioral aspects, making up the job, are left out.
3. Must not include surplus elements, i.e., not attainable through their own efforts; not go beyond what each strategy maker can do to affect outcomes.
4. Must be devised rationally in accord with long-range plans and goals.
5. Must be clearly defined according to actual tasks necessary for accomplishing goals; highly specific; nonambiguous.
6. Must be based on job behaviors that are observable and measurable.

No single set of dimensions has yet been found which satisfies all these criteria. But some rather specific behavioral dimensions* have been identified by research as related to managerial and organization success. They are expressed in researcher's language as follows:

1. *Order and Structure.* Behaviors that are orderly, systematic and well structured; e.g., he responds to his men's questions with firm and conclusive answers.
2. *Group Achievement.* Behaviors associated with team action, group leadership, morale, group goals, and group advancement; e.g., his men work together as a team, setting goals and targets.
3. *Personal Enchancement Oriented.* Behaviors which seek to gain status, power and recognition; e.g., he uses his authority to assure that people follow instructions.
4. *Personal Interaction.* Behaviors involving social interaction supportiveness and acceptance of support; e.g., he spends much time chatting and counseling with his men.
5. *Achievement.* Behaviors related to goal setting, self-improvement, independent advancement in work and innovation; e.g., he attempts to be aware of major

progress points rather than specific activities.

Some other dimensions are suggested from a recent study of 52 managers in U.S. government agencies.* The most essential attributes, selected from over 100 attributes for top managers, were as follows:

1. Delegates authority and accepts consequences.
2. Recognizes when a problem exists.
3. Inspires the loyalty and confidence of subordinates.
4. Effectively selects and uses information to make decisions.
5. Assesses the advantages and disadvantages of alternative courses of action accurately.
6. Effectively uses manpower resources.
7. Defines problem correctly.
8. Acts decisively.

These various dimensions, though some are not very specific, along with Steiner's strategic factors in success and the information-processing program of management strategy behavior previously discussed, may provide some clues for a beginning point for study of strategy makers' effectiveness. Additional research and analysis are needed to determine other dimensions, specific tasks associated with each dimension, the appropriate language or words to use, and the relative impact of each of the dimensions of behavior in various organization situations.

In the meantime, for practitioners and for students studying cases or doing field projects it would seem that a useful way to proceed would be to identify behavior effectiveness dimensions for strategy makers in the situation. In other words, it would seem appropriate to attempt to identify what is helping and what is hindering in the strategy-formation process. A critical incident approach might be used (see Appendix to Chapter 8), perhaps simplifying the previously mentioned retranslation method resulting in:

1. A systematic recording of perceptions across the whole domain of "desired" behavior and "not desired" behavior of strategy makers.
2. A tabulation of how often agreed-upon

*D. G. Bowers and S. E. Seashore: Predicting organizational effectiveness with a four-factor theory of leadership, *Administrative Science Quarterly*, 2:238–263, 1966; J. Woffard: Factor analysis of managerial behavior, *Journal of Applied Psychology*, 54 (No. 2):169–173, 1970. These dimensions need adjustments to focus specifically on top management or policy makers.

Managerial and Executive Development Needs in the Federal Service and *Recommended Systems for Meeting Those Needs*, Washington, D.C.; U.S. Civil Service Commission, 1972.

objectives in critical areas of the strategy makers' behavior are accomplished.

3. Bearing in mind the limits of time, cost and direct knowledge, ratings of the top echelon of the unit or units from various sources (i.e., superiors, peers, subordinates, independent assessors, clients).

In other words, a list of behavior patterns would be developed for managers who (1) tend to reach their objectives, and (2) tend to be rated as effective.

With the caution that we do *not* have and do need a research-based set of fundamental dimensions to describe or measure the top management role desired at a particular time and for a given situation, we turn to some ideas that seem to be helpful in strategy making.

OUTLINE OF CORPORATE STRATEGY

FORMULATING OBJECTIVES FOR
CHANGE
    Priority of Objectives
    Making Trade-offs on Objectives
    Problems to Overcome

THE ACTION PLAN: SETTING
STRATEGIC ALTERNATIVES
    Developing and Profiling
    Alternatives
    Major Opportunities
    Obvious Limitations

Narrowing the Choice
Synergistic Possibilities
Strategic Changes and
    Corporate Policies
Detailing Provisions for
    Procuring and Allocating Resources:
    Linking Overall Strategy with
    Operations

A COMPUTER PROGRAM FOR
REFORMULATING CORPORATE
STRATEGY

SUMMARY

5

REFORMULATING CORPORATE STRATEGY: OBJECTIVES FOR CHANGE AND THE ACTION PLAN

Strategy (or policy) makers have been seen as interrelating important or critical decisions in a continuous process of mediating and allocating among conflicting sets of interests. Corporate strategy that results from the process is viewed here as an integrative concept encompassing not only the objectives but also a selection of combinations of resource deployments for achieving those objectives. The corporate strategy may be determined formally in a strategy planning program or intuitively in the brain of a top manager in the organization. Frankly, there is no complete certainty at this point on the best approach to use.

No certainty on best approach.

However, the assessment guides presented thus far (i.e., organizational mission, basis of support, resources, present and potential organizational objectives and outcomes, policy-generating structures, opportunities or problems) provide a sound basis for analysis of strategic choices. Though much staff work may be done by others and though there may be much line involvement, the strategic choices frequently are made by top executives working at the conference table. The primary keys to success seem to be judgment, experience, and well guided discussion rather than staff work and mathematical models.* The joint conference effort is especially suc-

Judgment, experience and well guided discussion are important to success.

---

*See P. Holden, C. A. Peterson, and G. E. Germane: *Top Management*, New York, McGraw Hill Book Co., 1968; R. Mann (ed.): *The Arts of Top Management*, New York, McGraw Hill Book Co., 1971, and W. Klein and D. Murphy (eds.): *Policy: Concepts in Organizational Guidance*, Boston, Little, Brown and Co., 1973.

cessful for smaller and medium-size companies.* Larger organizations, of course, may do extensive staff work with mathematical and statistical analysis, but still rely heavily on discussion and judgment.

In some cases the corporate strategy is written down as a planning document. This chapter will present an outline of such a document to illustrate the elements (or phases) of a corporate strategy. Following the outline is a discussion of various aspects of those elements or phases. The objective is to provide general direction focused on Part C of the Assessment Guides—Reformulating Corporate Strategy: Objectives for Change and the Action Plan. Subsequent chapters will provide a more specific methodology for information gathering and processing toward developing, evaluating, and implementing a corporate strategy.

General direction.

More specific methodology later.

OUTLINE OF CORPORATE STRATEGY

The outline of a corporate strategy is suggestive. It may (and should) be adapted to the particular and unique situation of the organization under consideration. The outline follows:

1. Objectives for Change

A specification of objectives with an indication of relative priority for each. The specification could include what performances (standards, limits, practices, procedures) will be enforced and reinforced or punished.

2. Analysis of Capabilities and Environment

An organizational resources analysis and potential basis of support for products or services. An indication of the desired mission or scope of activities as it may be defined by the market. Opportunities or problems in the environment.

3. Strategic Alternatives

An inventory of major strategic alternatives or major combinations of resource deployments to solve problems or exploit the opportunities. The more promising alternatives would be described by adding more specifics to one or more of the general strategic alternatives following: (a) penetration or saturation of existing markets with existing products or services; and/or (b) diversification into new markets with new products or services through internal development or acquisition; and/or (c) expansion of geographic scope of operations from local to sectional, regional or national, or into international operations; and/or (d) greater integration of the organization by adding functions formerly purchased from other organizations (e.g., switching from subcontracting to one's

---

*See F. F. Gilmore: Formulating strategy in a small organization, *Harvard Business Review,* June, 1971.

own manufacturing or data processing); and/or (e) divestiture by cutting back or selling out; and/or (f) stability by maintaining present course (but doing it better with a change in distinctive competence).

4. Corporate Policies

Policies to serve as guides to select among strategic actions in major areas. Policy areas which are likely to provide highly significant guidance and require continuing attention include: (a) concentration or mix of products/services (product policy), (b) types and characteristics of customers or clients to whom products (or services) are offered (customer policy), (c) manner in which prospective users are informed and encouraged to purchase (promotion policy), (d) method of distribution from supplier to end user (distribution policy), (e) how and what to charge for products/services (pricing policy), (f) where and how to obtain short-term and permanent capital (financial policy), (g) where and how to allocate financial resources (investment policy), (h) how to select, develop, and reward key personnel (personnel policy), and (i) how and when to review and evaluate performance (review and evaluation policy). Other policy areas, of course, may assume temporary strategic importance to an organization, e.g., labor relations at a time of intense conflict.

5. Evaluation

A forecast and analysis of the potential of the more promising alternative policies and strategies in fulfilling objectives in certain performance areas (e.g., growth, stability, flexibility, self-interests). Integrating of alternatives into a selected course of action.

6. Provisions for Procuring and Allocating Resources: Linking Overall Strategy and Operations

Provisions might include: (a) projected major long-term moves to give general direction for various functional areas or divisions, (b) specific moves detailing the resources that must be gathered and used in functional areas or divisions, (c) a timetable of the moves, including sequencing lead times, and (d) operational programs for detailing functional or divisional plans and budgets.

7. Implementation

Methods for dissemination of the corporate strategy. Role prescriptions for systematically organizing the efforts needed to carry out the decisions. Provisions for monitoring the results and modifying the plan.

FORMULATING OBJECTIVES FOR CHANGE

In previous chapters we have discussed methods for setting objectives for the organization and defining an action plan to achieve those objectives. As we pointed out in those earlier descriptions of the planning process, these two factors are continuously interrelated in a feedback loop. However, we shall now attack each of those problems and try to give some effective guides to attainment of an acceptable overall strategy.

Why objectives need to be set.

The subject of overall objectives has been discussed by many people both as to their need and their effectiveness. The question still enters the analyst's mind, however, as to exactly why objectives need to be set. There are several specific reasons that enter into the strategy-formation process. The four reasons we outline include:

1. To break psychological sets within the organization.
2. To avoid waste in generating alternatives that may not be feasible for the organization.
3. To provide a motivating force within the organization.
4. To coordinate efforts and provide for consistent operations within the organization.

Breaking psychological sets.

One of the greatest problems when attempting to alter corporate strategies is the inability of many people within the organization to change their way of thinking regarding long-range objectives of the organization. Since we are primarily talking about change in an organization, we have somehow to overcome this natural tendency to maintain the status quo. The manner in which we set objectives can help us significantly to overcome this natural inertia. Breaking psychological sets is discussed in behavioral theory to overcome this status quo image. A simple (perhaps silly) anecdote could be used to describe not only what psychological set is, but also how it can adversely affect a corporate strategy (in a "one man show" organization).

The anecdote involves a professor at a well known school of business. He was faced one day, a Friday, with the necessity of going to his office to clear up some business before he had to take both himself and his wife to the airport for a trip to another city to attend his brother-in-law's wedding. He had planned the day so that he would have plenty of time to get to his office, clear up his business, pick up his wife, and arrive at the airport well in advance of the scheduled departure time. He proceeded to the university and his office, finished his work, and then went out to his car to proceed back to his home. He hadn't progressed more than about 100 feet before he realized that there was something wrong with the car's engine. The car he was using was one of the older model Volkswagens that didn't have a fuel gauge. After it sputtered a few times he determined that he was out of gas. He then switched on the emergency tank, or what he thought was the emergency tank, only to find that the sputtering continued. But when he looked at the emergency tank switch he realized that he had been using the emergency tank all along. This meant that there was no reserve gasoline left in the car, and he was truly out of fuel.

The professor realized that he now had a problem. He had to get gas and get back to pick up his wife to take her to the airport relatively quickly. He had a margin of time left, however, so he wasn't overly worried. Fortunately he had coasted to a stop in front of a dormitory. He got out of the car and went inside the dormitory to find a telephone so he could call somebody to bring him some gas. He ran into a young student, who turned out to be a freshman, and asked the student where the nearest phone was. The student, rather bewildered at being this close to a professor at such an early point in his career, sputtered that there was a pay phone around the corner. The professor then started to turn toward the phone. Before he got far, however, he realized that he didn't have any dimes for the pay phone. He turned back and, fortunately, caught the freshman before he disappeared. He asked the young man if he had change for a quarter. The student replied that he did and began to offer him two dimes and a nickel. The professor, however, after thinking his plan out realized that he might not be able to get somebody on the phone with just two calls, so he asked the freshman for change for two quarters. The freshman replied that he only had forty cents. The business professor then, realizing that it was worth the 10 cents loss to be sure he would be able to get assistance, took the freshman's 40 cents in exchange for the two quarters (which probably, therefore, also started some young man on his merry way toward capitalism at an early age).

The professor then found the pay phone and decided the first person to call should be his wife, since she had another car at home at her disposal. He dialed his number. It was answered by a strange woman. The professor was perplexed and asked whether this was his home. The woman answered yes but that the wife wasn't in. She said that she was the baby-sitter and that the wife wouldn't be back for some time. The professor explained who he was and that he was having difficulty with his car, but before he could think of anything else to say the babysitter replied that she would tell his wife what was happening, then promptly said good-by and hung up.

Next the professor tried his wife's mother. He did reach her. However, after explaining the situation and receiving some noncomplimentary replies, she stated that she was on her way to the airport at that very moment and could not solve his problem. She added that he had better get his wife, her daughter, to the airport, with the explicit threat that, otherwise, he would never be forgiven.

At this point the professor was feeling both very pleased with himself and very worried. He was pleased that he had thought to get extra dimes and he was worried that time was now starting to become a crucial factor. He tried to think of a person who would be sympathetic with his position. The person who came to mind immediately was the husband of his wife's sister, since he would be in a relatively similar position with regards to the wedding. He then called his wife's brother-in-law at his job which was about 10 miles away. He reached his wife's brother-in-law and explained the situation to him, including the conversation with their respective mother-in-law. The brother-in-law was sympathetic with the situation and explained he would be happy to help the professor. The main problem that the brother-in-law foresaw was that he was unfamiliar with the campus at which the professor was teaching. The professor then proceeded to give him directions to the campus, including the turns to take once he got on to campus. The brother-in-law still felt that he could not find the professor without further directions. The professor then gave him some landmarks as well as names of all the streets that the brother-in-law would have to travel on. He asked his brother-in-law if he could follow the directions as far as the main entrance of the campus. The brother-in-law stated that he could, but he needed much more information from there. The professor told him that the name of the street at the entrance of the campus was University Avenue. University Avenue should be followed for a short while through one major intersection, to another. At the second major intersection there would be a stop sign and a Shell sign on the left. He should take a right on that road which was called College Drive and the professor would be waiting approximately 100 yards up College Drive on the left side of the road. The brother-in-law said he thought he understood it now and would be there shortly after getting some gas.

The professor now felt quite satisfied with himself at having hopefully arrived at a suitable and acceptable plan of action for achieving his objective of getting someone to bring him gasoline. Although there was a light drizzle now starting to fall, he decided to stand by his car in case the brother-in-law neglected to take the last turn. The professor really didn't mind the drizzle, however, since he was experiencing a warm glow of accomplishment from what he thought was a job well done. He turned to look down the road when he realized he had a new problem to solve which could very well be more difficult than the first. He now had to explain to his brother-in-law why he didn't simply walk down to the Shell gasoline station which he had used as a landmark.

The objective of this anecdote is to demonstrate the effectiveness of thoughtfully defining objectives during the strategy-formation process. If the professor had fully defined his objectives he wouldn't have run up against the problem that he eventually encountered. The professor had defined his objective as finding someone to *bring him* gasoline. If he had set as his objective getting the gasoline for his car or even getting alternative transportation he might have been able to arrive at a much more efficient solution to his problem. In setting his objective too narrowly, he had overly constrained his solutions. He had set a pattern of action out of which he could not break. In this sense he had presented himself with a *psychological set* that inhibits creative or efficient problem solving. The ideal solution, therefore, would be to set objectives that leave enough room within the decision-making process to develop effective, creative solutions to problems.

Avoiding waste.

A problem that frequently arises, however, is that many organizations go too far in the opposite direction and set objectives that are too broad in nature. These broad objectives allow the individuals within the organization to generate alternatives that are either not feasible or ineffective for that particular organization. There are many organizations that have effective constraints placed on them either through the external environment or the internal organization. To state that American Motors had an unlimited number of actions open to it in 1967, when it was faced with a potential bankruptcy problem, large amounts of short-term debt, and a declining market share, is infeasible. Therefore, the objectives set for American Motors should present individuals in a decision-making capacity within the organization with constraints that would not lead them to waste their time looking for action plans that are contrary to the environment. We can see from these two examples, the Volkswagen story and the American Motors situation, that a decision maker has to walk a tight line between setting objectives that are too broadly based or too narrowly defined.

Providing motivation.

Objectives, however, also fulfill the function of providing motivation within the organization. Built into the objective-setting process should be an understanding of incentives desired in the organization. Objectives should be broad enough to allow individuals a degree of creativity in their work process, but they should also be specific enough so that the individuals know when they are able to achieve objectives. Objectives, therefore, should be feasible enough to be reached by the people who are responsible for the decision-making process.

Coordinating efforts.

Finally, as we have stated, objectives are also designed to coordinate efforts within the organization. There are many instances in industry and elsewhere when we can see different parts of an organization working at cross purposes. An example of this comes readily to mind in the power or energy crisis that the country is now going through. All petroleum and chemical firms find that they are operating under a shortage of certain materials. They find that, in many instances, certain products are not as profitable as other products. In particular, a situation can exist in which the salesmen handling home heating oil might find it very easy to expand sales as a result of restrictions placed on installation of new natural gas lines in many states, particularly the Northeast. This allows heating oil salesmen to press for the installation of home oil heating units in new housing developments. This, however, may not lead to the best alternative use of resources for petro-chemical firms, since home fuel heating oil is not the most profitable use of their total resources.

The point is that the proper use of objectives can aid the analyst to avoid the suboptimal use of the total resources of the organization because of apparent inconsistencies in the market place. The analyst must realize, however, that objectives are not always equally important at all levels of the organization, nor are they equally important across time within the same organization.

Priority of Objectives

The top manager or top executive will be more interested in the broad-based objectives of the organization, whereas the lower level manager is more interested in specific constraints defining the objectives. Likewise, the top manager is more likely to be interested in the objective-setting phase early in the strategy-formation process as well as in the evaluation stage after plans have been set in motion. Lower level managers are much less likely to be involved in objective setting at the earlier stages, but are probably going to be involved in implementing actions to achieve those objectives.

This implies that there are different levels of objectives within an organization. The primary objectives for the organization may be broad based yet provide clear-cut measurable goals for the organization to follow. For clarity of purpose, it is probably most effective to utilize just one objective at the primary stage. For a profit-making organization this type of objective could be return on investments, earnings per share, or some similar goal.

Primary objectives.

The secondary objectives or targets may be utilized at this point to further define and constrain the analysts in achieving the primary objective. The secondary objectives for profit-making organizations would include increases in sales, quality of product, control of the organization, size of the organization, and so forth.

Secondary objectives.

In nonprofit organizations the primary goal could well be the quality or amount of service, utilization of resources for a social goal, such as increase in G. N. P. for a government agency, increase in income for welfare organizations, or others. The secondary objectives or targets for such an organization could include size of staff, efficiency of staff, use of resources, number of people assisted, and so on.

Another benefit of using primary and secondary goals is that the fine line we referred to earlier between overdefinition and underdefinition is overcome to some extent. The primary goal provides enough breadth to allow creativity within the organization. The secondary goals or objectives, however, may provide the definition necessary to guard against suboptimization within the organization.

Making Trade-offs on Objectives

Many organizations recognize the necessity of making trade-offs among various objectives in developing policy alternatives. For example, Figure 5–1 illustrates three policies that might be considered to achieve, say, a primary objective of 15 per cent earnings per share. The alternatives are (1) a high volume policy, (2) a high asset

	Approach		
Target	High Volume (%)	High Asset Utilization	Aggressive Financing
Sales growth	15.0	7.0	10.0
Profit before income tax/sales	4.0	4.0	4.0
Inventory turnover	3.5	4.0	3.5
Dividend payout	60.0	60.0	40.0
Debt/equity	50.0	50.0	60.0

Figure 5–1 *Three policies for achieving 15 per cent earnings per share. (Adapted from L. V. Gerstner, Jr.: Can strategic planning pay off? Business Horizons, 15 (No. 6):12, December, 1972.)*

Why are trade-offs necessary?

utilization policy, and (3) an aggressive financing policy. Each of the alternatives implies a fundamentally different way of operating the company, yet each set of objectives is internally consistent and may allow the organization to achieve an identical overall earning per share target. In the high volume approach, emphasis may be placed on lower prices and heavy promotion. In the high asset utilization approach, emphasis may be placed on eliminating slow-moving products. In the aggressive financing approach, dividend payout may be held back, the percentage of debt to equity increased and new products added.

The interlocking of sales, earnings and return on investment targets is recognized in each approach. While trading off lower targets here for higher targets there, it may be possible to properly integrate these targets so that alternative ways of attaining a primary objective may be identified. The alternatives most consistent with the organization's situation may be proposed in an action plan.

Problems to Overcome

As we stated earlier, the objective-setting process is part of the larger corporate strategy-formation process. Not only are the objectives and actions continuously interrelated, but also the objectives in and among themselves are part of a continuously changing process. One problem encountered by the analyst is that objectives are, in part, determined by the values or self-interests of the individuals involved in the strategy-formation process. Values, as we all well know, do change. The analyst should realize that values are going to change. If at all possible he should take advantage of this value-changing process.

More importantly, however, the analyst may attempt to change the values of individuals within the organization. There is a need for attempting to alter values when those values might seriously affect the outcome of the plans. There are many approaches that might be used. Just one example will be given here. It involves use of an isolation technique that can quite often be effective. If you have a plan that is, as is usually the case, accepted by some, rejected totally by others, but finds most people some place in the middle, then one approach would be to work first with the people who are not definitely committed one way or the other. Bringing them together in small groups with the people who are strongly in favor of your plan will isolate them from the people who are not so much in favor of it. This isolation approach may be utilized until as many people as is necessary are convinced of the value of the objectives of the strategy.*

Isolation technique.

There are several potential problems in trying to change people's values, however. If your plans are not properly laid, and you have not worked out your own alternatives, you may have raised false hopes. This problem was evident during the early 1960's within the Civil Rights movement in the United States. Early backers of the movement had not fully formulated plans for implementing their objectives of achieving racial equality. Their followers were led to believe that those objectives would be achieved immediately. When the objectives were not fulfilled relatively quickly, the disillusionment and frustrations engendered were directed not only at the leaders, but at society as a whole. Hopes had been raised that could not possibly be achieved because of the inadequate planning.

Similar problems can arise within any organization. Objectives that are set too high with regard to the resources and opportunities available to the organization often lead to frustration and mistrust by subordinates. Analysis of internal strengths and weaknesses is particularly important to enable implementation of a given plan of action.

Consider resources and opportunities in setting goals.

Also important, however, is an understanding of the total environment that the firm faces externally. Whatever plan of action is finally chosen must be achievable within the constraints placed upon the organization by the external environment. This external analysis, combined with an understanding of the resources available within the organization, should lead to combinations of strengths and opportunities around which feasible corporate strategies can be implemented.

These obvious combinations of strengths and opportunities should not be the only basis for future plans, however. The analyst should always be on the lookout for methods of turning weaknesses into strengths and threats into opportunities.

The petroleum companies exemplify this last point. They have

---

*For discussion see H. A. Hornstein, B. B. Bunker, W. W. Burke, M. Gindes, and R. J. Lewicki: *Social Intervention: A Behavioral Science Approach*, New York, The Free Press, 1971; and P. Zimbardo and E. Ebbeson: *Influencing Attitudes and Changing Behavior*, Reading, Mass., Addison-Wesley Publishing Co., 1969. Also, we shall further elaborate upon developing individual and group involvement for implementation and change in Chapter 8.

considered the governments of the oil-producing countries as a potential threat to their organizations. Some forward-looking executives in that industry, however, can now view the same countries as potential opportunities and strengths. One of the more pressing problems for the industry has been the need to generate funding for new refining capacity as well as funding for exploration for new resources. The oil-producing countries, because of their increased wealth, at the expense (we may add) of not only the consumer but also the oil or petroleum companies, now are contemplating building or buying refineries in the western market. This increase in capacity at the refining stage would assist the producers who would no longer have to be constrained by cash or capital shortages. The petroleum firms would have less need to use scarce cash resources to build refineries, and this would free their presently available capital for marketing and for exploration for new sources of supply.

Don't be constrained by obvious pairings.

If the firms properly analyze the strengths and weaknesses along with threats and opportunities, not necessarily being constrained by obvious pairings of these factors, innovative development of corporate strategies could be effected. It is quite possible that the most effective ideas and strategies come from what seem, at first glance, to be pairings of unrelated factors within the total environment of the firm.

Strategy formation, therefore, requires a thorough analysis of the total environment even at the early stage of objective setting. This will help to produce clearly formulated objectives that can be used as a base from which strategic changes may take place.

THE ACTION PLAN: SETTING STRATEGIC ALTERNATIVES

As we stated earlier, the setting of objectives for change is only one part of reformulating corporate strategy, however. Another part of the process, determining the action plan to achieve those objectives, is often the most difficult. It is usually relatively easy for individuals to set objectives for an organization; determining how to achieve those objectives effectively and efficiently, however, requires not only creative direction, but also a need for definitive detail. Frequently the problem is exacerbated by ineffective objectives. Assuming that we have set sound and effective objectives, we must now define and determine effective alternative methods to achieve those objectives.

Develop contingency alternatives.

The question may be asked as to why we are suggesting that alternative actions be proposed as opposed to a single action approach. The setting of alternatives allows the analyst some contingency in the eventuality that one of his plans of action is unacceptable for some reason. Too often we neglect the generation of distinctive alternatives. In the final planning process we may find that we do not actually choose one total plan of action from among the alternatives proposed, but rather that we pick and choose from several sets of proposals. In this manner a corporate strategy is chosen that is not only consistent and feasible, but also is acceptable to more individuals within the organization responsible for strategic decisions.

These alternatives may need to be created rapidly and at a relatively low cost. However, we know from experience that the process of creativity is not necessarily rapid. It also does not always come at low cost. The organization, however, may be interested in defining alternatives that are both creative and effective without wasting the resources of the organization in the mere determination of these alternatives.

An effective analysis of the total environment will help the analyst in determining which action plans fail to satisfy constraints posed by the environment. The analyst will also save valuable political energy by not having to press for changes that would not be feasible or acceptable. As a result of this analysis the analyst will know which values actually need to be changed to obtain a commitment to the favored action plan associated with a corporate strategy.

Developing and Profiling Alternatives

Major Opportunities

Frequently a determination needs to be made whether there are major opportunities or product/market/customer segments, other than those presently being served, that would fit the organization and utilize its competitive strength. In addition, creative alternatives beyond the "limits" imposed by the organization's ability or inability to operate in the area may be a most important consideration.

The monitoring of the environment gives an indication of problems, opportunities and threats that the organization may face. *Generate ideas.* The importance of the generation of ideas about specific fields of endeavor in which to engage is stressed here. From the preliminary questioning the analyst will have a general, overall view of the organization and its current position in the environment. Then he will work toward creating, through an iterative process, feasible strategic moves by matching strengths with opportunities and suppressing or overcoming weaknesses and threats. As indicated, ideas may come from many sources both outside and inside the organization. For example, customers or clients or potential customers may be helpful if they are asked about their own self-interests; that is, what specific wants or needs can be satisfied effectively and efficiently now or in the future by the supplying organization? What scope or dimensions of the market might be overlooked?

Systematic forecasting of what competitors are likely to do, mentioned before, is something more and more organizations are starting to do. The use of the informal communications network of informed people is an effective method of generating such strategy information. We shall discuss this source of information (and others) in the next chapter.

Given the right support and assuming appropriate competence, research and development staffs within the organization will, of course, provide some ideas. If a policy analyst is going to be successful in improving the search process among the line and staff members he needs conditions to overcome blocks to idea production. One important block is the lack of ease felt by some participants in their dependency relationships to others in the organization. In group problem solving, for example, for some individuals to participate effectively in the work of the group, there needs to be a permissive, informal atmosphere. Otherwise, they may not be sure where they stand and fear immediate evaluation or devaluation of their ideas.* The supportive work environment† and the freedom to make honest mistakes does not mean that quality standards are reduced; the internal environment should make it seem natural and easy to express ideas in the search for additional or alternative endeavors.

Even brainstorming may be used on occasion to improve the idea production climate. Evaluation and criticism of any presented idea is supposed to be withheld during the brainstorming session. The orientation is on quantity of output of ideas for later synthesis and evaluation. Brainstorming is an example of the staging process that is associated with effective problem solving.‡ A manager or analyst may find it to his advantage in generating alternatives to state or to separate idea forming from idea testing in his individual or group problem-solving experience. One danger that should be mentioned in group sessions is the occasional occurrence of a common perceptual set or similar way of seeing policies and alternatives.§ Frequently various individuals or interest groups will be pushing and politicking for their own alternatives. The various audits of the environment and perceptions of the reward system and self-interests tend to generate alternatives competing for allocations of resources.

Students doing a case analysis or a field investigation will want

---

*See C. Argyris: Interpersonal barriers to decision making, *Harvard Business Review, 44* (No. 2):84–97, March–April, 1966.

†This environment may not be easy to attain. Various approaches have been suggested: Laboratory training, feedback, group therapy, systemic change. For a discussion of these and other methods see D. Katz and R. L. Kahn: *The Social Psychology of Organizations,* New York, John Wiley & Sons, Inc., 1966; and J. P. Campbell and M. Dunnette: Effectiveness of T-group experiences in managerial training and development. *Psychological Bulletin, 70:*73–104, August, 1968.

‡N. R. F. Maier and A. R. Solem: Improving solutions by turning choice situations in problems, *Personal Psychology,* 1962, pp. 151–157.

§M. Dunnette, J. Campbell and K. Jansted: The effect of group participation on brainstorming effectiveness for two industrial samples, *Journal of Applied Psychology, 47:*30–37, 1963.

to put themselves in the position of the manager to the greatest extent possible, gather and interpret relevant, accessible information,
and do some creative thinking about alternative fields of endeavor
for the organization.

Keep an open mind.

It seems important, then, to keep an open mind in generating
promising fields of endeavor that exist or may exist in the future.
However, we do need to check whether these product/service/mar-
ket/customer/geographic area segments fit our current basic missions and utilize or go beyond our current basis of support.

Obvious Limitations

While we should be careful about ruling out alternatives, it may
be helpful to consider whether the organization has obvious limitations in terms of environmental demands or requirements for success. To illustrate let us take one example of financial strength and
one of raw material strength.

Financial strength. Industries such as steel, public utilities, oil
refining and chemicals require large amounts of capital to build efficient facilities; therefore, it is foolish for small organizations to
even list this sort of action as a "field of endeavor." An example in
reverse is the large chemical company which, because it was producing the basic plastic sheets, attempted to make and sell decorated
shower curtains. The firm lost heavily on the experiment because
the smaller shower curtain manufacturers and distributors could
change their styles and policies more rapidly, meeting retailer
demands for many product variations and styles.

Raw material strength. Organizations that own or have as-
sured access to basic raw material resources can realistically consider business that requires these resources. As examples one need
only look at the history of the metal and petroleum companies.
Chemical and paper manufacturers usually attempt to control timber
resources. Large wallboard manufacturers usually control sources
of gypsum rock.

Narrowing the Choice

We may wish to narrow the choice of alternative strategic
moves by identifying the more promising kinds of activities with,
say, market dominance and growth possibilities. A forecast and
analysis of the potential of the endeavor(s) in fulfilling objectives in
the performance areas of interest may be made. Performances of
leading firms in an industry offer indications of industry potential. In
addition, developing a profile of the more promising strategic alternatives is an early action to consider. It could include:

Profile alternatives.

Conditions of entry (e.g., competitors, magnitude of the market,
capital requirements)

Preliminary break-even analysis

Simulation of first operating year (e.g., profit and loss, balance
sheet, cash flow)

Return on investment

In many cases it makes sense to start this profile planning earlier than one is seemingly "ready" to do it. The figures generated may bear little precise relationship to those on subsequent documents, but the earlier this requirement is made the sooner the proposed kinds of activities will be disciplined into financially sound and complete proposals.

Such evaluation of alternatives may be done readily with computer programs, which will be discussed in Chapter 7.

Synergistic Possibilities

It may be desirable to test possible combinations of the more promising fields of endeavor with each other. A more thorough analysis is arrived at by generating more alternatives combining fields of endeavor. These alternatives again are evaluated with respect to feasibility (e.g., flexibility, service, stability, growth, self-interest). Combined profiles of conditions of entry, break-even analysis, simulations of first year operations, and return on investment may be developed and analyzed for synergistic possibilities. A simple example of *synergy* is building a restaurant with a motel. Synergy arises when the two actions performed jointly produce a greater result than they would if performed independently. The motel contributes business to the restaurant and the restaurant makes the motel a more convenient place to stay. Synergy may be sought in the transfer of technical know-how; for example, skills and knowledge acquired on a government-military contract hopefully will be applicable to civilian business. The learning period, again hopefully, would be much shorter.

Test synergy.

There may be negative synergy; that is, the combination of two or more fields may have a negative impact.* We shall use an example of a debatable case of negative synergy. Some insurance specialists argue that if you combine variable annuities with established types of life insurance, the association of the two will lead to substantial reduction in life insurance sales. The rationale is that the life insurance image of stability and sureness would suffer from being associated with a gamble or speculation (variable annuities). More experience is needed to come to a firm conclusion as to whether, in this instance, the synergy would be positive or negative. However, the point is to examine carefully combinations of the more promising fields of endeavors for the advantages and disadvantages of the joint activity.

Negative synergy?

A brief inventory and profile of alternative endeavors, opportunities and synergistic possibilities may be constructed. This, together with an indication of the expected competitive advantage or basis for support may be included in the action plan.

---

*W. Newman and J. Logan: *Strategy, Policy and Central Management*, Cincinnati, Ohio, South-Western Co., 1971.

Strategic Changes and Corporate Policies

The alternatives to be considered in the action plan, however, will be affected by the market share-growth condition that the organization or division finds itself in. Important examples of how corporate strategies are changed and reformulated under various conditions can be derived using the matrix illustrated in Figure 5-2, Checking the Strategic Mix. The vertical columns differentiate between companies or products with high or low market shares in their industry. The horizontal rows differentiate between industries with high and low growth potential.

Check market share — growth conditions.

Many new firms start out in the upper righthand quadrant (I). They start initially with a new product (or service) in a new or growing industry (a single-product policy). As such their market share is low, but the growth potential is high. Their main objective for change is to move over to the upper left quadrant (II). Here, they have penetrated to become a dominant factor in a high growth industry. Eventually, if the product follows the typical maturation process, the firm will drop into the lower left quadrant (III).

Determine cost advantage of accumulating experience.

At this point the firm should consider restructuring its corporate strategy to accommodate a changed environment. Previously the firm may have needed a finance policy of acquiring large amounts of resources from external sources to keep pace with its rapid growth. Now the firm may find that the effect of accumulated experience on costs allows it to produce its own excess resources for expansion.*

---

*For a discussion of the effects of experience on costs, see Boston Consulting Group: *Experience Curves as a Planning Tool*, Boston, Massachusetts, Boston Consulting Group, 1972, pp. 8–9.

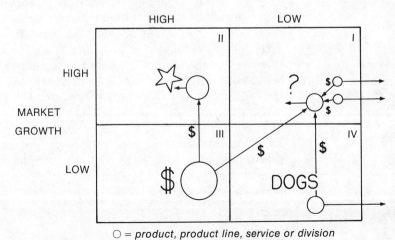

$\bigcirc$ = product, product line, service or division
Diameter of $\circ$ = annual volume
$\square\rightarrow$ = divest

Figure 5-2 *Checking the Strategic Mix. The authors are indebted to the Boston Consulting Group, from whose presentation at Stanford University this matrix was derived.*

What direction should the corporate strategy take?

What direction should the corporate strategy take? The organization may be guided by an investment policy of taking its excess resources and applying them to promising new quadrant I firms or products. The decision pattern in this case may indicate a diversification strategy through acquisition or development. Alternatively, the firm may invest in propitious quadrant II firms or products. In this case the firm may be attempting a penetration strategy through extra promotion or lower pricing. The firm may attempt to (1) expand its geographic scope and/or (2) improve its competence, say in distribution. The hope is to find the right combination of resources and products that will follow the path to excess resources and not tumble into the lower right quadrant (IV).*

The corporate strategy, therefore, has to be restructured as the firm (or division) follows a path from I, eventually, to IV. A comment here would be that at the stage at which maturation is about to progress from III to IV, a new corporate strategy would be desirable. Emphasis at this stage could be on preparing the product or division for divestiture. At this stage additional expenditures might be limited to only those making the division more appealing to potential purchasers.

Summary of changes.

Summarizing the strategic changes implied by the matrix, we have followed an organization from the inception of an idea through to the demise of the product or service. Each of the positions in which the organization finds itself requires a different emphasis in its corporate strategy. The early stage requires large inputs of resources and attention to shifting competitive and demand forces. Quadrant II requires a shift to maintaining dominance with only a few competitors (after a shake out period). At this stage, however, the revenues now starting to accrue still are not enough to offset the continued demands for resources brought on by rapid growth.

A corporate strategy for the mature organization (Quadrant III) is to maintain its stable position while supplying excess resources to the products or divisions in Quadrants I and II. Moreover, it has to constantly re-evaluate its market position so that it can divest itself of areas that threaten to lapse into a Quadrant IV position.

Provide guidelines for resource allocation.

Strong central control may be necessary to effectively carry out the revaluation and divestiture procedure. The person in charge of divisions or products moving into Quadrant IV is not likely to plan himself out of business. He may be more likely to argue that new growth is just around the corner; he may argue for additional promotion or other expenditures to get this payoff; he may devise calculations that actually meet the financial hurdle established on a traditional capital budgeting basis.

---

*See C. Hofer: *Some Preliminary Research on Patterns of Strategic Behavior.* Professional papers of the Academy of Management, Division of Business Policy and Planning, Boston, 1973. His preliminary research with a small sample (N-41) of firms indicates that changes in distinctive competence and/or geographic scope were more important aspects of corporate strategy for a significant proportion of the firms than were changes in product/market scope.

The central policy maker(s) may need to set explicit corporate policies or guidelines to follow in the overall resource allocation process. Use may be made of the simple but powerful approach of sorting products, services or divisions into the four broad *portfolio* categories (or Quadrants): I, sources of growth (future earnings); II, sources of intermediate earnings; III, sources of current earnings; and IV, potential divestitures (immediate cash flow). Using these categories to consider various parts of the enterprise as a group, policy makers are aided in checking that available resources do not flow to a mediocre division or product line at a rate equal to or greater than a high potential division.

Use portfolio approach.

Alternatively, there may be a concentration of the excess resources on a limited number of ventures where there are hopes to capture a large share of a fast-growing market. A limited number of new ventures may be desirable because of the fact that spreading resources among too many alternatives may result in a lack of market dominance for any of them. The solid dominant "winners" in the portfolio are likely to move to a cost and market position (Quadrant III) where they can provide excess resources for keeping a cycle of new ventures coming along.*

Seek dominant winners with cost and pricing advantages.

The organization, if it is at all diversified, needs to consider the balance of its portfolio among Quadrants I, II, III & IV. Particular attention needs to be given to the cash appetites and the cash flows of various divisions and/or product lines in the quadrants. It is true that debt can be used to finance successful growth and thus have a favorable effect on return on equity; it is also true that incurring heavy debt to finance new ventures with high cash appetites may be quite foolhardy, given the environmental uncertainties reducing the possibilities of attaining a dominant "winner." The organization may be wise to avoid acquiring substantial funds from the outside. Rather, it may attempt to move toward a balanced portfolio position which allows some reliance on reallocation of internal resources, as indicated in Figure 5-2.

Considerations of overall resource allocation guidelines and financing arrangements are not the only policy implications of a portfolio approach. The impact may be felt in many of the strategic or action moves made for individual divisions or product lines. For example, a Quadrant IV division may be managed for high asset utilization. A high asset utilization approach may emphasize elimination of low contribution products/varieties, adding products that

What are some other policy implications?

---

*For a discussion of market dominance see H. Boyd: Experience Curves, Pricing, and Strategic Planning. Paper presented at Stanford-Sloan Alumni Conference, October, 1972. See also S. Schoeffler: *Profit Impact of Marketing Strategy*. Marketing Science Institute, internal memorandum, November, 1972. His research on 35 manufacturing firms indicates that the desirable strong market position is expensive to obtain, especially when there is a market slowdown, the number of customers is low, the customer importance is uniform, and the business has a medium position to begin with. Also, earning position by high relative quality seems to be less expensive than "buying" it with low relative price.

are only sure winners, avoiding promotion expenditures and raising prices even at the expense of volume.

Strategic moves for a Quadrant I product line or division may include adding extensions to the product line by acquisition or development, promoting heavily and lowering prices to build market shares. In a Quadrant III division there might be a shift in the product line to higher profit product categories. An illustration for Quadrant II would be targeting efforts to build market dominance in the high growth segments.

There are, of course, numerous other variations, depending on individual organizational circumstances.* For example, different types of pricing policies could be incorporated in the action plan to take advantage of environmental opportunities.

If the firm is well ahead of competitors in developing new products, it might opt for a "*skimming*" pricing policy. This type of policy allows the firm to take advantage of lack of competition by setting high prices for the short term. This skimming price policy encourages the development of competitive products, however. The originating firm may not have gathered enough brand loyalty to maintain its dominance of the market. What frequently follows is severe price competition and a shake out of marginal firms (sometimes including the originating firm). This eventually leads to stabilization within the industry, with a much smaller number of competitors.

An alternative pricing policy would be to charge a price for the product that is based on favorable costs of production. The originating firm should be able to maintain its *dominance-oriented pricing* in the industry provided it can continue to improve its efficiency as it gathers experience. There is a risk that the firm will not be able to determine the proper price to set. Too high a price will encourage competition; too low a price will unduly restrict profits.

Whatever policy is chosen, the firm must constantly evaluate the position of the product in the maturation cycle. Changes in the direction, not only of pricing, but also of the product itself, must be made at each stage of the product cycle, from initiation through maturation and demise.

Check the research for ideas.

These several examples of change-oriented strategies and policies are designed to demonstrate the need for an effective set of strategic moves in the overall strategy. The manager or analyst uses his knowledge of, say, marketing, finance and/or management to de-

---

*See W. Freehan: Pyrrhic victories in fights for market share. *Harvard Business Review*, Sept-Oct., 1972. His research indicates that for some organizations (or divisions) it may not be economically worthwhile to seek to increase market share through internal expansion. This tended to be the case where (1) extremely heavy financial resources are required; (2) the expansion strategy may have to be cut off abruptly; and (3) regulatory agencies continuously place new restrictions on the types of competitive behavior which firms can follow. Freehan analyzed the main-frame computer industry, the retail grocery industry and the domestic air transport industry.

velop strategic moves appropriate for the organization or division under consideration.*

Detailing Provisions for Procuring and Allocating Resources: Linking Overall Strategy with Operations

The action plan that is developed will consist of different levels of detail. It will include short-range operations linked with long-range moves, both aimed at achieving objectives for change.

Detail varies with level and with time dimension.

The long-range segments of the plan are usually more general in nature. They provide the overall direction for the strategy as a whole. They are designed to outline the general directions that are expected to be followed by the various functional areas within the organization (e.g., distribution through direct sales force).

The short-range or operational aspects of the plan are designed to provide specific moves within these functional areas (e.g., number, type, and location of specific sales outlets to be developed). Along these lines, specific budgets detailing the resources that must be gathered and used during the action phase of the corporate strategy are needed. Included in this detailed action plan, typically, is a projection of the timing and sequence of these moves.

Timing is a critical factor.

Timing of the various moves included in the corporate strategy can often provide the critical factor in determining the success or failure of the actions. It is possible that the electronics firms we discussed in Chapter 1 could have had a higher probability of success had they been able to better determine the proper time to implement their moves. In some instances the firms just had not properly charted the relationship of the various phases of their corporate strategies from a timing standpoint, with regard to the total environment.

The amount of time required to implement many actions often comes as a surprise to managers as well as to students. New plants are not built or obtained overnight. Additional labor cannot be hired, trained and inserted into productive positions on short notice. Financial resources usually take time to muster (particularly if the need is acute). These factors must be considered if feasible corporate strategies are to be formulated.

In larger organizations, the action plan, similar to the objectives phase, involves different levels of management at different stages of its formation. These levels of management are also interested in different levels of detail of the action plan. Figure 5–3 demonstrates possible relationships.

---

*Schoeffler's research indicates some other examples; i.e., (1) if a business has a strong market position, it can further enhance profitability by increasing its product differentiation, maintaining a high debt/equity ratio, and maintaining a stable capacity/market ratio; and (2) trading increased short/term earnings for a diminished market share is feasible when there is a market slowdown, competitive position is weak, relative quality is high, and the number of customers and purchase frequency are low.

Management Level	Detail Level	Stages of Development
Top (Strategic) ↓	Direction ↑	Formation; evaluation
Middle (Coordinative) ↓	Functional or divisional plans ↑	Information
Lower (Operating)	Budget estimates	Implementation

Figure 5–3

The figure shows that top management decides on general directions of the corporate strategy at the early phases of the formation process.* This management level also evaluates the end product before it has to be implemented. Middle managers develop functional or divisional plans based on information they have been charged to gather. These plans are combined into the total action plan; they are derived from budget estimates supplied by lower levels of management.

Determine roles and programs needed at various levels and at various stages.

As we can see, the level of detail of the action plan increases as we go down the organization. The comprehensiveness of the plan increases as we go back up the organization, however. The responsibility for the various levels of detail incorporated within the action plan may need to be denoted prior to implementation of a formal strategy-formation process.

The organization must be designed to facilitate strategy formation at all stages of the process. This necessitates a knowledge of the role expected of all levels of the organization if the process is to proceed without extensive confusion.

Inclusion of various programs can help to ensure the success of this process at all levels. Top management may use a general information-processing program to generate objectives and direction for the firm. The result would be equivalent to the Univis Creed reproduced in the Appendix to Chapter 1, p. 33. Top management may also be expected to review all operating guidelines as well. At Univis, Inc., this would include an analysis of the document stating the standards for risk calculation. Also, they may perform overall review of the total corporate strategy such as the one alluded to in the text of the Univis case.

It becomes apparent by reading the comments of the various executives in this case that some are, at best, paying lip service to some of these roles. It is doubtful whether they even understand

---

*The roles at various levels of management are not completely understood at this time. J. L. Bower, for example, has observed a "bottom up" process operating in such a way that undesirable projects are screened before they get to top management. Hence, the actual role of top management in strategy formation generally may be one of approval. See J. L. Bower: *Managing the Resource Allocation Process,* Cambridge, Harvard University Press, 1970.

the content of some of the documents being generated by the planning process. The planning program probably should have been presented in a form that was acceptable to and more readily understood by those concerned.

Other levels of management also require programs to assist them during the strategy-formation process. As we noted earlier, they are more involved in filling in detail to the overall strategy reviewed by top management.

Typically, the operational programs used by middle or lower management involve a detailing of functional or divisional plans. Two examples of the types of programs they might use to facilitate the flow of information are presented in Figures 5–4, Division Five-Year Plans and 5–5, Financial Summary. These forms provide summary information to appropriate levels of management concerning resources and timing needed to achieve objectives which may already be agreed upon.

These forms show some estimates that may be needed so that corporate strategy could be transformed into long-range (two to five years) plans, or reflected immediately in short-range (one year) operations.

Develop estimates.

In a divisionalized company the general manager may be delegated authority to do environmental and capabilities analysis for his product line or service. This analysis would be used, together with whatever objectives, policies and other inputs he gets from headquarters, to make his long-range plans. A close linkage may be developed between overall corporate strategy and the subobjectives and substrategies developed by the division manager.

Environmental and capabilities analysis in each division?

It may be advisable, as well, to have a close link between the first year of the long-range plans and the short-range operational budget summary. Such a link may help to keep long-range plans realistic. However, such a tight relationship may divert attention from long-range to short-range matters, such as this year's rate of return. As described earlier, this may present a serious problem if the manager involved sees his rewards based primarily on short-term results (e.g., he may avoid developmental expenditures). If the organization is serious about its long-range plans, care needs to be taken to see that those plans are reflected in the current operational budget making.

How close a link?

In addition, various flow-charting and critical path techniques* may be used to link or integrate the necessary resource procurements and allocations with timing and sequencing of specific moves. For example, devising plans for implementation requires a detailed accounting of the personnel who will be required at each stage. The various financial and nonfinancial resources necessary to implement

---

*Examples of these techniques would be PERT (Program Evaluation and Review Techniques), first formulated for the U.S. Navy, and CPM (Critical Path Method).

Figure 5-4 *Division Five-Year Plans**

Item	This Year Last Year	This Year Forecast	Next Five Years First Year	Second Year	Third Year	Fourth Year	Fifth Year
Sales							
Marketing Expenditures							
Advertising							
Distribution							
Unit Production							
Employees							
Total							
Direct							
Indirect							
R & D Outlays							
New Products							
Product Improvement							
Cost Reduction							
New Facilities (Total)							
Expansion Present Prod.							
New Products							
Cost Reduction							
Maintenance							

*From G. A. Steiner: *Comprehensive Managerial Planning*, Oxford, Ohio, Planning Executives Institute, 1972, p. 17.

Figure 5-5 *Financial Summary**

DIVISION: _____

	This Year	19__	19__	19__	19__	19__
Sales—Units						
Gross Sales—Dollars						
Allowances						
Net Sales						
Cost of Goods Sold						
Gross Profit on Sales						
G & A Expense						
Selling Expense						
Advertising Expense						
R & D Expense						
Total Operating Expense						
Other Charges, Net						
Interest on Long-term Obligations						
Other						
Income Before Depreciation						
Depreciation						
Income Before Overhead Allocation						
Allocation of General Overhead						
Net Income Before Taxes						
Rate of Return on Assets						

*Source: *Ibid.* Page 19.

the corporate strategy must be budgeted so that they are available when they are needed. These can all be included in an overall planning chart with cash flows, cash appetites and key manpower requirements and assignments. The PERT chart in Figure 5–6 illustrates simply the tracing of a product development process from the early strategic decision stage through the shipping of the first product run.

Purpose of programs.

One purpose of all these programs is to provide the policy analyst with a method for determining the effectiveness of his plans at all levels of the organization. These programs are not meant to be unchanging; however, environmental factors do change. These changes should be reflected in the program as it is used for implementation purposes. The risk analysis exhibit referred to in the Univis case, as an example, must be revised as the perceptions of top management change. Just because Figures 5–4 and 5–5 are phrased in terms of annual projections does not preclude their being changed more frequently than annually. All these programs should provide the various levels of management with "bench marks" for evaluation of the progress of the corporate strategy. The programs, therefore, may be useful not only during the formation phase of corporate strategy, but also during the various evaluation and implementation phases as well.

A COMPUTER PROGRAM FOR REFORMULATING CORPORATE STRATEGY

The previous comments have demonstrated the possible need for a well thought out and clearly defined action plan if corporate

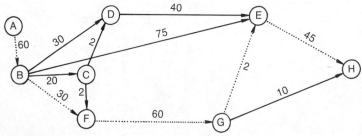

Events

A. Decision to add product
B. Engineering work completed
C. Financing arranged
D. Material purchase orders placed
E. Production started
F. Sales campaign arranged
G. Initial orders received
H. Initial orders shipped

A simplified PERT chart. Events—that is, the start or completion of a step—are indicated by circles. Arrows show the sequence between events. The time (in days) required to move from one event to another appears on each arrow. The critical path—the longest sequence (A→B→F→G →E→H)—is shown by the dotted lines (197 days).

Figure 5–6 *From W. H. Newman, C. E. Summer and E. K. Warren: The Process of Management, 3rd ed., Englewood Cliffs, N.J., Prentice-Hall, 1972, p. 617.*

strategy formation is to be a success. We have discussed some of the ingredients that make up a strong action plan. How to put these ingredients together is often an insurmountable problem for many analysts, however.

One method for overcoming this problem may be to use a heuristic computer program such as the STRATANAL technique discussed briefly in Chapter 3. Basically this program relies on a sound and thorough analysis of the "total environment" facing the organization.

The program then leads the analyst through a decision process of choosing the right mix of factors for an efficient corporate strategy. The program, through an interactive question and answer technique, requires the analyst to start with a re-examination of the basic objectives and mission of the firm, taking into consideration the effects of environmental trends and organizational capabilities. *Phases in program.*

The analyst then is asked to develop moves and actions covering short- and long-range time periods. Based on these initial alternatives, he is then pressed to include an innovative approach to any changing trends, either internally or externally. These various alternative plans are then supposed to be combined to present the organization with the best overall combination of actions.

At this point the program draws upon the previously stated environmental analysis to allow the analyst to test his combined action plan. This builds an evaluation phase into the process to ensure consistency between the various parts of the corporate strategy.

The final phases of the program are designed to help the analyst to evaluate the feasibility and efficiency of the newly designed corporate strategy. During this phase, the analyst is asked to fill in details required for implementing the strategy. This requires the analyst to determine if resources critical to the successful implementation of the corporate strategy are available. It also tests the acceptability of the total plan to key individuals.

A key factor employed in the program is an analysis of the replies by the analyst to determine if he has understood the planning process or format up to that point. Various prompts and supplemental questions are used if the analytical part of the program determines they are necessary for a better understanding of the strategy formation process.

Figure 5–7 follows the basic path taken by the STRATANAL program. The various analytical responsive points have not been included, however.

How effective are such programs? It is too early to make a positive conclusion. They do have merit; they do show promise. There is some evidence, however, to suggest that such programs at the present time are *not* significantly influencing the strategy-formation process within the firm.* In other words, for various reasons that we *Caution!*

---

*See W. K. Hall: Strategic planning models: Are top managers really finding them useful? *Journal of Business Policy,* 3 (No. 2):33–42, 1973.

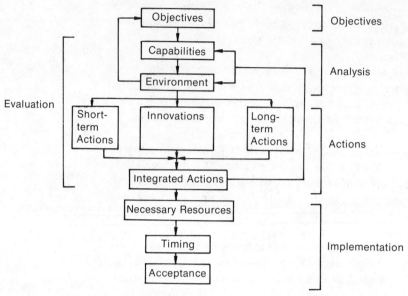

Figure 5-7 *The STRATANAL Program. (Source: W. Naumes.)*

shall discuss later (in Chapter 7) many top managers are not really finding them useful. Some modifications in content or methodology may be necessary.

SUMMARY

Corporate strategy is an integrative concept. As we have used the term here it refers to several elements (i.e., objectives for change, analysis of capabilities and environment, strategic actions, corporate policies, evaluation, detailing of provisions for procuring and allocating resources, and implementation) patterned into a reasonably unified whole. The process by which this unification is brought about is a continuous one involving redefining the organizational objectives and actions to adjust to a complex, ever-changing competitive environment. In earlier chapters it was seen that objective formulation is an interaction process between the structure and its environment and that the manager is a link between that structure and environment. The manager may initiate the development of objectives for change and an action plan to attain these objectives. Inevitably, as these actions are carried out they will be affected by influencers, technocrats, other managers, customers and competitors. These "others" will affect what priority of objectives is actually followed, what proposals and calculations are made, what performances are enforced and reinforced or punished, what policies are in fact relevant, and what products or services are supported. Therefore, corporate strategy development is a dynamic process that requires diligent consideration for effective performance of the manager's role.

In this chapter we stress some initiatives that a manager or analyst may take in reformulating that corporate strategy. They should be viewed as building upon the situational analysis suggested in the previous chapter. With a general overall view of the organization and its current position in the environment in mind, the analyst will work toward creating, through an iterative process, a feasible corporate strategy.

Various considerations in initiating corporate strategy are discussed. We have seen how a well laid set of objectives can be used as an agent for inducing change in an organization. The set also provides a unifying influence for individuals who are charged with forming and implementing action plans. Trade-offs among objectives may be made in developing various ways of operating the business.

Examples of how alternative strategies and policies may be changed and reformulated were given. We followed an organization through periods of change from the inception of an idea to various stages of growth and decline. The various positions the organization found itself in should suggest to the manager or analyst useful strategic changes in resource allocation (e.g., penetration, diversification, integration, divestiture and stability). The portfolio approach is highlighted. Several major policy areas that need continuing attention are suggested. We also stressed the need for initiating provisions for procuring and allocating resources, considering long- and short-term moves, timing, degree of detail and management involvement at various stages of development. Various operational programs for detailing of functional or divisional plans and budgets are presented. While the development of a corporate strategy is usually done following a rather loosely defined strategy planning program of considering in an iterative fashion the several elements previously discussed, another approach is possible. A computer program such as STRATANAL is designed to lead the analyst through the strategy and policy-formation process. The approach provides a framework for developing corporate strategy.

Portfolio approach is highlighted.

In summary, this chapter and the previous one give general guidance in formulating objectives for change and an action plan to reach those objectives. A more specific methodology for information gathering and processing aimed at developing and evaluating as well as implementing corporate strategy is given in subsequent chapters.

DISCUSSION QUESTIONS

1. What are the purposes for setting well designed strategic objectives?

2. Who is involved in setting strategic objectives? At what stages of the strategy-formation process?

3. Discuss the portfolio approach to resource allocation.

4. Discuss alternative policies suggested by trading-off various objectives.

5. Discuss the inputs affecting objectives.

6. What problems are encountered when attempting to change values?

7. Discuss the strategic changes and corporate policies presented in this chapter. Use your previous knowledge of marketing, finance and management.

8. Why are alternative action plans needed within the strategy formation process? What are the key factors necessary in generating these alternatives?

9. Discuss the participation expected of various levels of management when setting alternative action plans. How does the timing of the participation differ throughout the organization?

10. How can dynamic computer programs be designed to help the analyst develop corporate strategies? What steps should these programs follow in this process?

11. What timing techniques can be used to help in setting and implementing action moves?

Suggested Additional References for Further Research

Burns, T., and Stalker, G. M.: *The Management of Innovation.* 2nd ed. London, Tavistock Publications, Ltd., 1966.

Chesser, R. J.: *The Development of Behavioral Change Models of MBO Reflecting Moderation Effects of Personality Characteristics.* Presented at the Academy of Management, Boston, 1973.

Cooper, A. C., DeMuzzio, E., Hatten, K., Hicks, E. J., and Tock, D.: *Strategic Responses to Technological Threats.* Professional papers of the Academy of Management, Division of Business Policy and Planning, Boston, 1973.

Elbing, A. O.: *Behavioral Decisions in Organizations.* Glenview, Ill., Scott, Foresman & Co., 1970.

Elbing, A. O., Jr., and Elbing, C. J.: The Value Issue of Business. New York, McGraw-Hill Book Co., Inc., 1967.

Gilmore, F. F.: Overcoming the perils of advocacy in corporate planning. *California Management Review 15*(No 3):127–137, Spring, 1973.

Gross, B.: What are your organization's objectives? A general systems approach to planning, *Human Relations 18* (No. 3), Aug., 1965.

Hofer, C. W.: *Some Preliminary Research on Patterns of Strategic Behavior.* Professional Papers of The Academy of Management, Division of Business Policy and Planning, Boston, 1973.

Howell, R.: Plan to integrate your acquisitions. *Harvard Business Review,* Nov.-Dec., 1970.

Johnson, S., and Jones, C.: How to organize for new products, *Harvard Business Review, 35* (No. 3), 1957.

Kitching, J.: Why do mergers miscarry? *Harvard Business Review,* November/December, 1967.

Mace, M. L.: The president and corporate planning, *Harvard Business Review, 43*:49–62, January/February, 1965.

Moder, J. J., and Phillips, C. R.: *Project Management with CPM and PERT.* 2nd ed. New York, Van Nostrand Reinhold Company, 1970.

Nemhauser, G. L.: *Introduction to Dynamic Programming.* New York, John Wiley & Sons, Inc., 1966.

Rucker, L.: Using computer models for short- and long-range planning: A case study, *The Business Quarterly 34*:29–37, Autumn, 1969.

Schein, E. H.: Organizational socialization and the profession of management, *Industrial Management Review,* Winter, 1968.

Shuford, E. H., Jr.: A computer-based system for aiding decision making. *In* Spiegel, J., and Walker, D.E. (eds.): *Information System Sciences.* Washington, D.C., Spartan Books, Inc., 1965.

Stagner, R.: Corporate decision making: An empirical study, *Journal of Applied Psychology 53*:1–13, 1969.

Stevenson, H.: Defining Corporate Strengths and Weaknesses: An Exploratory Study. Unpublished doctoral dissertation, Harvard Business School, March, 1969.

Tosi, H. L., and Carroll, S. J.: Some structural factors related to goal influence in the management by objectives process, *MSU Business Topics 17* (No. 2):45–50, 1969.

Wynne, B. E., Jr.: CPM – An effective management Tool. *The Controller,* June, 1962.

WHY ASSESSMENT AND
DEVELOPMENT?

EVALUATION APPROACHES

WHAT IS AN ORGANIZATION
DEVELOPMENT APPROACH TO
POLICY FORMATION?

ACTION-RESEARCH PROGRAM

USE AND LIMITATIONS OF METHODS

INFORMATION GATHERING AND
PROCESSING
    Forecasts
    Publications and Reports
    Informal Information Networks

Observation
Interviews
    Interview Item Content
    Sample of Structured
      Interview
Questionnaire
    Questionnaire Item Content
    Content Related to
      Organization Effectiveness
    Policy-Formation Practices
      Questionnaire
Breakout of Returns and Use of
    Results
Market Segmentation
    Breakouts

SUMMARY

6

ASSESSMENT AND DEVELOPMENT METHODS—AN ACTION-RESEARCH PROGRAM

Until now we have discussed conceptualizing and learning about the strategy-formation process and have provided a program (or a set of programs) for improving corporate strategy making. But this general guidance and discussion must be supplemented with a more specific methodology directed toward developing a self-renewing, self-correcting strategy formation system—a system that will continue to expand and improve the choices available to and made by the organization as it copes with changing demands and challenges from the environment. As we have indicated, the organization goes through (perhaps informally) a more or less continuous process of evaluation, choice, coordination, implementation and re-evaluation.

You should be able to discuss models of evaluation, an organizational development approach, and information gathering and processing.

In this chapter we shall discuss, first, some models of evaluation and, second, an organization development approach to strategy formation. The organization development approach suggested includes a diagnostic phase that is data based. The data collection and analysis methods in this book are separated into those methods primarily associated with the behavioral sciences and those primarily associated with management science. In this chapter we shall cover some behavioral science methods; in the next, we shall cover some management science methods. In Chapter 8 the data generated and analyzed are designed to be useful as input to overall assessment and development activities.

The purpose of this and the next two chapters is to provide a readily available methodology for consideration by policy analysts or managers. The various methods subsequently described are not to be interpreted as being the only feasible methods. The collection represents those techniques which have had at least some testing and which seem, with the limited evidence available, at least somewhat effective in assessing and developing (1) strategies and policies, and (2) the policy-formation process. Development of innovative techniques or improvements in the techniques described is encouraged. The field of identifying policy problems and uncovering solutions to those problems is a rapidly changing and developing one.

This grouping of methods should *not* imply that all methods presented are to be used periodically in assessments. The policy analyst will be concerned with developing a methodology mix that meets the needs of a particular assessment in conjunction with programs and questions presented in previous chapters. The previous chapters have already alluded to and provided some methods. This chapter and those following will add to and elaborate upon the collection.

WHY ASSESSMENT AND DEVELOPMENT?

If we were to ask ourselves why the use of these assessment and development methods is desirable or necessary, it would appear that several reasons are related to corporate strategy. First, there is a need for the organization to adapt to the environmental changes and to develop new capabilities and perhaps structural alignments to accommodate these. Second, if the organization were to enter into new services and/or a new market as a result of a strategic decision about where the organization is going, then there might be the necessity to develop additional skills and certainly additional structures to accommodate this new domain of its service area or technological strategy. Third, the organization's status or current stage of development may be less than fully effective in achieving its current goals, let alone any changes in the environment that might have occurred or any changes in the domain of its operations. For example, differences in perceptions about corporate strategy and conflicts in these perceptions may cause ineffective performance. One of the difficulties may lie not in strategy formation but rather in the communication of the corporate strategy to lower levels and in the independence that coalitions at lower levels are able to exhibit in contradistinction to whatever corporate strategy has been established. It might be useful for an organization to discover the discrepancies between intended and actual perceptions of corporate strategy within an organization. Thus, in summary, an organization may need some sort of systematic assessment and development carried on

Reasons for assessment and development.

continuously (1) to adapt to environmental changes, (2) to adapt to a new domain of operations, (3) to maintain its current state, or (4) to improve its "steady state," so to speak.

EVALUATION APPROACHES

There are a number of ways to choose from in proceeding with assessment of and improvement in organization practices and policy formation in particular. We do not have in the field of policy a neat typology of evaluation approaches, but a few models can be identified. A Continuum of Management Behavior, Table 6–1, illustrates some of the possibilities. These range from an evaluator-centered compliance approach to the client-centered process approach. Some of the difficulties in each approach that may be encountered are indicated and have been discussed elsewhere.* There will be only a brief discussion here.

Compliance.

One of the most prevalent models of evaluation is certainly the evaluator-centered compliance approach. This compliance approach occurs when the evaluator examines the organizational situation, identifies the problem and the solution, and tells the relevant parties in the situation to comply with his solution. This model frequently works quite well when the evaluator is respected and has made an accurate diagnosis. Sometimes, however, the evaluator does not procure an accurate picture; he may have used unreliable sources; he may not have fully thought through the consequences of his recommendations. Sometimes there is resentment and resistance to the evaluator, who may appear to act in a condescending manner.

Doctor-patient.

Another popular model of evaluation is that of doctor-patient. Here the managers initiate the actions of bringing in evaluators (who may be managers themselves) to "look over" some part or all of the organization and to make recommendations. Again, this approach may work quite well. The evaluators have been invited in, and if they do a competent job of evaluation, their recommendations may carry some weight. However, numerous difficulties may be present. For example, the organizational unit that is defined as the patient may attempt to cover up information needed for an effective evalua-

---

*See for example: T. W. Costello: An Organizational Psychologist Looks at Change in Municipal Government, presented at the American Psychological Association Convention, San Francisco, 1968; W. J. Crockett: Team building—One approach to organization development, *Journal of Applied Behavioral Science 6* (No. 3):291–306, 1970; W. Dyer, R. Maddocks, J. W. Moffett, and W. Underwood: A laboratory-consultation model for organization change, *Journal of Applied Behavioral Science 6* (No. 2):213–227, 1970; W. Eddy: Beyond behavioralism organization development in public management, *Public Personnel Review 21* (No. 3):169–175, 1970; R. T. Golembiewski: Organization development in public agencies; Perspective on theory and practice, *Public Administration Review, 29* (No. 4):367–377, 1969; A. J. Marrow: Managerial revolution in the state department, *Personnel 43* (No. 6):2–12, 1966; E. Schein: *Process Consultation: Its Role in Organization Development,* Reading, Mass., Addison-Wesley Publishing Co., 1969.

TABLE 6-1 A CONTINUUM OF MANAGEMENT BEHAVIOR

Evaluator*-Centered			Client†-Centered
Compliance Model P! S!	Doctor-Patient Model P S	Purchase Model S	Helper or Process Model P? S_1? S_2? S_3? · · S_n?
Evaluator identifies problem and solution; tells client to comply	Managers ask evaluators what is wrong with organizational unit and what should be done	Managers identify problem and request information or service	Evaluator's activities help client to perceive, understand and act upon events in his environment; evaluators provide challenging alternatives; client decides
Possible difficulties: Resentment; resistance; problems tend not to stay solved effectively unless organization solves own problems	Organizational unit reluctant to reveal information; systematic distortion of information; lack of common diagnostic frame of reference; organizational unit unwilling to believe diagnosis; evaluators without exhaustive study unable to learn enough about organizational culture to suggest reliable courses of action	Managers do not correctly identify and/or communicate their own needs; build dependence on evaluator; assumption may be made that organizational change comes through transmittal of information (e.g., a report)	Evaluators may advance solutions prematurely; client may be unwilling or unable to see the problems, to share in diagnosis or to be actively involved in generating solutions; evaluators may not pass on diagnostic skills to client; client may not request services; evaluator may need right to come in

P = problems; S = solution.
*Evaluator may be the manager himself or a policy analyst.
†Client may be manager or a subordinate to the manager.

tion. The Watergate case illustrates this difficulty. Thus, the "doctor" may not be able to properly identify the problem and suggest an appropriate solution.

A third approach occurs when the manager identifies the problem and requests information or service to identify a solution. He may define a need—e.g., some activity he wishes carried out—and look for someone with expertise to fill the need. For example, he may wish to know the demands or requirements of a particular segment of consumers, or he may wish an analysis of the efficacy of some complex technology. The success of this approach depends on the appropriateness of the assumptions that (1) the manager has correctly identified and/or communicated his own need, and (2) the manager has accurately assessed the capability of the evaluator and the consequences of his recommendations. Many things have to go right for the purchase model to work.

Purchase.

Finally, an evaluation model we have illustrated in Table 6–1 is the helper or process approach. Here the evaluator's activities are aimed at helping the complex problem-solving process. In other words, the evaluator (who may be a manager or policy analyst) is trying to help members of the organization to perceive, understand and act upon events in the environment or the organization. The evaluator may assist in setting up a problem-solving process and he may suggest alternative courses of action. A key assumption is that if the organization members being evaluated *see* the problem, share in the diagnosis and are actively involved in generating a remedy, problems will tend to be solved more permanently. In addition, if the evaluator has effectively passed on his diagnostic skills to the evaluatees, they will be better able to solve new problems as they arise.

However, numerous difficulties may be encountered. For example, a trust relationship necessary for the success of this approach may not be developed. There may be an unwillingness or inability to see the problems, to share in the diagnosis or to be actively involved in generating solutions. Part of the problem may be that the evaluator has real power (e.g., he is the boss) and cannot easily switch to the collaborative helper role. Those being evaluated may distort their responses; they fear that the evaluator-boss may utilize negative information to their detriment.

Helper.

In an effort to develop ways of diminishing some of the many barriers to effective assessment and to deal with the variegated environmental changes affecting organizations, an organizational development technology has emerged in recent years. Organizational development practitioners have used, built upon and added to such traditional methods as interviews, questionnaires, forecasting and financial and operating data analysis. Such methods, traditional and new, may be fitted into the various models of assessment behavior—Compliance, Doctor—Patient, Purchase, and Helper. Such methods and models or combinations of methods and models may be applied specifically to the strategy formation process.

WHAT IS AN ORGANIZATION DEVELOPMENT APPROACH TO STRATEGY FORMATION?

It would be helpful to have a single, clear definition of exactly what organization development is and what it is not. However, there is no single definition; on the contrary, there are many. For example, the NTL Institute sees organization development as a "short title for a way of looking at the whole human side of organization life."* Others place more stress on its specific application to finance, market, and labor relations variables.† Examination of the literature in the field points up why, in fact, organization development is many things to many people, depending upon how broadly or narrowly they apply the term to their own purposes.

Organization development can be a broad label that includes many activities through which the manager or analyst may make better use of the organization participants. In this book these activities are viewed as both *problem solving* and *developmental* in nature in that they are helpful in solving policy problems while at the same time increasing the capability for solving future problems.

Problem solving and development.

Definition

To further elaborate, an organization development approach to strategy formation is defined as a process (1) planned, (2) organization wide, (3) managed from the top (4) to improve strategy formation through interventions, in that process using relevant analytical and developmental methods. In addition, (5) the approach suggested tends to focus more on coalitions of performers or groups than on individual performers.

Definition.

1. It is a planned effort.
   There is a systematic diagnosis using multiple methods of analysis, providing an indication of the forces, factors, effects and relationships that impinge on mission accomplishment; a set of action steps is developed for new or improved strategy formation and implementation.
2. It has organization-wide implications.
   Strategy formation is the focal point and, as indicated, involves the widest sort of ramifications in the organization. An organization development program involves the entire organization or coherent system or a significant part thereof.
3. It is managed from the top.
   Experience and research indicate that top management involvement, direction and commitment seem to be desirable‡ attributes of

---

*News and Reports, NTL Institute, Vol. 2, June, 1968; see also Bennis, W. G.: *Organization Development: Its Nature, Origin and Prospects,* Reading, Mass., Addison-Wesley Publishing Company, 1969; W. French: Organization development—Objectives, assumptions and strategies, *California Management Review 12* (No. 2):23–24, 1969.

†See R. Blake and J. Mouton: *Building a Dynamic Corporation,* Reading, Mass., Addison-Wesley Publishing Company, 1969.

‡See L. Greiner: Pattern of organization change. *In* Dalton, G., Lawrence, P., Greiner, L. (eds.): *Organization Change and Development.* Homewood, Ill., Richard D. Irwin, 1970.

successful development programs; thus, we include this element. Top managers may be the analysts themselves, or they may endorse the efforts of external advisors or those analysts internal to the organization.

4. It is designed to improve strategy formation through planned interventions and assessments, using relevant analytical and developmental methods.

   It is comparable to other organization development efforts. However, it focuses on strategy formation and places more emphasis on market, economic and financial variables than many other organization development efforts. It places somewhat less emphasis on human variables and values. The interventions designed are based on the behavioral sciences. Experience-based learning activities (e.g., sensitivity training and T groups) are not relied on; instead, a shared approach to problem identification and solution is used. Methods are selected and developed for auditing the existing environment and structure and helping the organization to examine its corporate strategy and its strategy formation process.

5. It focuses more on coalitions of performers rather than on individual management development.

   Management development aims at ensuring a constant supply of trained individuals to fill anticipated vacancies in the management ranks. The organization development approach here takes the point of view that the way in which participants adapt corporate strategies to the changing environment and deal with conflicting sets of interests has a great deal to do with the effectiveness of the organization. This approach includes concern with the establishment of appropriate systems and problem-solving processes for group and intergroup interaction in developing corporate strategies.

Core issue — prevent stagnation.

As indicated, one purpose of implementing an intervention within the organization is to encourage a renewal process. This renewal process must take place; otherwise, the organization may suffer deterioration. As John Gardner points out, an organization tends to have a predictable life-cycle of decline that may be offset by a struggle for renewal.* A built-in provision for self-criticism, for challenging present corporate strategies and practices, for auditing the environment and for revising and reformulating policies and strategies is needed. This is a core issue; the organization needs to deliberately seek a way of preventing dry rot or stagnation.

The organization development intervention therefore is seen as basically a problem-solving (anti-dry rot) *and* development approach, with its activity focused more on groups or coalitions than on individuals. Outside advisors, assessors or consultants often share the responsibility with managers for the problem-solving and development process, but they also work with managers toward increasing the organization's own capacity to diagnose the external and internal environment and to develop and carry through strategic plans of action.

---

*J. Gardner: Can organization dry rot be prevented? *Personnel Administration* 29:3–13, 1966.

ACTION-RESEARCH PROGRAM   *what + how ?*

An element frequently included in organization development activities is the *action-research* program of intervention. As the term is used in this book there are three processes in an action-research program applied to strategy formation, all of which involve extensive collaboration between the analyst and the organization:

Three processes in action research.

1. Information gathering from the internal *and* external environment.
2. Organization, analysis and feed-in of such information to relevant parties or groups in the organization.
3. Joint action planning based on the analysis and discussion.

Action research is designed to make data available about the organization and its environment and then to help the organization to use that information to make plans for the future.

A variety of sources and methods for an action-research program are covered in this chapter; e.g., personal contacts, publications and reports, observation, interviews, questionnaires and market segmentation. In the next chapter we shall consider models, simulations and statistical decision making. Methods for using data that have been generated for gaining individual and group involvement in *joint action planning* are covered in Chapter 8. The ideas covered in these three chapters seem to be useful in assessing, formulating and implementing corporate strategies based on the framework that has been suggested thus far in the book — *environmental forces, strategy-generating structure, organizational objectives and outcomes,* and *action plans.*

Multiple sources and methods useful.

The ideas are also seen as being useful in developing the strategy-formation process. For example, group and organization involvement would include a series of sessions including, if appropriate to the unique situation, such focal points as: stating and analyzing objectives, priority setting and action planning, policy group development, intergroup conflict management, and progress review. The plans for the future from action research may include parts that extend for a relatively short period (e.g., six months) and parts that are projected for the long run (e.g., two or five years).

Use questions from conceptual framework presented previously.

USE AND LIMITATIONS OF METHODS

We shall discuss the various methods and provide examples of actual instruments or procedures that have been used in business and government. It is worth reiterating that there is a lack of rigorous research (e.g., systematically controlled experimental studies) that would provide a better understanding of the actual effectiveness of the action-research approach in inducing organizational change and strategy improvement. Much reliance at this point (perhaps too much) is placed on before-and-after studies, self-reports and anecdotal evidence.

Lack of rigorous research.

The action-research approach, however, has been used in a variety of profit and nonprofit organizations with apparent success. For example, in a study of organization development–action-research activities in the 4000 employee "Sigma" plant, Blake et al. report significant improvement in: (1) productivity and profits, (2) management practices and behavior, and (3) attitudes and values.* Phases of the program included data collection feedback and discussion for group and intergroup development. The before-and-after evaluation, however, did not include a control group. Thus, any changes cannot be uniquely associated with the development activities.

Phillip H. Chase reports success in the utilization of an action-research design at Babcock and Wilcox, a manufacturing firm.† The holding of "Creative Management Workshops" at Babcock and Wilcox is reported to have resulted in an increased desire on the part of the executive participants to play an active role in future problem identification and problem solving.

Some research support.

A team development effort in a large investment and commercial bank is reported as a successful method for coping with overly centralized decision making and changes in the external environment that require concomitant change in the internal environment. Results from interviews and questionnaires and previously existing data on productivity, turnover and absenteeism were fed back and discussed, using teams of managers.‡ In addition, there have been a

A variety of applications.

variety of applications of action-research programs in large and small organizations in many countries, in government agencies, hospitals, and universities and school systems.§

From the point of view of the student analyst learning about policy there may be lack of opportunity to use some of the techniques (e.g., observation, interview, questionnaire, management science programs, conferences) being presented unless a cooperative organization is available. Nevertheless, the student should have

---

*R. Blake, J. Mouton, L. Barnes and L. Greiner: Break-through in organization development. *In* Dalton, G., Lawrence, P., and Greiner, L. (eds.): *Organization Change and Development,* Homewood, Ill., Richard D. Irwin, 1970.

†Phillip H. Chase: The creative management workshop, *Personnel Journal,* April, 1972, pp. 264–282.

‡Richard Beckhard and Dale G. Lake: Short and long range effects of a team development effort. *In* Hornstein, H., et al. (eds.): *Social Intervention: A Behavioral Science Approach.* New York, The Free Press, 1971, pp. 421–439.

§Numerous illustrations are provided by W. L. French and C. H. Bell: *Organization Development,* Englewood Cliffs, N.J., Prentice-Hall, Inc., 1973; thirteen studies are surveyed by L. Greiner: Patterns of organization change, *in* Dalton, G., Lawrence, P., and Greiner, L. (eds.): *Organization Change and Development,* Homewood, Ill., Richard D. Irwin, Inc., 1970; five case studies are presented in R. Beckhard: *Organization Development: Strategies and Models,* Reading, Mass., Addison Wesley Publishing Company, 1969; see also A. D. McCormick: Management development at British-American Tobacco, *Management Today,* June, 1967, pp. 126–128; B. F. White: A higher dimension for management development, *Report of the Presidential Task Force on Career Advancement,* November, 1966; and G. Foster: The managerial grid at Ward's, *Stores,* 48:42–44, 1966.

some familiarity with the full variety of sources and methods being used today. Of course, these information sources and the methods for assessment and development of organizations and strategy formation may change somewhat over time. Included in the approaches, however, is a durable characteristic; that is, a systematic way of finding out what any current reality is. The systematic way of learning the "state of things" in the organization and the conditions in the environment has lasting value. Thus, the sources and methods would appear to be useful to the analyst, be he a student or a practitioner.

Systematic way of learning about state of things.

INFORMATION GATHERING AND PROCESSING

A first step in the action-research program is information gathering from the internal and external environments. There are a wide variety of sources: customers, suppliers, subordinates, friends, colleagues, books, reports, forecasts, journals, and so forth.

Interviews and questionnaires may be used. The manager or analyst collects, organizes and interprets information to determine the status of those factors that seem to have greatest relevance to the organization.

Scanning status can be quite a job considering the explosion of information that is occurring in our society and the world. For example, the United States government publishes over 100,000 technical reports each year. The number of journals and the number of published articles are increasing rapidly.

The manager or analyst has several information-gathering and processing problems with which to deal. What information is needed? Where is the information? Has enough information been gathered? Is the information available to him? For example, he may feel that not enough relevant information is available within the organization itself. Even if the information is available within the organization, he may not know where to obtain it or, if he does, he may feel that for some reason it is unavailable to him.

Several problems with which to deal.

If this situation seems unrealistic, reference to the anecdote discussed in Chapter 1 might demonstrate some of the problems.

The financial planner (or technocrat) in that anecdote, working for a large electronics firm, found that he needed a certain amount of data concerning market forecasts to plan realistically for capital improvements. His first attempt at gathering this information within the firm led him to the Marketing Department; it seemed natural that market forecasts would be available there. He contacted the marketing manager, who referred him to the market forecasting group. The manager of that forecasting group, after some discussion, agreed to give the financial planner what information he had available. Upon returning to his own financial group, the planner used the information to develop his recommendations. He soon found, to his dismay, that the manufacturing manager disagreed with his action plan, primarily because the manager disagreed with the data on which the plans were based.

The financial planner asked the manufacturing manager what he felt were realistic sales forecasts. The manufacturing manager presented him with his thoughts. The financial planner then went back and asked the market forecasting group why there was some discrepancy between what they thought were sufficient data and what the manufacturing group thought were sufficient data. The market forecasting group stated that the planner had received an early version of the forecast, and that forecasts had changed since then. The planner then asked for the updated forecast, which the group promised to send him. A new set of data was forwarded to the planner relatively quickly. The planner, upon receiving this new information and comparing it to the old information, realized that the two sets of data were totally different. To ensure that he would not waste time, he presented the manufacturing manager with the updated forecast. The manufacturing manager proceeded to tell him that, just as the previous forecast was too low, these data were too high by almost the same amount.

The planner now found himself rather perplexed as to what was happening. Rather than go back to the market forecasting group he decided to try another route. He asked his own superior to attempt to find sufficient data for planning purposes. The superior then contacted the financial Vice-President, who, in turn, called back to the financial planner and asked why he had gone over to the marketing department to obtain this information in the first place. The financial planner stated that he thought that, since it was market forecasts that he needed, the right place was the market forecasting group. At this point, the financial planner learned that although the market forecasting group did indeed have data available to them, they did not originate this data. They were merely information brokers. This was the primary reason they were hesitant about giving this data to the financial planner. It turned out that the person who originated all this data was in actuality in the finance group. Once the source of the data was found, the planner no longer needed the market forecasting group. The upshot of this action was to decrease the importance of the market forecasting group. It became evident to everybody within the organization that if you needed good, up-to-date, effective data, then you should probably go straight to the source rather than to the broker.

The problems that we see here indicate the various reasons information can be very difficult to gather within an organization. The validity of gathered data may be used as an excuse if something goes wrong with the formulated plan. This is evident in our previous anecdote. The financial planner was contemplating relatively large capital outlays based on the data that were supplied to him. The market forecasting group was afraid that if their information was used for these large capital outlays, running into millions of dollars, and something happened to jeopardize the plan, then management would blame their data rather than the plan itself. The planned capital outlay was approved in that organization and something did go wrong with the plans. The organization found that it ran into the credit crunch and encountered a recession that it had not planned on in its forecasts. It did not have enough funds to carry through the investment. The plan had to be scrapped at a considerable cost to the organization in total resources. By this time, however, the planner had already left the organization and was not directly affected. It's to be expected that some of the people within the organization who supplied the information were adversely affected, however. One of the problems we can see from this example is that much of the information that should be used cannot be found within the organization. For instance, information concerning a potential credit problem in the environment was obviously not available within the company. Also, the future of the industry hadn't been thoroughly studied by people within the organization; they hadn't looked to the relevant external sources of information.

We talk frequently in the policy-formation process about changes in the direction of the organization. Quite often this means that we are looking for new and different methods of achieving expanded goals. The search may reveal that pertinent information is just not available from any sources within the organization. Sometimes the source is outside the organization; sometimes, within. The questions arise as to just what are good sources of information and how we utilize them effectively.

A study by Aguilar* indicates that the main source of information about the environment used by managers is the informal information network with subordinates and with friends in the industry. Impersonal sources such as publications and forecasts provided the second most important source.

Main source of information.

Forecasts

The manager or analyst, of course, may rely on a variety of forecasts. Some may be available to the public in the library and/or through subscription. Some may be privately conducted at his direction. For example, forecasts in the following areas may be available already, or, on the other hand, may be made by (1) sales (e.g., by industry or by corporate product/service), (2) general economic (e.g., Gross National Product, Personal Disposable Income), (3) technological (e.g., automatic data processing), (4) social values (e.g., attitudes toward materialism or human dignity), (5) social indicators (e.g., measures of "quality of life" phenomena such as noise pollution or personal security), and (6) competition's intentions (e.g., plans to enlarge an agency's scope of operations). Accurate forecasting in such areas is likely to give the organization an obvious advantage in striving for success.

Several forecasts that may be useful.

---

*Francis J. Aguilar: Scanning the business environment, *In* Columbia University Graduate School of Business: *Studies of the Modern Corporation,* New York, The Macmillan Company, 1967. See also H. Mintzberg: The myths of MIS. *California Management Review 15*(No. 1):92–97, Fall, 1972.

Important progress is being made in "futures" forecasting.* We shall discuss such forecasting in the next chapter.

Publications and Reports

Written or published information includes several different subcategories. The sources in one subcategory include various research organizations that are available for both business and nonbusiness sectors. One that comes to mind would be the Stanford Research Institute's long-range planning series. It is available to organizations at a fee. Some libraries carry this series, but many large organizations subscribe to it. The series can be very costly, but is of relatively high quality. There are similar types of series and reports from consulting firms, other research organizations, such as the Brookings Institute, and others that are of equally high quality. The major benefit of these reports is the quality of their research. The research writers usually go to great lengths to determine whether the environment is conducive to various strategic moves in a particular industry or area. The reports are also relatively unbiased in their point of view.

Quality. ✓

The problem with these reports, however, is that they are often quite costly and, also, their material is usually dated. The researcher who writes these reports usually gathered the information from other published sources, so that the combination of publication times built into the various reports and their data lead to, in some instances, considerable lags between the original data sources and the time of reading by the user. It is often impossible to determine just how many sources the material has gone through; whether the reports are second, third-, fourth-, or even fifthhand information is never really known.

Material dated?

A second source of public information is the entire list of business and specialist publications. Included in this list would be publications such as *Business Week, The Wall Street Journal, Fortune,* and various technical and industrial publications. The advan-

✓

---

*Several illustrations are included in the following: John C. Chambers, Satender K. Mullick, and Donald D. Smith: How to choose the right forecasting technique, *Harvard Business Review* 49:45–74, July–August, 1971; Nestor B. Terleckyj: Measuring progress toward social goals: Some possibilities at national and local levels, *Management Science* 16:765–778, August, 1970; Robert U. Ayres: *Technological Forecasting and Long Range Planning,* New York, McGraw-Hill Book Co., 1969; Kurt Baier and Nicholas Rescher (eds.): *Values and the Future,* New York, The Free Press, 1969. Also see such journals as *The Journal of General Management, Technological Forecasting, Marketing Research, The Futurist, Public Administration Review, Dun's and Modern Industry, The Wall Street Journal,* and *Business Week.* The case analyst, of course, may not have an informal information network or be able to have his own forecasts made, but he, as well as the manager, can rely on published reports and forecasts such as the Department of Commerce: *Survey of Current Business; Standard and Poor's Current Statistics;* Bureau of the Census, *Statistical Abstract of the United States;* National Industrial Conference Board, *Economic Almanac;* Bureau of Labor Statistics, *Monthly Labor Review and Robert Morris Associates, Annual Statement Studies.*

tage of these publications is that their data are usually up-to-date. They are also easy to come by and relatively inexpensive. The problem with their information is that they can often be biased in their interpretation of potential opportunity areas, and also their information has varying degrees of quality.

Up-to-date.

Bias?

A third source of information includes the documents published by governments. The federal government, in particular, publishes large amounts of information on just about any conceivable topic or strategic area. This information is readily available for use from large libraries. Vital information, however, is frequently hidden among large amounts of extraneous material in the government periodicals section. Most large libraries do have a government periodical librarian who is adept at researching any given topic in a particular strategic area. If the manager or analyst utilizes these reference librarians effectively he will find that they can be extremely useful to him. The reference librarians in these areas may have little contact with the "real" world. They often welcome contact with people who are trying to research actual problems through government reports. Their knowledge of the various government reports often enables them to spot, on a moment's notice, specific types of information that might be available.

The benefits of this kind of information are that it is readily available and covers millions of different topics. However, it is often unclear just how old this information is. The quality of the information also varies considerably from report to report. Much of the information may be open to bias. The various departments that carry out the research, such as the Departments of State, Interior, Labor, Commerce, and so forth, often have a major interest in the outcome of the report. When evaluating any particular report consideration must always be given to the reason for the research and the research agency that performed it.

Readily available.

A general problem that applies to the entire area of written reports is that, when the analyst does find a particular piece of information from a published report that appears to fit his corporate strategy effectively and properly, he should be wary of that information. If he has seen this information, then others have probably seen it also. Since we are talking about changes in corporate strategy, what we really want is a competitive advantage in the strategy-formation process. If the information relating to the corporate strategy is readily available, then competitive advantage could very well be lost.

Any competitive advantage?

Informal Information Networks

If we need new information that is specifically appropriate to future objectives (e.g., on market potential, competitors, pricing, customers, technical tidings, government actions, acquisition leads, etc.), where is that information available? Certainly some of the in-

Where is new information available?

formation can be obtained from written reports. Quite often, however, when considering new approaches or new directions, human resources must be utilized. The problems here are, first, finding relevant and reliable human resources or informants, and then utilizing those resources effectively and efficiently.

The first problem involves two separate phases: Initially we have to be able to spot the informant and, second, we have to be able to approach him. (The first phase could be handled in advance.)

Build an information network.

We all have a relatively good idea of the potential areas in which we might need material in the future; therefore, *informal information networks* or potential networks should be built in advance. There are three types of informants which could be potentially useful in achieving this purpose.

Deviant.

The first type of informant can be called the *deviant*. The deviant is the analyst who has tested out new or untried ground. He has attempted to implement change in a particular area. Examples of this type of person would include inventors, innovators, entrepreneurs. People like Bill Lear of Lear Jet and stereo fame and Howard Head of Head Ski fame exemplify this type of person. An advantage of the deviant is that he makes good copy for the press. This means that it is relatively easy to spot him in the environment. This advantage should be utilized by the analyst by accumulating the names of deviants and situations under which they are operating.

Transitional individual.

The second type of person can be called the *transitional* individual. This person has gone through a rapid change or is in the process of going through a rapid change in his organization. His particular area of expertise lies in his knowledge of the incremental problems of change. He also is in the public eye, which makes him easily identifiable. On the way up, he is usually the hero for the journals; on the way down, he is usually the goat. An example of this type of person would be Jimmy Ling, formerly of LTV, Inc.

Marginal individual.

The third type of informant is the *marginal* individual. He is marginal not because his information is weak, but because of his position. He is the type of person who works on the fringes of an industry or area, not specifically within it. Examples of marginal informants are lawyers, consultants and accountants. They are easy to find, but from a different standpoint; they advertise themselves quite frequently. Also, they are frequently more than willing to discuss the area around which they work. They often give a fresh approach to that particular area; they often see the entire picture rather than just a small portion of it, such as in the forest-for-the-trees syndrome.

Advantages.

These various types of individuals provide certain advantages as information sources. The first two categories of informants are usually too busy with what they are doing at any given time to make immediate use of any information you might impart to them. The third individual usually does not want to actively participate in any given area since he makes his living working for people within the area. In this case the consultant, accountant or lawyer could not operate in his traditional capacity if we were also considered a competitor for the market.

One of the key problems in obtaining information from such human sources is discretion. Discretion must be used in the information-gathering process to ensure that the environment won't be changed by merely trying to gather information. The individual who attempts to buy land, for instance, in advance of a large expansion in a particular geographic area will find that if he doesn't use discretion in gathering information about that land, the price may increase simply because of the way he is asking questions.

Use discretion.

Likewise, the analyst gathering information may utilize the strategic alternatives he has previously developed for the information-gathering process. If the individual from whom he is gathering information cannot determine which of the alternatives will actually be utilized, it would be more difficult for the informant to become a potential competitor. Also, if the potential competitor believes that the analyst is creative enough to develop several different alternatives, he may be wary of trying to steal any ideas for fear that the analyst will be able to creatively prevent the informants from using those ideas effectively.

Need for strategic alternatives

The question now arises as to how to find this type of individual. Informants are usually very busy people and therefore don't like to waste their time listening to unrealistic or worthless ideas. They guard themselves from this problem through the use of screening devices. Screens are set up to keep out unwanted individuals and to allow in desired individuals. An example of a process of this type can be shown by looking back to our previous example of the financial planner in the large electronics firm. We saw that he went from individual to individual within the organization until he finally found the person who could actually give him the information he needed. The information-gathering process in this instance, however, took him in several wrong directions and, at one point, gave him incorrect information. Therefore, one of the most important phases of the information-gathering process, where humans are concerned, is not only to find the individual you want to talk to but also to find the screen that will get you through to him.

How to approach informant?

The student has a ready supply of potential screens available to him in the faculty of his school. Many business or public administration professors have had dealings with individuals of importance of the type we are talking about during their careers. In many instances, professors and college administrators can act as screens. Students with good ideas can quite often utilize their contacts with faculty members as screens. Other people who act as screens are the same people referred to as marginal individuals when describing informants. Accountants, lawyers, consultants and others of that type perform the screening function for other informants. The main factor to be remembered is that discretion throughout this process is of prime importance. Also remember the desirability for developing alternatives before reaching the informant. The informant and his screen may be much more enthusiastic about talking to someone they feel has more to offer. Increased worth to the informant can be demonstrated by the use of several different alternatives.

Observation

In addition to forecasts, published reports and the informal information network, the policy analyst or manager may use an observer approach.* For example, in studying how an organization goes about its policy-formation process, the observer would stay on the sidelines and watch individuals and coalitions going about their daily tasks for a period of time. The observer might then be qualified to answer such questions as:

1. What is the pattern of distribution of perceptions of the corporate strategy?
2. What are the positions and makeup of relevant coalitions?
3. Which are the dominant coalitions for various issues?
4. How much do the coalitions practice effective teamwork and effective intergroup cooperation?

Gain firsthand knowledge.

5. To what extent are goals and targets challenging, clearly understood and accepted?
6. What are the competencies of various relevant strategy initiators?

The observer approach would be useful if it is accepted and skillfully applied. The major advantage to this method is that the observer can gain firsthand knowledge and a "feel" for the process at hand. However, normal standards of validity (the degree that a char-

Validity and reliability?

acteristic of an individual or a situation reflects what is felt to be the true characteristic) and reliability (the degree of consistency in a behavior or measure over an extended period of time or recurring number of repetitions) may be prevented by:

1. Lack of formal criteria of assessment.
2. Lack of independent checks on observation.
3. Lack of recurrence or replication of phenomena.
4. Bias of manager trying to observe phenomena in his own organizational unit.

Observation of external environment.

In addition, those truly skilled in the observation approach are in scarce supply and expensive. However, the observations or impressions of managers or policy analysts are relied on frequently in making judgments about the organization's policies and the strategy-formation process. The judgments are, of course, not limited to just those based on in-house observations. Feelings or impressions are used and sometimes are quite useful, for example, in judging com-

---

*See E. J. Webb, et al.: *Unobtrusive Measures: Nonreactive Research in the Social Sciences,* Chicago, Ill., Rand McNally & Company, 1966.

petitors' corporate strategies, customer behavior or labor union activities.

Interviews

Another frequently used method in analyzing policies and strategies is the face-to-face interview. Interviews may be conducted with managers, staff, employees, employee or union representatives, clients or customers, and community organizations and leaders, as well as informants outside the organization being examined. Other sources of obtaining information, such as published reports or observations, provide information about areas of interest that will prompt further investigation, but the interview remains as a significant method for gaining in-depth information on strategy formation.*

Advantages and disadvantages.

The basic interview requires that the analyst actually speak with the other party and question him as to his reactions, impressions, feelings, and so forth before, during or after his experience. The interview has a major advantage of high information yield. It can be highly flexible and can facilitate the investigation of highly complex management issues. However, the interview, as is well known, may involve difficulties in validity, reliability, question bias, retrospective bias and investigator bias.†

Structured interview.

Two types of interviewing procedures are of particular use in studying complex strategy issues. The first is the standard structured interview. Attention is paid to standards of reliability by developing standardized questions and asking them of all respondents in the same manner. If the questions have been carefully selected and limited in number with appropriate preliminary analysis, this approach can yield a rich volume of information while saving considerable interview time. A systematic way can be developed to "add" together the descriptions from each respondent. The sum total of their reports compensates for individual bias and distortions skewed by poor or prejudiced reporters. This approach could be considered for *lower and perhaps middle* managers and staff (and for first line supervisors if appropriate).

Focused interview.

A *less* structured approach that may be appropriate for outside informants and for *middle to high level* strategy makers is termed "the focused interview." An interview guide may provide a set of foci for the interviewer, but the interviewer himself determines the exact form and structure of the interview as he sees fit. This approach allows much deeper probing and is sensitive to unan-

---

*See W. Keegan: Scanning the International Business Environment: A Study of the Information Acquisition Process. Unpublished doctoral dissertation, Harvard Business School, 1967; and R. Collings: Scanning the Environment for Strategic Information. Unpublished doctoral dissertation. Harvard Business School, 1968.

†For discussion of difficulties, see R. A. Bauer and K. J. Gergen: *The Study of Policy Formation.* New York, The Free Press, 1968.

ticipated responses. It has a special advantage with persons of prominence. Such persons may resent an overly structured approach and may play such an important policy-making role in an organization that greater flexibility in questioning is desirable. This approach, though perhaps preferable for informants and top management officials, does suffer in terms of bias, validity and reliability.

Kahn and Connell* have dealt with the issue of selecting between an open "focused" interview (open-ended) and a standard structured interview (fixed alternative). They list the key factors to be weighed in deciding between the two approaches as:

Factors in choosing approach.

1. The objectives of the interview (classification of respondents vs. understanding).

2. Respondent's degree of information about the topic.

3. Degree to which the topic has been thought through and opinions crystalized.

4. Respondent's motivations or ability to communicate.

5. Interviewer's prior awareness of the respondent's situation.

The main criterion they present, however, for using one format over another is that relatively complex and ill defined issues should be evaluated through an open-ended technique.

The interview depends heavily on the interviewer's knowledge of the environment and the interviewer's skill in sensitive probing. Intensive training is necessary for excellence in "focused" interviewing and also, to a lesser extent, for the standard interview.

The many variations in corporate strategies and in emphases of different assessments make it impractical to define precisely the scope and direction of each interview or to establish any single formula for conducting an effective interview. The following listed guides seem to have general application to interviews on strategy issues:

Guides to interviewing.

Because of the sensitivity of some respondents to possible invasion of privacy, not only should an interview be treated in confidence, but the interviewer himself should avoid delving into or giving any impression of delving into areas not related to organization matters or strategy issues. Some situations would dictate that respondents should be advised that their expression of opinion will be treated in complete confidence (keep it "off the record").

Interview findings should be used with regard to the limitations of interviews. The manager or analyst should consider interview findings as one source of information that tends to confirm or to cast doubt upon findings reached through other methods. Interview findings often suggest the need for further study. When it is necessary to base a finding primarily on information gained through an interview, the findings should be appropriately qualified. In the case of group interviews, consideration should also be given to the extent to which one or two domi-

---

*R. L. Kahn and C. F. Connell: *The Dynamics of Interviewing,* New York, John Wiley & Sons, Inc., 1957. See also R. L. Gordon: *Interviewing: Strategy Techniques and Tactics,* Homewood, Ill., Dorsey Press, 1969.

nant personalities within the group may have influenced the responses of the other members of the group.

Interviews should sometimes be conducted at different levels in the organization. Strategy formation and implementation issues may be seen differently at various job levels in the organization.

There are many techniques and methods that can be used to manage conflict between different interest groups and to accomplish objectives. The emphasis and theme of interviews may be on success in attainment of objectives rather than on procedures and techniques.

The phrasing of the questions is important in the interview (as well as a questionnaire). To obtain a more accurate description of strategy formation practices, for example, consider phrasing the question so that the respondent is not describing what he thinks *his* policy or *his* behavior is like. Phrase questions so that he is describing decisions or the way decisions are made when he looks at his peers and when he looks at his boss. The rationale is that, though the objective superior can pinpoint some of the issues in the situation, the subordinate is assumed to see the "real" world a shade more clearly.

Developing and asking good questions for an interview (or questionnaire) is not easy. Many of the pitfalls and suggestions for overcoming this have been discussed elsewhere.* A brief listing of suggestions would include the following:

1. Be honest and utterly objective.
2. Avoid complex or abstract concepts that may obscure the meaning (e.g., some people may not know what a Norwegian correlation is).
3. Avoid too many open-ended questions (some people are hard to shut off).
4. Avoid loading the question (e.g., "You encourage innovations, don't you?").
5. Avoid double-barreled questions (e.g., "Are you rewarded on productivity and creativity or on competent leadership and good investment spending?").

Interview Item Content

Ultimately, however, the usefulness of the interview rests with the type of question asked. The type of question could vary with the kind of issue under study (e.g., market tidings, product or service, distribution, investment, competitor's intentions, social responsibility) and the kind of respondent who is being used as a source of information (e.g., customer or client, informant, subordinates, public official, union leader, manager). When measuring how an organization goes about its strategy formation, for example, the objective is to ask about activities that are (1) descriptive of the strategy process, (2) related to the organization's effectiveness, and (3) capable of being changed by the action of the strategy maker.

To illustrate we shall describe and discuss a hypothetical focused interview approach and then a structured interview ap-

---

*For example, see F. N. Kerlinger: *Foundation of Behavioral Research,* New York, Holt, Rinehart & Winston, Inc., 1964; and M. Dunnette and W. Kirschner: *Psychology in Industry,* New York, Holt, Rinehart & Winston, Inc., 1968.

proach to measuring aspects of strategy formation. A "focused interview" approach might involve two general stages.* The first might be to identify strategy formation issues of interest, individuals involved in the issues, and phases through which the issues pass (e.g., initiation, staffing, data collection, and so forth). The second stage would build on the information so gathered and add to it. Subissues could be specifically delineated and identification and evaluation of useful practices made.

Stages I and II of the hypothetical interviewing project on strategy formation are described in more detail below.

Stage I
A. Identify issues involved in policy or strategy formation. Initial interviews will be with those in formal positions of leadership in relevant organizational units, including such considerations as:

What is crucial to know about the internal and external environment?

1. Are competent leadership, greater productivity, creativity and initiative encouraged in the organization?
2. Are there systematic critique and evaluation of mission accomplishment, and is high achievement in meeting organizational purposes expected, required, rewarded and publicized?
3. Is management sensitive to community interests and standards of reasonableness both in routine and unusual situations and in generating and adapting to changes?
4. Do the managers ensure that participants understand and accept the policies and goals, and do managers learn of and use participants' attitudes in making corporate strategy?
5. Do managers learn of and use attitudes and requirements of customers or clients, employee organizations, relevant public agencies, stockholders and the general public in making policy?

Many additional questions could be constructed from the corporate strategy considerations brought up in the previous chapters.
B. As a second step, information could be gathered concerning other participants in the issue area who have important roles in the strategy process (including people not in positions of formal leadership).
C. Between the inception of an insight into an opportunity and its ultimate implementation many events transpire. These events may be conceptualized as overlapping temporal phases, each of which may affect the effectiveness or outcome. Information could be gathered on the phases through which issues pass (e.g., initiation, staffing, data collection, feedback, analysis, standards, corrective action).
D. Each respondent might be asked to sort a number of individuals on the basis of the subphase in which they are most influential.
E. Respondents could be questioned on the degree to which each strategy issue was salient to him and his own position on the issue.

Developing map of strategy issues, phases and leverage points.

Combining information from Stage I would provide a map of corporate strategy issues, phases and leverage points in the strategy-formation process in an organization or in a segment of it.

Stage II

On the basis of the information collected, the next step would be to sharpen the questioning and analysis on a set of specifically delineated issues and subissues. For example, issues or subissues might include decentralization, goal clarity, guidelines for interpreting results, and functional excellence for its own sake.

---

*These stages have been adapted from R. A. Bauer and K. J. Gergen: *The Study of Policy Formation,* New York, The Free Press, 1968.

Respondents would be asked to what extent, and how, changes in specific practices should be made to improve organization effectiveness and efficiency.

Thus, our "focused interview" example will provide for discussion and analysis of: (1) significant corporate strategy issues and subissues identified in the words of the respondents, (2) an indication of the significant phases that corporate strategy issues go through, (3) a map of leverage points in the organization or part of it and, finally, (4) an indication of suggested changes for improvement. *Suggested changes for improvement.*

In contrast, our example of a structured interview will include content relevant to corporate strategy effectiveness such as feedback on planning, the adequacy of staff meetings, the degree of conflict and consistency among objectives and policies, overall organization effectiveness, equity of rewards, adequacy of communication and intragroup and intergroup cooperation. This content is modified from part of a structured interview that was used recently in a federal government agency to assess its management policies and practices. The Instructions to Interviewers are included along with a sample of the questions as follows: *Example of structured interview.*

Sample of Structured Interview

INSTRUCTIONS TO INTERVIEWERS

You are to fill out the interview schedule. The interviewer is not to write at all.

There are several rating questions such as "On a scale of 1 to 5, please rate how clear the quality of work expected is. 1 indicates very poor; 5 very good." *Make sure* that the interviewee gives you only one number.

In general, the format of the interview is to ask closed questions such as in the above example followed by open-ended questions in which the interviewee is allowed to express his opinions in an unstructured manner. Please follow this format. However, do not allow the interviewee to ramble. Throughout the interview schedule, special instructions for the interviewer are placed in parentheses.

The entire interview should take approximately ____ minutes; you should not exceed ____ minutes per interview.

At the end of the session, you may write down any observations you would like to make on a separate sheet. Please complete this structured interview sheet immediately after the completion of an interview.

STRUCTURED INTERVIEW

LEAD-IN BY INTERVIEWER: This survey is being conducted by

_____. The purpose of the survey is to review and evaluate the effectiveness of corporate strategy in the

Sample of Structured Interview—Continued

_____. We are concerned with the whole set of organization and management policies. After we finish the survey, we are going to report the grouped results to the top management of _____. No one in _____

_____ will see your individual answers.

First, I'd like to ask you a few background questions.

What is your full name? _____
                          FIRST   MIDDLE   LAST

What is your job title? _____

(Instructions to interviewer: Please note the position of the interviewee, that is, staff, assistant director of the unit, or director of the unit)

_____ staff

_____ assistant director of the unit

_____ director of the unit

How long have you worked for the _____

_____ years and _____ months approximately

The name of the unit is (Interviewer: Please fill in; don't ask)

_____

It is located in (Interviewer: Fill in; don't ask)

_____

How long has it been since your boss sat down with you to discuss your overall planning formally? _____ years and _____ months and _____ days

In general, how often does your boss sit down with you to discuss your overall planning? Every _____ years and _____ months and _____ days

Think of a scale of 1 to 5. One represents very bad impressions, five very good impressions. Now I want you to rate the feedback you receive from your boss regarding your planning. First, how helpful do you feel this feedback is? _____ points. Second, how fair do you feel the feedback is? _____ points. On the 1 to 5 scale, would you say that your boss's evaluation is based on solid facts? _____ points. Do you

Sample of Structured Interview—Continued

feel that the boss is too critical? _____ points. Overall, how would you rate the feedback your boss gives you? _____ points. Why do you feel this way?

In general, how often do you have staff planning meetings? _____ never or about every _____ weeks. Again think of a scale of 1 to 5 where 1 represents very bad impressions and 5 represents very good impressions. How would you rate the amount of participation in these staff meetings? _____ points. How would you rate the contribution of your boss during these meetings? _____ points. Do you feel that the real planning problems are discussed at the staff meetings? _____ points. Finally, on the 1 to 5 scale, do you feel that there are enough planning meetings? (1 represents too few meetings, 5 too many meetings) _____ points. Overall, how would you rate the staff meetings? _____ points. Why do you feel this way?

Again using the 1 to 5 scale where 1 represents strong agreement, and 5 represents strong disagreement, how would you rate the inconsistency or contradiction among policies and guidelines? _____ points. Do you feel that there is conflict between objectives that groups are expected to accomplish? _____ points. To succeed it is necessary to play politics. _____ points. If a project is going badly it would be better to keep it quiet. _____ points. Good ideas get serious consideration from top management. _____ points. Information is dealt with secretively. _____ points. Overall, how do you feel about conflict and communication in the organization?

Now I'd like you to respond to each of the following questions in terms of the 1 to 5 scale.

This organization is improving. _____ points.

The people in this organization generally do a good job. _____ points.

Sample of Structured Interview—Continued

People with whom I work are interested in improving their job per-

formance. _____ points.

Overall, this organization is doing a good job. _____ points.
There is cooperation among the people in this organization in develop-

ing policies. _____ points.

There is good cooperation among the people in this organization in

carrying out the work. _____ points.

On the 1 to 5 scale, how do you feel about the fairness of promotions

in the _____ ? _____ points.

If 1 is very unfair and 5 is very fair, how do you feel about the pay you

receive for the work you do? _____ points.

Again on the 1 to 5 scale, do you believe that people get credit for

doing a good job? _____ points.

Compared to other people who are doing the same work you are

doing, how do you feel about your pay? _____ points.

Using the 1 to 5 scale, how do you feel about the cooperation between

members of your workgroup? _____ points. Again using this scale,
how do you feel about the relationship between your boss and the

workgroup? _____ points. On this scale, how would you rate the

cooperation between your workgroup and other workgroups? _____

points. Overall, how would you rate your workgroup? _____ points.
Why do you feel this way?

On the 1 to 5 scale, how would you rate your boss regarding the communication of information and new developments that directly affect

corporate strategy? _____ points. On the same scale, how would you

rate managers of the _____ who work in the regional

offices? _____ points. Why do you feel this way?

Questionnaire

An alternative or supplementary approach to information gathering is the questionnaire. The questionnaire survey for assessment requires a set of questions—open-end and/or closed-end, structured or unstructured—to be answered and returned by the relevant parties under study. Some assessors* have little faith and trust in the questionnaire approach for purposes of developing organizations. This may be for several reasons: too impersonal, the difficulty in giving objective and meaningful interpretation to results, attempted improper use as a scorecard, and unrealistic expectations about the ease of developing leads for assessment from descriptive data.

Many analysts (e.g., Likert)† are more favorably inclined toward the questionnaire. Perhaps the situation here is similar to many other instances in organizations where assessment (or training) techniques seem to follow a pattern of rise in interest and use and then decline or abandonment, and then a rebirth, and so on. The questionnaire approach has probably not been developed to its fullest potential as an important diagnostic device.

Two types of questionnaire procedures may be of use in studying complex policy issues. The first is the self-administered, fixed alternative questionnaire. It is praised for requiring the respondent rather than a coder or interviewer to make an attitudinal judgment, for giving greater clarity to the dimensions for answering the question, and for easing data handling via precoding. On the other hand, fixed alternative items may be detrimental in the sense that they provide irrelevant or meaningless frames of reference. That is, the wording may not be appropriate to the respondent. *Choosing a format.*

The other type of questionnaire uses an open-ended format. This type is usually criticized and praised for opposite reasons; e.g., data handling is cumbersome because of the need for coding responses, and response freedom is allowed without researcher-based sets. With advantages and disadvantages for each type, it means that the appropriateness of the response format (open, fixed or a combination) is left to the judgment of the questionnaire developer. Though the open format is cumbersome, this approach has proved useful in assessments; for example, "Write-in responses were extremely valuable in a large government industrial facility. A recurring theme in the write-ins was conflict and polarization, skilled vs. unskilled labor, white vs. black, union vs. nonunion, etc. This polarization lay at the root of numerous problems, including lack of cooperation, poor morale, and even potential violence at the installation.

---

*See E. Shein: *Process Consultation: Its Role in Organization Development,* Reading, Mass., Addison-Wesley Publishing Company, 1969.

†R. Likert: *The Human Organization,* New York, McGraw Hill Book Co., Inc., 1965.

This issue was isolated as one of the primary barriers to organizational improvement, and later fact finding during the survey was aimed at identifying potential solutions in terms of planned management action.*

Questionnaire Item Content

As with the interview, the usefulness of the assessment and development questionnaire rests with the type of questions asked. The type of questions could vary with the kind of policy under study and the kind of respondents who are being used as a source of information. For example, a questionnaire on consumer attitudes toward products or services may be helpful in identifying challenges and opportunities in the external environment. The following is a sample of items that were used in a study of consumer attitudes toward alternative transportation modes in Baltimore (N = 550) and Philadelphia (N = 471).† The respondents were asked to indicate the importance of several factors (time, convenience, reliability, state of vehicle, and so forth) for work trips and nonwork trips. Each respondent was also asked to check how satisfied he was or would have been if he took (1) *auto* and (2) his most likely form of *public* transportation (bus, subway, train, taxi). For example:

Consumer attitudes.

How satisfied were you with

	Very Little	Little Satisfied	Some- what	Gener- ally	Very Well
The time it took to travel					
auto satisfies					
public transportation satisfies					
The cost of the trip					
auto satisfies					
public transportation satisfies					
The feeling of independence					
auto satisfies					
public transportation satisfies					

Implications for strategy.

Some implications for possible strategic moves to change mode use patterns were developed from the study. For example, the researchers concluded that perceptions of travel time, susceptibility to weather, avoidance of changing vehicles, avoidance of waiting, avoiding the unfamiliar and independence were *more* significant

---

*See *Evaluating Personnel Management,* FPM Supplement 273–73, U.S. Civil Service Commission, Washington, D.C., 1973.

†F. T. Paine, A. N. Nash, S. J. Hille and G. A. Brunner: Consumer attitudes toward auto versus public transport alternatives, *Journal of Applied Psychology* *53*(No. 6):472–480, 1969.

than cost, reliability of destination achievement, state of vehicle, congestion and diversions in choosing between auto and public transit.* Also, significantly different preferences were found between the inner-city segment and the suburban segment of respondents.

However, for our main example of a questionnaire let us use the same concept as we did with the interview; when measuring how an organization goes about its policy-formation process, the objective is to ask questions about activities that are (1) descriptive of the policy process, (2) related to organization effectiveness, and (3) capable of being changed by the action of the policy makers.

The policy-formation questionnaire that follows is one such instrument. It attaches an agreement-disagreement scale that can be used to measure such dimensions as planning adequacy, reward orientation, goal consensus and clarity, conflict and inconsistency in policies and standards, and skill utilization depth. (Additional dimensions could be added.)

Content Related to Organizational Effectiveness

A large body of research has shown these dimensions to be associated with organizational effectiveness.† It is recognized that for any particular organization all of these dimensions may not be appropriate criteria of effectiveness. The choice of criteria will depend on the objectives of the organization and the requirements imposed on it by its environment for continued survival and mission attainment.

In fact, these are measures of the organization climate. The theoretical construct of organizational climate according to Forehand and Gilmer refers to the environment within which organization participants operate.‡ The significance of this construct lies in the longstanding proposition that behavior is a function of the interaction of a person and the environment. The combination of items (or scales) proposed are possible methods for assessing organization effectiveness to be used along with gross end results or economic measures. Organizational unit outcomes and economic measures may be difficult to obtain and frequently are contaminated by irrelevant factors such as economic conditions, windfall innovations, fortuitous competitive conditions, and political or governmental variations.

These measures of organization climate seem to be important

Measuring organization climate.

---

*It is interesting to note that the DIAL-A-RIDE bus system has been developed to take advantage of some of the more important travel considerations.

†See, for example, J. Price: *Organizational Effectiveness,* Homewood. Ill., Richard D. Irwin, 1963; C. Perrow: *Organizational Analysis: A Sociological View,* Belmont, Calif., Wadsworth Publishing Co., 1970; T. Mahoney and W. Weitzel: Managerial models of organization effectiveness, *Administrative Science Quarterly 14*(No. 3):357–365, Sept., 1969.

‡G. A. Forehand and B. Von Haller Gilmer: Environmental variation and studies of organizational behavior, *Psychological Bulletin 62*:361–382, 1964.

correlates of organizational effectiveness. If managers were to institute changes so as to maximize such phenomena as clarity and acceptance of goals and improvements in planning adequacy, research suggests that organizational effectiveness would be favorably and significantly affected.

However, the correlates of organizational effectiveness are only a first approximation of the tasks that must be accomplished by top managers if the organization is to be successful. As stated before, additional study and discussion and research need to be conducted to determine clearly defined and highly specific tasks appropriate in various situations. On the following pages is a sample of items from a policy-formation questionnaire that has been tested in business and government.

Policy-Formation Practices Questionnaire

The statements listed on the opposite page describe some policy-formation practices. Rate each item, using the 1 to 5 scale of agreement-disagreement on the degree to which the condition described in the item exists in the organization.

The 20 questions listed in the policy-formation questionnaire examine each of five previously identified dimensions from several perspectives. For example, the four questions 1, 6, 11 and 16 relate to the planning adequacy dimension. The questions have been arranged in mixed sequence for better reliability. However, they may be reshuffled into the dimensions or groupings indicated.* To obtain a composite picture of how those practices are rated, the data are extracted from the questionnaire and consolidated into a policy-formation practice summary form as follows:

Processing the data.

1. Transfer the scores (1 to 5) that are associated with each dimension.
2. Add the scores of all questions associated with each dimension and enter the total.
3. Divide the total by the number of questions in each dimension and enter the average score.

Finally, the average scores are transferred to a Policy Formation Profile Form where they are graphically displayed. These previous procedures, of course, may be handled with a computer program. It may be appropriate to develop such a policy-formation practices profile for each component and/or unit that is being studied. An alternative or supplementary approach would be to develop breakout tables for comparison of superior and subordinates responses and for comparison of unit and component responses. These compari-

---

*The groupings are based on factor analysis. See F. T. Paine and M. J. Gannon: Job attitudes of managers and supervisors, *Personnel Psychology,* Winter, 1973.

1. Important factors are frequently overlooked when plans are made.   YES   yes   ?   no   NO

2. People get credit for good planning.   YES   yes   ?   no   NO

3. People know pretty clearly what is expected of them.   YES   yes   ?   no   NO

4. There is inconsistency or contradictions among policies and standards.   YES   yes   ?   no   NO

5. People have freedom to use their abilities on the job.   YES   yes   ?   no   NO

6. Important information is not considered when basic policies are made.   YES   yes   ?   no   NO

7. Promotions are based on ability and talent.   YES   yes   ?   no   NO

8. People know what they must do to make better plans.   YES   yes   ?   no   NO

9. There is a conflict between objectives or directions that people or groups are expected to accomplish.   YES   yes   ?   no   NO

10. People have enough authority to modify plans as they are implemented.   YES   yes   ?   no   NO

11. Opportunities are missed because of poor planning.   YES   yes   ?   no   NO

12. To succeed it is necessary to play "politics."   YES   yes   ?   no   NO

13. The mission of _____ groups is clearly defined.   YES   yes   ?   no   NO

14. Policies and strategies conflict with each other.   YES   yes   ?   no   NO

15. People must get approval for decisions they should be able to make themselves.   YES   yes   ?   no   NO

16. Policies and plans are made with great care.   YES   yes   ?   no   NO

17. Getting ahead is a matter of luck and pull.   YES   yes   ?   no   NO

18. Specific targets for improvement are made and understood.   YES   yes   ?   no   NO

19. People give assignments or directives that conflict with each other.   YES   yes   ?   no   NO

20. People can use their good ideas.   YES   yes   ?   no   NO

sons could be made on an item by item basis or by grouping of items. The following abbreviated tables suggest one way in which the data may be organized and analyzed in preparation for discussions with managers or groups being assessed or in preparation for a report on the policy-formation process. After the examples of tables for grouping survey data, we turn to other programs for processing information from both the internal and external environment (e.g., market segments).

POLICY-FORMATION PRACTICES SUMMARY FORM

Planning Adequacy	Reward Orientation	Goal Consensus and Clarity	Conflict and Inconsistency in Policies	Skill Utilization Depth
Question Value	Question Value	Question Value	Question Value	Question Value
1 _____	2 _____	3 _____	4 _____	5 _____
6 _____	7 _____	8 _____	9 _____	10 _____
11 _____	12 _____	13 _____	14 _____	15 _____
16 _____	17 _____	18 _____	19 _____	20 _____
Total _____	Total _____	Total _____	Total _____	Total _____
Average _____	Average _____	Average _____	Average _____	Average _____

POLICY-FORMATION PRACTICES PROFILE FORM

Dimensions

Planning Adequacy	YES	yes	?	no	NO
Reward Orientation	YES	yes	?	no	NO
Goal Consensus and Clarity	YES	yes	?	no	NO
Conflict and Inconsistency in Policies	YES	yes	?	no	NO
Skill Utilization Depth	YES	yes	?	no	NO

TABLE OF RESPONSES TO QUESTIONNAIRE ITEMS

Unit _____

There are _____ managers and _____ staff in the unit.

Significant conditions in unit _____

Component _____

There are _____ managers and _____ staff in the unit.

Significant conditions in the component _____

TABLE OF RESPONSES TO QUESTIONNAIRE ITEMS (Continued)

These are the percentage responses to the questionnaire administered in this unit. An asterisk designates that superiors and subordinates *in the unit* responded in a significantly different manner; a double asterisk indicates that supervisors and subordinates in the entire component had significantly different responses.*

*Significant differences in responses between superiors and subordinates can be ascertained by means of a statistical test (t-test). Where possible, efforts should be made to explore the reasons for differences within the unit.

		YES	yes	?	no	NO	No. of Responses
(Conflict)	There is conflict between objectives that people and groups are expected to accomplish						
	Unit	____%	____%	____%	____%	____%	( )
	Component	____%	____%	____%	____%	____%	( )
(PLN)	Important factors are often overlooked when plans are made	____%	____%	____%	____%	____%	( )
		____%	____%	____%	____%	____%	( )
(GC)	People know pretty clearly what is expected of them						
	Unit	____%	____%	____%	____%	____%	( )
	Component	____%	____%	____%	____%	____%	( )

Breakout of Returns and Use of Results

Results from questionnaire, interview, observation and other sources are often useful when comparisons can be made between responses of participants in major components of the organization. By comparing attitudes or behavioral indications from major departments, divisions or satellite units, valuable leads may be discovered as to specific policy problems that are unique to one or more segments of the organization. For example, it may be useful to compare whether respondents in the unit answer in a manner significantly different from the respondents in the entire component. Feedback of such unit-component comparisons may be meaningful to the superior in charge of the unit in question.

In addition, a check could be made to see if there are any significant differences between those responding as superiors and those responding as subordinates. There is a tendency for persons to be clear about how much influence they have, would like to have and are encouraged to exercise when they are subordinates looking upward. It may be more difficult for them to fully accept the same operating guidelines when they look downward at their subordinates. Therefore, they may operate by a double standard. They may want to be involved and have influence with their superior but are unwilling to recognize and accept that their subordinates feel the same way in the organization. Breakouts of data comparing superiors' responses with subordinates, may be helpful in getting such double operating standards out in the open for discussion. Bringing a group together to examine and interpret such policy-formation practices data may lead to the development of some policy-formation practices to correct the situation.

The group may need *practice* and *training* before it can achieve the full potential in this process. Interestingly, as a questionnaire is used with the same group of respondents over time the results may become more reliable and even move backward in terms of favorability of results, even though the environment has not changed significantly or at all. The results may move backward for another reason, namely, because of higher expectations in the group as to effective policy-formation practices.

Catalyst.

Because of such reasons, the actual levels of descriptions, as indicated by the responses on the scale, are of less interest than what the policy-formation group in question (and other such groups) are doing to bring about improvements. Used as a basis for group discussions, the questionnaire's main purpose is to serve as a catalyst to start the improvement process, rather than as a research or analytical instrument.

Market Segmentation Breakouts

Breakouts of questionnaire, interview, sales or other data from relevant parties who are not normally considered members of the organization (e.g., clients or customers) need to be as carefully considered as the data breakouts from those within the organization. For example, it may be useful to breakout groups who are similar in their reasons for needing or wanting or not needing or not wanting a particular type of service or product. The characteristics (i.e., age, sex, income, education, geographic location) of the various groups may give an indication that different strategies or policies could beneficially be adopted for various groups.

An important factor in determining the scope of a corporate strategy involves the decision by analysts as to the key market segments to be exploited. The definition of market segment often presents the organization with artificial constraints that are difficult to overcome. This constraint can be similar to the situation discussed earlier in which the professor limited his potential solutions by his definition of objectives.

The key question asked here is what business the organization is in.* This determines the markets or segments of markets on which the organization will concentrate its efforts. Various methods of determining which segments to attack have been suggested by many authors. Traditionally, market research breakouts have been employed to spot these segments. The key question for the policy analyst involves what the basic types of segments might be.

Again, what business is the organization in?

One form of market segmentation involves differentiating geographic tastes, preferences and requirements. The housing industry understands that different geographic regions require or can withstand varying product standards and that local government regulations provide constraints on the type of building materials, styles and sizes of products that can be offered to the consumer. Other differences involve the needs of the consumer. Housing in the South requires less insulation to the cold than similar housing in the North. A similar example would involve the producers of flavored soft drinks. In the outset of the marketing of these products, it was determined that certain ingredients, particularly caffeine, were more desired by consumers in some areas (the South) than in other areas. Firms engaged in these industries, and others affected by similar types of problems, have adapted their products to these geographic preferences or requirements.

Geographic segments.

Another form of segmentation involves producing the same basic product for several different types of customers. This policy is appropriate when different customers are using a basic product in different ways. An example would include the widespread practice of producing a product for both private label and brand label marketing. Food processors supply the same product to supermarkets for sale under different labels. The product remains the same, but the package and, usually, the price differ. The same practice is followed by many other industries supplying products to the consumer—tires, petroleum and clothing.

Same product for different types of customer.

This type of segmentation allows the organization to utilize its production capacity more fully. Problems arise, however, in that the organization may become overly dependent on one segment to the detriment of the others. Many organizations have found, after entering the private label market, that they have become captive suppliers to one customer. They become dependent on one large customer to absorb their increased capacity. It is also possible that attempting to reach different markets may dilute the efforts of the firm in some one segment.

A third type of segmentation finds an organization attempting to attack several different markets with variations of a similar product. The organization perceives that customers do not all want exactly the same product. The firm attempts to tailor its product line to sat-

Vary product for several markets.

---

*T. Leavitt: Marketing myopia, *Harvard Business Review*, July-August, 1960, pp. 45–56.

isfy as many different customers as possible. The auto industry exemplifies this product and customer policy. The major producers all offer an extensive line of different models through different outlets to appeal to the broad range of tastes and preferences of the consumer. Even with the proliferation of models and lines by the major producers, there is still unfilled demand being captured by foreign producers and small specialists such as the Lotus Europa.

This type of policy may become expensive. Unless large production runs can be utilized, inefficiencies can develop within the organization. In the auto industry there is the need for large scale duplication of marketing and distribution efforts. This type of segmentation requires large investments in all phases of the organization. It also forces the organization to diversify its efforts among several different products and markets. The chance arises that if the various market segments are not large enough, resources may be misallocated among the various products. The policy analysts, while aware of potential difficulties, may find that experimenting with different breakouts of information from informants, clients or customers may give some clues to design market segmentation policies.

What are some potential difficulties?

To reiterate, managers and other policy analysts frequently use multiple sources and multiple methods in gathering and processing information. The results may serve as a vehicle to begin discussion and analysis. For example, the information network, report, observation and interview are regarded as assessment and development tools for identifying indications of possible strategy problem areas or leads to be explored. The results may be used:

As an opener for management discussions and conferences. Discussion of, say, interview results with key participants may be aimed at joint diagnosis of the situation to provide a basis for evaluation.

As an indication of potential demands and opportunities in the external *and* internal environment where in-depth analysis appears to be warranted. Questionnaire results may be considered before a product or customer policy is developed. Interviews and forecasting, for example, can be structured to follow up on the leads generated from the informal information network.

In Chapter 8 we shall explore the use of results from information gathering and processing activity in an interlocking chain of conferences down the hierarchy.

SUMMARY

An organization may need some sort of assessment and development approach for a variety of reasons, such as to aid in: (1) adapting to environmental changes, (2) adjusting to a new domain of operations, (3) maintaining its current position, or (4) improving its "steady state."

A number of approaches (or models), sources, and methods for proceeding with assessment and development are presented in this chapter and the next two chapters. We are stressing a broadly defined organization development approach to policy formation, including management science as well as behavioral science programs. The activities in this approach are viewed as both problem solving and developmental in nature.

In particular, the action-research program is introduced in this chapter. Action research, as the term is used in this book, is a generalized procedure, including three parts: (1) information gathering from the internal and external environment; (2) organization, analysis and feed-in of such information with relevant parties or groups in the organization; and (3) joint action planning based on the analysis and discussion. The generalized procedure may be based (using considerable judgment in selecting content) on the framework suggested thus far in the book, e.g., environmental forces, strategy-generating structure, organization objectives and outcomes and action plans.

This chapter has emphasized that while there is some supporting evidence validating the effectiveness of an action-research program approach for improving some aspects of the policy-formation process, a cautious "I don't know for sure" approach to prescriptions must be maintained. With additional study of the wide variety of applications of action-research programs in both large and small organizations in many countries, in business, government agencies, hospitals, universities and school systems, better insight and understanding may be developed in the next few years.*

This chapter also has paid considerable attention to sources and methods for information gathering and processing, i.e., the informal information network, forecasts, publications, observations, interviews and questionnaires. We have provided several examples and illustrations so that the reader will have some familiarity with a variety of ways of finding out about the "state of things" in the organization and expected conditions in the external environment. Careful judgment and expertise are needed in selecting and using the appropriate sources and methods.

Finally, we introduce some programs for the processing and use of results of our information-gathering activities. Special recognition of the existence and importance of *market segmentation* as a part of corporate strategy formation is given.

Next we shall turn to some management science programs (statistical decision making, models, simulations) that may be useful in generating and analyzing information for the action-research program.

---

*See, for example, the recent study of D. G. Bowers: OD techniques and their results in 23 organizations: The Michigan ICL study, *The Journal of Applied Behavioral Science* 9(No. 1):21–43, Jan./Feb., 1973.

DISCUSSION QUESTIONS

1. Select an organization with which you are familiar. Discuss why this chosen organization may need some sort of systematic assessment and development activities on a more or less continuous basis. What type of information is needed?

2. What is meant by an organization development approach to strategy formulation? In your judgment, how would it differ from more traditional approaches to strategy formation?

One of the many programs in the strategy-generating structure is an action-research program. What does this program involve? How might this program be linked or coupled with other programs?

4. Give an example of how the action-research program might be used in an organization with which you are familiar. Discuss possible difficulties that might be encountered. How would you overcome such difficulties?

5. Compare and contrast the observer approach for data gathering with the interview approach.

6. Identify some of the correlates of organizational effectiveness discussed in the chapter. These variables are measures of organizational climate. What is meant by organizational climate?

7. Organizational unit outcomes and economic measures are frequently said to be contaminated. What does this mean? Why are they contaminated?

8. Discuss two types of interviewing procedures that may be used for data gathering about strategy formation. Under what conditions would you recommend each type?

9. Identify and discuss several guidelines for effective data gathering with survey instruments in an organization.

10. Discuss a top management information system. What are some of the most effective methods and some of the more important sources? What cautions should be observed in using the system?

11. How does the type of question asked affect the usefulness of the assessment interview?

12. Take an organization of your choice. Explain precisely how you would assess the effectiveness of the strategies of that organization. What would be some of the more significant questions you would ask? What sources of information would you use? What methods of data collection would you use?

13. Why is it useful to break out results from data collection by major components of the organization?

14. Discuss the use of results from data collection with survey instruments. Why is the feedback process so important?

15. Identify some of the most useful sources of information for top managers and analysts.

Suggested Additional References for Further Research

Athanassiades, J. C.: The distortion of upward communication in hierarchical organizations. *Academy of Management Journal 16*(2):207–226, June, 1973.

Barrett, R. S.: *Performance Rating.* Chicago, Science Research Associates, 1966.

Campbell, D. T., and Stanley, J. C.: *Experimental and Quasi-Experimental Design for Research.* Chicago, Rand McNally & Company, 1966.

Cochran, W. G.: *Sampling Techniques.* 2nd ed. New York, John Wiley & Sons, 1963.

Hyman, H.: *Survey Design and Analysis.* Chicago, The Free Press of Glencoe, Inc., 1955.

Kelly, J.: The study of executive behavior by activity sampling. *Human Relations 17*:277–287, 1964.

Kerlinger, F. N.: *Foundation's of Behaviorial Research.* New York, Holt, Rinehart & Winston Inc., 1964.

Kish, L.: Survey Sampling. New York, John Wiley & Sons, Inc., 1965.

Labovitz, S., and Hagedorn, R.: *Introduction to Social Research.* New York, McGraw-Hill Book Co., Inc., 1971.

Lopez, F. M., Jr.: Evaluating executive decision making: The in-basket technique. *American Management Association Research Study No. 75, 1966.*

McNaughton, J. B.: Work sampling at executive level. Advanced Management, 1956, 21, 12–13.

Merton, R. K.: Continuities of Social Research. Chicago, The Free Press of Glencoe, 1950.

Mintzberg, H., Raisinghami, D., and Theoret, A.: *The Structure of "Unstructured" Decision Making.* Professional papers of the Academy of Management, Division of Business Policy and Planning, Boston, 1973.

Newell, A., and Simon H. A.: *Human Problem Solving.* Englewood Cliffs, N.J., Prentice-Hall Publishing Co., 1973.

North, R. C., et al.: *Content Analysis.* Chicago, Northwestern University Press, 1963.

Sawyer, J.: Measurement and prediction, clinical and statistical. *Psychological Bulletin. 66*:178–200, 1966.

Simon, J. L.: *Basic Research Methods in Social Sciences: The Art of Empirical Investigation.* New York, Random House, 1968.

Torgerson, W.: *Theory and Methods of Scaling.* John Wiley & Sons, Inc., New York, 1958.

Webb, R. J.: *Organizational Effectiveness in Voluntary Organizations: A Study of the Institutional Church.* Unpublished dissertation, University of Maryland, 1973.

Weick, K. E.: Systematic observational methods. *In* Lindzey, G., and Aronson, E. (eds): *Handbook of Social Psychology.* Rev. ed. Reading, Mass., Addison-Wesley Publishing Company, 1968, 357–451.

USE OF MANAGEMENT SCIENCE
APPROACHES IN STRATEGY
FORMATION
    Quantitative Problems in Policy
    Discounting and Present Value
    Personal Probability
    Establishing Priorities and
      Rates of Return
    Cost of Delay
    Tracing Decisions into the
      Future
    "What If" Questions
    Forecasting Models and
      Methods
    Simulations
    Combining Expert Opinion
REASONS FOR SUCCESS AND
FAILURE OF MANAGEMENT SCIENCE
PROGRAMS

COMPUTER-AIDED DECISION
MAKING
    Applications of Computers
    Creativity and the Computers
    Complex Systems
      Human Reaction to
        Complex Systems
SUMMARY
DISCUSSION QUESTIONS
APPENDIX 1. SOLUTION TO PROBLEM
1
APPENDIX 2. SOLUTION TO PROBLEM
2

7

MANAGEMENT SCIENCE AND COMPUTER PROGRAMS

Some information-gathering and processing aspects of an action-research program have been discussed as a way to measure how an organization goes about its policy-formation process and as a way to assess environmental forces and market segments. The action-research program has been discussed also as a way to obtain an indication of what should be done to improve corporate strategies and policies and to improve the process by which they are made. In addition to, or supplementing, the action-research program there is a broad range of programs available to aid the manager or analyst in playing his role. The range covers a spectrum from rather ill defined qualitative programs (e.g., some scanning or intelligence activities, Chapter 6) to traditional procedures such as financial analysis (Appendix 1 to Chapter 4) to rather sophisticated quantitative programs such as capital budgeting, statistical decision making and simulations. These programs, of course, vary in their degree of usefulness, depending on the type of organization and the type of policy problem. Furthermore, in some situations these programs may be viewed as part of an action-research program, e.g., when they include information processing or analysis that is fed into the action-research program itself. Or, the generalized procedures may be considered as a group of programs that are part of the overall strategy-formation program used to design, implement and review integrated corporate strategies for the organization.

USE OF MANAGEMENT SCIENCE APPROACHES IN STRATEGY FORMATION

We have recognized that if feasible and effective corporate strategies are to be developed and utilized, evaluation programs must be built into the policy-formation process. An understanding of some of the evaluation programs available to the analyst or manager is, thus, a necessity. This chapter will illustrate and briefly discuss some of the rather sophisticated programs for determining if the corporate strategy fits the total environment. We shall consider (1) various management science or quantitative programs for dealing with environmental uncertainties, performing futures forecasting and evaluating alternative corporate strategies, and (2) computer programs for improving creativity in strategy formation.

After study of this chapter the reader should be able to see the relevance of these programs for the manager or analyst, understand where and when they can be used, and recognize some of the limitations and difficulties in applying them. Our objective does *not* include teaching how to actually utilize the management science programs. This is done in functional courses. However, in Appendix 1 to Chapter 4 enough information is given about financial analysis so that it could actually be applied in case discussions or in field projects.

Objectives of this chapter.

The reader, if he processes the information, say, in the Univis case, may gain skill in utilizing the financial analysis program. Furthermore, enough information is given about certain aspects of capital budgeting and statistical decision making so that application may be made directly to specific cases and field investigations.

The basis for much of the evaluation stage of strategy formation lies in various management science programs. Quite often, evaluation involves analyzing the quantitative relationships between the objectives of the organization and the action plan designed to achieve those objectives.

Although these programs can have great value, it must be remembered that there is no substitute for the informed intuition and judgment of top management and influentials. Management science programs are only to supplement, not to replace, the manager's judgment in strategy and policy formation.

Part of the complexity of the problems facing the policy analyst lies in the fact that he must deal with *environmental uncertainties* and he must evaluate *future consequences*. In order to explain these problems and to illustrate some of the assumptions made and some of the generalized procedures that have been proposed to help the analyst, we shall use a simple example of a policy situation involving capital budgeting and statistical decision theory. We shall describe the situation, then ask some questions about it. Then we shall answer the questions and indicate some additional quantitative problems for practice. A policy analyst may want to try to answer the questions before proceeding to the discussion that is provided.

Dealing with uncertainty and future consequences.

Quantitative Problems in Policy

One problem we shall discuss involves financial investment and a change in technology in a very small organization.*

The decision required may be viewed as one of a cluster of decisions. The cluster might include decisions about the product, the market and the source of funds, as well as technology and financial investment. For this very small firm the decision may be viewed as a strategic decision. The problem is as follows:

In the past, all financial investment decisions made in the Larroc Corporation have been based on the "intuitive" hunches of its president, A. N. Renim. Recently the president, heeding the advice of his astrologer, hired a young financial analyst, Mr. M. Nonnag, who, since he has been with the organization, has spent considerable time extolling the virtues of present value analysis to Mr. Renim. In a recent conversation between the two on this subject, the president made the following comments: "Your present value model is theoretically unsound because it assumes that future returns realized from investments are known for certain, whereas, in real life, they're not. For example, I have a chance to buy for $5,000 a new machine with an economic life of three years that will (1) effect labor savings of $2,200 in the first year, $3,630 in the second, and $2,662 in the third if business is good, but will (2) effect savings of only $1,100 in the first year, $2,420 in the second, and $1,331 in the third if business is bad. Our cost of capital is approximately 10 per cent."

Mr. Nonnag asked, "What probabilities do you assign to business being "good" as opposed to being "bad"?

"About 50–50," responded Mr. Renim.

"Well, then," said the analyst, "solving your problem is not difficult at all."

1. What do you suppose Mr. Nonnag's conclusion was? Why? Show all calculations.
2. What would the analyst's conclusion have been had the president assigned a probability of: (1) 0.3 to "good" business conditions and 0.7 to "bad" business conditions? (2) 0.4 to "good" conditions, and 0.6 to "bad" conditions?
3. What are the weaknesses of such management science programs for policy formation?

Discounting and Present Value

One way to handle the problem would be as follows:

The pattern of benefits (savings) occurs over a three-year period. We recognize that a dollar today is worth more than a dollar next year, because we have the option of investing the present dollar and obtaining a positive return during the time period in which we would have to wait for the other dollar. A way to take the time value of money into account is called discounting or present value calculating. The simple arithmetic of compound interest may be relied on

Present value calculation.

---

*This problem was adapted from M. Richards and P. Greenlaw: *Management Decision Making*. Homewood, Ill., Richard D. Irwin, 1966.

in calculations for an approximate solution (approximate because an assumption is made that the benefits are received at the end of each year). If the interest rate is r between year 0 and year 1, then $1 can be converted to $1 + r dollars in year 1. In similar fashion a dollar return in year 1 can be exchanged for $1/(1 + r)$ dollars in year 0. Thus, the present value of $1 in year 1 is $1/(1 + r)$ or, more generally, the present value of $1 in year n is $1/(1 + r)^n$.

For the problem given we would come up with the present value for each of the years' savings and then add them together for a total present value associated with a decision to invest followed by good business conditions. Follow a similar procedure for bad business conditions. But what is the r? The interest rate (r) is the cost of using money, and our indicated cost of capital is 10 per cent. We proceed as follows:

If good business, PV=2,200/1.1 + 2,630/1.21 + 2,662/1.33 = $7,000
If poor business, PV=1,100/1.1 + 2,420/1.21 + 1,331/1.33 = $4,000.

The $7,000 and the $4,000 are referred to as present values (PV). They may also be referred to as conditional values (CV), that is, benefits dependent or conditioned on the business climate. Two alternative business climates have been indicated as possible; only two, of course, is a simplification.*

What is a conditional value?

Personal Probability

So far the likelihood of probability of occurrence of each alternative climate has not been taken into account. In using management science procedure from statistical decision theory one may take the probability of various outcomes into account by explicitly using the personal judgment of the decision maker as to the likelihood of the various outcomes. The policy analyst should carefully audit the environment and estimate this likelihood. Then the value of the outcome (or present value of outcome) should be weighted by the probability of occurrence of the outcome. The result is called the *expected value* (EV). Thus, the expected value of a conditional benefit is equal to the perceived probability of occurrence times the conditional benefit. In the problem that we have:

What is an expected value?

If good business: $7,000 × 0.50 = 3,500
If poor business: $4,000 × 0.50 = 2,000

The two expected values ($3,500 and $2,000) may be added together, based on the assumption in our procedure that there is a

---

*The problem may be adapted to a government organization by determining the financial value of benefits of services to the client under various conditions. The calculation of benefits, of course, is difficult and inexact.

100 per cent probability of good business *or* poor business: $3,500 + $2,000 = $5,500. $5,500 is the total expected value of the benefits. Thus, the benefits have been adjusted for the time pattern of distribution and for uncertainty. We have used discounting to present value and personal probability to make these adjustments.

Before we go further it should be mentioned that in simplifying the problem we have ignored depreciation and corporate income taxes. These might be taken into account by subtracting annual depreciation from gross benefits, obtaining taxable income (if a profit is being made). The taxable income times the income tax rate would give the taxes, and subtracting the taxes from the gross benefits would give us the net savings. The main thrust of the discussion here, however, does not have to do with taxes and depreciation.

The reader may wish to proceed with the calculations with part (2) of the problem to check the effect of variations on probability estimates that might be used. In addition, there are some variations in calculation procedure, but these are outside the scope of this book. For a discussion of the possibilities there are numerous books on statistical decision theory.*

Present value decision rule.

Thus, present value is one procedure to be used in making the choice. It says, in summary, that a project should be undertaken if the sum of future returns minus costs discounted back to the present is positive; that is, if PV > 0.

Case Problem I

The following problem illustrates the application of present value techniques to a strategic decision-making process:

A staff planner has been presented with three alternative strategic moves to offer to top management. The three strategic moves appear to be feasible relative to the external environment. He is not sure that they are financially feasible, however.

They all have differing cash flows, so that comparison is not obvious. The planner would like to know if any of the moves would be profitable and which would provide the greatest return based on net present value (NPV) criteria. He has already determined that the cost of capital for the firm is 7 per cent. The cash flows for the three moves under the same probability are shown below.

Strategic Move	Initial Outlay	Net Returns			
		Year 1	Year 2	Year 3	Year 4
A	100,000	15,000	45,000	60,000	55,000
B	125,000	50,000	40,000	25,000	20,000
C	75,000	30,000	25,000	20,000	15,000

*For example, see R. Schlaifer: *Applied Statistical Decision Theory.* Boston, Division of Research, Graduate School of Business Administration, Harvard University, 1961; and S. Kassarf: *Normative Decision Making,* Englewood Cliffs, N.J., Prentice-Hall, Inc., 1970.

Which of the strategic moves are economically feasible? If the firm can make only one strategic move, which should it make and why? Solutions can be found in Appendix 1 of this chapter.

Establishing Priorities and Rate of Return

Projects seldom occur in isolation. The choice is not just whether we accept or reject this specific project; what is needed is a priority approach for ranking competing projects. The present value method may be converted to a priority approach; or another criterion, the rate of return, may be used. Some readers may be familiar with this alternative approach, which asserts that a project should be undertaken if the rate of return is greater than the cost of capital (r > cost of capital). The rate of return (r) is the rate that equates the present value of the future stream of benefits with the present value of the future stream of costs; that is, $PV = 0$.

Why do we need priorities?

This rate of return criterion will indicate the same choice as the present value criterion for accept-reject policy problems. Furthermore, as indicated, the rate of return provides a basis for establishing priorities among competing projects. The present value also provides such a basis, but these methods do not always indicate the same order of rank; that is, under certain time patterns of benefits and costs, the present value rank order will not be the same as the rate of return rank order. This occurs because of the differences in the assumptions about the rate at which the benefits will be reinvested. Simply stated, according to the statistical decision theory, a decision maker in selecting an approach should check to see which assumption comes closer to his situation.*

Rate of return.

Cost of Delay

Another difficulty with the rank order approach may be that the cost of delaying certain alternatives may not be considered. Some strategic moves may be better suited to present needs; others can be delayed profitably if, for example, the interest rate is expected to come down. A simple example using present values and assuming a $1,000 yearly budgetary constraint (a very small organization) is shown below.

Strategic Move	Cost	Present Value Year 1	Year 2	Cost of Delay
A Divest product line x	$1,000	$2,100	$1,800	$300
B Phase out distributors	$1,000	$1,300	$1,100	$200
C Begin search for sites	$1,000	$1,700	$1,050	$650

*For a more complete explanation of situations in which the two methods produce different results, see H. Bieman, Jr., and S. Schmidt: *The Capital Budgeting Decision*, New York, The Macmillan Company, 1966.

Different choice?

If we select the strategic move on the basis of rank order for each year, we select move A in the first year and move B in the second year (A has already been selected). Examining the cost of delay, however, would lead us to a different choice, that is, C in the first year and A in the second year. This illustrates for us that choices cannot be made in a vacuum. As we discussed in Chapter 5, a

Portfolio approach.

portfolio of strategies (and budgets) should be taken into account that ties together short- and long-range opportunities and resources. The effects of alternatives should be closely analyzed to determine what interactions will occur in the long run. Strategic moves that appear beneficial in the short run can often become constraining influences in the long run.

Tracing Decisions into the Future

Decision tree procedure.

Decision trees are one application of statistical decision making that is particularly useful for tracing decisions into the future, especially for capital budgeting decisions. Decision trees help the analyst to structure his decisions under conditions of uncertainty. By indicating the many possible events and the decision-making requirements that will be encountered, and using estimates of probability that each event will occur, this procedure helps the manager to assess the probable payoff from his decision.

The following diagram traces a simple decision tree problem. The analyst can make one of two investment decisions. Decision A has a 50 per cent probability of returning a net profit of $7,000 and a 50 per cent probability of returning $3,000. Decision B has a 60 per cent probability of returning $10,000 and a 40 per cent probability of no profit. The initial diagram would be drawn as follows:

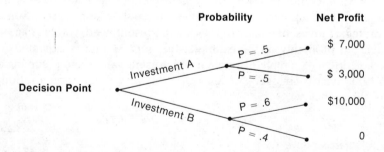

Probability	Net Profit
P = .5	$ 7,000
P = .5	$ 3,000
P = .6	$10,000
P = .4	0

Investment A
Investment B
Decision Point

The solution would find the expected value for both investments, and a decision would theoretically be made based on the highest expected profit. (In this case, investment B would be chosen, since it has an EV = $6,000 versus an EV of $5,000 for investment A.)

A realistic view of the decision-making process, however, would consider how the various outcomes might affect the decision maker's future. The decision maker might decide to choose investment A regardless of the fact that investment B has a higher expected value. He might be led to this conclusion because there is a positive net profit from one, whereas there is a potential for no profit from the other. If, as we discussed in earlier chapters, individual rewards are based on not incurring negative results, then this would provide a "safer" decision.

Are managers finding statistical decision making useful? The situation is changing rapidly. However, a recent survey* of 40 United States companies indicates that 12, or 30 per cent, use general statistical decision-making procedures for planning for the following types of applications: to analyze factors in markets outside the U.S. to be considered in marketing lighting and home-entertainment products, to estimate costs, and to make general forecasts of economic conditions, deposits, earnings, and so on.

The survey also indicates that 15, or 38 per cent, use decision trees for planning for the following types of uses: to select research and development projects, to evaluate alternative new business opportunities, and to evaluate the outcome of strategic moves that are conditional, particularly in regard to product-planning decisions. Decision trees have become more commonly used by business managers, but they still have not achieved widespread acceptance. The main reason seems to be the difficulty in obtaining accurate information about the kinds of problems management faces and the computational complexity for all but the simplest problems. The following decision tree problem demonstrates the uses of this method in the strategy-formation process.

Case Problem II

A chief executive has requested his planning staff to analyze potential alternatives available to the firm. The alternatives involve expansion into new product lines related to their present efforts. They cannot afford to enter both areas at the same time, however. Both areas are relatively new, and information is not perfect. The expected returns under best and worst conditions are as shown below.

	Product A	Product B
Best results (0.4 prob.)	$7,000,000	$10,000,000
Worst results (0.6 prob.)	$6,000,000	$ 5,000,000

*E. C. Miller: *Advanced Techniques for Strategic Planning*, AMA Research Study 104, New York, AMA, 1971. This excellent study has provided many examples and ideas, some of which are paraphrased in the following sections. See also B. W. Denning: *Corporate Planning: Selected Concepts*, New York, McGraw-Hill Book Co., 1972; M. K. Starr: Planning models, *Management Science 13* (No. 4):115–141, 1966; H. Mintzberg: The science of strategy making, *Industrial Management Review 8*:71–81, 1967.

The planning staff has to decide if it is worthwhile to gather more information at a cost of $1 million. The estimated effectiveness of this research is not perfect, however. The staff estimates the probability of obtaining information favoring Product line A under the worst results is 0.7. Likewise, the probability of information that favors Product line B under the best conditions is 0.8.

Which product line should be chosen and why? The solution can be found in Appendix 2 at the end of the chapter.

"What If" Questions

Models.

In the adoption of any management tool the critical test is the test of usefulness. One great value is to enable management to ask "What if . . ." questions. The major contribution of models is their ability to ask questions and obtain answers that are an approximation of what might actually happen if a particular corporate strategy is followed. This makes it possible for organizations to experiment with new strategies and policies before they select the one they will ultimately adopt. Models, therefore, are frequently designed to evaluate outcomes of corporate strategies, given various forecasts of future events. A simplified example of an attempt to evaluate the strength of a proposed corporate strategy against what a competitor might do is shown in Figure 7–1. In many cases analysis of this kind leads to a better understanding of contingencies which need to be taken into account.

A model you see is merely an artificial representation of a possible or actual occurrence. It is an abstraction used to represent conditions, relationships and processes. The model may be expressed in mathematical form. Although many managers tend to shy away from anything mathematical, they have, in fact, worked with a mathemat-

KEY ELEMENTS OF PROPOSED CORPORATE STRATEGY

What if Competitor A's Basic Strategy is	Build Continental Production Capacity	Expand Continental Sales Force	Concentrate R & D on Applications
Component supplier	Effective	Neutral	Neutral
Domestic only	Neutral	Strong	Neutral
Leader in technology	Neutral	Neutral	Weak
Specialized/high price	Weak	Neutral	Weak

Figure 7–1 *Assessing corporate strategy against what each competitor might do. (Adapted from L. V. Gerstner, Jr.: Can strategic planning pay off?* Business Horizons 15 *(No. 6):11, December, 1972.)*

ical model of their business if they have worked with a budget. The budget is actually a quantitative forecast of future actions. Therefore, there should be nothing inherently threatening in the use of models.

Mathematical models vary in complexity from simple linear relationships used in break-even charts to highly complex linear programming techniques. The equation $y = k + av$ is an example of a simple model, where y equals total costs, k equals fixed costs, a equals variable costs per unit, and v equals volume in units. The equation is a symbolic representation of a real-world process.

Modeling has been aided by computers that process and store the tremendous quantities of data involved in modern business operations. The very act of constructing models, however, generates new insights into the nature of the factors that make it successful, or not.

Models can also be used to test the sensitivity of the end result *Sensitivity* sought, such as present worth or return on investment; to change *analysis.* certain input factors; and to test the impact of alternative courses of action. Some specific applications of models that have been reported include the following:

(1) to evaluate the effect of alternative corporate strategies on profit; (2) to forecast cash flow; (3) to develop a corporate profit model; (4) to contribute to determination of research priorities and to estimate improvements in productivity from automation.

The North American Rockwell Corporation, as an example, uses corporate models to assist it in acquisition planning.* They first use the model to uncover promising sectors of the economy in which it is anticipated that future growth will be above average for the economy as a whole. This is done with a model of the United States economy projected to 1975–1980. The company then carefully screens possible acquisitions. Once a promising possibility has been found, the company uses a computer-based financial model to determine what the effect of the acquisition would be on its overall financial resources.

Boston Edison also built a corporate financial model, from which the following six major guidelines evolved:

"1. It is possible to start with a gross, simple model and work systematically to refine it.
2. The total task of building an overall corporate model can be divided into a number of submodels, which are more manageable to work with. If this is done, however, care must be exercised to see that the various submodels are properly integrated; that is, that each one is consistent with the others.
3. Here, as in any major effort, top management support is indispensable.

*See Ansoff, H. I., *et al.*: Does Planning Pay? The Effects of Planning on Success of Acquisitions in American Firms, Long Range Planning, 3, December, 1970. This study of 93 firms provides some quantitative evidence supporting the effectiveness of long range planning (for acquisitions).

4. It is important to work on the problems top management wants worked on. Once the model has proved its usefulness in helping to make the long-term decisions that are important to the business, management will seek the guidance of the model for decisions of lesser priority.

5. Team effort is a particularly effective way of going about building a complex corporate model. A team ensures the expert inputs needed and also helps to win acceptance for the model and the new methods of analyses that a model provides.

6. A workable financial model can be constructed without recourse to complex mathematics. The essentials of a good computer model of the financial aspects of a business are effective systems for processing the financial affairs of the company, sound accounting advice, and expert computer programming."*

Any kind of model is limited by the realism of the variables used to describe the actual occurrence. Too often models have been developed based on the perceptions of these occurrences by only one or a few individuals. The perception of the market, as an example, may differ substantially within different levels and functions within the organization. Some individuals may perceive many market factors, such as competitive reactions, pricing, and to some extent, even demand for the product, as external to the decision process of the firm. Others, however, may view these same factors as being key determinants of their actions.

If the model is to be an effective tool for answering "what if" questions, these differing perceptions must be coalesced into a consistent explanation of the effect of decision on outcomes. If they are not, using the previous example, the model would be invalid for at least one of the groups, at best. One group would be evaluating decisions with a model that did not express their views of the environment. Those policy analysts would be falling into the standard trap faced by anyone who uses models, computerized or not. That is the garbage in—garbage out syndrome; the results are only as effective as the inputs.

Garbage in, garbage out.

Forecasting Models and Methods

A variety of management science models and methods may be useful to the manager in forecasting.† Econometric methods, for example, involve measurements of economic variables, frequently including correlation analysis. Using such analysis (and other techniques) the technocrat (an econometrician in this case) constructs equations that relate relevant variables to the factor being predicted and therefore to develop predictive equations. Such equations have

---

*E. C. Miller: *Advanced Techniques for Strategic Planning*, op. cit., p. 59.
†L. T. Sitmister and J. Turner: The development of systematic forecasting procedures in British industry, Journal of Business Policy *3* (No. 2), 43–52, Winter, 1972–1973. See also discussion and references in Chapter 6.

been used: (1) to forecast market sizes, (2) to forecast prices, (3) to forecast the relationship between volume of activity and costs, and (4) to relate profit to supply of raw materials.

These forecasts may be useful in the portfolio approach.

Econometric forecasting is a rapidly expanding field. Moreover, the models currently in use are no longer limited to short-range (six- to 18 months) forecasts of the economy as a whole. Long-range (up to five years) models are being built to forecast trends and changes for the entire economy, such as the Hickman-Coen model at Stanford. Short- and intermediate-term models for specific industries are also being developed.

When fully developed, these techniques could be of great assistance to the policy analyst in attempting to forecast future demand. A key factor, however, involves the determination of just how well the particular econometric model fits with the objectives of the analyst. The industry represented by the model must correspond specifically with that of the firm. The time span encompassed by the model must also correspond with the time span dealt with in the corporate strategy.

Does model fit objectives of analyst?

The policy analyst must realize that no econometric method is infallible; it is only as good as its component parts. All econometric models are based, in large part, on past experience. They cannot predict sudden changes in policy such as wage and price controls. The results of econometric models must be constantly analyzed and updated if they are to be used effectively in forming and evaluating corporate strategies.

Another rapidly growing field is *technological forecasting.* Technological forecasting has been defined as "the prediction, within a stated level of confidence, of the anticipated occurrence of a technological achievement, within a given time frame with a specified level of support."* Each forecast comprises five categories:

Technological forecasting.

1. *Background.* This section should identify the organizational objectives to which the fields of technology being forecast can contribute.
2. *Present Status.* The field of technology's current state-of-the-art should be quantitatively described.
3. *Forecasts.* Consists of a projection of the state-of-the-art as a function of time and cost with an indicated level of confidence.
4. *Product Implications.* This section should describe the effect on the corporation of the technological advances projected in the forecast.
5. *References and Associated Activities.* List the technical documents in the field that add credibility to the forecast.

The methods used to forecast the future state-of-the-art are generally categorized as intuitive, growth analogy, and trend correlation, with several techniques existing within each of these categories.

---

*Marvin J. Cetron and Donald N. Dick: Technological forecasting: Practical problems and pitfalls, *European Business* 21:13–24, April, 1969. See also J. R. Bright: *Technological Forecasting for Industry and Government.* Englewood Cliffs, N.J., Prentice-Hall, Inc., 1968.

Technological forecasting has been utilized by public as well as private organizations. The U.S. Navy first prepared and published a technological forecast in 1968. This has aided them in determining what types of armaments might be possible in the future. This is particularly useful because of the long lead times involved in developing sophisticated weapons systems. Other public and private organizations have used technological forecasting for similar ends.

Input-output models.

Still another forecasting technique, which may grow rapidly in the near future, is the use of *input-output* models. Input/output analysis is a method for analyzing the interrelationships of a particular economy to uncover existing interdependencies. Through this method of analysis, the trend of development of the technical coefficients among the various economic sectors included in the input/output table can be combined to forecast the growth or decline of these sectors by some specified time in the future. Technical coefficients are ratios that show the proportion of each economic sector's output that is made up of inputs into that sector and all the other economic sectors under study. In broad terms, input/output analysis shows where all purchases by an industry come from and where all sales end up, as inputs either to other industries or to final-demand markets. This indicates the interdependencies that exist in the economy. It is only since the development of large computers that input/output analysis has become useful to the businessman. Even today it is not widely used. However, many feel it will be one of the essential planning tools of the near future as analysts become more sophisticated in their design and analysis of these techniques.

What do technical coefficients indicate?

The main advantage of input/output analysis is that the interindustry forecasting provides detail by industry and by markets, which the aggregative econometric models do not.

The National Steel Corporation and the Celanese Corporation use input/output analyses developed specifically for their industries. By using forecasts of the technical coefficients that are projected for some specified time in the future, the input/output models contribute in both cases to the companies' long-term forecasts. Combustion Engineering, Inc., also uses input/output analysis for long-term economic forecasting.

Simulations

Simulations involve the use of models to investigate what would result if we used different assumptions and forecasts about the organization and its environment. To the degree that the model is accurate, the simulation runs will show what would happen if the circumstances represented by the interactions occurred in the real world. In this sense, any model can be used to simulate. Analysts talk of using their models to ask "what if" questions; the operations involved in answering these questions define simulations.

Monte Carlo simulations are based on the laws of probability implicit in games of chance such as poker, dice, or roulette. The values assigned to each of the variables on each run of the model are selected at random from probability distributions developed to represent the likelihood of occurrence of each of the values. The simulation provides a distribution of the end result that would be obtained given the assumption of the different sets of values run with the model. The manager can then calculate the most likely end result and decide, on the basis of whatever criteria he selects, whether this result would be acceptable to him.

What are Monte Carlo simulations?

In business gaming, the models used may be all verbal or part verbal and part mathematical or entirely mathematical. The essential element is that participants in the game assume roles and act out these roles in the patterns or circumstances posed by those running the game. The participants' judgments at each successive stage become the inputs to the next stage of the model.

Simulation has a long history. It is possible to trace the technique back to early war games. Although simulation is quite popular in other fields, it seems to have caught on as a useful business tool only recently.

Some examples of the use of simulation for strategy formation include the following: evaluating a new product, evaluating planning alternatives, assisting research and development planning and project selection, and studying possible divestments and consolidations. The Burroughs Corporation has a simulation model of the financial structure of the entire company. Xerox Corporation uses simulation to aid in marketing decisions. American Can developed a family of models to help to make the many different planning decisions it faces.

Risk analysis is a kind of simulation that managers are using more and more to assess the relative attractiveness of alternative plans.

Risk analysis.

Alternative plans typically depend on many inputs that will occur in the future. Among these may be market size, selling prices, market growth rate, share of market, investment required, operating costs and useful life of facilities. Risk analysis allows an evaluation of the plans that take into consideration the uncertainties surrounding the inputs.

In applying risk analysis, the analyst would generate a probability distribution for values of *each* significant input (indicating the chances that the value would be achieved). Then sets of the inputs would be selected (at random) according to the chances they have of turning up in the future. The rate of return would be determined for each combination, and the process repeated until there is a clear portrayal of the investment (chances that the rate will be achieved).*

How to apply risk analysis?

---

*For elaboration, see D. B. Hertz: *New Power for Management.* New York, McGraw-Hill Book Co., Inc., 1969.

The analyst with a number of alternative plans and his own sub-jective schedule of levels of the risks he is willing to accept has a basis for choosing among the alternatives.

The Univis case in Chapter 1 describes a rather simplistic method of attempting to use levels of risk in the planning process. The risk table at the end of the case attempts to put limits on the po-tential opportunities open to the firm. These limits are the percep-tions of some individual as to the appropriate degree of risk accept-able for a particular action. It is unclear just how the risk table was arrived at; also, the risk table appears to be extremely conservative. This would seem contradictory to the expressed desire by the com-pany to be considered a growth-oriented organization by investors; this points up a problem in using risk analysis.

The risk factors used by a firm such as Univis must be consist-ent throughout the corporate strategy. They also must be consistent throughout the firm. While it may be relatively easy to determine the degree of risk acceptable to an individual, it is far more difficult, if not impossible in some instances, to do this for an entire organiza-tion.

Some examples of the use of risk analysis include the following: To evaluate medium and large capital investments, to evaluate new product proposals, and to evaluate diversification opportunities. Exxon International, Inc., uses risk analysis to investigate whether it would be more advantageous for the company to build or to charter a vessel to transport the company's goods. McKinsey and Co., Inc., uses risk analysis for helping a client select among a number of different patterns of investment in the development of a sugar cane plantation.

Restricted use?

Risk analysis provides a rational approach for evaluating stra-tegic alternatives by reflecting the uncertainties affecting the inputs. The cost of applying the techniques so far has restricted its use (usually to substantial problems). Standard computer programs are being developed, however, so that it will be possible to use this help-ful way of looking at alternatives more frequently.

Combining Expert Opinion

One problem that has been discussed in conjunction with using management science programs is obtaining a consensus on the direc-tion of growth for the firm. What apparently is required is a method of combining the opinions of key individuals within the organization for those purposes.

Delphi method.

The Delphi method, as developed by the Rand Corporation,* is a decision-making technique that is designed to gather expert con-sistent opinions from group members. The final decision, or analy-

---

*N. C. Dalkey: *The Delphi Method: An Experimental Study of Group Opinion.* Rand Corp., 1969.

sis, should provide a consensual group point of view. Typically the problems attacked are ones in which uncertainty, through lack of complete information, is a key factor.

The technique requires three key ingredients: The first involves the precept that all responses by the expert members of the group should be anonymous. In this way undue emphasis is not placed on who originates the information, but on the content of the information itself. This is particularly important where the expert opinions are originating from individuals within the organization. Without anonymity of responses, formal or informal leaders would probably exert undue influence during the process.

What are three key ingredients?

The second factor involves the ability of the group members to refine their decisions and analyses through feedback of prior information. All members of the group are given an overall figure or piece of data (such as a median response) representing the responses of the group. They may then base their next decision on this overall information. This provides the experts with the ability to refine their assessments based upon more information than was originally available. In this manner they can reassess their personal probabilities.

The third factor requires presentation of the results of each interaction in a statistical form that allows for breadth of opinion as well as noting what the consensus might be. The purpose is to allow for differences of opinion while also indicating the trend of the thinking of the group. This allows the experts to further adjust their projections based on their own analysis of future trends, consensus of other individuals and the spread of opinions. In this manner, diversity of thought is allowed in the decision-making process. The possibility of following diverse opinion is open to the respondents.

The purpose of the Delphi method is to combine these factors to aid the decision-making group in arriving at a consensus concerning the environment facing the firm. This process is designed to make arrival at the decision impartial and participative. Because of the results derived from this method, its application to risk analysis, personal probability and other forms of statistical decision making is enhanced. The Delphi method can help to overcome some of the previously noted problems of using management science programs.

This process is also particularly useful in arriving at a consistent projection of future trends. This is of assistance in determining if the various parts of the corporate strategy, both objectives for change and the action plan, are feasible relative to environmental trends. For an example of projections of future trends based on a Delphi approach using 70 experts at the Institute for the Future see Table 7-1.

If these projections are accurate how will they affect your organization?

REASONS FOR SUCCESS AND FAILURE OF MANAGEMENT SCIENCE PROGRAMS

Although schools of business have been teaching management science programs for some time, effective implementation of these

TABLE 7-1 WHAT'S LIKELY TO HAPPEN BY 1985

Event	Per cent probability
Many chemical pesticides phased out	95%
National health insurance enacted	90
Spending on environmental quality exceeds 6% of GNP	90
Insect hormones widely used as pesticides	80
Community review of factory locations	80
Substantial understanding of baldness and skin wrinkling	40
A modest (3%) value-added tax passed	40
Wide use of computers in elementary schools	25
Development of cold vaccines	20
Autos banned in central areas of at least seven cities	20
Breeder reactors banned for safety reasons	20

*Source: Institute for the Future, as presented in Business Week, 70 August 25, 1973.

programs has not occurred on any large scale. There are several reasons associated with this lack of success.

Understanding of strategy-formation process?

Quite often a key problem involves the inability of the management science expert to fully understand how the strategy-formation process operates. This failure causes misunderstandings between these technocrats and the managers who eventually have to use the programs.*

Conflict between the manager and the technocrat.

Both these groups have their own languages as well as perceptions of what the programs should do. Until the technocrat and the manager can agree in a conversant manner as to the process itself and the applicability of management science programs to that process, effective use will be seriously impeded.

Furthermore, the role of the technocrat in the strategy-formation process must be clearly defined. All too often, the technocrat is pressed into making decisions since he is the only one who can interpret output from what are perceived by other analysts as complex decision-making programs. When this occurs, antagonisms can develop between the two groups within the organization. Managers often view the technocrats as purposefully trying to usurp power within the organization on the basis of their technical expertise. This inhibits communications and exacerbates the problems noted previously.

Adequate data?

A complaint often voiced by the technocrat, however, is the lack of accurate data to use in the programs. Strategy formation, as we have noted, is not a precise science. Managers have learned to try to make decisions based on limited data. This "seat of the pants" type of decision making is usually abhored by the technocrat; he often feels frustrated by this inability to use management science

*See W. K. Hall: Strategic planning models: Are top managers really finding them useful? *Journal of Business Policy* 3(No. 2):33–42, 1973; E. C. Miller: *Advanced Techniques for Strategic Planning*, op. cit. and C. J. Grayson: Management Science and Business Practice. Harvard Business Review, *51*:41–48, July-August, 1973.

programs in the ideal manner for which they were developed. This frustration may lead to a failure to adapt these programs to the data that are available.

Also, the technocrat often complains that the traditional manager does not want to use new techniques. The technocrat feels that the manager's fears of unknown programs inhibits their application to business problems.

The manager replies that the main problem is that the technocrat is interested only in using a particular program. The manager feels that the technocrat is not interested in the problem posed by the strategy process. He is viewed as being interested primarily in experimenting with his program, often at the cost of an effective or efficient decision-making process.

All too often, when it is decided to use management science programs, sufficient preparation is not made within the organization. Top management sometimes decides for reasons of status, or simply because competition has implemented a particular program, that it is necessary for their organization to do likewise.

Preparation for use?

Management science programs, like any other type of innovative program, must have more than top management commitment. They must be understood by the managers who will eventually be required to use these programs. The organization can't simply hire a new group of managers who already understand the programs; it also can't wait for a new generation of managers who are trained in these programs to gradually replace current managers. What may be needed is a thorough training program for managers already within the organization.

At this point in time, however, most management science programs are used solely for evaluation purposes. A corporate strategy has to be devised by traditional methods before programs can be used to test its feasibility relative to constraints facing the organization. Too often the manager relies solely on imitation to develop the corporate strategy. This leads to an inability to properly analyze the corporate strategy through the use of management science programs. The corporate strategy has not been developed on a rigorous basis and, therefore, doesn't lend itself to quantification. The variables inherent in the strategy are not fully defined.

Full defining and integrating the variables in the corporate strategy.

If management science programs are to be used effectively the various phases of strategy formation must be defined and integrated. Strategy development and evaluation must be defined so that one can build on the other in a rational and well defined manner.

Many of the programs we have discussed may seem simplistic and commonplace to the student or teacher of Business Policy. It is becoming increasingly important, however, for most upper and middle level managers to utilize these programs to maintain their competitive posture.

In fact, the manager who utilizes these methods now finds himself with a comparative advantage in the marketplace. The position of the manager must take cognizance of the human factors and influences caused by use of sophisticated programs, however. Quite often the problems posed by implementation of new methods are increased through the introduction of computer-oriented approaches. Most management science programs are, after all, most efficiently used with computer facilities.

Applying programs to a creative process.

The key to these problems lies in applying formalized procedures to a creative process. Strategy formation must be viewed by managers as an uninhibited and nonthreatening procedure if it is to succeed.

COMPUTER-AIDED DECISION MAKING

The use of management science, especially through computers, for all types of management functions has been proposed for some time. The first step in utilizing the computer, be it for simple mechanistic tasks or for more complex purposes, has been to attempt to understand the particular process. Our analysis of the strategy-formation process to this point has demonstrated several areas where the computer could potentially be of use.

There isn't total agreement as to the effectiveness of the computer over the full range of management decision making; however, the creative world of top management decision making resists quantification or model-building efforts, in many areas.* This has been true because management decisions, particularly at the top, are seldom routine. The capacity of the computer to store knowledge and guidance procedures must be expanded if it is to be of greater use. More importantly, however, as mentioned, the strategy-formation process requires much better and more insightful understanding before use of the computer can be expanded in this area.†

We do understand the strategy formation process much better than it might appear. The process, as we have noted in earlier chapters, can be divided into several phases or stages. All these stages share common characteristics. Probably the most important characteristic involves the need for creativity on the part of the individuals involved in the strategy formation. This creativity must be present not only in the formulation stage, where alternatives are generated, but also in the evaluation stage, where the corporate strategy is refined to its final forms.

If we attempt to study the problem in parts, we might find our task a bit easier. Creativity appears to be a significant factor in the strategy-formation process. Creativity, particularly in conjunction with the computer, requires confidence, knowledge, and effort on

*See Tom Alexander: Computers can't solve everything, *Fortune, 80*:126–129, October, 1969.

†See Martin L. Ernst: Stage three for computers: Management decision making, *Illinois Business Review 27*:6–7, April, 1970.

the part of the strategist; however, the key here is that the individual must be willing to follow some form of set procedure.* In line with this, however, the manager must have the knowledge necessary to be able to ask the types of questions most relevant to the problem at hand. Also, he must be willing to perform, at least to some extent, the function of combining, screening and recombining the data that are already available. Obviously this requires the potential for hard work and effort.

Must follow a set procedure.

Applications of Computers

Much of the application of the use of computers in management decisions has not really utilized the full potential of the computer. Most applications to date have used algorithmic types of programs. These are mainly of assistance in the evaluation phase of management decisions, as with the types of quantitative techniques discussed earlier in this chapter.

Many observers have felt, almost from its inception, that the computer was being underutilized for a variety of reasons. One area for furthering the utilization of the computer is as a tool to help top managers in interrelating strategic decisions as illustrated with the STRATANAL program in Chapter 5.†

Middle management now is using the computer as a tool to generate and evaluate the data necessary to present top management with more alternatives from which to choose. The computer now allows top management to ask more "what if" types of questions of subordinates and expect rapid answers.

In addition, complex, interactive computer systems are now utilized in an effective manner over a whole range of managerial problems. This can be done, moreover, with individuals who have no strong background in the use of computers.

What applications to strategy formation?

Creativity and the Computer

If it is true that many types of programs don't cause excessive fears, then it appears that the computer can be of significant assistance in interrelating strategic decisions. First, the memory capacity of the computer can be of great assistance in the more mechanical phases of combining and, to some extent, screening data. Most of the previous references have shown how the computer is being used in this area now, and its use could be spread among higher levels of

---

*Roman R. Andrus: Creativity: A function for computers or executives? *Journal of Marketing* 32:1–7, April, 1968.
†For more information, see James B. Boulden and Elwood S. Buffa: Corporate models: On-line, real-time systems, *Harvard Business Review* 47:65–83, July/August, 1970.

management, given the proper system and language. Of greater significance is the use of the computer as a guide during the creative phases of the strategy-formation process. A form of creativity can be built on a flexible framework that could be followed during the process.

There have been significant changes in computer technology which may overcome many of the utilization problems noted by their many detractors. Boulden and Buffa back this up strongly by stating:

> We feel that on-line, real-time decision systems are of great appeal to managers, partially because they do not require a basic structural change in a manager's role. He is not replaced by a supposedly optimizing mathematical model. On the contrary he remains the focus of the decision-making process, with a high premium placed on his judgment and intuitions.*

The main objection to this type of thinking is in use of the terms "nonrepetitive" or "nonprogrammable" problems. It may well be true that some problem, as a whole, may be nonprogrammable. But this does not necessarily mean that there are not individual subdivisions of the problem in which the computer can be of assistance in analysis. In particular, it appears that interactive computer programs might well be of assistance in providing the guidance required for a consistent and creative analysis of a strategic problem.

Complex Systems

The types of programs that would be useful along these lines would require an integrated, complex system. Systems must be designed with the ultimate goal in mind of the specific interaction desired; however, both the human and machine participants involved in the system must accept a common goal for the system if it is to be effective. Fortunately the human participant is adaptable to many environments and objectives. The question usually revolves about determining the proper incentives to encourage the man to adapt to a particular environment.

Human Reaction to Complex Systems

As we have discussed earlier, one of the primary difficulties encountered involves the individual's fear that the program is actually performing the decision-making function itself. Ward Edwards states, "Since we want machines to help us solve problems, the more intelligent we are able to make it (the computer), the more

---

*James B. Boulden and Elwood S. Buffa: op. cit., p. 83.

unobtrusive it should be in providing this help."* Hopefully, by making the program as natural an aid as possible, adverse reactions to the use of a computer program as an aid can be held to a minimum or eliminated entirely.

This implies that the programming involved in the stragety-formation process should be as flexible as possible. This presents a further problem. In actuality, the human is infinitely more programmable and easier to change than the computer. His flexibility and the ease and ability with which he can change increase the difficulties involved in attempting to produce a program that will maintain as little visibility as possible. The program, to do this effectively, should be able to adapt to each of the individuals using it as an aid.

To be able to adapt to the user requires a knowledge of the types of responses that one would expect a policy maker or strategist to produce for these types of decisions. It also requires a knowledge of the format of an efficient and acceptable strategy-formation process. This follows the belief held by Edwards that man should be used to set up the basis for the decisions and hypotheses. The computer program should then be assigned the task of performing the heuristics necessary to achieve acceptable forms of solutions. The human policy maker can then decide, from a set of alternatives, which one he feels is the most appropriate for the structure and the environment that he is facing. Hopefully, the computer program would be able to assist him in this phase as well.

The key to the problem of computer-aided strategy making is to maintain the individual as the center of the strategy-making process. The storage and speed of the computer should be used to provide guidance to the strategist. The memory of the computer can be used to augment the memory of the strategist. In this manner, he can be totally concerned with questions of corporate strategy and leave to the computer the task of maintaining data as well as the more important task of attempting to ensure that the user does not make the same mistake more than once. Hopefully, the guidance function performed by the system would be able to accomplish this.

What is the key to the problem?

SUMMARY

Although strategy formation may never be a science, there are aids to the process available from management science and quantitative methods. The formation of objectives and actions for strategic and policy-making purposes relies primarily on the creative ability of the manager. This kind of creativity is usually learned as an art,

---

*Ward Edwards: Men and computers. *In* Psychological Principles in System Development, Robert N. Gagné, editor. New York, Holt, Rinehart and Winston, 1962, pp. 91–92.

rather than as a science. To enhance this creative ability, however, the manager requires a sound analysis of the total environment. Also, the effects of any projected moves by the organization on the environment and ensuing reactions must be known as much as possible if the manager is to be able to ensure the success of his projects. It is in this area, the evaluation process, that management science can provide useful programs that save the analyst time and aggravation.

In many situations, modeling of the organization and its environment can be of great use. Generalized procedures such as economic, technological, financial and market forecasts can be more easily tested if a realistic simulation of the total environment facing the organization can be formed.

The method by which these simulations and forecasts are built is crucial. Input-output analysis should be used cautiously to determine what critical factors affect the firm and, therefore, should be included in the model.

Simulations, models and forecasts are not infallible, however, They are only as good as the information used to form them. Most of these programs rely on a continuation of past trends for accurate results. Many situations in which trends are changing drastically or rapidly cause these programs to lose much of their validity. They do serve as a reasonable base from which to predict changes and the effects of those changes.

Of particular help in conjunction with modeling is the case of various types of risk and statistical analysis. Those programs allow the analyst to build confidence intervals about his projections. These types of programs allow the analyst to input the concept of the amount of risk acceptable to the individuals in the organization responsible for strategic moves.

Of equal assistance in analyzing the input and feasibility of strategic moves is knowledge of the financial condition of the organization. Various financial analysis techniques give the manager this type of knowledge. Widely used capital budgeting and cost analyses are not the only tools available, however. Some of the more mundane types of analyses such as ratio analysis are equally helpful in analyzing the condition of the firm.

It must be understood, however, that all these programs must be utilized within the context of an organization presided over by individuals. These individuals often fear the implementation of these programs by management. Methods must be found to make sophisticated analytical tools less threatening and, therefore, more acceptable to managers responsible for strategic moves.

The next chapter will discuss methods of gaining cooperation and assistance from members of the organization for strategic moves. Methods of structuring the activity of managers and staff for discussions based on available information and analyses will be highlighted.

DISCUSSION QUESTIONS

1. During what phase of the strategy-formation process have management science programs found the highest degree of application to date? Why?

2. Which programs suffer greatest from a communication gap between technocrats and managers?

3. Is personal probability directly applicable to strategy formation for an organization? How can it be adapted for direct application?

4. What are some of the basic programs that are often used as building blocks for more complex management science programs? Are these basic programs fully understood yet?

5. What are some of the greatest problems faced in implementing management science programs in modern organizations?

6. How can the modern analyst help to gain acceptance for modern approaches within the organization?

7. What are the key factors inhibiting use of computers in the strategy-formation process? Are they behavioral or physical?

8. Can creativity really be assisted through use of the computer, or is it hindered through computer interaction?

9. What is an input/output model and how can it be used in the strategy-formation process?

10. Why is creativity so important for strategy makers?

Suggested Additional References for Further Research

Alexander, T.: Computers can't solve everything. *Fortune 80*:126–129, 168, 171, October, 1969.

Andrus, R. R.: Creativity: A function for computers or executives? *Journal of Marketing 32*:1–7, April, 1968.

Boulden, J. B., and Buffa, E. S.: Corporate models: On-line, real-time systems. *Harvard Business Review 47*:65–83, July/August, 1970.

Brady, R. H.: Computers in top-level decision making. *Harvard Business Review 45*:67–76, July/August, 1967.

Campbell, D. T., and Stanley, J. C.: *Experimental and Quasi-Experimental Designs for Research*. Chicago, Rand McNally & Company, 1966.

Campbell, R., and Hitchin, D.: The Delphi Technique: Implementation in the corporate environment. *Management Services* Vol. 5, Nov., 1968.

Carrell, D. C.: Implications of on-line, real-time systems for managerial decision-making. *In* Myers, C. A. (ed.): *The Impact of Computers on Management*. Cambridge, The MIT Press, 1967.

Churchman, C. W., Ackoff, R. L., and Arnoff, E. L.: *Introduction to Operations Research*. New York, John Wiley & Sons, Inc., 1958.

Colby, K. M., and Enea, H.: Inductive inference by intelligent machines. *Scientia 102*:1–10, January/February, 1968.

Dalkey, N., and Helmer, O.: An experimental application of the Delphi method to the use of experts. *Management Science 9*:458–467, 1963.

Ernst, M. L.: Stage three for computers: Management decision making. *Illinois Business Review 27*:6–7, April, 1970.

Evan, W. M., and Miller, J. R.: Differential effects on response bias of computer vs.

conventional administration of a social science questionnaire: An exploratory methodological experiment. *Behavioral Science 45*: May, 1969.

Ezekiel, M., and Fox, K. A.: *Methods of Correlation and Regression Analysis*. 3rd ed. New York, John Wiley & Sons, Inc., 1959.

Ferguson, R. L., and Jones, C. H.: A computer aided decision system. *Management Science 15*:B-550–561, June, 1969.

Gold, M. M.: Time sharing and batch processing: An experimental comparison of their value in a problem solving situation. *Communications of the A. C. M. 12*: May, 1969.

Grayson, C. J.: Management science and business practice. *Harvard Business Review, 51*:41–48, July-August, 1973.

Hatten, K. J., and Piccoli, M. L.: "An Evaluation of a Technological Forecasting Method by Computer-Based Simulation. Academy of Management Proceedings, Boston, Mass., 1973.

Holmberg, S. R.: Utility corporate planning. *Public Utility Fortnightly, XC*, July 6, 1972.

Jones, C. H.: At last: Real computer power for decision makers. *Harvard Business Review 47*:75–89, September/October, 1970.

Kaufmann, A.: *Methods and Models of Operations Research*. Englewood Cliffs, N.J., Prentice-Hall, Inc., 1963.

Klein, W. H., and Murphy, D. C.: *Policy: Concepts in Organizational Guidance*. Boston, Little Brown, 1973.

Kriebel, C. H.: The strategic dimension of computer systems planning. *Long Range Planning 1*:7–12, September, 1968.

Levin, R. I., and Kirkpatrick, C. A.: *Quantitative Approaches to Management*. New York, McGraw-Hill Book Co., Inc., 1965.

Licklider, J. C. R.: Man-computer partnership. *International Science and Technology*, May, 1965, pp. 18–26.

McKinney, G. W.: *An Experimental Study of Strategy Formulation Systems*. Stanford, California, Stanford University Graduate School of Business, 1969. (Unpublished thesis).

Meadow, C. T., and Waugh, D. W.: Computer assisted interrogation. *Proceedings of the American Federation of Information Processing Societies Conference, 39*:381–394, Fall, 1966.

Messick, D. M., and Rapoport, A.: Computer-controlled experiments in psychology. *Behavioral Science 9*: October, 1964.

Morton, M., and Scott, S.: Interactive visual display systems and management problem solving. *Industrial management review 9*:70–81, Fall, 1967.

Murdick, R., Eckhouse, R., Moor, R. C., and Zimmerer, T. W.: *Business Policy: A Framework for Analysis*. Grid, Inc., Columbus, Ohio, 1972.

Rue, L. W., and Fulmer, R. M.: "Is Long-Range Planning Profitable?" *The Academy of Management Proceedings,* Boston, Mass., 1973.

Sackman, H.: *Computers, System Science and Evolving Society*. New York, John Wiley & Sons, Inc., 1967.

Salveson, M. E.: Of models, computers and chief executives. *Management International* Oct.-Nov., 1963.

Schlaifer, R.: *Probability and Statistics for Business Decisions*. New York, McGraw-Hill Book Co., Inc., 1959.

Simon, H.: *New Science of Management Decisions*. New York, Harper & Row, 1960.

Swinth, R.: Organizational joint problem solving. *Management Science 8*:(No.2): Oct., 1971.

Theil, H. J., Boot, C., and Teun Kloek, G.: *Operations Research and Quantitative Economics, An Elementary Introduction*. New York, McGraw-Hill Book Co., Inc., 1965.

Vasonyi, A.: *Scientific Programming in Business and Industry*. New York, John Wiley & Sons, Inc., 1958.

APPENDIX 1 TO CHAPTER 7

SOLUTION TO PROBLEM I

The following are the calculations needed for arriving at Net Present Value (NPV) decisions:

Year	NPV of $1 Received in Year ...	Net Present Value of Returns		
		Strategic Move A	*Strategic Move B*	*Strategic Move C*
1	.9346	$ 14,019	$ 46,730	$28,038
2	.8734	39,303	34,936	21,835
3	.8163	48,978	20,407.5	16,326
4	.7629	41,959.5	15,258	11,443.5
		$144,259.5	$117,331.5	$77,642.5
Initial outlay		−100,000	−125,000	−75,000
Net present value		$ 44,259.5	−$ 7,668.5	$ 2,642.5

If only one strategic move can be chosen, A should be the one. If resources are not that limited, A and C should both be followed, since they both offer positive net present values, i.e., they both offer returns greater than the cost of capital to the firm.

APPENDIX 2 TO CHAPTER 7

SOLUTION TO PROBLEM II

P = Probability
Worst = Worst outcome
Best = Best outcome
Res = Research
A = product A
B = product B
EV = Expected Value

P[Worst] = .6   P[Best] = .4
P[Res A/Worst] = .7
∴ P[Res B/Worst] = .3
P[Res B/Best] = .8
∴ P[Res A/Best] = .2

$$P[Worst/Res\ A] = \frac{.7 \times .6}{(.7 \times .6) + (.2 \times .4)}$$

$$= .84$$

∴ P[Best/Res A] = 1 − .84 = .16

$$P[Worst/Res\ B] = \frac{.3 \times .6}{(.3 \times .6) + (.8 \times .4)}$$

$$= .36$$

∴ P[Best/Res B] = 1 − .36 = .64

Alt. 1 $\begin{cases} .6 \times 6 = 3.6 \\ \qquad\qquad + = 6.4 = EV \\ .4 \times 7 = 2.8 \end{cases}$

Alt. 2 $\begin{cases} .6 \times 5 = 3.0 \\ \qquad\qquad + = 7.0 = EV \\ .4 \times 10 = 4.0 \end{cases}$

Alt. 3a $\begin{cases} .84 \times 6 = 5.04 \\ \qquad\qquad + = 6.16 \times .5 = 3.08 \\ .16 \times 7 = 1.12 \end{cases}$

Alt. 3b $\begin{cases} .84 \times 5 = 4.20 \\ \qquad\qquad + = 5.80 \\ .16 \times 10 = 1.60 \end{cases}$

Alt. 3c $\begin{cases} .36 \times 6 = 2.16 \\ \qquad\qquad + = 6.64 \\ .64 \times 7 = 4.48 \end{cases}$

Alt. 3d $\begin{cases} .36 \times 5 = 1.80 \\ \qquad\qquad + = 8.20 \times .5 = 4.10 \\ .64 \times 10 = 6.40 \end{cases}$

Alt. 3a + Alt. 3d = 7.18
Alt. 3 − cost of information =
7.18 − 1 = 6.18

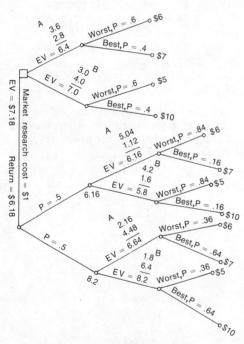

Product B with no
market research provides
the best solution.

PATTERNS FOR EFFECTIVE CHANGE
AND IMPLEMENTATION

INDIVIDUAL AND GROUP PROBLEM
SOLVING

OVERALL STRUCTURING OF THE
ACTIVITY

TIMING OF THE ACTIVITY

SELECTING PROBLEM-SOLVING
SITUATIONS

TYPES OF STRUCTURED
ACTIVITIES – INDIVIDUAL AND
GROUP

EFFECTIVE GROUP SESSIONS

FEED-IN OF ACTION RESEARCH AND
MANAGEMENT SCIENCE DATA

QUESTIONS AND ANSWERS
REGARDING THE ACTION
COMPONENTS

SUMMARY

DISCUSSION QUESTIONS

APPENDIX 1. QUESTIONNAIRE ON
MANAGERIAL FUNCTIONING

APPENDIX 2. ORGANIZATIONAL
EFFECTIVENESS FORM

8

THE ACTION THRUST IN STRATEGY FORMATION: DEVELOPING INDIVIDUAL AND GROUP INVOLVEMENT

We have discussed previously several generalized procedures, including an overall strategy-formation program, an action-research program and various management science programs for data gathering and analysis. These programs (and others) may be coupled or linked together in a variety of ways. First, they may be arranged in pyramidal order with, say, the more general strategy-formation programs at the top and the more specialized management science programs lower down. The action-research program, as a general data gathering–feed-in–action-planning program, may construct and maintain control over lower level programs. The output from a management science program (e.g., a simulation) might serve as an input into the second process of the action-research program — the analysis and feed-in of data. In addition, the management science programs may be linked horizontally, with the output of one being the input of the other. For example, the forecasting program would provide input for the capital budgeting program at the Univis, Inc., organization that was discussed in the first chapter.

Used in appropriate combination for a given organization, these programs will generate useful input for those concerned with strategy making, implementation and evaluation. In a "one man show" organization, for example, the individual strategist could use such input to plan and to evaluate his actions. Most often, however, in larger organizations, and even in the case of the "one man show," more than one person will be involved in using such data input. Frequently the manager will not be acting alone. He will need the support and assistance of others, not only to aid in the complex problem-solving process, but to assure that "the message gets through" to (and up from) various levels in the organization and to (and from) various divisions or groups.

Action components.

The manager may rely on the *action* components of the action-research program to gain such support and assistance. The action components include involving others in planning actions, coordinating actions, executing actions and evaluating actions. Data for such activity may be fed in from the other programs that have previously been mentioned.

Structured activities for implementing organization change in strategy situations.

This chapter will take up the matter of reliance on the action-research program for organization and strategy-improvement activities. First, however, we shall present a general discussion of various patterns that may be used in implementing organizational change. Then we shall turn to the action component of the action-research program and discuss some structured activities or organization development interventions available to managers and to analysts or consultants, internal or external.* Though there are a large number of structured activities,† the main emphasis here will be on individual *and* group activities that are related directly to strategy reformulation and implementation.

PATTERNS FOR EFFECTIVE CHANGE AND IMPLEMENTATION

The organization development approach to strategy formation, as indicated, is basically a complex problem-solving process, with its activity focused more on the group or coalition than on the individual participants. As a process it deliberately attempts to set up effective group, intergroup and sometimes individual activities to:

Develop goals and plans of action.
Gain understanding, acceptance and implementation of those plans throughout the organization.
Increase the capability of the organization for solving problems dealing with environmental changes in the future.

Group interaction does *not* mean that strategy decisions are turned over to subordinates as some might think; to follow this

---

*Some student analysts may find only limited access to these activities but should have knowledge of the ideas put forth.

†See W. L. French and C. H. Bell, Jr.: *Organization Development, Behavioral Science Interventions for Organization Improvement,* Englewood Cliffs, N.J., Prentice-Hall, Inc., 1973, P. A. Clark: *Action Research and Organizational Change,* New York, Harper & Row, 1973, and E. K. Warren: Long-Range Planning: The Executive Viewpoint. Englewood Cliffs, N.J. Prentice-Hall, Inc., 1966.

course of action might cause the organization's effectiveness to deteriorate. Group interaction does refer to the process that transforms an aggregate of individuals into a cohesively functioning team or group. In this context the word group means a face-to-face work or strategy-formation group that is characterized by its orientation to a series of objectives to achieve or problems to solve. Thus, the group of executives at Univis, Inc., who form a committee are a work group, as are the top official and those subordinates who report directly to him.

Group interaction but strategy decisions not turned over to subordinates.

Another example of a work or strategy-formation group is a temporary or ad hoc team that is brought together for problem identification and solution activity. The team might be brought together by a manager or, alternatively, by an analyst or group of analysts interested in helping the organization. The team members might represent different divisions, functions or groups. Thus, we would have intergroup interaction.

These kinds of work group or conference activities have become the target for organization development practitioners and researchers. Many empirical studies have dealt with the attempts to improve organizational functioning, using to one extent or another the group structure and functioning. Greiner* has examined 13 such studies in an attempt to separate those organizations that have successfully dealt with implementing change and those that were not so successful. (In Chapter 6 you read several examples of these studies in various organizational situations.) These studies indicated that there were many patterns for introducing change and gaining implementation that could be placed along an Authority Distribution Continuum. Such a continuum is pictured below.

Authority Distribution Continuum.

Greiner's continuum starts with unilateral authority compliance but extends beyond the helper or shared approach to a delegated authority approach. Unilateral action can be accomplished in three ways: The most common approach is called decree. It has its roots in centuries of military and government bureaucracies. It appears in the form of a policy statement, lecture, memorandum or verbal com-

Unilateral Authority	Shared Approaches	Delegated Approaches
By decree	By decision making	By case study
By replacement	By problem solving	By T groups
By structure		

*L. Greiner: Patterns of organizational change. *In* Dalton, G., Lawrence, P., and Greiner, L. (eds.): *Organizational Change and Development,* Homewood, Ill., Richard D. Irwin, Inc., 1970. See also P. Buchanan: Crucial issues in organizations development. *In* Watson, G. (ed.): *Change in School Systems.* Washington, D.C., National Education Association, 1967, pp. 51–67.

mand. It is impersonal and task oriented. The second approach in unilateral action is "by replacement." This rests on the idea that if a few key people cause a problem, their removal is the solution. The third form of unilateral action is "by structure." Currently this approach is under much study by behavioral scientists. Katz and Kahn,* for example, argue that changing the system (structure) is the most efficient way to introduce durable organization change. A basic assumption is that the way people behave can be importantly affected indirectly by changing the system or technology. Examples of this approach include engineering the job to fit the man and adjusting formal authority in line with informal authority.† Later we shall discuss the issue of restructuring the organization for action.

Sharing the power is accomplished in two general ways, according to Greiner: First, by group decision making in which the assumption is made that, given a problem, individuals develop more commitment to action when they have a voice in the choice of alternative solutions that affect them. Second, in group problem solving, in which both the definition and the solving of the problem are shared.

In delegated authority there is almost complete responsibility for defining and acting on problems. One form in which delegated authority appears is the case discussion. The teacher often does not impose analysis or solutions on the group. A second type of delegated authority is seen in sensitivity or T group sessions.‡ The purpose here is to increase the individual's self-awareness and sensitivity to group social processes. One assumption is that the method will unleash unconscious emotional energies, leading to self-analysis and therefore behavioral change.

Now that we have identified the authority yardstick let us look at the results of the comparison of the organizations attempting significant change and adaption. The organizations were compared on the conditions leading to change, the critical blocks and/or the facilitators encountered during implementation, and the more lasting results over a period of time. The comparisons were made on the basis of published reports. Perhaps unsuccessful attempts at change would tend not to be published.

Nevertheless, given the limitations of the data, the successful changes (those that accomplished stated organizational goals) generally appear to be those which:

---

*D. Katz and R. Kahn: *The Social Psychology of Organizations.* New York, John Wiley & Sons, Inc., 1966; see also, Bennis, W. G.: Theory and method in applying behavioral science to planned organization change, *Journal of Applied Behavioral Science* 1:337–360, 1965.

†See F. Fiedler: *A Theory of Leadership Effectiveness,* New York, McGraw-Hill Book Co., Inc., 1967; and F. Herzberg: One more time: How do you motivate employees? *Harvard Business Review,* Jan.–Feb. 1968, p. 59.

‡For a discussion of the evidence see M. Dunnette and J. Campbell: Laboratory education: Impact on people and organizations. *In* Dalton, G., Lawrence, P., and Greiner, L. (eds.): *Organization Change and Development,* Homewood, Ill., Richard D. Irwin, Inc., 1970.

1. Spread throughout the organization to include and affect many people.
2. Produce positive changes in line and staff attitudes.
3. Prompt people to behave more effectively in solving problems and in relating to others.

Moreover, the relatively successful changes tended to use a shared approach to collaborative problem solving. The collaborative effort seemed to be more effective than organization change attempted unilaterally (e.g., by decree) or through delegation (e.g., T groups). The pattern of successful change can be viewed as a sort of filter, with external and/or internal forces causing pressure which then arouses management. That would be the first step, be it planned or unplanned. The second step is an intervention and top management endorsement of an evaluation or re-evaluation. Third, there is a reorientation by management and a willingness to take a new look at "what things need to be different around here." Fourth, there is a specific shared diagnosis and recognition of problems. The less successful attempts at change seemed to avoid this step. If they took a unilateral approach, they tended to already "know" the problem. Those who took the delegated approach tended to abdicate responsibility by urning over authority to lower levels in such a nondirective way that subordinates questioned sincerity. The fifth step is sharing in the invention of solutions and becoming committed to them. The successful changes were characterized by widespread and intensive search for creative solutions. None of the less successful attempts at change reached this stage. Sixth, there is a process of experimentation and continued search. Some solutions were developed and tested and found creditable on a small scale before the scope of change was widened. Seventh, there is a period of reinforcement and acceptance. Early success experiences in experimentation bolster the confidence of the analysts and managers; they seem more willing to proceed with organization improvement.

In short, then, according to this evidence successful patterns of change tend to follow a well outlined series of steps. These steps are characteristically seen as shared among the various levels in the organization. The bulwark of this sharing was cooperation and involvement. The extremes of unilateral authority and the delegated approach were avoided. There was heavy reliance on collaborative group problem solving.

Successful changes sometimes use shared approach to collaborative problem solving.

Well outlined series of steps to change.

INDIVIDUAL AND GROUP PROBLEM SOLVING

We would caution that though group activity was relied upon, the importance of initiative and creativity in *individual* problem-solving efforts should not be downgraded or ignored. Individual brainstorming, for example, has consistently been shown to be supe-

Individual problem-solving efforts and creativity.

rior to group brainstorming.* Time should be allotted for both individual and group problem-solving efforts. Some individuals are inhibited in group situations; furthermore, group participants sometimes tend to develop a similar perceptual set (people use the same framework in viewing the problem). Thus, creativity, which is a very important element in strategy making, may be reduced unless independent individual problem-solving activity takes place.

There is some evidence to suggest, however, that individual problem solving or creativity is improved if individual problem-solving activity follows a group problem-solving effort.† Some ideas may be picked up from the group activity that may be pursued and elaborated upon when one is alone. Recognition and support should be given to individual problem-solving activities. This holds true for the practicing manager, for the policy analyst, and for teams of students studying cases or conducting field projects.

Reasons for relying on the group.

There are, however, a number of reasons for relying on group activity for implementation and change in existing organizations. They are discussed by organization development specialists French and Bell‡ as follows: "First, much individual behavior is rooted in the socio-cultural norms and values of the work team. If the team, as a team, changes those norms and values, the effect on individual behavior is immediate and lasting. Second, the work team possesses the 'reality of configuration of relationships' that the individuals must in fact accommodate to and learn to utilize and cope with . . . . Effective (or ineffective) relationships with these people can have far-reaching effects on the individual's performance and behavior. Third, the work team is the source of most of individual's knowledge about organizational processes such as communications, decision making and goal setting. These processes are the processes that most influence the individual's behavior. Fourth, it is commonly believed that many of the individual's needs for social interaction, status, recognition and respect are satisfied by his work group, consisting of both peers and superior. Any process that improves the work team's processes or task performance will thus probably be related to central needs of the individual members."

Caution.

It needs to be said, however, that though working through groups can be a powerful instrument in implementing organization change, poor handling of the process can have negative effects. Con-

---

*D. W. Taylor, P. C. Berry and C. H. Block: Does group participation when using brainstorming facilitate or inhibit creative thinking? *Administrative Science Quarterly* 3:23–47, 1958; M. D. Dunnette, J. Campbell and K. Jaasted: The effects of group participation on brainstorming effectiveness for two industrial samples, *Journal of Applied Psychology* 47:30–37, 1963; M. D. Dunnette: Are meetings any good for solving problems? *Personnel Administration* 27:12–29, 1964; T. J. Bonchard, Jr., and M. Hare: Size, performance and potential in brainstorming groups, *Journal of Applied Psychology* 54:51–55, 1970.

†M. D. Dunnette, J. Campbell and K. Jansted: op. cit., pp. 30–37.

‡W. French and C. Bell: *Organization Development, Behavioral Science Interventions for Organization Improvement,* op. cit., p. 61–62.

siderable expertise should be available if group intervention activities are being considered.

OVERALL STRUCTURING OF THE ACTIVITY

Using organizational change evidence and assumptions, practitioners and academicians have devised structured activities or interventions to improve individual, group, intergroup and organization functioning. These interventions are sets of structured activities in which selected organization units (individuals or groups) engage in tasks that constitute *the action thrust* in strategy formation. In other words, the activities (including planning actions, coordinating actions, executing actions and evaluating actions) are the means for implementing change. Our discussion here will focus on the structuring of activities, beginning with a highly flexible group program — the conference. Then we· shall discuss several other group *and* individual activities that seem to be useful.

Action thrust.

Some organizations have structured the group activity into sessions that can generally be called *problem-solving conferences.* Such conferences, using joint collaborative problem solving, fall into the process model category on the continuum for assessment behavior in that they aim at helping the participants perceive, diagnose and act upon events in their own environment. In other words, they aim at helping the problem-solving process.

Problem-solving conferences.

Recently in an attempt to make "all cylinders function at the same time" and to avoid surprises, Sperry Rand set up a formal arrangement for quarterly, in-depth review meetings between the divisions and top management.* They report success with this approach, which was initiated for the first time by Chairman of the Board J. Paul Lyet. The approach includes a long-range planning system and a heavy emphasis on determining what the market needs before developing products. Lyet says about the meetings,

We are not controlling in a restrictive sense; we want to be sure the divisions are doing all the things necessary to grow and that they are not taking the short term view, generating profits now at the expense of the future. And we want to avoid surprises.

The new approach apparently has played some part in helping the company to avoid such surprises as "horrendous write-offs," which had previously been habitual in the company. Sperry Rand has experienced a solid turnaround after two straight declines in annual profits.

It is assumed, as mentioned before, that these collaborative

---

*The winning strategy at Sperry Rand, *Business Week,* February 24, 1973. pp. 50–58.

meetings are more effective than organization change and implementation attempted unilaterally (e.g., compliance, or by decree) or through delegation (e.g., T groups). The lever that is used in attempting to change organizational behavior is the opportunity to obtain intrinsic rewards through influencing important activities in the organization. (Some might argue that this power distribution means a structural change.)

The group activity should be structured so that the relevant people are there. The relevant people are those most directly affected by the opportunity or the problem and those with necessary skills and knowledge. The consequences may involve intact work teams or ad hoc work groups. There may be a utilization of a joint team of managers and/or staff with internal or external analysts. Or the conference team, or a part of it, may represent a *diagonal** slice from top management down through the organization, including relevant functional or program areas. There may be separate action planning by teams at all levels.† Preplanning of the group composition is, of course, an important feature in structuring the activity.

May use diagonal slice.

Or a "bottom up" approach.

The group sessions should be structured to open lines of communication and, through the use of group dynamics, to establish personal and group commitment to improving strategy development and implementation. The aim is to identify major strategy issues and opportunities, to identify barriers to organization effectiveness, to establish a readiness to act, and to develop a plan of specific action for relevant parties.

Supplemental to these goals, the conference design should strive to emphasize that the re-evaluation activities are worthwhile and the outcome should have some important effects on the organization. Encouragement from top management through involvement, or at least endorsement, of the activities seems to be quite helpful. It does seem wise, though, to openly recognize the limits of manpower and money and to point out that there is no guarantee of acceptance of all or any results or outcomes. After all, the top official or officials will undoubtedly have veto power over important plans of action.

It is quite important that the conference goals be clear, as well as the way to reach the goals. Members of the organization are likely to be more highly motivated if they know what they are working toward and that what they are doing will contribute to goal attainment.

Link to various parts of organization.

The team (teams) is (are) to provide major input to the group session or sessions† and to be a major implementation link between

---

*The diagonal slice may be used for the purpose of improving communication by avoiding the possible inhibiting effect of the direct superior-subordinate relationship.

†See Vancil, R. F.: The Accuracy of Long-Range Planning. Harvard Business Review, 48, 98–101, September-October, 1970, and Formal Planning Systems, Cambridge, Mass., Harvard Business School, 1972. This research on the structuring of strategy formation indicates that long-range forecast accuracy seems to be greater when a "bottom up" approach is used than when a "top down" approach is used.

various parts of the organization. It is hoped that organization members will establish a continuing series of activities for auditing the internal and external environment and improving their problem-solving ability. Policy analysts may provide support and assistance in helping the continuation of group interaction. At Univis, Inc., some additional series of activities to generate better understanding and acceptance of the plans and the planning procedures might have been helpful.

TIMING OF THE ACTIVITY

We have discussed the assessment process as well as the other phases of the policy-formation process in discrete terms. This is not to state, however, that these various phases are carried on in a discrete manner. The entire policy-formation process, including evaluation of alternatives, is followed on a continuous basis. Without continuous evaluation of alternatives and outcomes we would soon find ourselves with an outdated corporate strategy and direction for the organization. There are, however, three particular points in time during the policy-formation process when structured activities should be considered on a formalized basis: (1) the formation stage, (2) the postacceptance stage, and (3) the postcommitment stage. Structured activities during the formation stage may be extremely beneficial in that added information from external sources either within the organization or outside the organization will aid in formulating the action plan. It is frequently easy to obtain criticism of the action plans at this stage. The individuals to be involved in the action plan will often be wary of anything that might upset the status quo. These managers will often be eager to point up weaknesses in the proposed plan. This type of criticism can be extremely valuable for determining what additional information is needed for developing a feasible, acceptable plan. The key here is not to allow the criticism to harden into solid opposition to desired and required changes in the direction of the organization.

When should structured activities on a formalized basis be considered?

Structured activities during the postacceptance stage can often be most crucial. At this point, the plan has been formulated and accepted by the individuals affected by it within the organization. Quite often, great enthusiasm has been generated for this new direction. At this time, also, there is more information available to the analyst. Time has passed since the formation stage. The economy has entered new stages, the organization has progressed (hopefully), and the market may have changed in the interim. Also, more importantly, valuable market research programs may have been progressing at the same time. This additional information should be utilized to present a more feasible, consistent overall strategy. The prime danger here is that pent-up enthusiasm generated so far may be stifled. A fine line has to be followed between the conservatism of assessment and the enthusiasm of conviction.

What information is available at each stage?

The third key stage for structured activities occurs after the plan has been implemented. In real terms, for example, the Edsel is on the showroom floors. The Ford Motor Company has already spent millions of dollars, and the auto buying public is staying away from Edsel dealers in droves.

It is at this stage that information is relatively easy to come by. Actual reports from the field are in and are easily analyzed. The decision must be made as to what the future course of action is to be. The organization must decide whether to continue with the original plan or to alter it to meet a changing environment or occurrences unforeseen during the formation of the orginal plan.

It was at this period, for instance, that Ford officials finally decided to cut losses on the Edsel and formulate new strategic moves for the future. Fortunately they were able to learn from their mistakes; they also were not frightened by the large losses incurred by this error. This was evident from their next attempts at finding and filling a new auto market. The Mustang and the Capri were developed and proved extremely successful.

Attention should be paid to this last point. Results achieved from implementation of a new strategic move should not overly influence the willingness of the organization to attempt further moves. Inhibitions caused by failure, or overenthusiasm caused by success, should play no part in future decisions, although these will be influenced by changes brought about in the resources available to the firm or changes in the external environment.

Structured activities, therefore, may be integrated into the formal policy-formation process on a periodic basis, and they should be given special consideration at certain points in time.

SELECTING PROBLEM-SOLVING SITUATIONS

The time it takes to reap the rewards that may result from the group sessions will depend to an extent on how often the opportunities are provided for the groups to interact. This means selecting situations wherein group problem-solving activity can be applied. (You will recall that the importance of individual problem-solving activity is fully recognized.)

Periodic staff or committee meetings are tailormade for beginning group problem solving because such meetings are frequently held quite regularly, and the participants are probably more or less comfortable at them. This presents an opportunity to begin by suggesting something like an examination of operating practices in order to improve acceptance and implementation of overall strategy. The group will need time to think about it and respond. Each member may be given a chance to contribute information and pose questions to other members. Some members may take an assignment to develop more detailed information about the various operating practices and to discuss the results at a subsequent meeting.

Regular group sessions or special purpose sessions.

In other words, no big deal has been made of the problem-solving conference approach. The group has been allowed to interact informally to a subject that presumably is of high interest to them. A goal is established (collection of data) that encourages communication and coordination among the participants. A reason for further discussion of the subject is established (interpretation of data). This low key approach, using regular meetings as a basis for action research and group problem solving may be quite helpful. The discussion of the strategy-making process as well as the strategy output (goals and plans of action) is made a normal part of business.

However, to highlight the importance of *avoiding organizational stagnation,* it may be appropriate to put a special emphasis on the regular group sessions or even to set up special purpose sessions. Analysts with specialized expertise, say, in forecasting or in the problem-solving process may be brought in. *Orientation* and *"deciding what to do"* discussions with relevant parties seem to be especially appropriate before such sessions. To aid the subsequent communication of conference results, the relevant parties may include managers and staff not included in the actual conference sessions, along with conference participants. Several sessions may be necessary to provide enough information and experience pertinent to formulating "what to do."

Orientation and "deciding what to do."

The discussion time is used to clarify the purposes of the overall action-research program, including the conferences. Some time may be spent briefing participants and others about what alternative assessment and developmental methods (e.g., conferences, interviews, training sessions) could be used before the serious commitment was made to engage in the present effort. The participants may be allowed to decide the extent and the manner in which they feel the developmental programs should extend.

If special policy analysts are to be included, time may be spent discussing an acceptable role for them.* Following the helper or shared approach to development, the analysts, be they external or internal, would be there to aid the problem-solving process, not to unilaterally identify problems and give their solutions. The analysts' role may include one or more of the following patterns of behavior: (1) to help the operating managers design and implement methods for obtaining information on the state of the environment and the organization; (2) to summarize all pertinent information collected; (3) to feed back information to individual managers and to the total conference groups; (4) to provide skill and expertise in designing meetings and in chairing such meetings or in sharing the chairmanship with operating managers; (5) to share in the analysis of information in the development of solutions; (6) to identify developmental methods for improved communication and problem solving; and (7) to act as part of the staff for the development program—preparing

Role of external analyst and internal analyst.

---

*See W. Athreya: Guidelines for the Effectiveness of the Long-Range Planning Process, unpublished doctoral dissertation, Harvard Business School, June, 1967.

minutes, delivering background material, polishing language, streamlining presentations, as well as evaluating the views of operating managers.

An external analyst may have been engaged to add professional skill, experience and objectivity to the role, whereas an internal analyst may be relied on for his knowledge of the organization's environment or culture, his continuity of support and his availability for timely assistance.

Other subjects may be brought up during these initial sessions also. Based on past experience, it may be judged advisable to discuss with and inform the participants that the meetings:

1. Are a key part of a joint continuing assessment of policies and strategies.
2. Are an opportunity to influence important strategies and policies in the organization.
3. Have endorsement of top management (some top managers may be present; in fact, the conference may be chaired by a top manager).
4. Need openness and frankness. (State — and mean it — that there will be no penalty for expressing frank opinions.)
5. Are confidential* (including all working papers and discussion).
6. May include analysts who are there to help (not to report to certain people).
7. Will include issues of special interest to the group.
8. Do not guarantee that all (or any) recommendations of the group will be accepted.
9. Should lead to certain outcomes (e.g., identification of priority issues, action steps for managers and staff, and a response from top managers where appropriate).

No one list of items to be covered in the initial sessions is appropriate for all situations; thus, judgment as to the unique circumstances will need to be used in ascertaining what to include in and what to exclude from the discussions.

TYPES OF STRUCTURED ACTIVITIES — INDIVIDUAL AND GROUP

Subsequent to the early orientation and "deciding what to do" meetings, the problem-solving activity may turn to one or more of a number of structured activities. As we see it, some of the structured activities that may prove helpful to the practicing manager, the policy analyst and perhaps to students doing field projects would include, but not be limited to, the following:

1. Strategy-formation process.
2. Assessment of leverage points.

---

*Reasons for this include: (1) avoiding premature release of information that is not thoroughly analyzed, and (2) the need for openness. A judgment has been made about when and to what extent other members of the organization and parties external to the organization (e.g., competitors, columnists) are going to share in the information and results.

3. Individual manager functioning.
4. Stating and analyzing objectives.
5. Priority setting and action planning.
6. Progress review.

Data collected from the previously discussed action-research program and the management science programs may prove useful as input to one or more of these structured activities.

Strategy-formation Process

Focus is on early identification of the developmental needs of the groups engaged in the process of strategic choice. Various assessments may be made: perceptions of strategy issues, role perceptions, self-interests, strategy-formation practices, communication skills and patterns, authority and hierarchical problems, and intra- and intergroup conflict management procedures. Questionnaire and/or interview data may be collected from the group itself and from others. It may be analyzed as part of an individual research study of strategy making. The data may be summarized and fed back to the group for discussion and analysis. Plans of action may be developed. For example, skilled parties may be designated to help in the diagnosis, understanding and resolution of conflict of interest problems, e.g., between different teams or groups that must work together in the formation of strategy, such as a federal government agency and a county school board, labor representatives and management officials, line and staff, sales and engineering or separate organizations involved in a merger.

Group discussion or individual study.

Assessment of Leverage Points

Focus here is on identification of those individuals within the organization or outside the organization (e.g., opinion leaders) who have the authority (formal or informal), motivation and competence to influence the output of the strategy process as well as the understanding, acceptance and implementation of that strategy output. For strategy issues various assessments may be made: leverage points, types and amounts of political resources, reservoir of goodwill, trade-offs, phases through which the strategy issues proceed. It should be recalled that these assessments may vary with the type of strategy issue and with the phase that the issue is going through. The information gathered can be useful for independent study or for group discussion and analysis.

These first two interventions, moreover, carried out by qualified analysts or managers, can serve not only to identify strategy problems, issues and individuals or groups of individuals that are judged to be important points at which to study the strategy process,

Organization learning also.

but also to improve that process. That is, there may be some *organizational learning* while dealing with relevant organizational issues. The data gathering, for instance, may help people to learn not only about the strategy-formation process, but also about some new ways of producing data about the process. From this point we turn to additional structured activities that are potential building blocks for improvement of that process.

Manager Functioning

This focus is on how individual managers are functioning. To provide input for such sessions data may be gathered on:

1. The network of others with whom they must work in order to get the job done. The network would include horizontal and diagonal as well as vertical relationships. Reporting this information seems to help the respondent to assess and to understand what his job is.

2. Functional* time allocation of managerial performance as it is and as it is perceived it should be. Comparisons of the two sets of answers may be made for various types of strategies or for various missions and may indicate leads to problems.

3. Examples of very important or critical actions that have helped the organization and examples of very important or critical actions that have hindered the organization.

Inventory of managerial strengths and problems.

The information gathered may be used as a basis for developing descriptions, definitions and evaluations of the managerial role. It may also be used as an inventory of perceived strengths and problems confronting a segment of the organization and may, in turn, be presented back to a relevant group for discussion. Together with other information, the "manager functioning" information may indicate training needs, such as knowledge acquisition, attitude change, problem-solving skill and interpersonal relations skill.†

One form for gathering such data is provided in Appendix 1 to this chapter, along with a discussion of how the results may be fed back to managers. A variation of the form has been used in a variety of government agencies with apparent effectiveness. No scientific evidence is available at this time to support the efficacy of its use.

---

*The set of functions provided on the form in Appendix 1 includes all management performance activities. The set has shown good reliability in tests with a variety of types of managers and supervisors. The functions are close to being mutually exclusive. See T. A. Mahoney, T. H. Jerdee and S. J. Carroll: The job(s) of management, *Industrial Relations* 4(No. 2): 1965, pp. 97–110.

†For a discussion involving the selection of appropriate training and development methods see S. J. Carroll, F. T. Paine and J. J. Ivancevich: Various training methods and training objectives: Research and expert opinion, *Personnel Psychology*, Fall, 1972, pp. 495–509.

Stating and Analyzing Objectives

Key parties (e.g., manager-subordinate pairs, groups and analysts) in major segments of the organization engage in systematic, periodic performance reviews and target setting. An illustration of an approach for doing this has been presented in the chapter on the assessment guides. As indicated, a good bit of research suggests that such goal setting affects performance positively.*

Priority Setting and Action Planning

The focus is on formulating and reformulating action plans. The question may be raised as to what needs to be changed around here — policies, strategies, structure, and so forth. Assessments may be made of such elements as the scope of support and resource deployment, what the scope should be, the basis of support for strategies, an inventory of organization resources and problems, changing environmental conditions, alternative opportunities and requirements for success, and possible combinations of alternatives for synergistic effects.

Use portfolio approach.

These priority-setting and action-planning sessions, of course, have many variations in their format and time schedule.† Special purpose sessions may be set up for (1) brainstorming on the effects of environmental or public policy changes, (2) devising an optimal plan of organization to implement a corporate strategy, (3) devising standards and a plan for progress review, (4) translating functional plans into financial terms in the form of a pro forma profit and loss statement and perhaps a pro forma balance sheet, and (5) linking the top management objectives and action plans with the objectives and action plans forged at lower levels in the organization. Depending on the magnitude of the problem and the exigencies of the situation, there may be one- or two-day marathons or meetings spaced over a period of weeks, months or years.

Variations in format and time schedules.

Progress Review

This is to keep managers focusing on strategic variables and environmental changes and to maintain positive tension in the system.
1. Officials report and discuss progress, if any, on major strategies and issues.

---

*H. H. Meyer, E. Kay and J. R. P. French, Jr.: Split roles in performance appraisal, *Harvard Business Review*, Jan.–Feb., 1965, p. 129.
†See R. Beckhard: *Organization Development: Strategies and Models.* Reading, Mass., Addison-Wesley Publishing Company, 1969, and F. T. Paine: *Organization Effectiveness Conferences*, Washington, D.C., Civil Service Commission, 1970.

 2. Cycle begins again with a review of issues, priorities, barriers to improvement, and so forth.
 3. Analysts and officials keep probing for specific examples, actions taken from results of action, unresolved difficulties.

For situations in which there is no progress to report, we present (with tongue in cheek) Figure 8–1, Standard Progress Report (For Those with no Progress to Report).

We have indicated some focal points and activities that might be included in an intervention in the strategy-making process. These activities are available to the practicing manager or the policy analyst. Some may be available to students doing field projects. In addition, students studying cases may find enough information in some cases so that partial analysis may be made. Both individual analysis and group discussion may be included.

The reader will note again that we are viewing the organization as going through a more or less continuous process of initiation, evaluation, choice, implementation and re-evaluation. The activities

---

STANDARD PROGRESS REPORT (FOR THOSE WITH NO PROGRESS TO REPORT)

During the report period which encompasses the organizational phase, considerable progress has been made in certain necessary preliminary work directed toward the establishment of initial activities. Important background information has been carefully explored and the functional structure of component parts of the cognizant organization has been clarified.

The usual difficulty was encountered in the selection of optimum materials, available data, experimental methods, etc., but these problems are being attacked vigorously and we expect that the development phase will continue to proceed at a satisfactory rate.

In order to prevent unnecessary duplication of previous efforts in this same field, it was deemed expedient to establish a survey and to conduct a rather extensive analysis of comparable efforts in this direction, to explore various facilities in the immediate area of activity under consideration, and then to summarize these findings.

This Committee held its regular meeting and considered rather important policy matters pertaining to the over-all organization levels of the line and staff responsibilities that develop in regard to the personnel associated with the specific assignments resulting from these broad functional specifications. It is assumed that this rate of progress will continue to accelerate as these necessary broad functional phases continue further development.

Source: *Anonymous*

Figure 8–1.

are not strictly limited to the action thrust of corporate strategy development; they include the diagnostic component of data collection about the external and internal environment.

EFFECTIVE GROUP SESSIONS

The structured activities that we are talking about include assembling an appropriate mixture of people "to work the problem." Certain assumptions are made. It is felt that if an aroused top management endorses a reorientation, others will develop an interest and readiness to act on strategy issues that are perceived as important. It is felt that open collaborative problem discussions on real organizational problems and opportunities will enhance involvement and commitment by group members. At the same time, it is assumed that the transfer to everyday work (implementation) is enhanced if the overall assessment and development design builds the expectation that strategy implementation activities will continue and expand, and if the design calls for periodic progress report conferences.

For some structured activities it is assumed that using small heterogeneous subgroup meetings would, on balance, help individuals to communicate and to use problem-solving skills as well as provide varied points of view for discussion. If successful experiences occur in the subgroups, a transfer of problem-solving efforts to groups in which the participants ordinarily work might also occur.

Many factors have a bearing on whether the conference groups develop into effective operating teams — previous experience together and expectations, heterogeneity of group, type of problems, size of group, time pressure, amount of information available, personality and orientation of members, number of previous meetings, degree of consensus demanded, and so forth. The many factors have been discussed elsewhere;* we shall not discuss all of them here. We shall indicate that the conferences seem to depend to quite a degree on the skill and perceptiveness of those exercising leadership functions in the group.†

Many factors have a bearing on effectiveness.

The role of chairman, for example, is a difficult one requiring patience, a sensitivity to how much conflict is healthy, and the tough-mindedness to keep focus on the problem. Though there is *no one best way* to function as a conference leader, some ideas based on research and experience provide clues to the process of developing appropriate knowledge and skill to function more effectively in

No one best way.

---

*B. E. Collins, and H. Guetzkow: *A Social Psychology of Group Processes for Decision Making,* New York, John Wiley & Sons, Inc., 1964. See also H. A. Shepard: Changing interpersonal and intergroup relationships in organizations. *In* March, J. G.: *Handbook of Organizations,* Chicago, Rand McNally & Company, 1965.

†R. F. Bales: In conference, *Harvard Business Review* 32:44–50, 1954.

such a capacity. Norman Maier* provides such a set of ideas for planning and leadership in problem-solving conferences. These ideas are presented as a series of steps or phases which some conferences go through, as shown on the opposite page.

Some research and experience-based ideas.

These steps may occur in a series of sessions over several months or years or may be condensed into a much shorter period of time.

FEED-IN OF ACTION RESEARCH AND MANAGEMENT SCIENCE DATA

There may be data collection both before, during and after group sessions. There is a need to be flexible and to design and redesign the data collection and data feed-in process as the situation dictates. Some situations seem to call for an aggressive structured approach, with much data input to the sessions prepared ahead of time. In other instances the conference members themselves will open the door, so to speak, and initiate the identification of problems and solutions. We should now illustrate different situations and conditions affecting data feed-in.

First, we shall give an example of an approach in which the participants themselves generate information about their own problems, analyze the root causes, develop action plans and set a schedule for progress review. It is called the *confrontation meeting.*† In the confrontation meeting the top manager gives an initial challenge to a large segment of his management group. The challenge is a reorientation question, "What things need to be different around here — strategies, policies, structure?" The agenda is wide open. Out of such reorientation may come an interest and a readiness to act on problems seen as important. It is assumed again that open collaborative discussions on real organizational problems will enhance involvement.

Confrontation meeting.

There is some evidence to indicate that the approach has worked successfully in business and government organizations. Conditions for its successful use are indicated by Beckhard:

There is a need for the management group to examine its own workings.

Conditions for successful use.

Very limited time is available for the activity.
Top management wishes to improve conditions quickly.
There is enough cohesion in the top team to ensure follow-up.

---

*N. R. F. Maier: *Problem-Solving Discussion and Conference Leadership Methods and Skills,* New York, McGraw-Hill Book Co., Inc., 1963; see also W. W. Burke and R. Beckhard (eds.): *Conference Planning,* Washington, National Education Association, 1970.

†R. Beckhard: The confrontation meeting, op. cit., p. 150. This article gives the steps to follow in such a meeting.

SOME STEPS IN CONFERENCE PLANNING AND LEADERSHIP

I. Provide orientation and explanation to relevant parties.
II. Provide for collection and sharing of appropriate data.
III. Discuss problems and issues with group.
   a. Check deviations from standards and goals.
   b. Ascertain factors impinging on mission accomplishment.
IV. Discuss problem priorities with group.
   a. Decide which problems to work on.
   b. Decide sequence of taking up problems.
V. Clarify problem(s) to be discussed.
   a. State in impersonal terms.
   b. Show how problem relates to their interests.
   c. State only one major objective (with limiting factors).
   d. State problem briefly and stop.
   e. Refrain from suggesting solutions yourself.
VI. Obtain possible solutions.
   a. Allow new idea evaluation.
   b. Be sure enough solutions are obtained; be patient; restate problem if necessary.
   c. Check understanding of ideas and solutions proposed.
   d. Write down solutions on chalk board or newsprint.
VII. Evaluate solutions.
   a. Get whole group involved. How?
      1. Ask by name how they feel about idea expressed.
      2. Create opportunities to indicate agreement or disagreement.
   b. Reward criticism.
   c. Bring hostility out into the open.
   d. Reduce list of solutions. How?
      1. Integrating solutions.
      2. Voting for best 3, and so forth.
   e. See if assumed cause is supported by the facts of the situation (get agreement on facts).
   f. See if solution addresses itself to assumed cause.
   g. List advantages and disadvantages of each solution on chalk board or newsprint.
   h. Eliminate solutions transferred from another situation unless situation is identical.
   i. Forecast effects of each solution.
   j. Use exploratory questions.
VIII. Choose solution.
   a. Choose one that most completely obtains the objective, one that does so most efficiently (least expenditure of time, money, energy).
   b. Choose one that is acceptable.
   c. Specify action to be taken.
      1. Duties of each member.
      2. Steps involved in implementation.
      3. Evaluation procedures to be used.
      4. Arrange for follow-up.
IX. Implement and test alternatives.
X. Provide for progress review sessions and further action.

There is real commitment to resolving issues on the part of top management.

The organization is experiencing, or has recently experienced, some major change.

As we have mentioned, it may be desirable to *feed in additional data* for the group to discuss during the sessions. The data may be fed in, allowing much leeway to the participants in interpreting the data and determining problems and solutions to the problems.

However, the relatively unstructured approach *may* fail if there are tight controls on delegation of authority, if there is perceived to be little or no articulated support from top management for openness in communications, if the purposes of the sessions are either not explained to or accepted by the conferees (i.e., if they feel they are participating in self-incrimination rather than in problem identification and solution), if there is little external or internal pressure for change, or if there is a need for more sophisticated data collection and analysis.

In these cases, more direction will be needed in order to develop the groups into effective operating teams. The direction may take the form of the session leader's initiating problem definitions and proposing solutions. Discussion, of course, is allowed. We call this generalized procedure the Situation Description Discussion Proposal Discussion (SDDPD) program. The program requires advance data collection and analysis, with preparation of situation descriptions and solution proposals. The program allows sharing in the refinement of the situation and in the development and elaboration of relevant solutions.

A more structured approach—SDDPD program.

The program has been used in various organizations (e.g., Babcock & Wilcox, Department of Treasury, Union Carbide, Department of Agriculture) and seems to increase involvement and commitment to action on the part of conference members.*

Specifically what is done is as follows:

An organization situation (e.g., opportunity or threat in environment) is described, checking with the group after each item in the description for agreement and discussion.

The situation description, which had been prepared ahead of time, is revised on newsprint as the group proceeds.

Similarly, the proposals are prepared ahead of time on newsprint and are revised as the group proceeds.

The proposals are presented and discussed, with the question, "Do we agree to do this?"

The most *valued* solutions or proposals are those that could be implemented by the conference group members themselves.

After each session a list of agreed-upon items is transcribed and distributed to each member of the conference as soon as possible.

The group is asked from time to time to stay with and bring up significant issues.

---

*See, for example, P. H. Chase: The creative management workshop, *Personnel Journal* April, 1972, pp. 264–282.

The conference leader keeps checking on the group process to see if what is being done is helpful. He checks on the accuracy of communication, protects minority points of view, keeps the discussion moving and summarizes from time to time.

This approach allows involvement as well as aggressive pursuit of problem areas in implementation of strategies or areas in which there may be opportunities for the organization to change practices or strategies.

An alternative way of feeding in data puts emphasis on debate and the examination of underlying assumptions, and the generation of new assumptions once old ones are exposed or demolished. The program for strategy formation that we mentioned in connection with role playing is the *dialectical approach*. Specifically what is done in this case is as follows:

Dialectical approach.

An individual or subgroup develops a set of objectives and a plan of action.

Another individual or subgroup develops a similar set of objectives and a counterplan to attain the objectives.

The objectives and plans are presented and advocated to the total group.

The total group examines the underlying assumptions as they relate to environmental demands and support and the strategy-generating structure.

Opposing advocates interpret relevant information as supporting their views.

The total group is asked from time to time to judge the suitability of the various assumptions, objectives and action plans.

As with the SDDPD approach, the session leader keeps checking on the group process to see if what is being done is helpful. He checks on the accuracy of communication, protects minority points of view, keeps the discussion moving and summarizes from time to time.

As reported by Mason,* in most cases in which this approach has been tried, what seems to develop is either clear support for one alternative or a new composite approach that is superior to either of the original objectives or action plans. Moreover, the assumptions underlying the plans are made explicit and given a thorough examination, and new assumptions are generated. (See Fig. 8–2.) As mentioned, this approach lends itself to role playing.

Test your assumptions!

The group activity may be preceded (or followed) by individual problem-solving activity. Thus, the advantages of both types of activity may be obtained.

To give more detail on some of the various activities in these sessions we shall give the guidelines and report and the measurement plan that resulted after orientation and discussion in a public organization.† The focal point in this particular illustration is

---

*R. O. Mason: A dialectical approach to strategic planning, *Management Science* 15:403–414, 1969.

†The plan is a modification of the "confrontation meeting" approach used frequently in consulting by Professor Richard Beckhard of Harvard University, to whom we have previously referred.

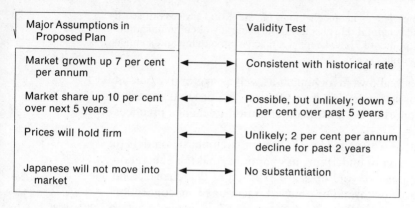

Major Assumptions in Proposed Plan	Validity Test
Market growth up 7 per cent per annum	Consistent with historical rate
Market share up 10 per cent over next 5 years	Possible, but unlikely; down 5 per cent over past 5 years
Prices will hold firm	Unlikely; 2 per cent per annum decline for past 2 years
Japanese will not move into market	No substantiation

Net Assessment
1. Plan is unrealistically optimistic.
2. Highly unlikely that market share can be increased without substantial price reduction.
3. Competitive threat from Japanese not adequately dealt with.

Figure 8–2 *Testing key corporate strategy assumptions. Adapted from L. V. Gerstner, Jr.: Can strategic planning pay off? Business Horizons 15(No. 6), 13, December, 1972.*

An example of guidelines and a report and measurement plan.

priority setting and *action planning.* You will notice that there are multiple sources of data and multiple methods used, i.e., (1) self-generated data in the sessions, and (2) data fed in from outside sources (interviews, questionnaires, analysis of strategic moves and practices). You will notice as well that the design pays close attention to gaining understanding and acceptance of the measurement plan.

PHASE I

(One or two half-day sessions.) Separate meetings across organization lines to collect information.

a. Separate top management group (perhaps exclude organization head).

b. Subgroups of five to eight people composed of others that they do not work with on a regular basis (may use a diagonal slice).

c. Assignment for each group. Example: "We think this is a very good organization. We think this organization is highly creative in developing policies and strategies and in managing its people. We want to experiment and try to make things even better. We all want to help. Considering the changing environment, your needs and those of the total organization, what things should be different around here—strategies, policies, ways of implementing policies, structure, and so forth?"

d. Each subgroup should develop a list for approximately one hour, put the list on newsprint and be prepared to report these back to the total group.

PHASE II

(One or two half-day sessions.) Total group meeting.

a. Each subgroup reports its discussion.
b. Areas of agreement and disagreement are identified and discussed.
c. Issues are assigned to categories by the group, for example, by type of issue and by area of their authority, ability and motivation to have an impact on the issue.
d. Barriers to improvement are identified and discussed (if time permits).
e. Indication is given by top manager that additional information about improving organization effectiveness is going to be collected in a variety of ways. Examples:
   (1) All participants will anonymously and independently fill out an organizational effectiveness form. (See Appendix 2 for an abbreviated version of this form.) They will rate identified issues on importance and on effectiveness and rate barriers to improvement.
   (2) Special questionnaires will be sent to a sample of all organization members.
   (3) Interviews and discussions will be held with a sample of managers and supervisors.
   (4) Strategic moves and practices will be reviewed by task forces.
   (5) Some additional conferences will be held.
   (6) Studies of the strategic environment may be made if appropriate.

PHASE III

(Two or three half-day sessions.)

a. Subgroups go through list of priority issues and select one which affects their group and which is susceptible to their own efforts. They determine action plans (dimensions and tasks) that their group will take on those issues and a time-table for beginning subsequent work.
b. Subgroups identify what other relevant parties, staff supervisors and lateral groups might do to assist them.
c. One assignment might be to design an "optimal" organization of work for their part of the organization; another might be to determine a tactical plan for communicating what happened at the conference to relevant parties.

PHASE IV

(One half-day session).

a. The groups reconvene and each subgroup reports out its list of priority issues and its plans for dealing with them. Then each group reports suggestions for other relevant parties. A cumulative list of specific suggestions is maintained.
b. Top management officials of the unit respond to the list, making some commitment on each major policy and issue.

REPORT AND MEASUREMENT PLAN

A record should be kept of important actions and statements in the conferences. The report(s) would include:

1. A brief statement of methodology used in identifying issues and courses of action.
2. An identification of policy issues discussed, including the perceived relative importance and the degree of agreement on the importance of the issue.
3. Perceptions of dimensions of the managerial job and the staff job as they relate to the policies and the issues identified.
4. Specific tasks for each type of position to improve organization effectiveness.
5. Minority comment on appropriateness of recommendations.
6. A timetable for their completion.
7. Tactical plan for communicating what happened at the conference to relevant persons not there.
8. Methods for estimating how much has been accomplished. It is highly important to gain *understanding* and *acceptance* of the measurement plan. A management performance accomplishment plan* might be developed by the conference groups as follows:
   a. Identify independent dimensions of

performance relating to issues identified. These could be individual group dimensions or interteam dimensions, e.g., managers support and reinforce investment spending among subordinates.

b. Provide descriptions of these dimensions.

c. Develop descriptions or samples of high, moderate and low levels of performance on each dimension, e.g., the manager isolates strategic work for objective analysis and profiling of strategies.

d. Transfer the dimension and examples to a second group knowledgeable about the issues for discussion and editing. Discard dimensions and examples for which there is a lack of consensus on definitions and on ratings.

e. Participants and outside analysts independently and anonymously rate organization and management performance as it stands at time of conferences and then rate again after a period of time, e.g., six months, 12 months.

9. Appendix could include summaries of information distributed.

10. Progress review sessions should be scheduled within six months.

---

*This type of plan has been referred to previously in Appendix 1 to Chapter 4, Determining Top Management Effectiveness Dimensions.

QUESTIONS AND ANSWERS REGARDING THE ACTION COMPONENTS

Numerous questions about structured activities and their effectiveness and efficiency may occur to the reader. We can only proceed *tentatively* at the time, but some appropriate guidance may be gained from experienced judgment. Some questions and answers arising out of experience with the interventions are presented below. (Also some additional relevant research findings are introduced.)

Do the approaches work?

Before-and-after studies, case studies, direct observation and anecdotal evidence (we have already referred to some of this evidence in Chapter 6) seem to indicate some outcomes associated with these types of structured activities which are judged as at least temporarily improving the strategy-making process. The approaches are being adopted by practicing managers (often with external advisors). Additional studies of the structured activities mentioned and variations of them are being conducted in a variety of business and government settings across the country. To fully understand the complexities and unique problems of application of these structured activities, however, requires systematic controlled research and constructive dialogue between specialists in the field. More data are needed, for example, on the cost benefit relationship, the limitations for size and type of organization, the effects of extended reliance on outside help and the limitations of group versus individual problem analysis.*

---

*See F. R. Wickert: Book review of Addison-Wesley Series on Organization Development, *Personnel Psychology* 23(No. 3):411–415, Autumn, 1970; D. C. Barnland: A comparative study of individual majority and group judgment, *Journal of Abnormal and Social Psychology* 58:55–60; R. Beckhard and D. Lake: Short and long range effects of a team development effort, *in* Hornstein, H. A., et al.: (eds.): *Social Intervention,* New York, The Free Press, 1971, pp. 421–439.

Is top management support needed?

As indicated before, the personal acceptance and endorsement of the structured activities by the top manager(s) in the organization or the unit* seem quite important. Not only does the top official probably need to endorse the approach personally, it is highly desirable that he unmistakenly communicate his belief in the need for identifying strategic issues and suggesting changes.

It may not be possible to get a high level of commitment, but the top man's failure to support or his active diagreement with the intervention may be fatal. Before undertaking an assessment, the concurrence of the top man may be gained. In asking for such approval, a low-key approach may be helpful. Approval of an assessment and development plan which as a matter of course includes individual work and group sessions may be requested.

How many organization managers should be included?

The desirable number will depend on such factors as how the unit's work is divided, what participation would contribute a good enough spread of experiences and viewpoints to give a good picture of the organization or the organizational unit. For break-out groups, approximately five to eight members tend to provide for a good balance. Greater resources are available for problem solving, which may result in improved group performance. However, there may be decreased member satisfaction and increased difficulty in reaching a consensus or a joint decision.†

Who should be organization participants in the session?

For regular meetings the normal participants in the meetings may be included. For special sessions consideration should be given to:

Type of strategy issues to be discussed.

Representation from significant strategy units.

Interests, knowledge and skills of potential members.

Heterogeneity of membership.

While heterogeneity will tend to increase the difficulty of building interpersonal relations, it will also tend to increase the problem-solving potential of the group, since errors are reduced, more alternatives are generated and wider criticism is possible.‡

Should there be substitutes for group session participants?

The policy and strategy issues being dealt with are important to the success of the organization. The conference members need to be

---

*Identification of the top officials may be a problem. For example, in the federal government "top" authority for certain activities may rest with various parties: the Secretary, the Executive Director, the Office of Management and Budget, the Civil Service Commission, Congressional Committees, the Government Accounting Office, the President, and so forth.

†E. J. Thomas and C. F. Fink: Models of group problem solving. *Journal of Abnormal and Social Psychology* 63(No. 1):53–63, 1961. See also A. P. Hare: *Handbook of Small Group Research,* Chicago, The Free Press of Glencoe, 1962.

‡See B. E. Collins and H. Guetzkow: *A Social Psychology of Group Processes for Decision Making.* New York, John Wiley & Sons, Inc., 1964.

made aware of the importance and to be personally present at each session unless there is a dire emergency. Experience indicates an increased risk of ineffectiveness if substitutes for conference members are sent to the sessions. Even a few substitutes seem to hamper the continuity of thought and interaction among participants.

What about timing and spacing of the sessions?

We have already discussed timing of the structured activities. We should add that group effectiveness seems to depend on the openness between participants. Such openness is a function of, among other things previously cited, the number of meetings the group has. There should be enough meetings to permit openness to develop, but not so many nor held so often as to make the meetings too time-consuming or nonproductive. It is difficult to say how many sessions should be held or how often; probably not more than one or two sessions a week seems to be a good guide based on experience thus far.

It seems desirable to have one session held just before presentation of findings and possible solutions to the top manager. At this time the group members need to discuss the key issues and the best manner of presentation.

How to present the plan or report?

This question is relevant when the higher level officials are not members of the group. The question may be answered by the participants themselves. Since the staff analysts tend to be more neutral in the face of possible conflict, some managers may prefer to have the analysts make the presentation. In any event, it seems desirable after the presentation for the official to respond and to discuss the report with the total group from his standpoint to attempt to gain agreement on timing and priority. The official, as indicated, along with the highest board (e.g., directors, commissioners, and so forth) has probably reserved the right to final choice.

What of findings that members fail to confirm or agree on?

As suggested before, various conflict management procedures may be used. Effort in the session is sometimes made to bring differing objectives, values and perceptions out into the open where they can be dealt with constructively. In addition, a basic tactic is to find the goals upon which the participants can agree and thereby establish an effective interaction.

If some findings are not confirmed or agreed upon there may be a need for further study, or the findings may be reported, with notations made of disagreements or lack of confirmation. This is a decision that will test the judgment of the participants and the analysts.

SUMMARY

We have covered some of the considerations necessary for developing group and organizational involvement and for selecting in-

dividual and group problem-solving situations. We have indicated:
(1) that individual problem-solving efforts are a very important part
of the action thrust in strategy formation; (2) that group interaction
does *not* mean that strategy decisions are turned over to the group;
(3) that relatively successful development efforts tend to include a
shared approach to information gathering and to collaborative problem solving following a well outlined series of steps; (4) that group
activity may permit participants to obtain intrinsic rewards while
perceiving, diagnosing and acting upon relevant strategy issues; (5)
that many factors, including the skill and perceptiveness of those exercising leadership functions, have a bearing on whether the groups
develop into effective operating teams; and (6) that it is assumed that
a transfer to everyday work would be enhanced if the development
design built expectations of continuation and expansion of strategy
formation and implementation beyond the meetings and if the design
called for periodic progress report sessions.

The structured activities, as posed, may be used in regularly
scheduled meetings, or special sessions may be set up. Using structured activities is a *highly flexible* approach that may be used in conjunction with training and development sessions or feed-in or with
observational, interview, questionnaire, report and management
science data. The information gathered may be useful for individual
research and independent study of strategy formation as well as for
group discussion and analysis. Expertise is needed and the problem-
solving process may be designed and aided by internal and/or external analysts. It may have several focal points, including (1) strategy-
formation process, (2) assessment of leverage points, (3) manager
functioning, (4) stating and analyzing objectives, (5) priority setting
and action planning, and (6) progress review.

These action components of an action-research program may
be relied on to gain support and assistance by involving others in
planning actions, coordinating actions, executing actions and evaluating actions.

DISCUSSION QUESTIONS

1. Can groups be used effectively and efficiently to create strategies within the organization? Why? Within what constraints does
this action occur?

2. Discuss how authority and leadership patterns affect the ability of the organization to react to strategy changes.

3. What criteria are satisfied by organizations that generally
deal successfully with strategic changes?

4. How can the group problem-solving activity be designed to
implement the "best" strategic changes within the organization?

5. What stages of the strategy-formation process require particular emphasis during evaluation? Discuss the problems and benefits
associated with structured evaluation at each of these phases.

6. Discuss the critical steps involved in setting up problem-solving conferences. Which key individuals should be included in this process? What should their roles be?

7. What types of activities lend themselves to group action? What is the focus of the group during each of these activities?

Suggested Additional References for Further Research

Athos, A. G., and Coffey, R. E.: *Behavior in Organizations: A Multidimensional View*. Englewood Cliffs, N.J., Prentice-Hall, Inc., 1968.

Blake, R. K., and Mouton, J. S.: The Managerial Grid. Houston, Gulf Publishing Co., 1966.

Cleland, D. I., and King, W. R.: *Systems, Organizations, Analysis, Management*. New York, McGraw-Hill Book Co., Inc., 1969.

Cyert, R. M., Simon, H. A., and Trow, D. B.: Observation of a business decision. *Journal of Business*, 1956, pp. 237–248.

French, J. R., Kay, E., and Meyer, H. H.: Participation and the appraisal system. *Human Relations 19*:3–20, 1966.

Gore, W. J.: *Administrative Decision-Making; A Heuristic Model*. New York, John Wiley & Sons, Inc., 1964.

Homans, G.: *The Human Group*. New York, Harcourt & Brace, 1950.

Hopkins, T. K.: *The Exercise of Influence in Small Groups*. Totowa, N.J., The Bedminster Press, 1964.

Kahn, R. L., and Katz, D.: Leadership practices in relation to productivity and morale. *In* Cartwright, D., and Zander, A. (eds.): *Group Dynamics — Research and Theory*. 2nd ed. New York, Harper & Row, 1960, pp. 554–570.

Katz, E., and Lazarsfeld, P. P.: *Personal Influence*. Chicago, The Free Press of Glencoe, 1955.

Lorsch, J., and Lawrence, P.: Managing Group and Intergroup Relations. Homewood, Ill., Richard D. Irwin, Inc., 1972.

Lorsch, J., and Lawrence, P.: Organizing for product innovation. *Harvard Business Review* Vol. *43*(No. 1): 1965, pp. 96–104.

Marrow, A. J., Bowers, D. G., and Seashore, S. E.: *Management by Participation*. New York, Harper & Row, 1967.

Newell, J. S., and Simon, H. A.: The process of creative thinking. In Gruber, J., Terrell, W., and Weitheimer, M.: *Contemporary Approaches to Creative Thinking*. New York, Atherton Press, 1962, Chapter 3.

Parker, T. C.: Relationships among measures of supervisory behavior, group behavior and situational characteristics. *Personnel Psychology 16*:319–334, 1963.

Patton, A.: How to appraise executive performance. *Harvard Business Review 38*(1):63–70, 1960.

Porter, D. E., and Applewhite, P. B.: *Organization Behavior and Mangement*. Scranton, Pa., International Textbook Co., 1964.

Richards, M. D.: "An Exploratory Study of Strategic Failure." Academy of Management Proceedings, Boston, Mass., 1973.

Sherif, M.: Experiments in group conflict and cooperation. *Scientific American 195*:54–58, 1956.

Shure, G. H., Rogers, M. S., Larsen, I. M., and Tassone, J.: Group planning and task effectiveness. *Sociometry 25*:263–282, 1962.

Smith, P. C.: The development of a method of measuring job satisfaction: The Cornell studies. *In* Fleishman, E. A. (ed.): *Studies in Personnel and Industrial Psychology*. Rev. ed. Homewood, Ill., Dorsey Press, 1967.

Soelberg, P. O.: Unprogrammed decision making. *Industrial Management Review*, Spring, 1967, pp. 19–29.

Stogdill, R. M.: *Leadership Behavior: Description and Measurement*. Business Research Monograph. No. 88. Columbus, Ohio, Bureau of Business Research Ohio State University, 1957.

Taylor, D., Berry, P. C., and Block, C. H.: Does group participation when using brainstorming facilitate or inhibit creative thinking? *Administrative Science Quarterly,* Vol. 3, 1958.

Thompson, J. D., Truden, J. A.: Strategies, structures and processes of organizational decision. *In* Leavitt, H. J., and Pondy, L. R̂. (eds.): *Readings in Managerial Psychology.* Chicago, University of Chicago Press, 1964, pp. 496–515.

Tilles, S.: *Making Strategy Explicit.* Boston, The Boston Consulting Group, 1967.

Tuason, R.: "Corporate Life Cycle and the Evalulation of Corporate Strategy." Academy of Management Proceedings. Boston, Mass., 1973.

Vroom, V. H.: *Some Personality Determinants of the Effects of Participation.* Englewood Cliffs, N.J., Prentice-Hall, Inc., 1960.

Whyte, W. F., Jr.: *The Organization Man.* New York, Doubleday & Company, 1956.

APPENDIX 1 TO CHAPTER 8

QUESTIONNAIRE ON MANAGERIAL FUNCTIONING

Features of the Questionnaire

— Questions on management functions are given which include a list of performance activities. The set of functions has been tested for reliability with a variety of types of managers and the functions are close to being mutually exclusive. The respondent is asked for: (1) The per cent time he spends on each function; (2) what per cent of time he feels he should spend on each function; (3) his comments.

Answering the questions on time allocation can help the respondent to assess and understand what his job is.

The respondent is also asked to help to provide an inventory of the forces, strengths, problems and expectations in his part of the organization by answering questions on the following items:

1). What kinds of specific actions contribute most to his job.
2). What kinds of specific actions contribute least, or impede, his effectively doing his job.
3). What things should management be most concerned with in regard to how the organization now functions.
4). What are his expectations about the future of the organization?

Guidelines for Use of the Questionnaire

The questionnaire should be used toward the beginning of an evaluation, as it is designed to provide leads to problems and follow-up is necessary.

Emphasize the importance of the questionnaire in the evaluation process based on the goal of determining managerial effectiveness. A letter from a top manager in the organization should be sent, informing respondents of the importance of the form and the need for its timely completion.

(Attachment 1 gives part
of the questionnaire)

Analysis and Evaluation

Data taken from the questionnaire should provide a useful component of the total evaluation of the various managerial elements through description, definition and measurement of the manager's performance.

To correctly classify data and determine directions for problem solving, information should be compiled along the following lines:

— The analysis should be arranged by work groups and levels.
— Inventory the strengths, problems and expectations for each work group and perhaps for categories of level. The evaluator's judgment can be used on the most appropriate arrangement for a specific unit.
— Using the same categories, inventory functions as they exist in a unit, and as the managers perceive they should be.
— A summary of the analysis may be fed back to individuals or groups of individuals in the relevant work groups for their comment and discussion. Feedback of information *should not* be ignored.

(Attachment 2 gives an example for reporting data)

Attachment 1

PART 1

Functional Time Allocation

The allocation of your time is determined by many factors: policies, structure, management style, etc. Estimate the usual allocation of time at your level in the organization. Then indicate what you think the allocation should be.

FUNCTIONS

	IS NOW	SHOULD BE

1. *Planning:* Determining goals, policies, and courses of action. Work scheduling, budgeting, setting up procedures, preparing agenda, programming.

2. *Investigating:* Collecting and preparing information, usually in the form of records, reports, and accounts. Inventorying, measuring output, preparing financial statements.

3. *Coordinating:* Exchanging information with people in the organization other than subordinates in order to relate and adjust programs. Advising other departments, expediting, liaison with other managers, informing superiors, seeking other departments' cooperation.

4. *Evaluating:* Assessment and appraisal of proposals, reports, or of reported or observed performance.

5. *Supervising:* Directing, leading, counseling, developing, and training subordinates, explaining work rules, assigning work, disciplining, handling complaints of subordinates.

6. *Staffing:* Maintaining the work force of a unit or of several units. Recruiting, employment interviewing, selecting, placing, promoting, and transferring employees.

7. *Negotiating:* Purchasing, selling, or contracting for goods or services. Collective bargaining, contacting suppliers.

8. *Representing:* Advancing general organizational interests through speeches, consultation, and contacts with individuals or groups outside the organization.

9. *Doing the Work:* Personally carrying out operational assignments for which your unit is responsible.

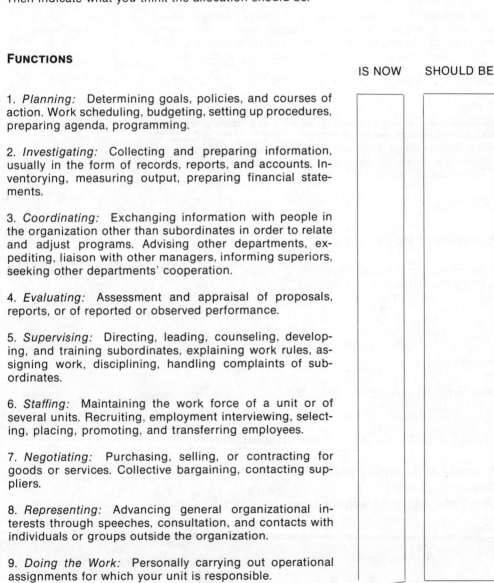

COMMENTS:

	Total:	100%	100%

PART 2

Performance of Functions

In order to begin to study management at your agency we are looking for specific illustrations of the kinds of management or supervisory actions in the functions that are unusually good or unusually poor.

Give specific recent example(s) of *very important* action(s) or behavior(s) which are *unusually good*. Indicate function(s). Do not indicate names. Your individual responses are *confidential.* Only totals will be reported back to top management. | Function(s)

Give specific recent example(s) of *very important* action(s) or behavior(s) which are *unusually poor.* Indicate function(s). Do not indicate names. Your individual responses are *confidential.* Only totals will be reported back to top management.

PART 3

Concerns of Management

What things do you feel management should be most concerned with in regard to the way the organization now functions?

Expectations

What are your expectations about the future of the organization?

Attachment II

Example of Reporting Data
Organizational Unit   X
(N = 7 managers, 35 supervisors)

Listing sequence: Category with the most respondents first; that with the least, last.

THE KINDS OF ACTIONS THAT CONTRIBUTE OR IMPEDE THE
SUPERVISOR'S OR MANAGER'S JOB

FUNCTION	HELPING	NO. OF RESPONDENTS
Coordinating (3)	Keeping other depts. informed of current operations	27

| Staffing (6) | Work force is sufficient to do the job | 17 |

FUNCTION	HINDERING	NO. OF RESPONDENTS
Supervising (5)	Poor supervision	15
Evaluating (4)	Delay in assessment of proposals	14
Planning (1)	Always working crash situations	13

FUNCTIONAL TIME ALLOCATION

TOO MUCH TIME SPENT	NO. OF RESPONDENTS
Staffing	25
Doing the work	15
Coordinating	2

MORE TIME SHOULD BE SPENT	NO. OF RESPONDENTS
Planning	18
Supervising	15
Evaluating	9

The actual percentage for functional time allocation is not too important unless very unusual. Of more importance is the perceived need to change allocation of time. Further investigation is needed before a firm conclusion on changes in the allocation of time can be made.

MOST IMPORTANT THINGS FOR MANAGEMENT CONCERN	NO. OF RESPONDENTS
Properly using the work force	24
Establishing priorities in advance	18

The evaluator should check the importance of the helps and hinderances in problem analysis. For example, perhaps management should promote proper use of the work force and establish a planned program of priorities since these were the specific items that were hindering managers' jobs.

FUTURE EXPECTATIONS FOR THE ORGANIZATION	NO. OF RESPONDENTS
Plodding along in the same old fashion	30
Going downhill slowly	7
Slowly improving	5

Here, respondents indicate that the organization is not really striving for upward development. This might make the respondents feel the situation is hopeless and extinguishes creativity and innovation. The analyst might check the type of people hired into managerial positions and the latitude permitted in experimentation with new ideas and new directions.

APPENDIX 2 TO CHAPTER 8

Organizational Effectiveness Form

In previous conferences the importance and the need to work on certain issues has been expressed. So that we can begin to sort out these issues in terms of their priority, we would like to obtain your ratings of the *importance* of each of them.

We would also like you to identify various factors, from the attached list, that may operate as *barriers* to carrying out the intentions you or the group may formulate in regard to each of the issues.

Please show your assessment of the importance of each of the following issues by marking the number in the scale to the left of the issue statement. Circle the number in the scale that corresponds to the number of the *importance statement* that best approximates your own judgment. If you feel any important issues have been overlooked they may be entered in the space provided at the end of this list.

In the column to the right of each issue statement please identify, by number, the factor or factors that may operate as *barriers* to work related to that issue. If you feel any factors have been overlooked they may be entered in the space provided at the end of the list.

Please do not sign this form.

Importance of Issues

Is further work on the issue quite important?

Importance

1. It no longer seems important.
2. We have adequately resolved the issue.
3. Not sure.
4. Continue at the present level of effort.
5. Put more effort on it.
6. Needs much more effort.
7. Top priority.

Importance	Issues	Barriers
1 2 3 4 5 6 7	( )	
1 2 3 4 5 6 7	( )	

Importance of Issues (*Continued*)

Barriers

Which of the factors listed below operate as barriers to carrying out the intentions you or the group may have formulated in regard to the previously identified issue?

1. Lack of clarity as to what should be done.
2. Pressures of day-to-day work.
3. Resistance or lack of support from peers or associates.
4. Resistance or lack of support from subordinates.
5. Difficulty in collaborating with people outside the department or division.
6. Conflict with policies that are outside our control.
7. Lack of trust.
8. Unqualified personnel.
9. Lack of direction, instructions or guidelines.
10. Lack of delegation.
11. Lack of enthusiasm.
12. Inadequate feedback.
13. Task interference.
14. Punishment or extra work if you do.
15. Other.

Suggestions

If you have a solution to an important problem or problems please explain it briefly in the spaces provided below. Please indicate who would be involved, how the problem would be solved, and when action would be taken.

_____

_____

_____

_____

_____

_____

_____

_____

_____

_____

_____

_____

_____

_____

TRENDS IN STRATEGY AND
STRUCTURE

DESIGNING THE ORGANIZATION
    Environmental Demands
    Related Influences on Design
    Differentiating by
        Organizational Level
    Keeping the Corporate Strategy
        in Mind

OVERALL SUMMARY
    Practical Prblems for You to
        Solve
    Questions to Answer
    Policy Makers

DISCUSSION QUESTIONS

APPENDIX 1. SOME ACTION
STEPS

9

STRATEGY AND STRUCTURE

Up to this point we have concentrated on a model of strategy and policy formation, guides for assessment, and methods for assessing and developing strategies and policies and the policy-formation process. A variety of ideas and methods have been presented. Their use as given or in revised form, alone or in combination, rests with the judgment and skill of the manager, analyst or student. Of course, there will be some "muddling through" owing to various uncertainties and pressures. We are assuming, however, that the planning and structuring of activities would be helpful.

What you should learn.

In the preceding chapter we discussed some structured activities that might help the organization both to initiate and to implement corporate strategies. In this chapter we shall discuss some general trends in strategy and structure (for large corporations where there is significant evidence), some external environmental considerations in designing the organization and some related internal influences on a structure. We shall also provide an overall summary of the book. Finally, in the appendix to this chapter we shall summarize some action steps along with several categories of questions that, when answered, should be a help in starting a planned approach.

TRENDS IN STRATEGY AND STRUCTURE

We have discussed earlier that strategy may be linked to aspects of the structure in a coherent organization design. A historian, A. D. Chandler,* has pointed out that as firms grow larger over time and diversify into new businesses or integrate their operations they have to decentralize because the business has become so

---

*A. D. Chandler: *Strategy and Structure,* Cambridge, MIT Press, 1962.

complex that top management does not have the technical knowledge or because it just takes too long to send the problems up to the top for a decision.

In addition, the hypothesized relationship between strategy and structure has received strong support from an analysis of firms in the Fortune 500 (1967) by Wrigley* (see Table 9–1). The analysis, as reported by B. R. Scott, indicates that among the largest industrial corporations in the United States all the single product firms were found to be functionally organized, all the highly diversified and 85 per cent of the related product diversified group to have a divisional organization.

Furthermore, previous analysis† of organizations in the United States indicated a trend over the last several decades toward the growth of markets involving increased volume in a product or service line associated with more specialized manpower and equipment. The development of an integration strategy and a centralized, functional structure to exploit the opportunities occurred frequently.

Integration and a functional structure.

However, a more predominant recent trend, which also stems from the growth of markets, includes the development of new products and services to serve them, the increased impact of product- or service-oriented research and development activities within the organization, and the development of a strategy and a structure to exploit the market, namely, diversification and divisionalization. Growth via diversification has become the most common corporate strategy in Western Europe as well.‡

Diversification and divisionalization.

The evidence (of Scott) also indicates that diversified compa-

TABLE 9–1 RELATIONSHIP BETWEEN STRATEGY AND STRUCTURE*

Stage	Product-Market Scope (Degree of Diversification)	Number of Companies	Structure	
			Functional	Divisional
I.	Single product	30	30	0
II.	Dominant product	70	25	45
III.	Related products	300	15	285
IV.	Unrelated products	100	0	100
		500	70 (14%)	430 (86%)

*Adapted from B. R. Scott: *Stages in Corporate Development, Part II,* Harvard Business School, 4-371-295 BP 999, 1971.

---

*As reported by B. R. Scott: *Stages in Corporate Development, Part II,* Harvard Business School, 4-371-295 BP 999, 1971.
†See, for example, J. K. Galbraith: *The New Industrial State,* Boston, Houghton Mifflin Company, 1967.
‡They're sniping at Galbraith again, *New York Times,* March 11, 1973, p. 16.

nies (e.g., E. I. Dupont, Eastman Kodak, General Electric, General Foods, Olin Textron) have performed better in growth by sales, earnings and earnings per share (especially if they had related products) than nondiversified companies (e.g., U.S. Steel, Scott Paper, Texaco). There are some exceptions, of course, such as the high-performance, vertically integrated* and dominant-product enterprises like IBM, Polaroid and Xerox.

These exceptions have occurred where the organization was able to gain a leadership position in a single, rapid-growth industry and to retain that position. The "diversifiers" were able to achieve a redistribution of sales and assets toward more favorable growth and profit prospects by using a multi-industry strategy and a divisional form of management.

While the trend toward diversification and divisionalization for large corporations is clear, the transition is quite difficult for an organization (e.g., Jones & Laughlin, Goodrich, and Armour) "caught" with large investments in vertically integrated operations in an industry with a low to moderate growth rate. For these companies it takes very substantial investments in new areas in order to achieve significant diversification. Many of the companies do not have a high price/earnings ratio and are not in a strong position from which to diversify by acquisition. Yet "to diversify into attractive areas with rapid growth prospects they almost surely face the prospect of buying companies with a high price earnings ratio. The result is a dilution of earnings per share, and possibly further downward pressure on the price of their stock. To pay cash, on the other hand, places a burden on the treasury in industries where recourse of outside capital is typically a continuing need. In addition, cash transactions may require a premium price in order to offset tax advantages for the seller."† Financially speaking, therefore, some dominant product companies (with low or moderate growth) are somewhat boxed into a situation where a significant redistribution of sales and assets is a slow process.

Nevertheless, many firms (dominant product and otherwise) seem to be going through this process and likewise toward the use of a divisional form of management. Continuing research is needed to describe more fully the trend toward increasing product market diversification and divisionalization.

Success of "diversifiers."

Transition may be difficult.

DESIGNING THE ORGANIZATION

While recognizing the limits of our current knowledge, it has been demonstrated that policy analysts need to give careful consid-

---

*Vertical integration may include growth by adding units closer to the final end-use market (forward integration) or to its original raw material sources (backward integration).
†B. R. Scott: *Stages in Corporate Development, Part II,* op. cit., p. 6.

eration to the corporate strategy *and* the organizational structure. Moreover, earlier in discussing aspects of our policy-formation model we have noted the accelerating pace of change in the economic, technological, social, political, competitive and social responsibility forces. Organizations significantly affected by this kind of turbulent environment would need a corporate strategy that allows more rapid modification of itself now than in the past. And with each shift in strategy the appropriateness of the existing elements in the overall structural design (i.e., the interlinking of roles and programs) for each organization situation will need to be re-examined.

Refer back to the policy formation model in Chapter 2.

There are several important considerations for the analyst. Determinations need to be made on the specialization by level and/or function plus coordination of specialized jobs in order to focus activity on organizational objectives. What is the most effective way to divide the work—functional group, product division or geographic division? Will it be helpful to group closely the units that are now required to integrate their activities? What procedures are appropriate for coordinating specialized jobs and for managing conflict situations? Will a wide or narrow span of control be most useful? What management information-gathering procedures will generate relevant and timely data? Are managers playing leadership roles that are appropriately matched to the situation? Are the measurement and motivational programs designed to encourage role orientations that are appropriate to the unit task? The action research program previously discussed will help to answer those questions on structural design.

Your previous learning should help in judging some significant considerations.

Structural design, however, is an involved topic that requires much refinement and amplification. The complexities are examined in organization theory courses and we shall provide only rather brief additional comment here.

Environmental Demands

The new roles and programs necessary to implement the corporate strategy vary along with the external environmental demands, as well as internal factors. We shall discuss the external environmental situation first. Perrow* suggests using three different types of environmental-technological demands as considerations in preparing an organizational design. The environmental-technological demands as used here include all sorts of methods for con-

Again—a contingency approach.

---

*C. Perrow: A framework for the comparative analysis of organizations, *American Sociological Review*, April, 1967. See also T. Burnes and G. M. Stalker: *The Management of Innovation*, London, Tavistock Publications Limited, 1966; J. Woodward: *Industrial Organization*, Oxford, Oxford University Press, 1965; D. H. Hickson, D. S. Pugh and D. C. Pheysey: Operations technology and organization structure: An empirical structure, *Administrative Science Quarterly*, Sept., 1969.

verting resource inputs into products and services for customers or clients. The inputs can be labor, knowledge and capital, as well as raw material. The three environmental types are:

1. Stable — organization confronted with rather *familiar* processing problems, *infrequent* need for change; e.g., retirement division of Civil Service, paper mill, firms processing large volumes of raw material.
2. Regulated flexibility — organization confronted with rather *familiar* processing problems, *frequent* need for change; e.g., job shops, hospital, newspaper office.
3. Adaptive — organization tends to be confronted with *unprecedented* processing problems, *frequent* need for change; e.g., research lab, aerospace firm, organization development consultant group.

Each of these three environmental types seems to be associated with a set of characteristics for the organizational situation. A sample of the suggested (or hypothesized) relationships is shown in Table 9–2. You will notice that we have included the policy formation elements — mission, organizational objectives, policies, strategies — along with programs (or procedures) and roles.

Hypotheses about these relationships have not been proved via substantial empirical research. Tentative patterns of relationship are identified. The stable situation seems to fit the more "bureaucratic" organization with risk aversion, centralization, programmed activity and tight control. Regulated flexibility seems to fit with some decentralization, separate planning and scheduling technocrats and limited use of participation in planning. The adaptive type of situation seems to fit the "organic" organization, with more risk-taking strategies, less programming of the work, more participation in decision-making activities and planning, and control with emphasis on objectives and results. Of course, it is not proposed that each organization will fit exactly into one of the environment-organization design types that have been described. The examples, however, do suggest that the policy analyst consider how environmental-technological demands provide one basis for designing a suitable organization for implementing a corporate strategy.

Related Influences on Design

Although the analysis of environmental demands in terms of *frequency* and *uniqueness* of problems seems helpful, the dynamic set of relationships in the organizational situation should not be underestimated. Other influences are at work. Richard Hall,* after

---

*R. Hall: *Organizations Structure and Process*, Englewood Cliffs, N.J., Prentice-Hall, Inc. 1972. See also J. P. Gibbs and H. L. Browning: The division of labor, technology, and the organization of production in twelve countries, *American Sociological Review, 31*(No. 1):81–92, February, 1966.

TABLE 9-2 POSSIBLE CHARACTERISTICS OF ORGANIZATIONAL SITUATION FOR THREE TYPES OF ENVIRONMENTAL DEMANDS*

Some Characteristics of Organizational Situation	Nature of Environmental-Technological Demands		
	Stable	Regulated Flexibility	Adaptive
Environmental uncertainty	Low	Medium	High
Degree of environmental influence on organization	Low	Medium	High
Mission	Fixed and well defined	Relatively fixed	Varied and not clearly defined
Organizational objectives	Efficient performance, stability, maintenance	Effective performance, punctuality	Effective problem solving, innovation
Policies	Stable	Fairly stable	Flexible
Strategies	Predictability, security, risk aversion, fully planned, detail specified	Flexible, some risk taking, fully planned, schedules and specs detailed	Adaptability, responsiveness, risk taking, main steps covered, adjusted to feedback
Specialization of activities	Highly specific by function	Specialized	Scope may vary, overlapping of activities
Centralization versus decentralization	Centralized	Mostly centralized	Decentralized
Procedure for coordination and conflict management	Built-in, programmed	Separate planning unit	Face-to-face within operating unit
Size of self-sufficient operating units	Large	Medium	Small, if equipment permits
Management information gathering procedure	Heavy upward flow	Flow to headquarters and operating unit	Flow mostly to and within operating unit
Leadership role	Autocratic, task oriented, desire for certainty	Mixed	Democratic relationship oriented, tolerance for ambiguity
Emphasis on on-the-job motivation	Limited scope	Craftsmanship and professionalism encouraged	Opportunity for involvement
Performance criteria and methods emphasized	Efficiency, dependability, "how" is specified	Quality, punctuality, efficiency, results at each step specified	Results within resource limits, end results stressed

*Adapted from W. H. Newman: *Strategy and Management Structure,* paper presented at the Annual Meeting of the Academy of Management, Atlanta, Georgia, 1971, and from F. Kast and J. Rosenzweig: *Contingency Views of Organization and Management,* Palo Alto, Science Research Associates, 1973.

reviewing extensive empirical research on organization structure, concludes that the aforementioned environmental-technological factors, together with the related consideration of the nature of participants and the stage of development and complexity, are important determinants of the form of an organization at any particular point in time. We shall give a few examples of such influences in strategy and design situations.

Also consider nature of participants, stage of development and complexity.

An example of how organizations may change with variations in the environment has been demonstrated implicitly in the discussion of the science fiction case given in Chapter 3. We saw there how an entrepreneur might have to change the structure of his enterprise as its complexity increased rapidly. This type of change is not limited to some fictitious future enterprise. Examples of organizations in change can be seen today.

There are many case studies that have explored the ways in which firms have tried to adapt to changing environments. We often see the problem encountered by the entrepreneur when he realizes that his organization has outgrown his ability to control it. He views the company as his pet and is unwilling to give up control of all aspects of the policy-formation process. In many instances, he struck upon a new product or an improved method of producing or supplying a particular product or service. Howard Head, inventor of the metal ski and founder of Head Ski Company, would be an example of this type of individual.

The type of organization usually developed by these individuals is highly centralized, but loosely structured. The innovator, or entrepreneur, frequently makes all significant decisions himself. There is rarely a formal organizational structure. The individual will define his task in relation to the environment, "plan" his activities over the long and short run and and then carry them out to achieve his objectives.

As the organization grows and becomes more complex, a formal structure is usually imposed. The entrepreneur will usually try to maintain control as long as he can. Frequently some crisis, such as sustained losses, forces him to relinquish that control. The organization is then often turned over to managers who play a professional role and implement formal controls within a centralized structure. The organization may be small enough so that a centralized structure is still the most effective method of operating the firm. Most organizations stay at this level of operations. Sometimes the family of the founder will maintain control of the organization and continue as its managers even after a formal structure has been imposed. Often, however, as mentioned, professional managers are brought in and perpetuated within the formal organization.

Differentiating by Organizational Level

Occasionally the products or services supplied by the organization will develop increasing environmental support and will provide for a high rate of sustained growth. The managerial team is presented with a critical decision concerning organizational structure. The continued growth often leads to more levels of management being introduced into the organization. The organization may, as

How do roles vary with organization level—strategic, coordinative and operating?

mentioned earlier, be differentiated into three levels; strategic, coordinative and operating.*

The primary role of the manager at each level is as follows: At the strategic level the manager is involved in relating the organization to its external environment through missions and goals and in designing comprehensive plans. At the operating level the managerial activity is aimed at accomplishing stated objectives effectively and efficiently, i.e., "getting out the work." At the coordinative level the manager is involved in a range of activities from strategic to operating, with the prime concern toward the integration of internal activities that have been specialized by function and/or level.

The complexities of a multilevel organization often increase coordination and communication problems. At this stage, top management has to consider decentralizing some of the operating and coordinative decisions. Strategic decisions may be made centrally. If the organization becomes geographically dispersed, coordinative and operating decisions may be made by regional managers with policy guidance being given centrally. In a diversified, divisionalized organization all operating decisions may be made locally, with broad corporate strategies and interdivisional coordination developed centrally. More detailed coordinative management may be carried on within divisions.

In the previous sections we have described the organizational characteristics (e.g., degree of decentralization) that may be related to environmental demands: stable, regulated flexibility and adaptive. This approach suggests that roles and programs as well as objectives and strategic moves should be adjusted to fit the environmental situation. In this section we have looked at related influences on characteristics of an organization. Differentiating by role expectations and competencies (say, of entrepreneurs or professionals), by stage of development and complexity, and by various levels, as well as by the environmental situation, compounds the difficulties in identifying patterns of relationships and/or configurations among organizational characteristics.

We have also discussed the structure for the whole organization. For example, we have assumed that there is one set of environmental demands for processing inputs and that one design predominates. For some single function organizations this holds true. However, many organizations do not fall into a single type of design. Firms often have more than one type of structural arrangement operating at the same time. An example would be a hospital. The medical staff is highly decentralized. Each physician expects to play a professional role, having the responsibility and authority to make

Organizational forms co-exist.

*T. A. Petit: A behavioral theory of management, *Academy of Management Journal*, Dec. 1967, pp. 341–50; and T. Parsons: *Structure and Process in Modern Societies*, Chicago, The Free Press of Glencoe, 1960.

his own decisions involving patient care. The administrative staff, however, is often centralized and reports to a single individual, the hospital administrator. The administrator sets policies for his subordinates. The two organizational forms coexist and are able to implement their combined, overall mission of providing medical care.

Matrix organization.

There are other examples of this type of coexistence of different organizational forms. The matrix organization, where products or project-orientated groups are superimposed on a functional organization, is probably the best known. Defense-related industries often use this type of design to achieve collaboration, teamwork and integration among participants where needed. The defense-related industries are committed to supplying a constant array of new products. The firms within these industries, moreover, have environmental support to continue to produce older products. They, therefore, have adopted the matrix organizational form to achieve their strategic objectives.

Keeping the Corporate Strategy in Mind

Consider key elements in corporate strategy.

Basically, changes in the direction and strategy of the organization have direct effects of the organization's design. Coherence in that organization design seems important whether the organization is simple or complex, large or small, private or nonprofit. The policy analyst has the difficult task of considering a whole mosaic of factors in planning a structure. While considering arranging the many parts of the organization, he may refer back to key elements in the success of the corporate strategy and then ask whether the organization design gives proper emphasis to those elements. In thinking through the refinements of a design he would not want to lose sight of the results expected or the specifically defined objective, goal or statement of future accomplishment that contributes to the organization's overall socioeconomic purpose.

New knowledge.

For example, "new knowledge" may be a key element in a corporate strategy to attain the objectives of growth and survival. The designed relationship between research and development and marketing and production depends upon the prime focus of the new knowledge. If new technological innovations develop rapidly, closer grouping of activities for integration between research and development and production than between research and development and marketing should be considered. On the other hand, if the technology for making new products is widespread and the new knowledge consists primarily of rapidly changing market information, the research and development department probably would be integrated to a greater extent with marketing than with production.

Financial synergy.

Another key element in an overall strategy may be financial synergy or the ability of organizational combinations to obtain external funds and to be able to allocate capital to various divisions. Some firms with unrelated products do *not* attempt to achieve operational and coordinative integration among various divisions. However, they do attempt to achieve financial synergy with centralized allocation of financial support to the most promising divisions. This approach to strategy and structure has important advantages for the firm with unrelated products: it makes it much easier to divest existing divisions and to acquire new organizational units. Substantial integration at the operating and coordinative levels would make such changes more difficult.

Use contingency approach.

The foregoing discussion suggests that organization design is contingent upon a number of factors. The policy analyst is required to make an effective matching of the overall strategy with the environmental-technological situation as well as a number of related considerations, including the stage of development and complexity of the organization and individual role expectations and competencies.

OVERALL SUMMARY

This book is concerned with what the analyst (student, manager or assessor) can do in a business or nonprofit institution to study and to improve the process of dealing with policy and strategy issues. Policy or strategy formation is seen as a complex problem-solving process by which the organization makes choices relating to the internal and the external environments. The policy activities have wide ramifications, have a long-time perspective, use critical resources, and include a social process as well as an intellectual process.

The book was written for use as a conceptual framework for information gathering on policy and for organizing and analyzing such information. It has been our experience in a variety of situations that use of the book with additional practice materials for information processing seems to be helpful in several ways, such as (1) conceptualizing the policy-formation process; (2) developing comprehension, skill and knowledge for diagnosing and dealing with specific strategy situations; (3) analyzing the organization's environment and its policy-generating structure; (4) developing administrative and communication skills in presenting and developing solutions to policy problems; (5) integrating or tying together concepts, principles and skills learned separately in more specialized courses; and (6) being cautious in accepting the many prescriptions that exist in the literature on policy.

Conceptual framework.

Practical Problems for You to Solve

In this book we have asked you to assume you were being hired to design and implement an approach for solving policy problems in a business or public body. You would be asking questions about what needs to be done, what resources are available, what characteristics of the environment would be worth knowing, and so forth. To elaborate, suppose that it was an organization whose rate of growth had leveled off in the last few years that had hired you to increase that rate of growth. You might first want to know if the organization merely wanted to increase the growth or whether it was also important to change the image of the organization for the stockholders or the general public. Does the organization want to be seen as an aggressive, innovative yet stable organization in addition to increasing the growth rate? It would be important to know the time period within which you had to work. Changes that are meant to occur quickly would probably be more expensive and difficult to produce. As a policy advisor, hired to develop significant changes, the questions you might want answered before you proposed and implemented your approach would be numerous.

Questions to Answer

In this book we have developed sets of questions concerning the policy or strategy situation. One set has to do with preliminary information on how significant choices in policy "should be" made and how significant choices are made. Another set has to do with further conceptualization of the policy formation, including how the environment and the organization (a coalition) interact to form organizational objectives, resource allocations, and so forth. A third set that you would surely want to consider deals with ways of learning about policy through case study, field and library projects, field research, dynamic computer games, simulations, observation, informal contacts, publications, and so forth.*

Multiple guides, sources and methods.

The remaining sets of questions that you might want to ask would deal with (1) guides that could be used for assessing the current situation and the changing environment and for reformulating organizational objectives and actions; (2) assessment and development methods from behavioral science and from management science; (3) processes by which there is an action thrust in corporate strategy formation for involving others in planning actions, coordinating actions, executing actions and evaluating actions; and (4) factors related to the overall design of the organization as it develops in the environment. These are the main questions for which this book has tried to provide some answers.

---

*See D. E. Schendel and K. J. Hatten: Business Policy or Strategic Management: A Broader View for an Emerging Discipline. Paper presented at Academy of Management National Meetings, Division of Business Policy, August, 1972.

Policy Makers

We have seen policy or strategy makers as planning and coordinating to find solutions to policy issues that will (1) satisfy environmental demands or requirements, (2) win external and internal support (coalitions are formed), and (3) partially satisfy self-interests. The coordination and planning have been described as sometimes like muddling through, with an impossibility of determining in advance exactly what the solution should be. Thus, policy makers are sensitive to feedback from the environment. They analyze their present situation and forecast what environmental demands and support will be. Then, with their self-interests as basic premises, they make choices that may emerge into patterns of decisions or strategies that influence future decisions.

Some policy makers seem to dominate and seek bold opportunities to reach established goals (the entrepreneur); some are more adaptors or reactors in a nondominated coalition (the adaptor); some seem to rely more heavily on an analytical, highly integrated, one-point-at-a-time approach to formulating strategy (the planner).

The entrepreneur, the adaptor and the planner.

We have suggested in this book that the analyst can go about the process of strategy formation more effectively by using the conceptual framework previously discussed and by using technology, some of which is associated with applied behavioral science and some with management science.

It appears that *action research,* a behavioral science program sometimes associated with organization development, holds promise for helping to initiate successful change in the strategy-formation process. Although the literature includes an inventory of self-reports, anecdotes and some before-and-after studies, there appears, so far, to be very little data to provide a firm base for prescription. Our approach has been a cautious one, suggesting that keen judgment is needed in making choices of variables to emphasize and methods of assessment and development to use. As mentioned, there will be some muddling through owing to various uncertainties and pressures.

Action research.

Keen judgment needed.

In summary, however, the process of action research applied to strategy formation can be described in the following way:

First, it involves the generation and explanation of pertinent information regarding the organization's environment, structure and functioning, and corporate strategy. It includes the use of various *management science* programs. In other words, outputs from management science programs feed into the action-research program.

Management science needed.

Second, it involves an evaluation of that information and a diagnosis of the current position and what the position *might* be.

And, *finally,* it involves the reformulation of organizational objectives and a plan of action based on the diagnosis that can bring about changes in the corporate strategy, the structure and the strategy-formation process. This plan of action provides for continuing assessment of the opportunities, challenges, problems and progress reviews in an attempt to avoid organizational stagnation and deterioration.

DISCUSSION QUESTIONS

1. Discuss the structure (i.e., roles and programs) of an organization with which you are familiar (e.g., a university or a restaurant).

2. How does this organization adapt to changing environments?

3. Discuss the relationships between product line, diversification and organizational structure. What has been the traditional line of development of structure and internal factors?

4. Discuss the benefits and problems of decentralization versus centralization, particularly as the structure relates to strategy formation.

5. Discuss the external variables affecting the design of stable versus flexible and adaptive organizations.

6. How can organizational design be blended to perform effectively under varying environmental conditions?

Suggested Additional References for Further Research

Baker, F., editor: Organizational Systems: General Systems Approaches to Complex Organizations. Homewood, Illinois, Richard D. Irwin, Inc., 1973.

Bennis, W. G.: *Changing Organizations.* New York, McGraw-Hill Book Co., Inc., 1966.

Bos, A. H.: Development principles of organizations. *Management International Review 9*:17–30, 1969.

Carroll, S. J., Paine, F. T., and Miner, J. B.: The Management Process: Cases and Readings. New York, Macmillan Company, 1973.

Chandler, A. O.: *Strategy and Structure.* Cambridge, Mass., MIT Press, 1962.

Filley, A. C., and House, A. J.: *Managerial Process and Organizational Behavior.* Glenview, Illinois, Scott Foresman & Company, 1969.

Guth, W.: "Toward a Social System Theory of Strategic Planning." Proceedings of the Midwest Meetings of the Academy of Management, April, 1973.

Hutchinson, J. G.: Management Strategy and Tactics. New York, Holt, Rinehart and Winston, Inc., 1971.

Katz, D., and Kahn, R. L.: *The Social Psychology of Organizations.* New York, John Wiley & Son, Inc., 1966.

Likert, R.: *The Human Organization: Its Management and Value.* New York, McGraw-Hill Book Co., Inc., 1967.

Litschert, R. H.: Some characteristics of organization for long-range planning. *Academy of Management Journal 10*:247–256, 1967.

Miner, J. B.: The Management Process: Theory, Research, and Practice. New York, Macmillan Company, 1973.

Parsons, T., and Shils, E. A. (eds.): *Toward a General Theory of Action.* Cambridge, Harvard University Press, 1951.

Pugh, D. S., et al.: Dimensions of organization structure. *Administrative Science Quarterly,* June, 1968, pp. 65–105.

Starbuck, W. H.: Organizational growth and development. *In* March, J. G. (ed.): *The Handbook of Organizations.* Chicago, Rand McNally & Company, 1965, pp. 467–533.

Thompson, J. D.: *Organizations in Action.* New York, McGraw-Hill Book Co., 1967.

APPENDIX 1 TO CHAPTER 9

SOME ACTION STEPS

Earlier we asked you to assume that you were hired to design and implement an approach for improving the strategy-making process. For the manager, analyst or student who makes this assumption and who accepts the concepts of this book, it would be helpful to have a plan of action. We are assuming that such a plan will improve the muddling through process. Here we summarize a sample of some action steps along with several categories of inquiries that, when answered, should help you to get started with a planned approach.

I. *Establishing an Internal Resource*
(Utilize skills, knowledge and contacts of member(s) of the organization. Or is relevant material available in cases?)

II. *Education and Deciding What to do?*
Needs and interests of participants?

	Importance*	Time Schedule† (Indicate sequence and timing)	Implementation Structure‡ (Describe procedural steps)
Alternative A and D methods?			
Effort worthwhile?			
What way willing to participate?			
Role of analyst and internal resource?			
Assessment and development design?			
III. *Data Collection*			
Pattern of perceptions of issues			
Leverage points			
Self-interests			
Conflict management approaches			
Strategy-formation practices			
Scope of support and resource deployment			
How organization defines scope and what scope should be			
Basis of support for strategies (primary distinctive competence)			
Legal basis for activities and degree of concurrence with public policy			
Stated objectives and goals			
Performance data compared to standards			

	Importance*	Time Schedule† (Indicate sequence and timing)	Implementation Structure‡ (Describe procedured steps)
Trends in performance indicators			
Records and practices of comparable units and/or comparable organizations			
Management functioning and functional time allocation helps and hindrances			
Alternative opportunities and missions from audits of the environment			
Requirements for success in alternative opportunites			
Inventory of strengths and weaknesses of unit or organization			
IV. *Feed-in and Action Planning* Priorities identified			
Inventory and profile of most promising strategies, alternatives and opportunities			
Combinations for synergistic effects			
Stating, analyzing and clarifying organization scope, objectives and strategies			
New activities			
Redeployments			
Plan of organization to implement corporate strategy			
Plan for progress review (criteria and methods for assessing organizational and managerial performance)			

*Importance Rating: Based on your situation rate each element low (1) to high (7) as you see its potential value for assessment and development of policy formation.

†Timing: Indicate sequence and timing of when they should be attempted.

‡Implementation Structure: Describe the procedural steps to follow. For example, have questionnaire completed, analyze forecast data, who is going to take action.

AUTHOR INDEX

Ackerman, R. W., 61
Aguilar, F. J., 183
Aiken, M., 48
Aldag, R., 48
Alexander, T., 228
Amory, C., 121
Andrews, K. R., 12, 62
Andrus, R. R., 229
Ansoff, H. I., 12, 219
Argyris, C., 154
Athreya, W., 247
Ayres, R. V., 184

Baeda, R. A., 91
Baier, K., 184
Bales, R. F., 253
Barnes, L., 180
Barnhill, J. A., 12
Barnland, D. C., 259
Bass, B. M., 56
Bauer, R. A., 18, 47, 52, 127, 189, 192
Baumol, W. J., 45
Beckhard, R., 180, 251, 254, 259
Bell, C. H., Jr., 180, 238, 242
Bennis, W. G., 177, 240
Berry, P. C., 242
Beverly, G., 90
Bieman, H., Jr., 215
Blake, R., 177, 180
Block, C. H., 242
Blumberg, A., 57
Bonchard, T. J., Jr., 242
Bonge, J. W., 68, 75
Boston Consulting Group, 157
Boulden, J. B., 229, 230
Bower, J. L., 62, 162
Bowers, D. G., 141, 207
Boyd, H., 159
Brayfield, 19
Bridges, F. J., 12
Bright, J. R., 221
Broom, H. N., 12
Browning, H. L., 276
Brunner, G. A., 198
Buchanan, P., 239
Buffa, E. S., 229, 230
Bunker, B. B., 151

Burke, W. W., 151, 254
Burns, T., 48, 275
Buskirk, R. H., 12
Butler, E. D., 69

Campbell, J. P., 115, 140, 154, 240, 242
Cannon, J. T., 12
Carlson, S., 140
Carroll, S. J., 69, 90, 109, 140, 250
Carter, E. E., 16
Cetron, M. J., 221
Chambers, J. C., 184
Chandler, A. D., 10, 68, 272
Chase, P. H., 180, 256
Christensen, C. R., 12
Clarke, P. A., 238
Cohn, J., 62
Cole, E. N., 52
Coleman, B. P., 68
Collings, R., 189
Collins, B. E., 253
Connell, C. F., 190
Costello, T. W., 174
Crockett, W. J., 174
Culbertson, F., 91
Cyert, R. M., 16, 116

Dahl, R. A., 53
Dalkey, N. C., 224
Dalton, G., 57, 177, 180, 239, 240
Denning, B. W., 217
Dexter, L., 52
Dick, D. N., 221
Dill, W. R., 89
Doppelt, M., 89
Drucker, P. F., 105, 110
Dunnette, M. D., 115, 140, 154, 191, 240, 242
Dyer, W., 174

Easton, D., 49
Ebbeson, E., 151

Eddy, W., 174
Edwards, W., 231
England, G. W., 20
Ernst, M. L., 228

Fenn, D. H., Jr., 127
Fiedler, F., 240
Filley, A., 55
Fink, C. F., 259
Ford, H., II, 62
Forehand, G. A., 199
Foster, G., 180
Fouraker, L. E., 19
Fox, W. M., 69
Freehan, W., 160
French, J. R. P., Jr., 251
French, W. L., 177, 180, 238, 242
Friedman, M., 62

Gagne, R. N., 231
Galbraith, J. K., 273
Gannon, M. J., 200
Gardner, J., 178
Gergen, K. J., 18, 189, 192
Germane, G. E., 143
Gibbs, J. P., 276
Gilmer, B. V. H., 199
Gilmore, F. F., 12, 144
Gindes, M., 151
Glueck, W., 12
Golembiewski, R. J., 57, 174
Gordon, R. L., 190
Grayson, C. J., 226
Green, M. J., 45
Greenlaw, P., 212
Gregory, C. E., 81
Greiner, L., 57, 177, 180, 239, 240
Grinyer, P. H., 3, 67
Gross, N. C., 51
Guetzkow, H., 253
Guth, W. D., 12, 20, 67, 89

Hage, J., 48
Hall, R., 48, 276
Hall, W. K., 167, 226
Hare, A. P., 259
Hare, M., 242
Harsangi, J. C., 53
Harvey, O., 90
Hatten, K. J., 282
Heleriik, L. W., 140
Hemphill, J. K., 140
Herold, D. H., 87
Hertz, D. B., 223
Herzberg, F., 240
Hickson, D. H., 275
Hill, W., 106
Hille, S. J., 198

Hofer, C., 158
Hoffman, C. R., 91
Holden, P., 143
Hornstein, H. A., 151, 180, 259
House, R. H., 55, 140
Hutchinson, J. G., 68

Ivancevich, J. J., 69, 90, 250

Jansted, K., 154, 242
Jerdee, T. H., 140, 250

Kahn, R. L., 100, 154, 190, 240
Kast, F. E., 18, 48
Katz, D., 100, 154, 240
Katz, R. L., 12, 115
Kay, E., 251
Keegan, W., 189
Kendall, L. M., 140
Kerlinger, F. N., 191
Kerr, S., 109
Kirschner, W., 191
Klein, W., 143
Kolasa, B. J., 45

Lake, D. G., 180, 259
Lawake, C. H., 91
Lawler, E. E., Jr., 115, 140
Lawrence, P. R., 48, 55, 57, 177, 180,
    239, 240
Learned, E. P., 12
Leavitt, T., 205
Lewicki, R. J., 151
Likert, R., 45, 197
Lindblom, C. E., 54
Lirtzman, S., 55
Locke, E., 107
Lodge, G., 45
Logan, J. P., 12, 156
Lorsch, J. W., 48, 55
Lynton, R. P., 80, 81

Maddocks, R., 174
Mahoney, T. A., 140, 199, 250
Maier, N. R. F., 91, 154, 254
Mann, R., 143
March, J. G., 16, 52, 116, 253
Marrow, A. J., 174
Mason, R. O., 92, 257
Mason, W. S., 51
McCormick, A. D., 180
McEachern, A. W., 51
McGowan, J., 45
McKenney, J. L., 89
McKinney, G. W., III, 15

McNichols, T. J., 12
Messick, 19
Meyer, H. H., 251
Miller, E. C., 217, 220, 226
Mintzberg, H., 20, 80, 81, 83, 114, 115, 116, 183, 217
Moffett, J. W., 174
Mouton, J., 177, 180
Mullick, S. K., 184
Murphy, D., 143

Nash, A. N., 198
Naumes, W., 89
Newland, C. A., 113
Newman, W. H., 10, 12, 156

O'Connell, J., 12
Olm, K. W., 12

Paine, F. T., 57, 69, 90, 198, 200, 250, 251
Pareek, U., 80, 81
Parsons, T., 279
Patchen, M., 44
Perrow, C., 107, 199, 275
Peterson, C. A., 143
Petit, T. A., 16, 114, 279
Pheysey, D. C., 275
Pool, I., 52
Prakash, S., 45
Price, J., 199
Pugh, D. S., 275

Raia, A. P., 89, 108
Raisinghani, D., 116
Rescher, N., 184
Richards, M., 212
Rizzo, J. R., 55, 140
Rosenzweig, J. E., 18, 48

Saunders, C., 100
Sayles, L., 115, 140
Schein, E., 56, 174
Schendel, D. E., 282
Schmidt, S., 215
Schoeffler, S., 161
Scott, B. R., 273, 274
Seashore, S. E., 141

Selznick, P., 19
Shein, E., 197
Shepard, H. A., 253
Sherif, M., 56
Shils, E. A., 50
Simon, H. A., 52
Sitmister, L. T., 220
Smith, D. D., 184
Smith, P. D., 140
Solem, A. R., 69, 91, 154
Stalker, G. M., 48, 275
Starr, M. K., 217
Steiner, G. A., 75, 115
Stewart, R., 140
Storey, R., 48
Sumner, C. E., Jr., 12

Tagiuri, R., 20
Taylor, B., 58
Taylor, D. W., 242
Terleckyj, N. B., 184
Theoret, A., 116
Thomas, E. J., 259
Thompson, J. D., 48, 50
Thune, S., 87
Tosi, H., 48, 109
Turner, J., 220

Ulmer, S. S., 49
Underwood, W., 174

Vancil, R. F., 244
Van Schacck, H., Jr., 91

Wallich, C., 45
Warren, E. K., 238
Watson, G., 239
Webb, E. J., 188
Weick, K. E., 115, 140
Weitzel, W., 199
White, B. F., 180
Wickert, F. R., 259
Wildavsky, A., 58
Woffard, J., 141
Woodward, J., 48, 275

Zand, D., 118
Zimbardo, P., 151

SUBJECT INDEX

Abt Associates, Inc., 127, 128
Action plan. See *Plan of action.*
Action-research. See *Organization, development of.*
Action Thrust, 4, 237–272. See also *Organization, development of.*
  defined, 243
Agriculture, Department of, 256
American Can, Inc., 223
American Motors Corp., 11, 13, 148
Assessment, 4, 97–142
  and development methods, 172–209
  guides to, 97–142
    main types of analysts using, 98, 100
  objectives of, 98
Authority distribution continuum, 239

Babcock & Wilcox, Inc., 180, 256
Baldwin Locomotive Works, 119
Bargaining, 56, 106, 111
Budgeting, 161–166
Burroughs Corp., 223

Case Study(ies), 21–23, 69–80
  effectiveness of, 69
  live, 79
Celanese Corp., 222
Choice process, 10, 15, 18. See also *Decision making* and *Problem solving.*
  collective, 20
  individual, 20
  policy formation and, 1–43
Climate, organizational, 199, 200
Coalition, 17, 18, 45, 50, 106, 283
  bargaining and negotiating to maintain, 18, 46, 56
Computer, decision making and, 228–231
  models from, 88–99
  programs from, creativity and, 228–231
Conditional value, 213
  defined, 213

Conflict, 17, 54–57
  management, 54–57, 113–114
  over unshared goals, 17, 55, 56
Contingency approach, 47–49, 275–279
Cost, effect of accumulated experience on, 157–159
Creativity, 12, 241–242
  related to computer programs, 228–231

Decision making, 44–47, 228–231. See also *Problem solving.*
  assumptions of typical model violated, 44, 45
  computer aided, 228–231
  diagnosis, 72–79
  theory of, descriptive, 18–20
    elite, 20
    group, 20
    normative, 18–20
  typical model of, 44, 45
Decision tree. See *Program(s).*
Delphi technique. See *Program(s).*
Diagnosis, 72, 73
  cautions in, 76
  defined, 75
  identifying causes in, 75, 76
  pinpointing problems in, 75
Dialectical approach. See *Program(s).*
Digital Equipment Corp., 11, 12
Diversification. See *Strategy(ies).*

Eastman Kodak, Inc., 7, 124, 274
Entrepreneur. See *Policy makers.*
Environment, 47–50
  adaptive, 276
  assessing basis and location of support from, 101–106
  competitive factors in, 124–125
  demands from, 47–50
  economic considerations, 119–121
  interdependence of factors in, 49, 50
  monitoring of, 49, 101–129
  observation of, 188
  political inputs, 123–125
  regulated flexibility of, 276

Environment (*Continued*)
　　social influences on, 122–123
　　social responsibility of, 61–63, 125–129
　　stable, 48, 276
　　support from, 47–50
　　technological advances and, 121–122
　　technological demands of, 275–278
Evaluation, 158, 174–176, 251–253
　　approaches to, 174–176
　　of objectives and outcomes, 106–111
　　timing of, 245–246
　　using qualitative evidence, 73, 74
　　using quantitative evidence, 74, 212–225
Expected value, 213–214
　　defined, 213
Exxon Corp., 224

Field projects, 80
Field research, 83
Forecasting, 99, 100, 153, 183, 220–223, 225
　　about 1985, 225, *226*
　　economic, 183, 220, 221
　　input-output models for, 222
　　social, 183
　　technological, 183, 221–222

General Electric Corp., 105
General Foods, Inc., 274
General Motors, Inc., 52, 100, 105
Goals. See *Objective(s)*.

Head Ski, Inc., 186, 278
HMH Publishing Co. (Playboy), 11, 12

IBM, 11, 104
Implementation. See *Strategy(ies), implementation of.*
Information, gathering of, 68, 103, 181
　　questionnaire in, 197–203
　　　　organizational effectiveness content related to, 199–200
　　　　processing results of, 202–206
　　restrictions on, 103
　　processing program for, 117
　　source(s) of, deviant individual as, 186
　　　　main, for policy analyst, 183, 184
　　　　marginal individual as, 186
　　　　transitional individual as, 186
Interviews, 189–196
　　choosing approach for, 189, 193–196
　　focused, 189, 191–193

Interviews (*Continued*)
　　guides to, 190–191
　　pitfalls in, 191
　　structured, 189

Leadership, 275
　　of policy conferences, 253–258
Lear Jet, Inc., 186
Lotus Europa, 206
LTV, Inc., 186

Management, function(s) of, 267. See also *Role, of management.*
Management science. See *Program(s).*
Market growth, 157–161
Market share, 157–161
McKinsey & Co., Inc., 224
Mission(s), 5, 6, 101, 144
　　defined, 6
　　identifying, 101–103, 204–205
Models, 45, 48
　　computer, 88–90
　　of policy formation, 47–61
Motivation and self-interest, 51–53, 112–113, 148, 150–151

National Affiliation of Concerned Business Students, 62
National Distillers, 102
National Steel Corp., 222

Objectives, 47, 55, 106–111, 144–152
　　assessment of outcomes and, 106–111
　　defined, 6
　　derivation of, 6, 106
　　need for, 146–149
　　primary, 149
　　relation to means-end chain, 5–10
　　secondary, 149
　　trading off of, 108, 149–150
Observation, in action-research program, 188–189
Office of Management and Budget, 102
Olin Textron, 274
Organization, climate of, 199, 200
　　development of, 177–181
　　　　action-research in, 179–209
　　　　defined, 177
　　　　processes involved in, 179
　　　　use of results of, 254–258

Plan of action, 12–17, 31–40, 74, 75, 143–145, 152–169, 179, 238, 251, 260–263, 282–287

Plan of action (*Continued*)
  as part of corporate strategy, 143–145
  detailing provisions of, to link over-all strategy with operations, 161–166
  developing and profiling alteratives for, 153–157
  steps to take for, 285–287
  strategic changes and corporate policies for, 157–161
Polaroid Corp., 124
Policy(ies), 6, 105, 149, 150
  as result of incremental process, 57, 58
  corporate, 145
  defined, 6
  differences in, 110
  distribution, 110, 145, 161
  financial, 105, 110, 145, 149–150
  formation of, 13–15, 44–65, *48*, 275
    and choice process, 1–43
    defined, 4
    normative framework for, 13–16
    use of probabilities in, 212
  investment, 145, 150–151, 157–161, 212
  personnel, 105, 145
  pricing, 145, 149–150, 160
  product, 110, 145, 157–160, 205–206
    differentiation, 161, 205–206
  promotion, 145, 157–160
  review and evaluation, 145, 158–160, 251–253, 261
Policy makers, 47, 50–52, 143, 276–280, 283, 284
  as adaptors, 50–58, 283
  as entrepreneurs, 50–58, 283
  as planners, 50–58, 283
Political resources, 48, 53–54, 111
  defined, 53
  tactics in using, 53
Portfolio approach, 157–161, 216, 221, 251
Present value of business, calculation of, 212–214
  decision rule in, 214
  defined, 212
Problem solving, 56, 57, 177, 241–243.
  See also *Decision making*.
  brainstorming in, 241, 242
  diagnosis, 72–79
  group, 241–245
  individual, 19, 20, 241, 242
  policy, effective groups sessions in, 253–255
    selecting situations for, 246–248
    types of structured activities for, 248–253
  testing assumptions in, 257, *258*
Product maturation cycle, 157–160
Program(s), 8, 50, 51, 111, 116
  action-research, 179–209
  capital budgeting, 210, 212–216, 237
  computer, creativity and, 228–231

Program(s) (*Continued*)
  decision tree, 216, 217, 218, 236
  defined, 8
  Delphi method, 224
  dialectical approach, 92, 257
  division five-year, 163, *164*
  financial analysis, 131–142
  financial summary, 163, 164
  information processing, 116, 117, 118
  management science, 210–236
    reasons for success and failure of, 225–228
  PERT, 163, *166*
  sensitivity analysis, 219
  STRATANAL, 89–90, 166–168, *168*
Psychological sets, 146–148

Rand Corp., 224
Rate of return as basis for priority, 215
Reward(s) as influence on behavior, 112–113
Role, 8, 50, 51, 55, 111–119, 161–166
  conflict, 51
  consensus, 51
  defined, 8
  of management, at various levels and stages, 114, 161–166, 267, 278, 279
    general, 114
  of technocrat, 114, 220, 226
  resolution of conflict in, 51, 55
Role-playing, 90–92
  Slimey Oil Co., 59–61
Rules of conduct, hierarchy of, 5

Scope. See *Mission(s)*.
Scott Paper, Inc., 274
Sears, Roebuck Corp., 104
Self-interest(s), 13, 51–53, 150–151.
  influences on behavior, 112–113
  motivation and, 51–53, 112–113, 148, 150–151
  need to determine, 112
Simulation(s), 222–224. See also *Program(s)*.
  Monte Carlo, 223
  risk analysis, 223, 224
Slimey Oil Co. (role play), 59–61
Social responsibility, 61–65, 125–130
Southern Pacific Railroad Co., 6
Sperry Rand, Inc., 243
Strategy(ies), 7, 11, 83, 105, 110, 212, 218, 283
  cluster of, 7, 8, 157–158, 212, 218
  continuity of, 83
  corporate, 7, 11, 143–171, 218, 280, 281
    defined, 7, 168, 169
  defined, 7

Strategy(ies) (*Continued*)
  developing map of, 192
  diversification, 12, 144, 158–160,
    272–274
    sources of, 274
  divestiture, 145, 157–161
  expansion, 144, 157–160, 218, 219
  formation of, defined, 4–5. See also
    Policy(ies), formation of.
    framework for, 13–15, 97–171
    holistic, 15
    incremental, 15
    integrative, 16
    portfolio approach to, 157–161,
      216, 251
    push-pull model of, 85
  global change in, 83
  implementation of, 84, 237–265,
    272–287. See also *Action thrust*
    and *Organization, development of.*
  integration of, 85, 144, 272–274
  niche or segmentation, 11, 153,
    204–206
  penetration, 144, 157–160, 218
  periods of development of, 83, 283
  periods of groping for, 83
  related to structure, 272–287
Structure, organizational, 9–10, 50–58,
    272–287
  assessment of strategy generating,
    111–119
  bureaucratic, V 48, 276, 277
  centralized, 48
  decentralized, 48
  defined, 9
  divisionalization of, 273, 274
  functional, 273
  matrix, 280

Structure (*Continued*)
  organizational, organic, 276, 277
    roles and programs as, 9
Synergy, 156, 280, 281
  defined, 156
  financial, 280
  negative, 156
  product, 156
  technological, 156

Technology, forecasting changes in,
    121–122
  demands of, 48, 275, 276
Treasury, Department of, 256

Union Carbide, 256
U.S. Navy, 222
U.S. Steel, Inc., 274
Univis, Inc., 21, 22, 25–43, 46, 47,
    108, 166, 224, 239, 245

Values, 13. See also *Self-interest(s).*
Volkswagenwork, 84, 85

Western Union, 102

Xerox Corp., 223